ISRAEL
AND
SOUTH AFRICA

THE MANY FACES OF
APARTHEID

EDITED BY ILAN PAPPÉ

Zed Books
LONDON

Israel and South Africa: The Many Faces of Apartheid was first published in 2015 by
Zed Books Ltd, The Foundry, 17 Oval Way, London SE11 5RR, UK

www.zedbooks.co.uk

Typeset in Adobe Garamond Pro by seagulls.net
Index: John Barker
Cover designed by roguefour.co.uk

A catalogue record for this book is available from the British Library.

ISBN 978-1-78360-590-3 hb
ISBN 978-1-78360-589-7 pb
ISBN 978-1-78360-591-0 pdf
ISBN 978-1-78360-592-7 epub
ISBN 978-1-78360-593-4 mobi

Printed and bound by CPI Group (UK) Ltd, Croydon, CR0 4YY

CONTENTS

Part 4: Future Models and Perspectives

ABOUT THE CONTRIBUTORS

Amneh Badran is a lecturer at the Department of Political Science at of Al-Quds university. Her recent book is *Zionist Israel and Apartheid South Africa: Civil Society and Peace Building in Ethnic-National States* (2013).

Oren Ben-Dor is a professor of law and philosophy at the University of Southampton School of Law. His publications deal with law and art and the one-state solution. His books include *Constitutional Limits and Public Sphere: A Critical Study of Bentham's Constitutionalism* (2001)and *Thinking about Law: In Silence with Heidegger* (2007).

Jonathan Cook is a British writer and a freelance journalist based in Nazareth, Israel, who writes about the Middle East and, more specifically, the Israeli–Palestinian conflict. His books include *Blood and Religion: The Unmasking of the Jewish and Democratic State* (2006); *Israel and the Clash of Civilizations: Iraq, Iran and the Plan to Remake the Middle East* (2008) and *Disappearing Palestine: Israel's Experiments in Human Despair* (2008).

Leila Farsakh is an associate professor of political science in the College of Liberal Arts at the University of Massachusetts. She has published extensively on Palestinian labour and the peace process. Her book, *Palestinian Labour Migration to Israel: Labour, Land and Occupation* was published in 2005.

Steven Friedman directs the Centre for the Study of Democracy at both Rhodes University and the University of Johannesburg. He is a South African academic, newspaper columnist, widely quoted public intellectual, activist, former trade unionist and journalist. He was appointed the national head of the Independent Electoral Commission's Information Analysis Department during preparations for South Africa's 1994 election. His books include *Building Tomorrow Today: African Workers in Trade Unions, 1970-1984* (2010); *The Long Journey : South Africa's Quest for a Negotiated Settlement* (2010) and *Race, Class and Power: Harold Wolpe and the Radical Critique of Apartheid* (2014).

Ran Greenstein is an associate professor in the Department of Sociology at the University of the Witwatersrand, Johannesburg, South Africa. His books include *Geneaologies of Conflict: Class, Identity, and State in Palestine–Israel and South Africa* (1995) and *Zionism and Its Discontents: A Century of Radical Dissent in Israel–Palestine* (2014).

Ronnie Kasrils is a South African politician. He was minister for intelligence services and now is a political activist. He was a member of the National Executive Committee of the African National Congress from 1987 to 2007 as well as a member of the Central Committee of the South African Communist Party from December 1986 to 2007. Kasrils has written several early books on Bertrand Russell and poetry as well as many articles on politics, defence and water and forestry issues. His autobiography, *Armed and Dangerous*, was first published in 1993 and updated and republished in 1998 and 2004. First published in 2010, *The Unlikely Secret Agent* gives a personal account of Ronnie's late-wife Eleanor's courage against the apartheid powers. It won the 2011 Alan Paton Award.

Anthony Löwstedt is an assistant professor in the Media and Communication Department in Webster University in Vienna. He is the author of *Kultur oder Evolution?: Eine Anthropologische Philosophie* (1995) and *Apartheid Ancient, Past and Present* (2014).

Virginia Tilley is an American political scientist specialising in the comparative study of ethnic and racial conflict. She is chair and professor of political science at Southern Illinois University–Carbondale. Her books include *The One-State Solution: A Breakthrough for Peace in the Israeli–Palestinian Deadlock* (2010) and *Seeing Indians: A Study of Race, Nation, and Power in El Salvador* (2005).

INTRODUCTION

The Many Faces of Apartheid

ILAN PAPPÉ

In recent years, a common item in the Palestine solidarity campaign in the West has been the 'Israel Apartheid Week', which was often organised by students on campuses in Europe and the United States. This activity was one of many reflecting a wish to compare the reality of present-day Israel with that which existed in Apartheid South Africa. Activists all over the world felt that the analogy was not only valid but also inspirational for the continued struggle for peace and liberation in Palestine.[1]

However, such a comparison is not only an item on the agenda of activists or critical academics; it has been attempted by some unexpected people and organisations. Quite a few high-ranking Israeli politicians and generals referred occasionally to the analogy. A recent book by Sasha Polakow-Suransky about Israel's ties with the apartheid regime registers these references quite pedantically and systematically.[2] A typical example is one made by the former Israeli Chief of the General Staff, Rafael Eytan, in front of a student convention at Tel Aviv University:

Blacks in South Africa want to gain control over the white minority just like Arabs here want to gain control over us. And we too, like the white minority in South Africa, must act to prevent them from taking us over.[3]

The acknowledged similarity is probably one of the main impulses behind Israel's long-lasting support for the regime even at the time when Western governments began to shun it. This odd behaviour did not escape Nelson Mandela when he was finally liberated from Robben Island. When an Israeli of South African origin wrote to him, shortly after his release from prison, saying that he was a 'latter day Moses who was about to reach the Promised Land' (this was before the elections that brought Mandela to power as president of South Africa), Mandela replied: 'South Africa will never forget the support of the state of Israel to the Apartheid regime'.[4]

This book is also interested in such an analogy and comparison, but it is, of course, motivated by different impulses from those pushing Israeli leaders into the hands of the apartheid regime. It is moved by the same sense of duty that led academics, activists and generally interested people in the Israeli–Palestinian conflict to refer to South Africa as a favourite point of compassion and inspiration. What unites all those engaged in such a comparison – be it professional, journalistic or popular – is that they all accept the validity of such an exercise. What is missing, we felt, was a more thorough examination of this comparison.

One of the reasons why, academically, this comparison was late in coming is the strong opposition to it in the pro-Israeli Western academia – and, of course, among the Israeli research community. In fact, most Israeli scholars and politicians are still enraged, even if they belong to the 'Peace Camp', by any such comparison. This is not surprising: even a slight or indirect implication of Israel as an apartheid state has far-reaching implications for the international legitimacy of the Jewish state.

And yet even a cursory knowledge of Israeli policies and practices on the one hand, and familiarity with the definition in the international law of apartheid on the other, begs at least a serious consideration for the validity of such an analogy.

The International Convention on the Suppression and Punishment of the Crime of Apartheid, adopted by the UN General Assembly in

November 1973, regards apartheid as 'a crime against humanity' and a violation of international law. Apartheid means 'similar policies and practices of racial segregation and discrimination as practised in southern Africa'. Such policies are criminal as they are 'committed for the purpose of establishing and maintaining domination by one racial group of persons over any other racial group of persons and systematically oppressing them'.

Despite strong pressure from Israel and its friends not to use the language of apartheid about the Palestine situation, it does seem that worldwide, especially in the wake of Jimmy Carter's clear reference to Israeli policy in the Occupied Territories as an apartheid regime, the need for such a comparison is deemed not only legitimate but even helpful.[5]

This volume wishes to launch a professional and academic discussion less about the validity of the comparison, which this editor takes for granted, but more about the similarities and dissimilarities of the two case studies. This is just the beginning of this comparative search and therefore this volume is not a comprehensive project – for this to happen one needs more than one collection and a longer and sustained academic effort.

I have tried to combine the obvious angles of comparison with the less conventional ones – such as the role of femicide in both case studies or that of the peace activists among both 'white' communities. However, all these are discrete contributions to the debate, due to its novelty (in the academic world at least). Each contributor had to comment in general about the comparison and its value (my article departs from this, as I am doing it here in the introduction). Two major questions are asked and answered in an individual manner by all the contributors. The first concerns the geographical boundaries of the comparison: namely, does the analogy for South Africa refer to the Occupied Territories or to Israel as a whole? And secondly, is the analogy needed only in order to understand the Israeli case study better, or can it also serve as an inspiration for a prognosis and future solutions? I will come back to these two questions at the end of this introduction.

The book begins with a chapter by Ronnie Kasrils. We chose one of South Africa's bravest and leading activists against apartheid, as we – the contributors to this volume – do not shun the clear connection between the academic project we pursue here and the causes of peace and reconciliation in Israel and Palestine. I am sure readers of this book will recognise both the professionalism of the contributions and, at the same time and with various degrees of strength, the commitment to contribute to a better understanding of an urgent crisis and the wish to produce, modestly, a new thinking that could extricate all those involved from the misery and hopelessness that they are experiencing today.

Ronnie Kasrils was a member of the National Executive Committee of the African National Congress (ANC), a member of the Central Committee of the South African Communist Party, and recently the Minister of Intelligence Services in post-apartheid South Africa. What, however, is most important in the context of this collection is his long involvement in, and commitment to, efforts to bring peace and reconciliation to Israel and Palestine.

In his contribution, he sets the tone for this collection, by stating clearly the need to consider what happened in South Africa in the past and in the present, for the sake of a better understanding of the Palestine reality. In this he stands alongside the legendary leader of the ANC, Oliver Tambo, who stated, when addressing the UN General Assembly in November 1982:

> The parallels between the Middle East and Southern Africa are as clear as they are sinister. The onslaught on the Lebanon, the massive massacre of Lebanese and Palestinians, the attempt to liquidate the PLO [Palestine Liberation Organisation] and Palestinian people, all of which were enacted with impunity by Israel, have been followed minutely and with unconcealed

interest and glee by the Pretoria racist regime which has designs for perpetrating the same kind of crime in Southern Africa in the expectation that, like Israel, it will be enabled by its allies to get away with murder.[6]

Kasrils highlights certain aspects of both cases where the similarity in his mind is obvious: notably the colonialist past and the legal framework adopted very early on by both settler states. Political Zionism and the apartheid regime shared not only a colonialist past but also a colonialist agenda. In both cases, these agendas persisted long after colonialism was defeated elsewhere and was already considered a closed chapter of the past. The difficulty in grasping the meaning and menace of colonialism in the second half of the twentieth century is behind the Western world's confusion, even among progressive circles, with regard to how to analyse the oppressive regimes and how to confront them.

In the second half of his opening chapter, Ronnie Kasrils poses the question of whether the study of Apartheid South Africa is relevant to the case of Israel and Palestine. In answering this question in the affirmative, Kasrils covers other aspects that were crucial for the validity of both regimes; the most important of these was American support for them, which, in fact, produced a particular pro-American Pretoria–Tel Aviv axis (of which we recently learned more from the revealing book mentioned above by Sasha Polakow-Suransky).

He also expands on remarks he made on the ground in his frequent visits to the Occupied Territories. He notes the difference between apartheid's 'grand masters', as he calls them, who treated Africans as a colonialist economic resource, and the Israeli so-called 'masters', who view the Palestinians as an obstacle to be removed. In South Africa, as terrible as the treatment of Africans had been, over the years there was a development that improved, even if only to a meagre extent, the possibility of earning a living within the apartheid system. This was made possible once the 'grand masters' of apartheid allowed black

South Africans to leave the Bantustans and seek work outside, since these 'grand masters' recognised that the development of the apartheid economy was dependent on the sweat and cheap labour of landless black nationals.

In contrast, the State of Israel went in precisely the opposite direction: first, it allowed the occupied Palestinians to work, in slavish conditions, in the Israeli labour market, and then it denied them this right. But, of course, as Kasrils notes, the difference was even more profound: there was no place for the indigenous population, as exploited labourers or residents of Bantustans, in the future vision of Zionism. Consequently, South African leaders such as Archbishop Desmond Tutu felt that in many respects the situation in occupied Palestine was worse than that in Apartheid South Africa.

This chapter ends with a stress on a joint fate and a wish for an even more substantial role for South Africa in bringing an end to the conflict and the misery. As Kasrils writes: 'South Africa bears testimony that this can be done in Palestine and Israel'.

The next two chapters focus on questions of history and origins. My own chapter seeks to widen the comparative historiographical scope beyond South Africa. This is an attempt to stress the validity of depicting Zionism as a colonialist movement through comparative analysis. The comparison is done diachronically by comparing the Zionist project with the Templer colonialism that preceded it in Palestine, and synchronically with the Basel mission in West Africa. The comparison with a colonialist project in the same country and in the same continent, Africa, on which the other contributions focus leads to similar general assumptions that characterise this volume as a whole. Although the Zionist project had its own specific features, it can quite comfortably be located within nineteenth-century colonialisms. It is first and foremost comparable to the modern Christian colonisation of Palestine in the first half of the nineteenth century and that in Africa as a whole. Moreover, Zionism was profoundly inspired and influenced by these particular colonialist projects. It seems that apartheid as a discourse or a practice was never alien to the Zionist movement – not in its early stages, nor today.

Oren Ben-Dor claims in the second background chapter that apartheid as a concept is in fact not foreign to Judaism. In December 2010, the most racist campaign ever against the Palestinians in Israel, which included not only a call to expel them but also a refusal to allow them to live in the vicinity of Jews or to work with Jews, was conducted and led by a list of famous and important Israeli rabbis. The possible theological Jewish justification for apartheid or discrimination deeply disturbed the late Israel Shahak, who was convinced that if Israel were to be based on Judaic law, it would become an apartheid state.[7]

Oren Ben-Dor adopts the same perspective. He defines the Jewish notions of apartheid as 'originary apartheid'. Like many others in this collection, Ben-Dor makes a distinction between various kinds of apartheid. There is an occasional apartheid as policy and ideology that has a beginning and an end within certain historical circumstances; on the other hand, there is the 'originary' apartheid that 'obeys a deeper history, existential in nature'. This doctrine of 'essential separateness' would, warns Ben-Dor, be very difficult to challenge – any challenge would be much more difficult than the struggle against apartheid in South Africa. The main obstacle is a clear taboo in discussing Judaism with regard to Zionism. I would add that it is indeed important to challenge this taboo – no religion or faith is beyond criticism or reappraisal – but this requires sensitivity and caution.

This article is exceptional in this collection not only because it wishes to challenge even the accepted anti-Zionist criticism, but it also wishes to locate the Palestine case in a unique historical context – even more unique than that of Apartheid South Africa. Other chapters reflect the same sense of at least some of the aspects of the Palestine reality: namely, that apartheid in the case of Israel is even harsher and harder to overcome than the variety that prevailed in South Africa.

7

The next section of the book examines the analogy in two ways: compared with the situation inside Israel, and with the reality in the Occupied Territories. The Zionist and later Israeli fragmentation of Palestine leads us to examine these two regions discretely and, at the same time, to think about Israeli policy as stemming from the same historical and ideological origins. This fragmentation was the aim, and the end result, of the Zionist strategy in the land and has been solidified by Israeli policies of 'divide and rule' ever since the creation of the Jewish state.

The gist of this policy was to shift Israeli oppression from one group to another: the military rule that was imposed on the Palestinian citizens in Israel between 1948 and 1966 was transferred to the West Bank and the Gaza Strip after 1967, and the policies of ethnic cleansing in 1948 reappear, albeit in a smaller and different form, in the Israeli policy in Greater Jerusalem and southern Israel. This is why comparative analysis can be extremely elusive at times. On the one hand, the comparison triggers an understanding that in certain aspects the oppression in Palestine is worse and harder to overcome; on the other hand, on the surface the Palestinian citizens in Israel seem to enjoy a better life than that experienced by Africans in South Africa. And yet the comprehensive picture that the contributors to this book seem to draw is quite clear: in one way or another, all Palestinians – inside and outside Palestine – are still living under a variant of the South African apartheid system.

This notion appears very clearly in Jonathan Cook's article in this collection. His analysis reiterates the claim already made a few years ago by the scholar and activist Uri Davis that Israel within its 1967 borders is an apartheid state, or, as Cook puts it, 'Israel's policies [towards Palestinians inside Israel] have strong echoes of the policies pursued by South Africa's Apartheid regime'. The main reason for his conclusive assertion is the overall picture emerging from his systematic examination of the wide-ranging restrictions Israel has imposed on its Palestinian citizens ever since 1948, including the very recent ones that demand that Palestinian citizens swear an oath of loyalty and recognise Israel unconditionally as a Jewish state. With the new legislation, a new hostility felt by the state and Jewish society towards Palestinian citizens also increased – this had been on the ascent since the Palestinian minority had showed a clearer identification with the Palestinian resistance in the Occupied Territories.

Cook refers to the minority as a group of 'degraded citizens' in the eyes of Israeli laws, after he surveys closely the basic laws (constitutional laws) of the State of Israel. A common Israeli defence against this kind of depiction is that the Supreme Court in the country quite often balances these severe restrictions with its rulings. Cook brushes aside this apology and claims that, more often than not, the Supreme Court reaffirms this oppression. In fact, as Cook points out, the Palestinian community in Israel is particularly vulnerable as it is systematically denied any constitutional protection.

The Palestinians in Israel live in what Cook calls 'normative duality' in both the de jure and de facto spheres of the state's laws. What he describes in essence is how the *Hafrada*, the Hebrew term for apartheid which literally means separation or segregation, is an inevitable part of the reality in Israel. The most important state organ responsible for maintaining this separation is the Israeli 'Secret Service', the Shin Bet, which enjoys unlimited power under the emergency regulations of the state. When this section of the government is the principal agency dealing with a community of citizens, it means that they can only be deemed to be hostile and alien enemies.

Just as it is futile to consider the Supreme Court as a bulwark against apartheid in Israel, so the alleged rights granted to Palestinians, such as the right to vote and be elected, are hardly indicators of a 'balanced' reality. In a genuine democracy, voting and being elected are means to ensure political participation; in this case, they are just a façade that enables the exclusion rather than the inclusion of Palestinian citizens. Cook's historical survey shows that, at any given moment, this community lived and lives under an apartheid regime that confiscates its land, encloses it in segregated communities, sends its children to a separate educational system, and leaves the economic and natural resources of the state in the hands of the Jewish majority.

The fate of the Palestinians in Israel was intertwined with that of those living in the West Bank and the Gaza Strip, once Israel occupied these areas in 1967. The military regime was transferred from Israel to the Occupied Territories and was expanded in a way that reminded many of the apartheid regime in South Africa. However, what Cook, and others in this volume, claim is that apartheid also continued inside Israel proper, although it was more subtle and less visible.

However, even the assertion that life under occupation is as bad, if not worse, than under apartheid has to be tested. Leila Farsakh provides us with the most damning analysis of that reality in her contribution to this collection. Farsakh notes that the basic Israeli policy is no different from that pursued by Apartheid South Africa. This emerges from an analysis of Israel's policy towards Palestinian statehood and mainly through what she calls the Bantustanisation process of the Occupied Territories, especially under the guise of the Oslo Process. In many ways, this is one of the striking differences between the case studies – peace in South Africa slowly eroded the apartheid system; in the Occupied Territories, peace only strengthened the apartheid reality and infrastructure.

Farsakh nonetheless does not create an artificial separation between Palestinians on the two sides of the green line. She explains how the specifics of the apartheid regime apply to Israel as well as to the Occupied Territories, whether those specifics relate to ideological premises, the role of labour exploitation, or the historical way in which the two regimes developed.

Farsakh's chapter also provides us with the most elusive aspect of the Israeli apartheid policy – as a group of scholars, we are dealing with a phenomenon that is still there and still reconfiguring and changing according to the circumstances on the ground. The article stems from an early work that included past predictions about how the Israeli policy would develop in the future; today, these predictions unfold as a new reality in front of our eyes.

Farsakh also directs our attention to the fact that this creeping apartheid and separateness, which resulted in the Bantustanisation of the Palestinian landscape in the West Bank and the Gaza Strip, enjoy immunity as far as the international community is concerned. Finally, Farsakh mentions in passing an issue that may require further research in the future: a comparison between the internal strife in the ANC and the PLO and the role of the oppressor in accentuating these divisions and keeping them alive.[8]

Another overlooked aspect – one to which we do pay a considerable amount of attention in this volume – is the double oppression of women in a comparative study. Recently, some impressive literature on this subject in the Palestinian context has appeared and has enriched our knowledge, but there has been no attempt to investigate the topic within a comparative paradigm.[9]

In his article, Anthony Löwstedt compares the two ghastly phenomena of witch burning in South Africa and honour killings in Palestine and refers to the women targeted as the 'ultimate victims of double and sometime triple occupation – national and social'. This very sensitive subject is dealt with here in a way that challenges the common essentialist cultural explanations, by governments and mainstream academia alike, of these ugly incidents.

The article shows that apartheid and colonialist regimes in general gain from the prevalence of these practices. Their constant reappearance became an asset for the 'divide and rule' policies of the colonising empires. In comparing the policies in the two cases, Löwstedt found out that the Israeli policy is more callous and sinister. The Israeli authorities have used the crime as means of eliciting collaboration, by shaming young women and families as a way of putting pressure on potential collaborators.

In both cases, academics and politicians tried to cast the blame solely on the indigenous culture, adopting an essentialist attitude that ignored the role of the coloniser and the later apartheid state in increasing these phenomena. The political and judicial elites in the two countries showed disinterest, in the case of South Africa, and leniency towards the perpetrators, in the case of Israel, and explained their reasons for adopting such a stance in a similar way: namely, that this was a traditional custom that they did not wish to tackle or confront.

The comparison leads Löwstedt to consider the role of demography both in the policies of apartheid and in the resistance movement against them. Here, too, as noted by other contributors, when different aspects of the state's 'divide and rule' policies are compared, the Israeli practices seems to be more ruthless and inhuman. In Israel, demographic control is used as a supremacist weapon for maintaining the Jewish majority in the state. Such an institutionalised use was unheard of even in white South Africa. There was nothing comparable to the Israeli 'Council of Demography', a government body established to encourage growth in the Jewish birth rate, and indirectly to discourage an increase in the Palestinian one. In practice, this meant enthusiastically encouraging only Jewish women in Israel to increase their number of children and to stop abortions. However, as mentioned above, Löwstedt does not absolve the resistance movement from abusing demography as well; he takes issue with the pressure exerted in the past by Palestinian leaders on women to have more children in the struggle for survival.

Femicide is not part of either culture: it was a marginal occurrence that has been pushed to the centre by apartheid in the two cases as part of a more general phenomenon. The author calls this the 'de-secularisation' of societies that were more complex and dialectical in their attitudes to tradition and modernity in the past. The delicate checks and balances disappeared not only because of Zionism or apartheid, but also due to the accelerated processes of modernisation. However, the cynical manipulation of this reality for the sake of control and segregation will make it more difficult to confront the phenomenon in Israel. If there is hope in this respect, it lies in the brave and dedicated work of women's organisations, such as those who opened centres for the victims of violence against women within Palestinian society in Israel.

Another nuanced view on comparison is offered by Amneh Badran, who looks at Jewish and white protest groups in Israel and South Africa. Through the story of the peace movements in both cases one can learn about the common and different features of the regimes in both countries and their relationships with their constituencies. The departure point of the article is that, since we are talking about similar political systems, we can expect similar modes of resistance.

The article provides an original critique on liberal Zionism and the Israeli peace camp. Badran juxtaposes this with the very clear notion of resistance within the white community in South Africa, where the few who joined the ANC had deeply held convictions about the need to struggle against the regime and its victims. In the case of Israel, very few subscribed to similar notions of resistance. South Africa did not have the same phenomenon of a quasi or pseudo resistance movement, which, in a way, abused the concept of struggle and resistance. Peace camps that were in fact supporting the regime and merely rejecting some of its policies were a peculiar Israeli phenomenon, better understood within the context of a comparative study such as the one offered by Badran here. One should add that a stale notion of resistance was also adopted by the Palestinian citizens in Israel – for very different and more acceptable reasons. However, great numbers of Palestinians in Israel maintained contact with and allegiance to the PLO, while the white liberals, namely the Israeli Jews, regarded and still regard the organisation as the enemy.

The most important case study, which is dealt with extensively in this article, concerns the Peace Now movement, which is the largest and oldest lobby for peace in the Jewish state. The comparative angle enables Badran both to assess the significance of this movement and to provide us with a convincing explanation for its failure. Even more daring is Badran's analysis of *Gush Shalom* (the Peace Block). This latter group is far more committed and active than Peace Now in the struggle against the occupation but is still a long way from walking the extra mile that would put it on a par with the white organisations that opposed, and fought against, apartheid.

The small anti-Zionist groups, which make only an occasional, temporary appearance on the political map, are also considered by Badran. She points to their greater resemblance to those elements in the white community that helped bring about change in South Africa. This part of the article leaves us with a glimmer of hope – although even among these groups the standard procedure of anti-apartheid whites in South Africa, namely directly joining the ANC, was followed by only two or three individuals.

Engagement with a topic like this also relates, as did the previous chapter, to the issue of gender and women's struggles in both countries. The Israeli scene has more women's non-governmental organisations and movements that work directly or indirectly for the cause of peace. However, most of them are still reluctant to question the very nature of the regime and its basic ideology, or to support the campaign of BDS – Boycott, Divestment and Sanctions – against the state. Although this changed recently when local chapters of one of the main women's movements in Israel, Women in Black, around the world adopted such attitudes, the mother organisation in Israel is still unwilling to go that far. However, this could change in the very near future.

The book ends with three overviews by scholars who worked on South Africa and who lend us their insights about the future prospects of a change in Israel and Palestine modelled on the South African success.

The first is provided by Steven Friedman, one of South Africa's leading political analysts and observers, who draws some crucial lessons from his personal experience and his overall analysis of the struggle against apartheid in South Africa.

The main lesson Friedman draws from the radical transformation of South Africa is that one should believe in the impossible. He recalls how he was ridiculed and laughed at in academic conferences as late as 1987 for stating his conviction that the apartheid regime was about to end.

The key point of reference for him is the justification both regimes sought and paraded in their attempt to win international legitimacy. Both countries demanded recognition of their right to be ethnic states despite the fact that they were socially and practically multi-ethnic. The founders of these states also shared a similar wish to be included in the liberal democratic world despite their overriding concern to keep the state as ethnically pure as possible. This did not always lead to oppressive policies, and sometimes this contradiction was approached by what Friedman calls 'an admixture of reform and repression in the attempt to solve the impossible contradiction'.

No less intriguing is the future prospective scenario that can be envisaged on the basis of the historical experience in South Africa and Friedman's description of how Afrikaners eventually began to accept the inevitable change. In any future solution in Israel and Palestine, such a process would have to take place if one wanted to bring an end to the conflict there.

Similarly hopeful inspiration can be drawn from Virginia Tilley's article. Tilley tackles the question of comparison by confronting head-on the arguments of those who shun such an exercise, the most important of which is that the cases cannot be compared and that there is even less room for an analogy where Israel proper is concerned.

Tilley agrees that the case studies are not identical and concedes that there should be a distinction between a comparison of Israel per se with South Africa and a comparison between the occupied West Bank and the Gaza Strip with the apartheid regime (although, as we shall see, this does not mean that she rejects the former per se). In this particular chapter, her focus is on the Occupied Territories and, as already mentioned, her method is to take one by one the challenges put forward by those opposed to this particular comparison.

The main objection to the comparison stresses the extraordinary political status of the Occupied Territories. The claim is that a comparison between the Occupied Territories and Apartheid South Africa is invalid since the Occupied Territories are not a state and that Israel is not sovereign there.

Tilley confronts this challenge by including the story of Namibia in the mix, as this offers a much wider historical context of settler colonialism in both Israel and South Africa. This time span highlights some unexpected similar, and even identical, features in the two case studies.

The focus on the status and reality of the Occupied Territories in this article is not meant to absolve us from extending the comparison, as other articles in this book do, to pre-1967 Israel. On the contrary, the Israeli rule of the Occupied Territories and the South African presence in Namibia are episodes in, and inevitable consequences of, the settler colonialist history and nature of both societies.

This siting of the Occupied Territories within the wider historical perspective is essential for Tilley's article, since it allows her to transcend the diagnosis and offer some thoughts about a possible prognosis that stems from the comparison. Historically, one can see how the policies in the Occupied Territories from 1967 onwards, and in recent years, follow similar patterns to the history of the white strategy in South Africa. Rereading that history in a comparative way is the first step towards a better understanding of possible future solutions.

The common solution that has been, and still is, offered for the conflict in Israel and Palestine is the two-state solution. Tilley argues that, in whatever form this model were implemented, it would allow Israeli settler colonialism to continue throughout historical Palestine – 'allow' here being used in the sense of winning international legitimacy.

The de-legitimisation of the South African apartheid regime was the main achievement of the anti-apartheid movement globally;

this de-legitimisation was directed not only against apartheid rule but also against the continued practice of settler colonialism in the second half of the twentieth century. Anti-colonialism in the case of both South Africa and Palestine represents a wish to allow everyone remaining on the land to have a normal and equal life. The overall view of the Palestinian struggle as anti-colonialist is thus associated with the vision of a democratic state throughout Palestine as the just and honourable solution.

Ran Greenstein's article closes this collection. Greenstein redefines the questions that concerned Tilley and many other contributors to this collection. The most important of these seems to be the ease with which we associate the term 'apartheid' with the Occupied Territories while we are more hesitant in applying it to pre-1967 Israel. The second question concerns the clear distinction between using the analogy to analyse the two cases on the one hand, and as a model for future solutions on the other.

Greenstein feels that a productive way of clarifying any analogy is by juxtaposing two concepts: the 'historical' apartheid and a 'generic' apartheid. No less helpful is his assertion that comparative analogies are better when terms such as 'apartheid', as well as 'race' and 'ethnicity', are not treated as rigid definitions.

With these refinements in mind, Greenstein expresses his own conclusions with regard to the twin questions with which the volume as a whole is concerned. He does not separate the Occupied Territories from Israel in his analysis, and he uses the comparison as a basis for some tentative thoughts about the future.

Greenstein concedes that it is more difficult, but not impossible, to defend the analogy of pre-1967 Israel with Apartheid South Africa; it is easier to make such a comparison if the depiction of Israel as an apartheid state refers to what Greenstein calls the generic and not the historical apartheid. When apartheid is regarded as a generic term — that is, not a term for something that existed only in a given period in South Africa, but rather for any political system of separation and segregation that is based on race, ethnicity or religion – then, as Greenstein puts it, 'Israeli policies and practices meet many – not all – of the criteria identified in the international convention on apartheid, with the qualification that they are based on ethno-national rather than racial grounds'.

The perspective of the 'generic' apartheid enables Greenstein to also include in the definition aspects of life in Israel that were different, indeed better, than those experienced by the majority of South Africans during the days of apartheid. And when he examines the various aspects of Israeli policies, he finds that Palestinian citizens are granted rights that were denied to the majority of black people, while occupied Palestinians are treated in much the same way as black people were treated (especially residents of the 'homelands'). As far as Palestinian refugees are concerned, in this perspective they are excluded to a far greater degree than black South Africans ever were.

In Greenstein's view, therefore, it is less fitting to use 'historical' apartheid as the measure of analogy since the features of apartheid in Israel are not the same as those of historical apartheid, 'although they do bear family resemblances'. However, as Greenstein explains, this would be true of any case study chosen, as no one instance is like any other. So 'Israeli apartheid' is apartheid of a generic kind and yet a special one.

As for the other concern of this volume as a whole, Greenstein's concluding remarks represent well the editor's vision – and, I suspect, the vision of everyone else who contributed to this book. The first point, I think, emerges from all the articles, and it is that the 'Israeli apartheid' is 'of a special type different from historical apartheid, and more difficult to overcome'. The legacy and manipulation of the Holocaust memory in the West on the one hand, and the strength of the pro-Israel lobby in the United States on the other, are factors that did not exist in the case of historical apartheid. Moreover, the ANC did not have to grapple with an association with Islam, as the Palestinian national movement does. Islamophobia weakens the Palestinian resistance, whereas the emergence of political Islamic forces within the movement prevents it from acting in a unified and sustained manner. There are disempowering features that did not exist in the case of South Africa. More than half of the indigenous people are absent from the homeland and are dispersed all over the Middle East and beyond, and, while the resistance movement was born among them, it now has more than one centre of power inside the homeland, thereby creating confusion and disorientation.

However, the South African model – historical apartheid – serves as a source of inspiration for how to conduct wisely a struggle from within and from without, even when the conditions on the ground are so dismal and hard to overcome. It is a mixture of international pressure, including BDS, from the outside and education and confidence-building on the inside. The aim of such a struggle still has to be clarified, Greenstein reminds us – and not only in the now famous debate between those who support a two-state solution and those who endorse a one-state solution. Far more important is the need to build a bridge between the struggle for 'democracy, equality and human rights', as Greenstein puts it, and the Palestinian national struggle. For this to develop fully, we need a Palestinian resolution on the question of representation; this was solved very early on in the case of the struggle in South Africa. When this is achieved, we will – and we should – all be able to be part of a campaign that will not only be as successful as the one in South Africa, but could also be one that will improve on it for the benefit of the people who live in Israel, Palestine and beyond.

Notes

1   Nancy Murray, 'Dynamics of Resistance: The Apartheid Analogy', *MIT Electronic Journal of Middle East Studies* (Spring 2008): 133–6: www.palestinejournal.net/gmh/MIT_journal.htm.

2 Sasha Polakow-Suransky, *The Unspoken Alliance: Israel's Secret Relationship with Apartheid South Africa*, New York: Pantheon, 2010.
3 Ibid., p. 8.
4 Ibid.
5 Jimmy Carter, *Palestine: Peace Not Apartheid*, New York: Simon and Schuster, 2007.
6 Statement at the plenary meeting of the United Nations General Assembly, New York, 9 November 1982.
7 Israel Shahak, *Jewish History, Jewish Religion* (preface by Ilan Pappé), London and New York: Pluto, 2009.
8 See also the work of Mona Y. Younis, *Liberation and Democratization: The South African and Palestinian National Movements*, Minneapolis: University of Minnesota Press, 2000.
9 One rare example is the article by Roslyn Arlin Mikelson, Mokubung Nkomo and Stephen Samuel Smith, 'Education, Ethnicity, and Social Transformation in Israel and South Africa', *Comparative Education Review* 45(1) (February 2001), pp. 1–35.

PART 1
HISTORICAL ROOTS

CHAPTER 1

Birds of a Feather: Israel and Apartheid South Africa – Colonialism of a Special Type

RONNIE KASRILS

Victory over fascism in 1945 raised the hope of freedom throughout the world. The stage was set for the de-colonisation of Africa and Asia – yet 1948 proved to be an *annus horribilis* for both black South Africans and native Palestinians, with the hawks of war darkening their skies. For South Africans, May 1948 marked the election of the apartheid government, consolidating over three centuries of colonial conquest and subjugation, and the prelude to a forty-six-year maelstrom. For the Palestinians, 1948 opened a truly catastrophic era (*Al-Nakbah*) of brutal dispossession at the hands of a rampant Zionist project, resulting in expulsion from a land they had inhabited continuously for millennia, and the displacement by an exclusivist Jewish settler state whose unilateral independence was declared on 15 May that year. While apartheid was replaced in 1994 by a democratic, non-racist, non-sexist, unitary state of equal citizens, the suffering of the Palestinians only gets more excessive, and a just solution appears more distant.

While there are Zionist apologists who decry the likening of the policy and practices of the apartheid state with those of its Israeli counterpart, the blatant similarities of these two birds of a feather were vividly illustrated by the words of Dr Hendrik Verwoerd – former

South African prime minister and the architect of 'Grand Apartheid'. In 1961, when expressing his deep admiration for Israel's foundation and socio-political architecture – and, more especially, for its character as an exclusivist, ethnic state, with special privileges in law for Jews, and the displacement of native Palestinians by foreigners – stated that: 'The Jews took Israel from the Arabs after the Arabs had lived there for a thousand years. Israel like South Africa is an Apartheid state'.[1]

Much has been written about the similarities between the legal and legislative framework governing Israel and Apartheid South Africa, the seminal work of which is Uri Davis' *Israel: An Apartheid State* (which referred mainly to Israel itself).[2] The laws and measures adopted by Israel, whether civil or military, closely mirror those of South Africa before and especially during the apartheid period. Among these were the notorious nationality or race laws of both states which excluded non-Jews or non-whites, as the case might be, from the entitlement and privileges of full citizenship; the land and property laws that made it illegal for those same categories of people to own or lease land or own businesses, purchase or rent homes, except in specific areas; the issuing of identity cards based on strict racial classification and reinforced by obsessive Kafkaesque controls, which greatly limited the freedom of movement of Palestinians or black South Africans, including the right to live, work, study, play, relax, travel and be buried where they wished; and, scandalously, even laws affecting the rights of mixed-marriage couples, and so on.

The United Nations (UN) Convention Against Apartheid could have been written for Israel:

> Any measures, including legislative measures, designed to divide the population along racial lines by the creation of separate reserves and ghettos for the members of a racial group or groups, the prohibition of mixed marriages among members of various racial groups, the expropriation of landed property belonging

24

to a racial group or groups or to members thereof [is apartheid and illegal].[3]

It is necessary to note that this legal framework relates to all Palestinians, whether they live within Israel as second-class, discriminated citizens with limited rights, or they are in the Occupied Territories, or they are refugees who fled abroad. The similarities with apartheid are remarkable and abundant, including the master-race psychosis engendered; the cruelty and race hatred generated; and the systemic trampling underfoot of the dignity of Arab or African. It is this colonial-type symbiosis on which this chapter will focus. Israel, from its very conception and inception, embodies similar features ascribed to 'Colonialism of a Special Type' (CST), the term coined by the South African Communist Party in 1962 in its characterisation of Apartheid South Africa. The thesis helped shape the strategy and tactics of the national liberation struggle and bears repeating here:

The conceding of independence to South Africa by Britain in 1910 was not a victory over the forces of colonialism and imperialism. It was designed in the interests of imperialism. Power was transferred not into the hands of the masses of people of South Africa, but into the hands of the White minority alone. The evils of colonialism, insofar as the Non-White majority are concerned, were perpetuated and reinforced. A new type of colonialism was developed, in which the oppressing White nation occupied the same territory as the oppressed people themselves and lived side by side with them.

On one level, that of White South Africa, there are all the features of an advanced capitalist state in its final stage of imperialism … But on another level, that of Non-White South Africa, there are all the features of a colony. The indigenous population is subjected to extreme national oppression, poverty and exploitation, lack of all democratic rights and political domination ... The African Reserves[4] show the complete lack of industry, communications and power resources which are characteristic of African territories under colonial rule throughout the Continent. Typical too of imperialist rule is the reliance by the state upon brute force and terror ... Non-White South Africa *is the colony* of White South Africa itself.

It is this combination of the worst features of both imperialism and colonialism, *within a single national frontier*, which determines the special nature of the South African system and has brought upon its rulers the justified hatred and contempt of progressive and democratic people throughout the world ...[5]

If we were to replace the words 'South Africa' with 'Israel' or 'Palestine' depending on the periods; 'White South Africa' with 'the Jewish minority'; 'Non-White South Africa' with 'the Palestinian people'; and 'African Reserves' (i.e., Bantustans) with 'fragmented Palestinian territories', we find an uncanny resemblance between the colonial Apartheid South African model and that of Zionist Israel. The conceding of independence by Britain to the white minority in South Africa in 1910 is comparable to the 1947 partition deal that paved the way for the handing over of power in Palestine to the Jewish minority.

It is not at all difficult to demonstrate Zionist Israel's colonial agenda. Indeed, from the early so-called *political Zionists*[6] onwards, to Israel's first prime minister and the associated military strongmen, we learn straight from the horse's mouth about the true colonial nature and objectives of their project, which at definitive times they did not bother to conceal.

The founding father of *political Zionism*, Theodor Herzl, stated in 1896 that once a Jewish state was established the aim would be to: 'Spirit the penniless population [the Palestinians] across the borders and be rid of them'.[7]

According to Vladmir Jabotinsky, whose outspoken political radicalism of the 1930s has triumphed in Fortress Israel:

Zionist colonisation ... must ... be ... carried out in defiance of the will of the native population. This colonisation can therefore continue and develop only under the protection of a force independent of the local population – an iron wall which the native population cannot break through. This is, in toto, our policy towards the Arabs. To formulate it any other way would be hypocrisy'.[8]

Israel's first prime minister, David Ben Gurion, who normally went to great lengths to conceal the true agenda, stated in an off-the-record discourse in the 1950s:

Why should the Arabs make peace? If I was an Arab leader, I would never make terms with Israel. That is natural: We have taken their country. Sure, God promised it to us, but what does that matter to them? Our God is not theirs. We come from Israel, it's true, but two thousand years ago, and what is that to them? There has been anti-Semitism, the Nazis ... but was that their fault? They only see one thing: we came here and stole their country.[9]

Moshe Dayan, as outspokenly hawkish as Jabotinsky, unabashedly explained:

Before [the Palestinians'] very eyes we are possessing the land and villages where they, and their ancestors, have lived ... We are the generation of colonisers, and without the gun barrel we cannot plant a tree and build a home.[10]

Such statements, consistently expressed by Zionist leaders from the time of Herzl, reliably contextualise Israel's expansionist objective and provide the clues as to why it has not been interested in real peace terms. Given the consistency of such formulations, which are not simply isolated rhetoric since they have been realised in systematically consistent actions and serial aggression, it becomes obvious that Israel's existence has been based on colonial conquest, annexation (whenever the time is ripe), ever expanding settlement, and, in those words of South Africa's CST definition, 'constitute the reliance by the state upon brute force and terror'.

The question arises: does the CST analogy assist in understanding the Palestinian–Israeli situation and does it point to its resolution? We can examine this by referring to Shamil Jeppie, a South African academic, who has provided a useful analogy in the article 'Israel: A Colonial Settler State? What Kind of Decolonisation? Some Reflections from Africa'.[11]

Jeppie's starting point was the French historian Maxime Rodinson's celebrated essay on Israel, a 'colonial-settler' phenomenon, written forty years ago.[12] Jeppie writes that Rodinson's arguments 'remain persuasive and valid for scholars looking for conceptual language to understand the origins and practices of the Israeli state, and for activists whose sympathies lie with the cause of the Palestinians'.

I totally concur and am of the view that it is essential to grasp the colonial factor in understanding the Palestinian case: a national liberation struggle of the indigenous and uprooted Palestinians against a colonial-settler project whose community has come to acquire a *distorted* national identity within the same territory, i.e., the CST paradigm. It is Zionist Israel's racist, colonialist agenda that is the fundamental cause of the conflict, as was the case in the South African example. After dealing with the validity of this for analytical purposes, I will return later to the relevance for activism.

It stems from the Zionist world view: its belief in a perpetual anti-Semitism that requires that Jewish people around the world – a faith group – usurp as a national home the territory of another people. The biblical narrative was evoked to proclaim Palestine as the 'Promised Land' reserved exclusively for God's 'chosen people' and their civilising mission. It sounds all too familiar, as the vision of the South African colonial settlers and exponents of apartheid was similar. In history, this has consistently given rise to racism, segregation and a total onslaught on those who stand in the way, whether Africans or Arabs, native Americans, Asians or Aboriginals. As with those whites who joined in the struggle for South Africa's liberation, many Jews, within Israel and even globally, reject the Zionist world view, and declare that being anti-Zionist and critical of Israel does not equate with anti-Semitism – any more than the accident of possessing a white pigmentation meant one was a proponent of apartheid.

Far from being a land without people, as Zionist propaganda falsely proclaimed, to attract and justify colonial settlement, the fact was that an indigenous people – the Palestinians – lived there and had developed agriculture and towns from Canaanite times over 5,500 years ago. In South Africa, too, colonial and apartheid mythology taught generations of schoolchildren that, when the Dutch colonists arrived on the shores of the Cape in 1652, the 'Bantu tribes' in their migration from the north had barely arrived to cross the Limpopo River[13] into what later became South Africa.

Undermining the Zionist claims on Palestine, a delegation of sceptical Vienna rabbis travelled to the Holy Land in 1898 to assess the Zionist vision and cabled home: 'The Bride is indeed beautiful but already married'.[14] This did not deter the Zionists, who plotted to forcefully abduct the bride and do away with the groom by whatever means necessary; and then to defend what they had stolen at all costs by creating a supremacist 'Fortress State' (as best described by Jabotinsky).

This exactly sums up the bloody and tragic fate that befell the Palestinian people, and their Arab neighbours, at the hands of a predatory, expansionist Zionist project that has been the source of war and untold suffering in the Middle East for sixty-seven years or more (when we include the pre-1948 Zionist settler violence against the indigenous Palestinian population). This colonial dispossession inevitably has regional repercussions for it threatens the entire Middle East, in much the same way that Apartheid South Africa constituted a threat of destabilisation and aggression to the entire Southern African region and beyond with its invasions, use of proxy forces, destruction, assassinations and massacres within and across its borders. From the start, Zionists such as Herzl made no bones about placing a future Jewish state at the disposal of imperialism. Such a state, he promised, would constitute for Europe in Palestine 'a part of the wall against Asia, and serve as the vanguard of civilization against barbarism'.[15] This prophetic racism was amply demonstrated within eight years of Israel's independence, in the joint invasion of Egypt in 1956 with Britain and France, and in the temporary seizure of the Suez Canal. Little wonder that back in 1921 Winston Churchill, then Britain's Colonial Secretary, had observed: 'Zionism is good for the Jews and good for the British Empire'.[16] For the many years of the South African liberation struggle against apartheid, the West similarly saw in the Pretoria regime a bulwark and ally against Soviet communism. And Apartheid South Africa played that card – 'the red peril' – for all its shabby worth.

After the Suez fiasco, America soon demonstrated its willingness to become Israel's chief backer. The late Egyptian scholar Abdelwahab Elmessiri pointed out that Israel had become a 'functional' client state for US interests.[17] It is well documented that it was through America's more than generous assistance in developmental and military aid that Israel became a regional superpower. America has been providing approximately $5 billion in aid annually – $3 billion per annum for military requirements alone since 1967 – and sees Israel as its strategic ally of choice with regard to keeping the oil-rich Middle East under control. An American organisation, Jewish Voice for Peace, has pointed out that US military aid to Israel since 1949 'represents the largest transfer of funds from one country to another in history'.[18] It is estimated that this military aid had amounted to $100 billion by the end of the twentieth century.

As US President Ronald Reagan explained in 1981:

> With a combat experienced military, Israel is a force in the Middle East that is actually a benefit to us. If there were not Israel with that force, we'd have to supply it with our own.[19]

President George W. Bush demonstrated Washington's support for Israel with a $30 billion dollar military aid programme announced in 2007[20] – within a year of Israel's barbaric onslaught on the Lebanon. Then, of course, we have witnessed the scandalous manner in which Washington, with EU complicity, rallied to Israel's support, immediately replenishing its arsenal, after the onslaughts on Gaza from 2009 to 2014.

Israel's partnership with the Western powers ran in tandem with that of South Africa's apartheid state, which loyally proclaimed its service in the anti-communist, Cold War crusade and – like the Zionist state in relation to Egypt, Iraq, Lebanon, Syria and Jordan – sought to destabilise the perceived Sino-Soviet threat in Angola, Mozambique, Namibia and Zimbabwe. In fact, an unholy alliance between the two emerged when almost the entire world was boycotting South Africa as a leper state – and Israel became its closest ally. The two rogue states connived in secret arms deals and Israel enabled the apartheid state to upgrade its jet fighter squadrons, naval fleet and weapons systems, and helped in the development of seven nuclear devices. The arms industries of the two states became closely intertwined, with billions of dollars' worth of profits generated. It has taken some time for a democratic South Africa to cut this Gordian knot – but, unfortunately, not entirely and not as far as should be the case, ensnared, as a democratic South Africa is, in the grip of a neoliberal paradigm where rhetoric is one thing and action quite another.

During the heyday of the Jerusalem–Pretoria axis, following apartheid arms supplies to an Israel reeling after the reversals of the 1973 October War, the two states exchanged military advisers and training specialists in respect of both conventional and unconventional warfare, and mutually encouraged the many terrorist excesses they both perpetrated.

Oliver Tambo, African National Congress leader at the time, addressing the UN General Assembly in November 1982, stated:

> The parallels between the Middle East and Southern Africa are as clear as they are sinister. The onslaught on the Lebanon, the massive massacre of Lebanese and Palestinians, the attempt to liquidate the Palestine Liberation Organisation (PLO) and Palestinian people, all of which were enacted with impunity by Israel, have been followed minutely and with unconcealed interest and glee by the Pretoria racist regime which has designs for perpetrating the same kind of crime in Southern Africa in the expectation that, like Israel, it will be enabled by its allies to get away with murder.[21]

The November 1947 UN Partition Plan accorded 56 per cent of the Palestinian Mandate territory to a Jewish homeland, although the Zionist movement had by then acquired less than 7 per cent of the land (purchased from absentee Arab landlords over the heads of tenant farmers) and comprised one-third of the population (many of whom had recently arrived as Holocaust refugees from Europe). The indigenous Palestinian majority were allocated 44 per cent and were never consulted, nor had they had anything to do with the horrific suffering of the European Jews. The Zionists accepted partition with alacrity but never intended to honour the decision. The Palestinians understandably rejected a plan that ripped their homeland asunder.

According to the Zionist strategy, which has become public record with the declassification of many telling historical documents (but not the most sensitive), the intention was to roll out a systematic reign of terror, massacre, dispossession and expulsion. This drove out the Palestinian population in a diabolical episode of ethnic cleansing that saw over 750,000 Palestinians – two-thirds of the indigenous people at that time – becoming penniless refugees, exactly as Herzl had anticipated. By the 1949 Armistice, the Israeli state had expanded to 78 per cent of the territory. This fait accompli was accepted without a murmur of protest outside Arab countries. The Western world largely ignored the ethnic cleansing despite the graphic testimonies of UN and international Red Cross observers, who independently confirmed the heart-rending Palestinian accounts.

That was sixty-seven years ago. Israel's June 1967 war of aggression, a direct and dramatic extension of 1948, resulted in Israeli military occupation of the remaining 22 per cent of the former British Mandate territory of Palestine, including East Jerusalem, without any meaningful opposition in the West. While apartheid shocked Western sensibilities, Zionist colonial conquest was accepted as payback for Holocaust suffering and because of the absurd argument, still vociferously peddled by biblical fundamentalists, that Israel constitutes a mere two-hundredth or 0.5 per cent of the vast land a 'God of Real Estate' allegedly promised the ancient Israelites![22]

Palestinians within the West Bank and Gaza Strip are besieged and imprisoned under the most onerous conditions, suffering hardships and methods of control that are far worse than anything black South Africans faced during the most dreadful days of apartheid. In fact, any South African with integrity, visiting what amounts to enclosed prison ghettos under brutal military occupation, siege and collective punishment – imposed on behalf of a Jewish people who, ironically, suffered the Nazi Holocaust – will find a stark similarity with apartheid immediately coming to mind, and, even more shockingly, comparisons with some of the methods of collective punishment and control devised under tyrannies elsewhere.

An Israeli cabinet minister, Aharon Cizling, stated in 1948, several months after the Deir Yassin massacre: 'I often disagree when the term Nazi was applied to the British ... even though the British committed Nazi crimes. Now we too have behaved like Nazis and my whole being is shaken'.[23]

If any lingering doubts remain with regard to what the 1948 and subsequent so-called pre-emptive, defensive wars were about, listen to Ben Gurion, who predicted in 1938: 'After we become a strong force, as the result of the creation of a state, we shall abolish partition and expand into the whole of Palestine'.[24]

The following words of Moshe Dayan in 1969 clearly give the game away too:

Our fathers had reached the frontiers which were recognized in the UN Partition Plan of 1947 [56 per cent of the land]. Our generation reached the frontiers of 1949 [78 per cent of the land]. Now the Six Day Generation [of 1967] has managed to reach Suez, Jordan and the Golan Heights. This is not the end.[25]

Indeed, the saga of Palestinian and Arab agony continues with the 2006 aggression against Lebanon, the incremental genocidal onslaught against the Gaza Strip through the serial massacres of 2009–10, 2012 and 2014, and the rising racism and brutality of the Netanyahu regime. The result of such horrendous suffering caused by Israeli state terror is the inevitable creation of insecurity for Israelis as well: as has been seen in South Africa and in other historical experiences, injustice and repression generate resistance. It is no good blaming the victims when they stand and fight, fire retaliatory rockets and dig tunnels from which to launch combat operations. That retaliation is, in fact, a form of defence and is more understandable than the ignominy of living on one's knees and legitimising one's suffering. As in the struggle for South African liberation, the blame must be placed squarely on the state perpetrators responsible in the first place for the repression that makes noble human beings rise up. When the Israeli people and their supporters internationally cry about Jewish suffering and fear, it is Netanyahu and his cohorts at whom they should be pointing the finger.

The Palestinian people's fate clearly reflects that of South Africa's indigenous majority during the colonial wars of dispossession of land, property and rights, and the harsh discrimination and suffering of the apartheid period that were classified as crimes against humanity. Israel is as guilty according to international and humanitarian law as the apartheid regime was. Israel's illegal conquest and occupation, with the avaricious land grab of its monstrous 'Apartheid Wall' and relentless expansion of its illegal settlements (in violation of the Fourth Geneva Convention), have reduced the West Bank to several disconnected pockets amounting to a mere 12 per cent of former Palestine. No wonder that Jimmy Carter, Archbishop Desmond Tutu and others compare the situation with apartheid and the infamous Bantustans – which gave 13 per cent of the land to South Africa's indigenous people.

There is, however, one key difference here. Apartheid's grand masters, while initially seeking to keep black South Africans strictly confined to those Bantustans, recognised that the development of the apartheid economy was dependent on the sweat of cheap, landless black labour. This dependence led to the rapid growth of a burgeoning urban black proletariat, which, while severely restricted in its movement and rights, was nevertheless ever present in the mines, factories, farms and kitchens of 'white South Africa'. Temporary residence in the sprawling black dormitory townships alongside the exclusively white cities was allowed, while surplus labour was kept in reserve in the Bantustan homelands.

Israel, however, has sought to rid itself of the Palestinian workforce on its doorstep, and, in an age of globalisation, is able to draw upon cheap labour from as far afield as Thailand and Romania. This becomes apparent on entering the Gaza Strip through the Erez Crossing, with its huge but underutilised reception centre, originally constructed to process the daily movement of 20,000 Gazan workers who are no longer sought by Israel.

This makes for a situation in which segregation in Israel and its 'Palestinian' appendages – prison ghettos enclosed within Greater Israel – is far more severe but, in essence, no different from the apartheid example. Apartheid South Africa needed black labour. Israel reduces as far as possible its dependence on a Palestinian workforce and applies all means at its disposal to stifle the economy of the Occupied Territories with the intention of completely driving out the remaining inhabitants. This is a merciless and ghastly process, which can be reversed only through the resilience of a beleaguered people reinforced by international support.

South Africa's colonial apartheid order – its CST – lasted almost 350 years following Dutch and British intrusion, with many ebbs and surges of conquest. The Zionist colonial-settler project stems from the 1880s and therefore has been violently crammed into a relatively shorter time frame with its shock waves of mass repression over the last seven decades. The Israeli ruling class, corrupt and bereft of vision, like the diehard proponents of apartheid in its ailing years, are finding that they can no longer rule in the old way. The Palestinians are not prepared to live under the old conditions. Here, indeed, the CST thesis could provide the Palestinian national liberation movement, and all activists, with the inspirational analogy of the anti-apartheid experience and lessons from the strategy and tactics of that struggle as referred to by Shamil Jeppie earlier. Historical experience requires:

- unity in the actions of the Palestinian masses of all classes and strata – within Israel, Jerusalem, the West Bank, Gaza and the diaspora;
- determined leadership from the grassroots up, capable of winning mass support and trust;

- the correct theory and practice, with clear objectives and appropriate methods of struggle, reinforced by popular mass actions embracing progressive Israeli Jews;
- a powerful international solidarity movement based on BDS (Boycott, Divestment and Sanctions) that exerts pressure on Israel and the states that support that country.

Such a strategy – as was applied against apartheid – is waiting to crystallise and will emerge with the growing BDS movement and the renewed energy that the Palestinian national liberation movement will undoubtedly generate for as long as *sumud* and resistance persist.

As former beneficiaries of selfless international backing, South Africans – with an anti-colonialist and anti-racist heritage – have a duty to lend a supportive hand to encourage the international campaign and press for genuine negotiations for a hopeful peaceful solution in the interests of all Muslims, Christians and Jews living in the Holy Land. South Africa's experience bears testimony to the fact that previous adversarial groups, once locked in a seemingly intractable struggle, can find a way to cross the Rubicon, talk to one another and reconcile in a mutually beneficial solution of equals as a consequence of a just struggle that emancipates all.

In taking this process forward, South Africa's position remains clear. We join with freedom-loving people across the globe in calling for Israel's immediate withdrawal from the Occupied Territories, including Syria's Golan Heights and East Jerusalem – lifting the physical, economic and financial blockade and siege of Gaza and the West Bank; removing the impediments to the freedom of movement of Palestinians, including the monstrous 'Apartheid Wall' and over 500 checkpoints; utterly dismantling the illegal settlements; releasing thousands of political prisoners (women and growing numbers of children among them); negotiating a just solution with the elected representatives of the Palestinian people; and implementing the various UN resolutions, including Resolution 194 of 1948 concerning the inalienable right of return of the refugees. These are necessary steps to create lasting peace, justice and security for Palestinians and Israelis alike, reinforced by international guarantees, so that all may live in harmony.

The importance of the CST characterisation is that it demolishes the dangerous charade that Zionism is itself a national liberation movement, and that the claims of both Israel and the Palestinians should be treated by the international community in a balanced and even-handed manner, on a par with one another.

The CST thesis cuts to the bone. It lifts the veil on the true nature of this historic struggle for land and national rights, which requires full national determination and independence for the colonised people – the Palestinian people – before all else. This is fundamental: after this, all else will follow, for this is the basis for solving the national question. It is only based on the freedom and independence of the colonised nation that the settlers – those who are prepared to stay – will find security.

While the acceptance by Yasser Arafat's PLO of a state based on the 1967 borders (East Jerusalem, West Bank and Gaza) certainly limited the outright struggle for the whole of former Palestine, Israel's reluctance (with US support) to accept the Oslo compromise (some would say 'trap') has come to threaten the two-state option. Indeed, owing to Israeli prevarication, and downright sabotaging of the Oslo agreement – initially by Sharon and then by Netanyahu – many have come to see negotiations as a charade and the two-state solution as being as dead as the proverbial dodo. This has consequently seen a revival of the full national demands of the Palestinians, not only in the support Hamas has received but also in the fact that Palestinian and some Jewish intellectuals and progressives (few in number but symbolically important) are revisiting the original unitary, bi-national or single-state option of equal citizenship and security for all, as in the example of a democratic South Africa.

Let me conclude with the words of noted South African professor John Dugard, special rapporteur to the UN Human Rights Council, in a 2007 report on the situation in the Palestinian territories. His statement underpins the very reason for South Africa's commitment to and support for the just demands of the Palestinian people:

> For years the occupation of Palestine and apartheid South Africa vied for attention from the international community. In 1994 apartheid came to an end and Palestine became the only developing country in the world under subjugation of a Western-affiliated regime.[26]

Sixty-seven agonising years after the 1948 Nakba, it is high time that justice prevails; that the suffering Palestinians achieve, together with their fellow Jews, the freedom that all South Africans now enjoy – emerging as freed birds of a democratic feather based on fraternity and equity in a liberated context. The formulation of a particular state structure must finally be worked out by the Palestinian and Israeli people without outside interference. They have to live together in justice and peace. The stampede to the right by the Jewish electorate of Israel, and the racist fearmongering of Netanyahu and his cronies, is ultimately doomed to failure.

There are rising Jewish voices in Israel and worldwide, just as there were whites in Apartheid South Africa, who see this as the sane hope for the future. While this might not be the primary factor for change, the contradictions within the settler 'nation' are important. The struggle and determination of the colonised people are, of course, the key to bringing about change.

Notes

1   *Rand Daily Mail*, Johannesburg, 23 November 1961. Verwoerd was hitting back at Western countries' criticism of apartheid while they supported Israel and overlooked its dispossession of Palestinian land and rights. Of course,

he erroneously calculated Arab settlement from Islamic times, ignoring indigenous Palestinian settlement from time immemorial.

2 Uri Davis, *Israel: An Apartheid State*, London: Zed Books, 1987.

3 International Convention on the Suppression and Punishment of the Crime of Apartheid, United Nations General Assembly Resolution 3068 (XXVIII) of 30 November 1973, which came into force on 18 July 1976.

4 Later to be termed Bantustans, with sham independence. There were ten such 'homelands' comprising 13 per cent of South Africa.

5 South African Communist Party, *The Road to South African Freedom*, 1962.

6 The term dates from the late nineteenth century and denotes a political agenda to establish a Jewish national state as a homeland for all Jews. This contrasts with spiritual or cultural Zionism's view of Jerusalem: that is, Zion as a place of pilgrimage.

7 Theodor Herzl, *The Complete Diaries of Theodor Herzl*, New York: Herzl Press, 1961.

8 Nur Masalha, *Expulsion of the Palestinians*, Washington, DC: Institute for Palestinian Studies, 1992, p. 28.

9 Nathan Goldmann, *The Jewish Paradox*, New York: Grosset & Dunlap, 1978.

10 Benjamin Beit-Hallahmi, *Original Sins: Reflections on the History of Zionism and Israel*, Northampton, MA: Interlink Publishing, 1998.

11 Shamil Jeppie in Aslam Farouk-Alli (ed.), *The Future of Palestine and Israel: From Colonial Roots to Postcolonial Realities*, Midrand and Johannesburg: Institute for Global Dialogue and Friedrich-Ebert-Stiftung, 2007.

12 Maxime Rodinson, *Israel: A Colonial Settler State?*, New York: Anchor Foundation, 1973. First published in French as 'Israel, fait colonial' in 1967 in a special issue of *Les Temps Modernes* devoted to the Arab–Israeli conflict.

13 The Limpopo River forms present-day South Africa's northern border with Zimbabwe.

14 Avi Shlaim, *The Iron Wall*, New York: W. W. Norton and Company, 2001.

15 Uri Avnery, 'America's Rottweiler', *CounterPunch*, 26–27 August 2006: www.counterpunch.org.

16 David Schafer, 'Triumph and catastrophe', *The Humanist*, November–December 2002: www.thehumanist.org.

17 Abdelwahab Elmessiri, 'The Role Of Philosophy and Ideology in the Israeli–Palestinian Conflict: An Outsider's Perspective'. Paper presented at the Institute for Global Dialogue (IGD) conference, September 2006.

18 See www.peacenow.org.

19 Nasser Aruri, *Dishonest Broker: The US Role in Israel and Palestine*, Cambridge, MA: South End Press, 2003.

20 'US and Israel in $30bn Arms Deal', BBC News, 16 August 2007: http://news.bbc.co.uk/1/hi/6948981.stm.

21 Statement at the plenary meeting of the UN General Assembly, New York, 9 November 1982.

22 Rabbi Warren Goldstein, South Africa's Orthodox Chief Rabbi, argued this point in an article in the *South African Sunday Times* newspaper on 17 June 2007.

23 Tom Segev, *1949: The First Israelis*, New York: Henry Holt, 1998.

24 Goldmann, *The Jewish Paradox*.

25 *The Times*, 25 June 1969.

26 UN Human Rights Council Report A/HRC/4/17 by Professor John Dugard, special rapporteur on the situation in the Palestinian Territories, 29 January 2007.

CHAPTER 2

The Many Faces of European Colonialism: The Templers, the Basel Mission and the Zionist Movement

ILAN PAPPÉ

Ever since historiography was professionalised as a scientific discipline, historians have considered the motives for mass human geographical relocations. In the twentieth century, this quest focused on the colonialist settler projects that had moved hundreds of thousands of people from Europe into America, Asia and Africa in the preceding centuries. The various explanations for this human transit have changed considerably in recent times, and this transformation is the departure point for this chapter.

These early explanations for human relocations were empiricist and positivist; they assumed that every human action has a concrete explanation best found in the evidence left by those who performed that action. The practitioners of social history were particularly interested in the question, and when their field of inquiry was impacted by trends in philosophy and linguistics, their conclusions differed from those of the previous generation.

Research on Zionism should be seen in light of these historiographical developments. Until recently, in the Israeli historiography, the dominant explanation for the movement of Jews to Palestine in the nineteenth and twentieth centuries was – and in many ways, still is – positivist and empiricist.[1] Researchers analysed the motives for the first group of settlers who arrived on Palestine's shores in 1882 according to the testimonies in their diaries and other documents. The Palestinian historiography, also adhering to a positivist and empiricist approach, found ample historical evidence to show that this group of people had a very different set of motives from those attributed by the Israeli historiography. According to the Israeli interpretation, Zionism was a national liberation movement with a strong socialist past and more recent liberal tendencies that returned to its ancient homeland, derelict and empty since the exile of the Jews in Roman times, waiting to be resettled. According to the Palestinian explanation, Zionism was a colonialist movement that penetrated the Palestinian homeland by force, with the wish to colonise the country and with the possible expansionist ambitions to penetrate the heart of the Arab world.

While this book focuses on comparing Zionism to apartheid, and Israel to South Africa, in this chapter I wish to widen the conceptual as well as the historical scope and look at a preliminary question. Was and is Zionism a colonialist movement? The search for an answer is conducted here through a comparative study rather than using a conventional examination of the Zionist case study against the theoretical and abstract notions of colonialism. Both modes of examination are valid, but I felt that the former was less common. What is offered here is a fresh look at the historical case of Zionism through a comparative analysis of the movement. Zionism is contextualised here historically and thematically as a rather unconventional case of colonialism, diluted by strong nationalist features, but still one that existed elsewhere – and in particular in Palestine itself and in West Africa. It belongs more generally, as illuminated clearly by Gabi Piterberg in a recent book, within the family of settler colonialism.[2]

It seems that the Zionist settlers were motivated by national impulse but acted as pure colonialists. Such a depiction of Zionism is still strongly rejected by mainstream academia in Israel and the USA.[3] The immigration of Jews from (mainly eastern) Europe to the heart of the Arab Middle East is still described today in Israeli and American academia as a pure liberal national enterprise, and any attempt to attribute colonialist features to it is rejected out of hand. This is a bewildering phenomenon in the age of professional historiography. Zionism was not, after all, the only case in history in which a colonialist project was pursued in the name of national or otherwise anti-colonialist ideals. Zionists relocated to Palestine at the end of a century in which Europe controlled much of Africa, the Caribbean and other places in the name of 'progress' or idealism – something that was not unfamiliar to the Zionist movement. It happened in a century when French settlers colonised Algeria, claiming an atavistic and emotional link to the Algerian soil no less profound than that professed by the early Zionists with regard to *Eretz Israel*. Similarly, the cynical reassurances of the Zionist settlers to the native population had been made before by British settlers in Africa and Asia. Like the Zionists, the colonies built by Europeans in these continents became imperialist communities serving only the strategic interests of European powers and the settlers themselves. In the period of the white man's penetration into Africa and Asia, the Jews 'returned' to their 'homeland'.

Israeli historians hesitate to compare early Zionism with colonialism – although some of the more progressive among them are willing at least to apply the comparison to the Israeli colonisation of the Palestinian areas occupied in 1967. This reluctance is due to two principal reasons. First, they wish not to deviate from the empiricist and positivist approach that analyses the nature of an ideological and human movement according to its declared goals. This is a methodological preference of Israeli historiography to see the documents written by the forefathers of Zionism prior to the act of settlement as the exclusive historical explanation for that act. With its missionary and socialist overtones, the national discourse of the early Zionists does not include, as a rule, overt colonialist intentions, and thus the movement cannot be branded, according to mainstream Israeli historiography, as *colonialist.* The second reason is the bad reputation of colonialism in our times. Although, as I argue elsewhere, the worst crimes committed by Zionism against the local Palestinians were national in character and not colonialist, it is difficult to convince Palestinian historians that labelling Zionism as *nationalist* or *national* does not absolve it from accusations of dispossession and occupation.

In the 1990s, a more critical Israeli historiography challenged the established narrative and offered a less nationalistic deconstruction of the texts of such thinkers as Arthur Rupin, Menachem Usishqin and Otto Warburg. They were introduced in the new works as conventional examples of European colonialists who came to settle in Palestine's *terra nullius* and fight against mosquitoes, swamps, and the indigenous population. Baruch Kimmerling and Gershon Shafir led the thinking in this new direction. Kimmerling saw Zionism as a mixture of territorial nationalism and colonialism, and Shafir depicted early Zionism as a clear variant of colonialism.[4] This was followed, as already mentioned, by the clearest location of Zionism within settler colonialism by Gabi Piterberg and others.[5] Against them, the more established historians continue to argue that Zionism is a pure nationalist movement with no colonialist features. Israeli historians such as Anita Shapira, Ran Aaronson and others have examined the mechanism of settlement in the Palestinian land and labour markets and have concluded that it was motivated and enacted as a national project, innocent of any colonialist impulse.[6]

In this chapter, I try to understand the interplay between nationalism and colonialism by comparing Zionism with nineteenth-century European colonialism in order to find out how unique, or how conventional, Zionism was as a colonialist project.

METHODOLOGY

In the search for comparative cases, the natural choice would have been national colonialism of the kind that produced the nation-states of

Australia and New Zealand, and those in North and South America. But in these cases, British, Spanish and Portuguese nationals were sent by a mother country and then rebelled against it. I seek a movement that had no clear mother country and went across the world in order to fulfil a vision of a return to an ancient homeland, as if it were a national movement; however, in reality it had to dispossess other people, and, therefore, it essentially became a colonialist project. And although South Africa, the major theme of this book, is an obvious example, as mentioned before, the research here is expanded in other chapters.

At first, these impulses to move had little to do with the wish to colonise but rather indicated a strong desire to build an ideal life. The territorialisation, mainly the choice of Palestine, transformed Zionism from a national project into a colonialist one. I found two cases that fitted this paradigm: the pre-Zionist Christian colonisation of Palestine (referred to here as the 'peaceful crusade') and the Basel Mission's colonisation of West Africa. The former began in the 1850s and ended just before the Zionists arrived in Palestine, and the latter commenced in 1820 and lasted until 1950.

I will compare these historical cases according to three dimensions: self-image, discourse, and praxis on the ground. These three aspects are examined in relation not only to the local population but also to an adopted mother country that served temporarily as a metropole. In these cases, as in Zionism, regardless of the motivations or intentions, alleged or otherwise, the three dimensions appear to be clearly colonialist. It means that the 'isms' in this chapter – such as colonialism, socialism and nationalism – are treated not only as ideologies but as settlers' interpretations of the reality that is manifested in their self-images, discourses and action. The features of the settlers' world vary in nature: they can be the colonies themselves, the textbooks of the settlers' educational system, the economic praxis and so on. They are established according to nationalist impulse in the case of Zionism and missionary zeal in the case of the Christian colonisation of Palestine and the Basel Mission's West African colonisation, but they all become pure colonialist tools when actually implemented. Thus, for instance, a kibbutz symbolised a wish to lead a collective life, but in the way in which it was constructed, in the early twentieth century, it broadcast a wish to defend an aggressive settlement against a local population and a desire to utilise the space economically.

THE 'PEACEFUL CRUSADE' AND ITS IMPACT

The pre-Zionist European attempts to settle in Ottoman Palestine warrant a comparison with Zionism if only because of their similar territorial and chronological frameworks. Moreover, as they preceded Zionism and there is no known challenge to their depiction as colonialism, they may also have influenced Zionism as a colonialist phenomenon. The German settler Hermann Guthe described them as *friedlichen Kreuzzuges* (a 'peaceful crusade'), and they were motivated by the wish to return the Holy Land to Christian hands, but not in the brutal manner of the Crusades.[7] To Catholics and Protestants, this peaceful 'redemption' seemed similar to the conversion of the local population to Christianity, which, in turn, would precipitate the second coming of the Messiah – this fitted with the divine apocalyptic scheme that would also include the return of the Jews to Palestine. This millenarianist idea aided, and disguised, the economic interests and strategic ambitions of European powers in the area. The main drive was to have as many strongholds as possible in the heart of the disintegrating Ottoman Empire.

This crusade began with pilgrimages and journeys to the Holy Land and ended in the attempt to establish colonies. Among the first who tried to settle in Palestine was Victor Guérin, a famous French explorer of the land. In his writings, he predicted the creation of Christian colonies, and to that end he toiled over mapping the land and meticulously studying its history and ethnography. His coveted aspirations were almost identical to those expressed by Usishqin, one of the leading early Zionists, who, like Guérin, was a studious explorer of the land and its history. Guérin wished to revive the crusaders' kingdoms, while Usishqin dreamed of resurrecting the biblical empire of King David.[8]

Both the peaceful crusaders and the Zionists were primarily, and initially, troubled by the question of acquiring land; here the projects became colonialist. The Promised Land, in national or religious terms, had to be bought or forcefully taken from the local population. The Christian and Zionist colonialists approached the problem in similar ways. The purchase of land was described by both groups as 'redemption'. And in 1948, when the Zionist movement took over most of the land of historical Palestine by force, it was still referred to as 'redemption' of the land. However, in the nineteenth century, the settlers of both movements bought the land and did not expel anyone directly from it. This was due more to the fact that they lacked sufficient means to carry out such a forceful eviction than to any moral considerations. Usishqin's words echo the feelings of the peaceful crusaders regarding this question:

> The whole of Palestine, or at least most of it, must belong to the Jewish people ... this can be achieved by three means: by force, but we do not have it, governmental coercion or purchase.[9]

Of the three options, only purchasing the land was possible in the late nineteenth century. Possessing the land was a national or religious mission, but the means were colonialist.

Always lurking, of course, was the issue of the fate of the local population once the land had been successfully obtained. At the outset this was not supposed to be a question of great significance. Seen from the perspective of the initial impulse to settle in Palestine, the missionaries and the Zionists regarded the native population as marginal. The locals were hardly there in the early visions of the future, as is apparent in the utopian novel written by the founder of Zionism, Theodor Herzl. For Guérin, too, the locals were to disappear into oblivion once progress and modernity impressed themselves on the newfound land of Palestine. Whatever happened to them would pale in comparison to the advantages of the peaceful crusade of Zionism, the forces that would make the arid land blossom and transform the country into a civilised European entity.

But there was no way of ignoring the Palestinians. They were needed for their knowledge of the land, and they had to be considered when they forcefully rejected any attempt to take over their homeland. In view of the reality, and not the vision, the German colonialists advocated the exploitation of the locals for the benefit of the enterprise, and not their expulsion. *Das Heilige Land*, a German journal, promised its readers that the peasants in Palestine would be happy to sell their lands in return for bread and protection.[10] This was condoned more crudely by Claude Conder, the head of the Palestine Exploration Fund, who proposed to turn the locals into carvers of wood and fetchers of water.[11]

However, there were others who talked about dispossession. Some leading German missionaries advocated transferring the indigenous population. For instance, during the tenth convention of the Catholic societies in Germany, in 1855, most participants spoke of a 'missed opportunity' when referring to the failure to uproot the local population of Palestine during the Crimean War, thereby paving the way for the creation of a pure Christian state there.[12] Peaceful crusaders such as Scottish philanthropist Lord Laurence Oliphant also advocated expulsion. Oliphant wanted to establish a sort of colony in Balqa in Transjordan and suggested imprisoning the local nomads in reservations, like those prepared for Native Americans, so that law and order could be guaranteed for the settlers. Oliphant would have a considerable influence on the Zionist movement. Some of his ideas for the colonisation of the land would become Zionist projects, such as drying out Hula Lake to make it suitable for European settlement and driving away the semi-nomads who lived around it. These proved to be successful capitalist projects but ecological disasters.[13]

As already mentioned, the leaders of the Zionist movement spoke more openly about dispossessing and exiling the locals. Isaac Rolf, a leading German Zionist rabbi, called for the expulsion of the locals from the land:

> For the time being we only talk on settlement and only on settlement and this is indeed our near aim. We talk only on that. But it must be clear as 'England is only for the English, Egypt for the Egyptians, Judea is for the Jews'. In our land there is only room for us. We will say to the Arabs: move, and if they disagree, if they resist by force – we will force them to move, we will hit them on their heads and force them to move.[14]

Every articulation of dispossession can be juxtaposed with one of exploitation. Exploitation was always presented as a wish to advance modernisation in the native local population. Usishqin can be found advocating both. This ambiguity between the wish to expel and exploit as part of a desire to modernise produced in both cases concepts such as temporary exploitation. The Zionist movement wished to take over the labour and land markets but could not yet do so, so exploitation had to be temporary. Yitzhak Ben-Zvi, later the second president of Israel, and David Ben-Gurion, one of the leaders of the early Zionist settlers and the founder of the state as well as its first prime minister, explained it well when developing the concept of *avoda ivrit* (Hebrew labour). According to Ben-Zvi: 'My hope is that in due course we will grasp the decisive place in the Palestine economy and in its collective and social life'.[15] It is obvious who was to occupy the marginal role in the economy: the Palestinians who formed the vast majority of the population at the time. Ben-Zvi was a leading member of *Hapoel Hazair* (the Young

Worker), which formed the nucleus of the future labour movement. His colleagues' written legacies are far more colonialist than his. One of these colleagues, Yaakov Rabinowitz, saw no contradiction in heading a seemingly socialist movement such as *Hapoel Hazair* and arguing for a segregated, colonialist labour market:

> The Zionist establishment should defend the Jewish workers against the Arab one, as the French government protects the French colonialists in Algeria against the natives.[16]

But the impurity of his colonialism and his colonialist discourse appear in this statement: 'And as other governments defend their workers against Chinese cheap labourers'.[17]

Ben-Zvi talked about temporary exploitation; when not contemplating expulsion, Usishqin desired a superior role that would be recognised by the Semites of the East because of the racial similarities between the Jews and the Arabs. This would make Zionism a positive kind of colonialism:

> I have seen the colonies of the English in Egypt. The English introduced there their own administration and Capitalism ... but if you ask the Arabs, do they want to live under England's rule, you will get a negative answer since the English are only looking for their own good and not that of the local people. Our role should be entirely different. With this old world, the world of the East, we should unite. We should bring them, our brethren to the race, a real culture, a culture of existence not a fictional one. We should solve the problem of the East.[18]

As we have seen, the same Usishqin advocated the expulsion of these brothers; as the years passed by, the contradiction was solved. If the Palestinians were willing to convert to Judaism or totally succumb to the Zionisation of the land, they could be tolerated. If they resisted, then they would be uprooted. Usishqin reflected – and one assumes was influenced by – the self-praising discourse employed generously all over colonialist Africa. Whether in South Africa or in other parts of the continent, individual and local colonialist movements claimed to be not only beneficial to the natives but also better than other colonialist projects and movements. The leaders of the Basel Mission asserted that they had brought a fair and attractive gospel for the locals compared with those of other colonialists. Christian colonialists in Palestine felt the same. Conrad Schick, for instance, the German demographer who was mainly busy preparing a master plan for the Christian colonisation of Palestine – namely, a massive transfer of European immigrants to the land – believed that his schemes were the only way to improve the agricultural conditions of the country for the benefit of all its inhabitants.[19]

Among the peaceful crusaders, one group deserves particular attention: the Templers, who operated in Palestine from 1868 until the arrival of Zionism in 1882. They were a typical product of the Protestant Pietist movement that appeared in the seventeenth-century German state of Württemberg. This movement sought to arrest the modernisation of religion, cut short the way to doomsday and prepare believers for the second coming of the Messiah. It also regarded the Industrial Revolution as heresy and a threat. These beliefs were commonly accepted by the more traditional sections of the German-speaking Protestant society. The movement was particularly popular in Württemberg, which was a predominately rural state without many progressive urban centres. In Württemberg, Pietism bred the Templers' movement.

The Templers' first mission was to buy land, which was possible until the second half of the nineteenth century. In the mid-nineteenth century, land was privatised in the Ottoman Empire. What had been state land (quite often leased rather than owned directly) was transferred to the local elite. Much of the land coveted by foreigners in Palestine belonged to absentee landlords in neighbouring countries who were quite eager to sell the land to Germans and Jews. This was done despite the near ownership position of their tenants, who had been living there for centuries.

There were other common features with Zionism. The attitude and depiction of the locals as almost absent or marginal and a great belief in agricultural innovations (which benefited mainly the settlers and not the local population) were the two salient similarities. Also similar was a discourse of 'return' to a Holy Land that was 'theirs' by divine right and had been 'empty' for two millennia.[20]

THE BASEL MISSION

This kind of colonialism, which Gabi Piterberg identifies as 'settler colonialism', and in an earlier version of this article I named 'diluted' colonialism, was not particular to the Zionist movement or limited to Palestine itself. It can be found in the missionary Protestant colonisation in Asia and Africa. Protestant missionary work in general, be it British or German, is worthy of comparison with Zionism for two main reasons. First, such missionary work was often colonialist in outlook. In fact, it was realised through massive settlement colonies, whereas Catholic missionary work tended to entrust proselytising to a chosen few. Protestant missions brought whole families along and employed laypeople as heads of its operations. At the headquarters of the Protestant missions on both sides of the Atlantic, secular leaders were often deeply involved in the making and execution of policy. Second, it is a valid historical comparison because of the special role Britain played in the effort to allow the 'return' of the Jews to their homeland and bring Christianity to Asia and Africa. This is particularly relevant to Africa, where the two principal colonialist powers, Germany and Britain, used the missionaries to expand their influence. It seems that Britain was exploiting Zionism in a similar way in Palestine as part of the overall drive to take over the Ottoman possessions in the eastern part of the Middle East.

The utilisation was mutual. The British Empire needed the missionary network to penetrate Africa, and the missionaries were unable to exist initially without the imperial infrastructure supporting them. This interdependence served Zionism well too. Thus, for a while, Britain was the 'mother country' of these two colonialist movements. Eventually, the two movements turned against Britain, but Britain was there for them in the crucial formative years. For the purposes of this chapter, the most relevant of all the missionary groups was the Basel Mission. Before comparing the discourse, symbols and location of the Basel Mission and Zionism within a more conventional definition of colonialism (namely, their relationship to a mother country), I will compare the similar historical context in which both movements operated.

THE HISTORICAL CONTEXT

The Basel Mission was founded in 1730 in Basel and simultaneously in some cities in Germany. The founders were Pietists, like the Templers, who were determined to salvage their society from the perils of industrialisation. With a particular religious fervour and a strong collectivist, almost proto-socialist enthusiasm, the Basel Mission aspired to produce agricultural collectivism that was to stimulate what it called Christian agriculturalism, a mode of life that represented the purest form of devotion, as it demanded the harshest personal sacrifices from the believer, given the task at hand. As with other Pietists at the time, such positions were unacceptable to the established church, and the missionaries were forced to leave. They were deported first to the Caucasus and then to Africa.[21]

The movement of the missionaries to the Caucasus and then to Africa and the arrival of the first Zionists in Palestine were triggered by similar socio-economic processes. Both in Württemberg and in Eastern Europe, the traditional rural areas were badly affected by industrialisation, and the wrath of the local peasants was easily directed towards those sections of Zionism as a colonialism society that were different because of their religious convictions and ways of life. The inability to survive economically and religiously was a powerful factor in both cases.[22]

This movement out of Europe was not associated with any particular European colonialist or metropolitan state. Throughout its existence, the Basel Mission vacillated between Danish, German and British colonialism but always preferred London's umbrella to that of the other countries. The main reason was that its particular brand of agricultural mission work suited the strategic understanding of British colonialism in West Africa. But it was not an ideological affinity. Those working directly for the British Empire pursued policies of modernisation abhorred by the missionaries. Members of the Basel Mission saw themselves as the religious victims of rapid urbanisation and industrialisation advanced by Britain and Germany. Britain had very little interest in or patience with the socialist or Marxist message the Zionists were allegedly bringing to Palestine (although some pious British politicians such as David Lloyd George did share the dream of a return to the Holy Land). But the collectivist settlement helped Britain to deepen and expand initial footholds in Palestine and West Africa.

Agricultural collectivism played a major role in both cases. Long before a non-European territory was clearly targeted for colonisation, both the Zionists and Basel Mission members tried to live collectively in Europe – the Zionists in the name of socialism and the missionaries in the name of Christ. But the collectives were very similar in structure and ethos. When the pressure to leave grew, due to prosecution and economic hardship, the archetypical models were imported to Palestine and West Africa. Basel Mission members called colonies in West Africa 'model villages', which broadcast an interpretation of Christianity as a combination of family values and commonsensical ecological exploitation of the natural resources. When established in Africa, the villages became typical colonialist communities – similar to today's gated communities.

After their arrival in Africa, the missionary collectivists appealed to the Danish government that had begun to explore West Africa's Gold Coast (what is now Ghana) in the early 1820s. Under Danish auspices, the first Basel colonies were established in that part of the continent. The Basel Mission created a collective settlement of Europeans that aspired both to exploit its new native environment and to serve as a model for it. It was born in a similar cultural context as Zionism – a messianic, monotheistic justification of return (which, in the case of Zionism, was carried out by secular Jews). The mission expanded its activities beyond Ghana into today's Cameroon and Nigeria.

The 'model village' was presented as a means of preserving core African values, but in practice it became a tool for European control and supremacy through agricultural modernisation. The declared wish to preserve traditional agricultural values was never even attempted. When the settlements expanded, they became such a powerful factor in the local economy that they turned into a principal employer in the colony. Their arrival thus generated the process of semi-proletarianisation in rural Ghana and, to a certain extent, in Cameroon.[23] Similar processes were created by the agricultural and land policies of the Zionist movement. In Palestine, until 1948 the process was led by British development policies and Zionist land purchases that rendered agriculture an unsatisfactory source of livelihoods. After 1948, the Palestinian minority in Israel and the Palestinians in the Occupied Territories would undergo similar processes of semi-proletarianisation.[24]

In Africa, the local population responded ambivalently. Some heads of tribes cooperated and some resisted. As a whole, the environment was hostile. The Ashanti, the strongest tribe in the area, managed to resist the colonialist missionary until 1850. The mission had to wait patiently for British forces to defeat the Ashanti (just as the Zionist movement had to wait for Edmund Allenby's victory in the battle for Palestine in World War I). After the missionary colonialist movement was linked with British colonialism, a network of villages was established. In 1850, Britain 'bought' Ghana from Denmark and became the law and order in the land.

With this new wind at its back, the mission became more intent on taking over land from the Ashanti. Before they were finally defeated by the British, the Ashanti fought a bitter war. The mission had to wait for the first comprehensive military confrontation between Britain and the kingdom, which raged off and on for thirty-six years (1860–96). It ended when British troops occupied Kumasi, the kingdom's capital, which became the mission's principal station. As a result of the war, Kumasi had been completely destroyed by the time missionaries entered it. Similarly, the mission trailed behind British successes in Cameroon and Nigeria.

The connection with Britain further weakened the mission's association with Germany and Switzerland. Although its European headquarters remained in Berlin for most of the nineteenth century, the mission belonged to Britain politically. After World War I and the German defeat, the mission moved its headquarters from Berlin to Scotland. Coincidentally, a similar change in location took place in the Zionist movement, which moved from Berlin to London. The reasons and the motivations were the same. Finally, in this note on comparative historical contexts, it is worth mentioning an important difference between the two. The Basel Mission perceived itself as a tool for building an African Protestant Christianity. For this purpose, it hoped to lead the way in forming new national religions in the emerging colonies in West Africa. It wished to 'nationalise' Christianity for the sake of the local national movements, and in this respect it was very different from Zionism. For Zionism, nationalism meant total alienation from the local people, which eventually led to violent confrontations with them.

However, when viewed through their discourses, symbols and relationships with Britain, it becomes clear that we are examining two very similar versions of meta-colonialist concepts and perceptions.

DISCURSIVE AND SYMBOLIC PRACTICES

In both movements, discursive attributions to the Bible and agriculture were prominent. The holy book and the plough appear literally and visually in the speeches of the leading members and indirectly in the daily discourse of the grassroots members:[25] West African and Palestinian colonisation in the name of religion (the Bible), supported by the force of the 'sword' (colonial weaponry). The difference is that in Zionism the land was depicted as a desert made to bloom by Zionism (reincarnating the fertile land of the Bible), while the missionaries effected the wise and ecological cultivation of a very fertile land.

'Return' also occupies a central place in the two movements' discourses. Zionism referred constantly to the return to the Promised Land, while the Basel Mission stressed a return to the 'pure' land (almost in a Rousseauian sense of going back to pre-decadent civilisation or, in this case, a pre-decadent industrialisation). Common to both was the idea that God endowed Africa with natural resources, but only his true believers, or those who were about to become true believers, knew how to properly exploit such resources. This sounds very much like Ben-Gurion's utterances on the same subject:

> The land is waiting for a cultural, industrious people. Enriched by material and spiritual resources; armed with the weapon of Science and Technology. The country craves for this people to come and settle in it, bloom its arid mountains, fertilize its uncultivated land, forest its sands and the deserted country would become heaven ... The Jews, as can already be seen in their agricultural colonies, will introduce to the land improved tools,

updated agricultural methods and develop the land's drainage and transportation systems.[26]

Whereas 'return' in the case of the Basel Mission did not include total possession of the local people, in the case of Zionism it was more ambiguous. Ben-Gurion's words refer to Zionism as the harbinger of progress in Palestine for the sake of everyone living there. As he puts it: 'Our renaissance in Palestine would be the renaissance of the land; namely that of the Arabs in it'.[27] A few years later, this sentiment would die, and the major desire of Ben-Gurion and his colleagues would be to ethnically cleanse Palestine of its Arab population. This transformation indicated that it was impossible to reconcile the two images of 'return' in Zionism: 'returning' to the homeland for the sake of the progress and enlightenment of the indigenous population, and returning to the land in order to create a pure supremacist state for the newcomers.[28]

The various forms of agricultural collectives built by the Zionist settlement (*kibbutz*, *moshava* and *moshav*) and the 'model villages' erected by the missionaries had much in common. Both types of settlement were meant at first to serve as an ideal for the world – or at least for the closest reference group, Christians or Jews. Then the collectives were seen to serve solely and exclusively the needs of the settlers in a hostile environment. The settlers and missionaries were so overwhelmed by local antagonism and hostility, on the one hand, and by developed racist attitudes toward indigenous peoples, on the other, that the collectiveness was no longer a universal dream but rather a means of survival for the settlers and missionaries.

Using the collectives as paragons was stressed, while model habitations were experimented with in Europe. For the Zionist models, this continued to be emphasised, for as long as the true identity of the Promised Land was unclear. (Uganda, Azerbaijan and Argentina were three out of many possible destinations, as were several 'empty' spaces in the United States.) Another group of Jewish settlers, also moved by national feeling, were building a model village in America. This group was the Am Olam (the People of the World) movement, which strove to erect a model agricultural collective in Louisiana. This collective inspired the first model village, Gedera, of the early Zionist settlers (the Biluim).[29]

There were, of course, stark differences in the ways in which the colonies were run as collective agricultural units. The Basel Mission's recipe for ideal life was agriculture based on the extended family, a limited degree of mechanisation, and a Presbyterian way of life. For the Zionists, the Marxist world of sharing the means of production, possession and privilege meant that they had a strong anti-family and, indeed, an anti-tradition bias. But, as in the case of Zionism, missionary collectivism was not just an ideology but was in fact the best way to survive in Africa. Living in the early Zionist colonies in Palestine and in the 'model villages' of the mission was a colonialist praxis, informed by a colonialist – and not a Christian or a socialist – interpretation of reality. Moreover, for the local people, both Zionism and the Basel Mission were perceived as pure colonialist and the colonies as the principal manifestation of oppression and occupation.

Discursively and symbolically, the two movements were equally troubled by money and the way to deal with its corrupting potential. Anyone wishing to find a connection in the colonialist era between cynical economic considerations and an alleged ethic altruism will benefit from the comparison here. The missionaries were very troubled by their external and internal image, given the obvious affluence of their settlements. The 'model villages' proved to be very profitable. However, at first, the Basel Mission claimed that its financial dealings were not for profit but were for self-sufficiency and simple existence. In its early years, the mission, like the Zionist movement, relied mainly on donations from philanthropists abroad and then on the agricultural production of the villages. But this was soon expanded to other areas, and the mission developed its own banking and commercial systems and established a trade company. When it proved that it had the financial ability to maintain its economic independence, it became a sought-after investment market for former missionary groups.[30]

Actual and symbolic Zionist dealings with finance developed in very similar ways, as can be seen from the thorough research carried out by the Israeli economic historian Nahum Gross. In a 1990 article, he called for another look at the relations between capitalist profit considerations and 'Zionist considerations'. Gross described the complex relationship between external philanthropy, Zionist and non-Zionist investors, and the political leadership in Palestine. He concluded that the establishment of cooperative unions (the backbone of the agricultural Zionist settlement in rural areas) was a convenient economic substitute for capitalist corporations and not – as the Israeli historiography would have it, even today – the fruit of socialist ideology.[31] This echoes points made by both Ernest Gelner and Gershon Shafir regarding early Zionist socialism as a tactical way to survive in a hostile environment rather than a means of fulfilling utopian socialist dreams.[32]

The realm of education is another intriguing field of comparison, both in its actual structure and its symbolic content. For the Zionists, education was of the highest priority. Since the British allowed the Zionists to establish an autonomous educational system, while the Palestinian majority was subjected to a typical colonialist approach, the Jewish community was given a crucial advantage over the local Palestinians. The Zionists then wanted to make education the backbone of the fledgling state.

The impulse in the case of the Basel Mission was different. It also established its own educational system, independent of the colonialist one in West Africa. But it was driven by a fear of the growing power of Islam as an educating force. This anti-Islamic attitude was inherited from the Christian Missionary Society (CMS), which had been working in West Africa before the Basel Mission arrived. A British society, the CMS concocted the ethos of an anti-colonialist missionary with the aim of salvaging Africa. For the Basel Mission, education was to continue the propagation of trade for the sake of Africa, education for the sake of African nationalism, and agricultural reform for the sake of African peasants, provided all these efforts were Christian, not Muslim or pagan.

In the Zionist community, education did not have an overt anti-Islamic tone, but the discourse about and images of Muslims were very much the same as those of the Basel Mission. At the height of the anti-Islamic efforts of the CMS and the Basel Mission, during World War I, the language used would be familiar to anyone looking at educational products in the early years of statehood in Israel in the 1950s. The image and perceptions of Islam and Muslims relied, in both cases, on scholarly Western Orientalism.

In the late nineteenth century, the CMS funded anthropological research into West African society. The research concluded that, without converting to Christianity, the Africans would be unable to integrate in the CMS's development efforts: 'Christianity and Civilization have to go hand in hand in Africa, if both wish to progress'.[33] In the wake of this slogan, black churches in Canada seriously considered 'homecoming'.[34] The black community in Canada was excited by the idea that bringing Christianity to Africa was a modernising mission, which the community wanted to spearhead. A similar understanding of the link between the colonisation of Palestine and a correct and progressive practice of Judaism can be found in several of the national religious parties that formed a crucial part of the Zionist movement as a whole and that are an essential part of the political scene of Israel today.

The CMS had a lot in common with the pre-Zionist colonisation of Palestine. In a way, it preceded the Basel Mission, as did the peaceful crusaders and the Templers' Zionism. These groups also tried to create self-sufficient colonies. 'Rich Africa was not properly exploited until we arrived', they declared. The CMS began to grow cotton, which could not handle the tough climate. The Basel missionaries were more successful. They grew cacao and palms and, as a result of their success, moved from self-sufficient agriculture to an industrial model. The profits were invested in the creation of new colonies and in furthering the mission's influence in Ghana and Cameroon. At a certain point, the mission became the principal political force in those countries. 'We preach the gospel of Jesus, Coffee, Coca, Cotton and Labour', the missionaries declared.[35]

Such successes eroded the movements' original ideals and pure visions. The Basel Mission expanded in Nigeria with the help of agricultural projects and employed thousands of local workers.[36] Preachers who themselves used to work in the plants became supervisors and then owners of the businesses. Jewish labourers took a similar path. In both cases, it transpired that the colonisation would be much more successful and efficient if collectivism were to be substituted with commerce and industry. Both movements brought labour from the outside that was similar in origin to the native groups but ideologically acceptable to the settlers' world. In 1827, the mission brought men and women to Ghana from the West Indies to help with proselytising, and, in the twentieth century, together with the locals, they became part of the main labour force in this region of Africa.

THE FAVOURED STEPCHILDREN OF THE MOTHER COUNTRY

Finally, the British role cements the argument made here about the exceptional colonialism that characterised both Zionism and the Basel Mission's work. To all intents and purposes, Britain owned the lands in which the Zionists and the Basel Mission operated. As such, the two groups were not proper colonies of a mother country, Britain, but satellite movements. These satellite movements were typified by a temporary association with colonialism, quite often in the name of anti-colonialist ideologies, and this is why the satellite movements originally assisted by European colonialism eventually turned against it. The Creoles of North and South America, as they appear in Benedict Anderson's *Imagined Communities*, were such a satellite group; Anderson accords them a formative role in the emergence of modern nationalism.[37]

At first, the Basel Mission's relationship with Britain was very tense. In their recollections, the missionaries reported a lofty attitude and a constant friction between British government officials and the settlers. In due course, mutual respect developed, but finally the mission made a connection with the West African liberation movement that struggled against the British Empire. However, this was not a straightforward policy. Some of the missionaries served the government of British Ghana. Some were behind significant reforms in the way in which British colonies were run in Nigeria, Ghana and Cameroon. The mission's official narrative also accords the organisation a decisive role in abolishing slavery in West Africa. None of these characteristics are similar to those of the Zionist movement, but what is similar is the framework of existing as a satellite movement relying on the British Empire. The relationship between Zionism and the British developed differently, but at its core there was a similar ambivalence. Above all, it was British military might that enabled the 'return' of the Jews to Palestine and of the Basel Mission to 'the pure land of God'.

One of the main arguments against any attempt to examine Zionism as a colonialist phenomenon is that Zionism cannot be colonialist because there is no recognised mother country or metropole. The same is true for the Basel Mission, as we have seen. Indeed, the particularism of both – namely, their satellite status compared with ordinary colonies – lies in the complex way in which their relationship developed with Britain. The Jewish national homeland was built and survived due to British imperial support. Had London wished otherwise, the Jewish state would have been a fait accompli in 1917 – or it would not have come into being at all. The strategy finally adopted by Britain was to endorse the slow construction of a Jewish community in Palestine, with the hope that it could be integrated into a new Anglo-Arab Middle

Eastern political system. The British attitude towards the Basel Mission was quite similar.

This complex relationship was manifested in the preferential economic treatment granted by the mandatory government to the Jewish community. It enjoyed concessions that the Palestinians could only have dreamed of. The British government encouraged the heads of the Zionist project to be self-sufficient economically and entrusted to them the natural resources of the land. In this way, the Zionist economy was segregated from the Palestinian one, as was the land and labour market, and a Jewish economic enclave was created. The British had a similar attitude to the Basel Mission economy. Both Zionism and the Basel Mission were stepchildren, but, unlike Cinderella, they did not suffer from any discrimination; on the contrary, they were always chosen over the legitimate children of the family (namely, those who were properly the 'colonised' people). The economic enclave was protected by the Empire, which acted as a classical colonialist mother country. The natural resources of Palestine and West Africa were not exploited by any rival colonialist empire, and the same applied to the finance and real estate markets, which were defended against greedy profiteers from the outside. Britain was busy pursuing a protectionist policy that enabled both the Basel and Zionist economies to grow and develop at the expense of the local economy and interests.

The British allowed the Zionist movement to establish not only an economic enclave but also a separate administrative infrastructure for a future state. This is a unique feature in the conventional British colonialist praxis. Officials in London and Jerusalem did not have time to examine the Zionist settlement as part of the British colonialist world. The Zionist settlements were not made up of a typical group of natives that could easily be exploited for the Empire's sake in the name of 'the white man's burden'. The usual lofty and condescending imperial attitude did not work here. Moreover, with time the Zionist movement, very much like the Basel Mission, behaved as a rival colonialist force.

But it could not be engaged in a similar way to competing European powers: there was no room for negotiation over strategic interests or territories elsewhere as part of the imperial game of quid pro quo. It could not be bought by money alone, as it was generally not motivated by profit considerations. However we define national motivation, it operated powerfully behind the Zionist policy vis-à-vis Britain and more fatally against the Palestinians, ending in their dispossession.

Barbara Smith offers another intriguing explanation for the British willingness to allow such economic independence during the British Mandate. Most of the Jewish immigrants who came from Eastern Europe expected a certain level of services in the new country. The British were willing to provide only the minimal level necessary to prevent the colony from becoming an economic burden. The absence of modern services furnished by the government forced the Jewish community to supply them itself.[38]

Whatever the reason, the economic enclave allowed the Jewish minority to establish a state while the Palestinian leadership was dormant and naïve and relied on British governmental policies and false promises of protection and progress. British officials ran the Palestinian systems of life, and, as happened throughout the Empire, these were maintained at a very limited and low level of modernisation and development. Economic thriftiness suppressed the native population in Western and Southern Africa, as it did in Palestine.

As with the Basel Mission, the Zionists' positive connection to Britain was eventually replaced with confrontation. But whereas only some of the missionaries joined the African liberation movement while others remained with the British administration, the national component in Zionism did not allow such diversity. In this respect, Zionism more closely resembles white colonies in America and the Far East. The Zionist war of liberation against the Empire, which lasted for three years (1945–48), was one that was also fought by the American, Australian and New Zealander settlers against their mother country (and, more recently, by Ian Smith in Rhodesia). These are all examples of European colonialism that bred local territorial nationalism.

CONCLUSION

The story of the Basel Mission stretches over 130 years, and it is not easy to conclude whether it was a success or a failure. It is noteworthy that a sizeable part of the population in the three countries in which it operated is today Protestant. The three countries have a large number of African churches. Yet Christianity is not the state religion, and the Protestants do not constitute a majority (although, in these countries, there is no religious majority). What is clear is that turning West Africa into a Christian haven is no longer on anyone's agenda.

In the comparison here, between Zionism and the Basel Mission, success or failure is not the point; rather, it is how we evaluate the historical chapter today. If the verdict offered here is tenable, then the enterprises compared here in Palestine and in Africa, of Jews and Christians, were a far cry from the way in which they were portrayed and perceived by those who initiated and maintained them. In the case of Israel, the comparisons here are very different from how they are still narrated today by the established historiography. This is why the comparison was utilised – to understand Zionism as a historical phenomenon. The argument put forward here – that Zionism is a form of colonialism – is still rejected out of hand by the pro-Zionist scholarly community in the United States and, of course, in Israel.

But it does seem that, when compared with Catholic and Protestant colonialism in Palestine and Africa, Zionism appears to be a similar colonialist venture. In this chapter, a similarity has been found in the way in which land was taken over, the way the colonialist praxis was disguised using similar discourses of modernisation and religious morality, and, later on, in the adoption of an anti-colonialist self-image. As such, these cases were quite exceptional in the colonial arena – not only because one was nationalist and the other missionary, but because the pure colonialist examples were mainly motivated by economic considerations of profit and loss and were wholly dependent on the metropole.

Yet this comparison does not weaken the impact and role of nationalism in Zionism. While the Palestinian historiography depicts the phenomenon of Zionism as a pure colonialist case, the national ideology diluted the pure colonialist nature of Zionism. As colonialism is not just an objective but also a pattern of behaviour, it is important to ask whether it was colonialism or nationalism that turned the Zionist movement into a movement of dispossession (of the native Palestinians), a political force committed to the ethnic cleansing of Palestine. What justifications were used for the dispossession of the local people?

It seems that a pure colonialist movement would not seek the physical dispossession of the native and would remain steadfast in its self-image of bringing progress to the country. Only in its first stages did Zionism fit this pattern. Later on, its perception of the native population was drawn from the romantic nationalist world of discourses and images. It was a world in which the natural rights of one people totally negated those of another – even when the others had lived in that place for more than a millennium.

But this happened only in 1948. Until that moment in history, the tools employed by the Zionists were colonialist, and they were to be used once more towards the Palestinians in the West Bank and the Gaza Strip. It is thus a nationalist movement that employed, and still employs, colonialist tools to implement its strategy and vision. Only a universal methodology, a neutral terminology and a comparative perspective can allow for a serious analysis of the uniqueness of the Zionist phenomenon on the spectrum between colonialism and nationalism. Both are relevant terms: in the final analysis, neither of them promises anything positive or hopeful for the original people of Palestine.

Notes

1   For an exposure of this trend, see Ilan Pappé, 'Critique and Agenda: The Post-Zionist Scholars in Israel', *History and Memory* 7(1) (Spring/Summer 1995), pp. 66–91.

2   Gabriel Piterberg, *The Returns of Zionism*, London: Verso, 2009.

3   See John Mearsheimer and Stephen M. Walt, *The Israel Lobby and U.S. Foreign Policy*, New York: Farrar, Straus, and Giroux, 2007.

4   Baruch Kimmerling, *Zionism and Territory: The Socio-Territorial Dimensions of Zionist Politics*, Berkeley: University of California Press, 1983; Gershon Shafir, *Land, Labour, and the Origins of the Israeli-Palestinian Conflict, 1882–1914*, Cambridge: Cambridge University Press, 1987. Amir Ben Porat followed suit many years later in 'They Did Not Sit on the Fence: Opportunity, Longing, and Breakthrough to Palestine', *Iyumin be-Tekumat Israel* 4 (1994), pp. 278–98 (Hebrew).

5   Piterberg, *The Returns of Zionism.*

6   Anita Shapira, *The Elusive Struggle: Hebrew Labour, 1929-1939*, Tel Aviv: Am Oved, 1977 (Hebrew); Ran Aaronson, 'Philanthropy and Settlement: YKA and Its Activity', *Eretz Israel Studies in the Geography of Eretz Israel* 2 (1990), pp. 95–107.

7   A detailed description can be found in Alexander Scholch, *Palestine in Transformation, 1856–1882: Studies in Social, Economic and Political Development*, Washington, DC: Institute for Palestine Studies, 1992, pp. 95–107.

8   Victor Guérin, *Description géographique, historique, et archéologique de la Palestine*, Volume 1, Paris: Imprimerie Imperiale, 1868, pp. 270–3.

9   Menachem Usishqin, *The Usishqin Book*, Jerusalem: Committee for the Usishqin Publications, 1934, p. 105 (Hebrew).

10 Quoted in Scholch, *Palestine*, p. 71.

11 Claude Conder, 'The Present Condition in Palestine', *Palestine Exploration Fund Quarterly Statement* 8 (1879).

12 Quoted in Scholch, *Palestine*, p. 71.

13 Laurence Oliphant, *The Land of the Gilead with Excursions to Lebanon*, London: Dr Appleton and Company, 1881, p. 286.

14 Quoted in Ben Zion Dinur, *The Book of the Hagana*, Volume 1, Tel Aviv: Ministry of Defense Publications, 1965, pp. v–vi (Hebrew).

15 Yitzhak Ben-Zvi as quoted in Yossef Gorny, *The Arab Question and the Jewish Problem,* Tel Aviv: Am Oved, 1985, p. 84 (Hebrew).

16 Yaakov Rabinowitz, 'Defending the National Labour', *Ha-Poel Ha-Zair*, 10 March 1908 (Hebrew).

17 Ibid.
18 Usishqin, *The Usishqin Book*, pp. 116–17.
19 Konrad Schick, 'Studien über Colonisirung das Heiligen Landes',
    Österreichische Monatsschrift für den Orient 7 (1881), p. 37.
20 Alex Carmel, *The Settlement of the Germans in Palestine in the Late Ottoman
    Period*, Haifa: Haifa University Press, 1999 (Hebrew).
21 See Lamin Sanneh, *West African Christianity: The Religious Impact*, London:
    Allen and Unwin, 1983, pp. 107, 111–19,147–51; C. G. Baete (ed.), *Christianity
    in Tropical Africa: Studies Presented and Discussed at the Seventh International
    African Seminar, University of Ghana, April 1965*, London: Oxford University
    Press, 1968; Noel Quinton King, *Christian and Muslim in Africa*, New York:
    Harper and Row, 1971, pp. 47–57.
22 Such an explanation for Jewish immigration can be found in Shumuel
    Ettinger, *The History of the People of Israel in the Modern Era*, Tel Aviv: Dvir,
    1969, p. 148 (Hebrew).
23 This is the conclusion of Paul Jenkins in 'Towards a Definition of Pietism of
    Württemberg as a Missionary Movement' (paper given at the African Studies
    Association of the UK conference on whites in Africa, Oxford, September
    1978). See also Terence Ranger's note in Eric Hobsbawm and Terence Ranger
    (eds), *The Invention of Tradition*, Cambridge: Cambridge University Press,
    1994, p. 214.
24 See Sarah Graham-Brown, *Palestinians and their Society, 1880–1946*, London:
    Quartet Books, 1981.
25 Sanneh, *West African Christianity*, p. 160.
26 David Ben Gurion, 'Towards the Future', *Hatoren* 5 (1915), p. 1 (Hebrew).
27 Quoted in Shabtai Teveth, *Ben Gurion and the Palestinian Arabs: From War to
    Peace*, Jerusalem: Shoken, 1985, p. 48 (Hebrew).
28 Ilan Pappé, *The Ethnic Cleansing of Palestine*, London and New York:
    Oneworld, 2006.
29 Shmueel Neeman, 'BILU: An Emancipatory Movement and a Settler Body',
    Haziyonut 8 (1983), p. 30.
30 The information on the model villages is gathered from Baete, *Christianity in
    Tropical Africa*. See in particular the quoted memo on page 48 from M.M.S.
    (Mission Secretary) to Freeman, dated 10 July 1856.
31 Nahum Gross, 'Economic Enterprise in the Period of the Mandate and the
    State', *Yahadut Zemanenu* 6 (1990), pp. 293–304 (Hebrew).
32 Shafir, *Land, Labour*; Ernest Gelner, *Nationals and Nationalism*, Tel Aviv:
    Open University Publications, 1994, pp. 140–1 (Hebrew).
33 Quoted in Sanneh, *West African Christianity*, p. 159.

34 See Yossef Salmon, 'Tradition and Modernity in Early Zionist Religious Thought' in Yehoushua Ben-Zion (ed.), *Zionist Ideology and Policy*, Jerusalem: Shazar Centre, 1978, pp. 10, 26–7 (Hebrew).

35 Quoted in Sanneh, *West African Christianity*, p. 160.

36 Ibid.

37 Benedict Anderson, *Imagined Communities*, London: Verso, 1991, pp. 47–66.

38 Barbara Smith, *The Roots of Separatism in Palestine: British Economic Policy, 1920–1929*, Syracuse: Syracuse University Press, 1993, pp. 133–59.

CHAPTER 3

Apartheid and the Question of Origin

OREN BEN-DOR[1]

Origin here means that from which and by which something is what it is and as it is. What something is, as it is, we call its essence. The origin of something is the source of its essence.

Martin Heidegger, 'The Origin of the Work of Art'

Origin always comes to meet us from the future.

Martin Heidegger, 'A Dialogue on Language'

INTRODUCTION

In Afrikaans *apartheid* literally means 'apart-ness', 'keeping apart', 'separation'; often capitalised, apartheid then stands for 'a set of policies and practices of legal discrimination, political exclusion, and social marginalization, based on racial, national or ethnic origins'.[2] The question of *apartheid*, then, must be the question of separation – a question that calls for reflection on the notion of separateness.

We know that instantiations of *apartheid*, periods in history when a system of apartheid was put into operation, have been challenged as part of history, and that such durational manifestations of apartheid have successfully been opposed and overcome. Any given historical narrative and identification can be ruptured, making captivity within an uncritically accepted historicality radically contestable. Such rupturing, for the plurality and alterity it generates, becomes the very moment in which temporality is put out of joint. Rupture is instantiated as political struggle when genuine deadlock propels people to contest their uncritically accepted self-description and the domination and oppression of others it entails. When this happens, people leap out of their uncritically accepted history, as it were, and, on falling back into it, transform that history. The connectedness to such a process and the critical moral reflection it invokes signal perhaps the deepest common humanity possible and reveal the ethical condition at the core of that humanity. This ethical movement – the leap out of history and then back again, rejoining and transforming it – is an instantiation of the actuality that appears to reassure us that apartheid is always durational, never essential. But is this the case? Are we to assume that there is no such thing as enduring separation: that is, self-preserving *apartheid*? What would it mean, and what would it take, to *be essentially* separate? What would it mean, and what would it take, to belong to what I want to call *originary apartheid*? How can *apartheid* self-preserve in the face of rupture: that is, in the midst of ethical and political forces that are bound to mount a challenge against it? How does originary *apartheid* successfully manage to shield itself from those interconnecting forces so that it continues to obstruct the possibility of genuine deadlock and true forgiveness? In other words, is there perhaps a sense in which originary *apartheid* utilises the violence in history to ensure that, through its very involvement *in* history, it remains separate *from* history, while concealing the fact that it does so?

Thinking apartheid back to its origin in order to understand what future its operation may bring about is different from conventional historical analysis and requires a different attunement in approach. Within conventional histories of political struggle, whether viewed through a liberal, Marxist or postcolonial lens, we find originary *apartheid* merely hinted at. In order to attune to this presencing absence we must try to grasp the sense in which originary *apartheid* refuses such history – the kind of temporality originary *apartheid* gives rise to is not necessarily sequential in the way it unfolds, recurs, self-conceals and self-preserves.

When such essential separateness does existentially manifest itself, how should we then account for the historical and political conditions that help to preserve it? How does originary *apartheid* manage to self-conceal its self-preservation through its ostensibly successful participation in, and contribution to, historical change? To borrow from Jung, how does the collective unconscious that perpetuates such essential separateness reveal itself in one particular group of people vis-à-vis other groups of people, and at what price? Furthermore, when attempting to find the connective tissue between the forces that preserve originary *apartheid*, how adequate may it be to enlist legal, constitutional, even moral responses in support of our quest? How likely may it be that those kinds of responses do not just prove inadequate, but do themselves provide the very tool originary *apartheid* uses to create a 'safe haven' for itself?

My argument is that it is both necessary and morally compelling to ask the question of originary *apartheid* in relation to Palestine, as it is originary *apartheid* and its ability to self-conceal that conditions the denial through which the violent actuality there continues to be so well protected and which makes the existential connective tissue between that violent actuality and originary *apartheid* so difficult to spot. I argue that originary *apartheid* fails to be discussed in relationship to Palestine, not because it does not exist there, but because it remains effectively concealed. In other words, the case I wish to make is only the initial one of pointing out that there are forces operating to prevent the question of originary *apartheid* from being brought into the open.

In the final analysis, I want to argue that to contemplate the question of originary *apartheid* is to contemplate the Jewish existential condition, or, if you will, the Jewish question. Briefly put, originary *apartheid* can be contemplated only when Zionist violence is viewed as the sophisticated self-concealing instantiation of the Jewish condition and recognised as constituting the very vehicle for that existential condition's self-preservation. The Jewish question, I want to suggest, is the question of originary *apartheid*.

Zionism's immoral practices vis-à-vis the Palestinian people are grounded in the very elements of originary *apartheid* that permeate the Jewish existence in Palestine. Any attempt, then, to separate the Jewish question from the Zionist question in order to enable an individual to oppose or condemn 'immoral' Zionism as a 'good Jew' becomes itself a sophisticated way of protecting the question of originary *apartheid* from being asked.

Contemplating originary *apartheid* thus not only takes the analysis away from the ambit of existing Zionist narratives, but also calls for the reconfiguration of anti-Zionism to make it embrace the challenge to originary *apartheid* – in defiance of the accusation of being anti-Semitic that scares conventional anti-Zionists into avoiding that challenge. Indeed, the function that accusations of anti-Semitism serve is to minimise the enormity of originary *apartheid* and reduce the existential stake it has in its own self-preservation, forcing the discussion instead to take place within the reduced coordinates of racial hatred. Thus, even the critical survey of Zionism we find in this volume, where it identifies the *apartheid* of Zionism with *Apartheid* South Africa, avoids discussing the Jewish question in conjunction with the question of Zionism, as it fails to spot the connective tissue between the denial that infuses the establishment and actions *of* the State of Israel and the denial that inspires reactions *to* the State of Israel.

One of the achievements of the anti-Zionist campaign may well have been its success in demonstrating that, like South Africa, Israel too is an *apartheid* state. But this does not yet constitute an adequate response to the question of the originary *apartheid* that the State of Israel embodies. For the focal point of its anti-*apartheid* struggle, I argue, there is no *need* for anti-Zionism to rely on the comparison between South Africa and

Israel. Indeed, legal, constitutional and moral comparisons between the two states, however irrefutable they prove to be, will always remain inadequate – essentially, existentially and, crucially so, *practically*. When asking the question of originary *apartheid*, we should put aside comparisons of this kind and instead focus all our efforts on a direct analysis of its existential features. Only such an analysis can propel anti-Zionism to reconfigure and help it overcome the 'political correctness' that currently imprisons it. Reconfigured, anti-Zionism will no longer need to hesitate to bring the existential features of originary *apartheid* into the open and tackle them head-on.

In building my argument, I gradually link two common levels of comparison between South Africa and Israel. The first level of comparison looks at the legal and constitutional manifestations of *apartheid* in both states; the second explores the depth of the rationalisation and the denial of *apartheid* in Palestine. In this way, I hope to expose why, in Israel, both levels of comparison operate to eschew any discussion of the role originary *apartheid* plays in the way in which the State of Israel relates to the Palestinian people.

THE SKEWED LEGAL AND CONSTITUTIONAL FRAMING OF THE QUESTION OF APARTHEID

In South Africa, white supremacy was explicit long before the creation, on 31 May 1910, of the Union of South Africa, with the Afrikaners in the Orange Free State and Transvaal and the British Colonial Government pursuing a programme of religious, labour and, to varying degrees, spatial segregation.[3] Important for my purpose here is that in 1948 the National Party adopted an *apartheid* philosophy that explicitly *justified* the policy of separate development the state had introduced and was quick to legalise.[4]

Where, of course, the notion of explicit *apartheid* in Palestine is most apparently similar to that of Apartheid South Africa (1948–94) is in the Palestinian territories the State of Israel occupied in June 1967 and in the 'legal' reality it created there. This comes most clearly to the fore in the legal limbo that defines the status of the occupied Palestinian territories: on the one hand, Israel never *officially* annexed these areas to Israel (i.e., to 'pre-1967 Israel'); on the other hand, instead of calling them '*occupied*', it insists on defining them as '*held*' territories. Israel created this legalistic subterfuge to enable it to claim that articles 47 to 78 of the Fourth Geneva Convention that pertain to 'territories occupied in war' are not relevant there and to ensure that the state can be selective in the way it applies official Israeli law. The geopolitical upshot of this process is that, in the West Bank, Israeli policies of colonisation through illegal settlement have enforced the spatial segregation of the land to such a degree that Palestinian territorial contiguity is no longer possible today.

The history is well documented of the legal and constitutional separation between the laws that apply to Jewish settlers in the occupied Palestinian territories (Israeli law) and those (by and large emergency regulations) that govern the Palestinians whose country it is. Approximating open *Apartheid* South Africa, the resulting system is one of 'legal dualism'.[5]

This comparison between Israeli practices in the West Bank and the explicit *apartheid* that was practised by South Africa is typical of liberal and left-wing Zionist critiques, but it works only because it remains limited to the territories Israel occupied in June 1967 and neglects to include the Palestinians in Israel 'proper' (i.e., Israel within the 'Green Line' that delineates its pre-1967 borders), whom Israel categorises as '*non-Jewish* citizens' (some of them still living today as internally displaced persons).[6] The 'explicit *apartheid*' comparison also excludes the Palestinians Israel ethnically cleansed in 1948 and turned into refugees.[7] The first group of Palestinians, '*non-Jewish* Arabs', are *actual* citizens of the State of Israel, while the second group are *potential* citizens: the moment the descendants of the refugees will be allowed to realise their internationally recognised legal Right of Return (United Nations General Assembly Resolution 194, 11 December 1948), they will become citizens of Israel.

From this liberal left-wing Zionist perspective, Jewish settlers in the West Bank embody the *apartheid* people, while Jewish citizens within the borders of Israel 'proper' do not. And for people who hold this view, Israel would cease to be an *apartheid* state the moment it gave up the Occupied Territories – however 'painful' this might be – and enabled the creation there of a viable independent Palestinian state (the so-called two-state 'solution'). For them, the question of *apartheid* is decided within the context of the 'legitimate' (i.e., pre-1967) borders of Israel and not within the wider context of the very creation, nature and continued existence of the Jewish state. One imagines very few of them would have objected had Israel decided to erect the 'Separation Wall' *exactly* on the pre-1967 Green Line border, and even then they would never have called it the 'Apartheid Wall'.

Because they typically regard both the 'potential' citizens – the Palestinian refugees and their descendants – and Israel's actual '*non-Jewish*' Arab citizens as an existential 'problem', rather than acknowledging that they actually pose an essential challenge to the inherently exclusivist nature of the State of Israel, many people, even those who openly opposed *Apartheid* South Africa, fail to recognise the *apartheid* that persists *within* Israel 'proper'.[8] But, of course, legitimising Israel through the adoption of a two-state 'solution' effectively means legitimising a Jewish *apartheid* state, even as one agrees that the Green Line forms that state's permanent border.

In this context, it is bemusing that even scholars who tend to project a more nuanced approach and accept the comparison of Israel with South Africa confine the thrust of their argument to Israel's occupation of the Palestinian territories, including East Jerusalem, rather than acknowledging the *apartheid* mentality behind the Zionist movement that led it to colonise the whole of historical Palestine. Thus, while these scholars clearly signal that they are aware of the question of Israel's *apartheid* nature, they will never allow it to take centre stage. In refusing to do so, one could claim, they are concealing the effect their own scholarship has, here too, of legitimising Israel as an *apartheid* state.[9] Indeed, expressions such as 'criticising *Israel*' and 'peace between *Israel* and ...' immediately presuppose the legitimacy of the Jewish state, thereby excluding the possibility of asking the question of *apartheid* in relation to the very nature of the State of Israel. In other words, the hegemony of the '1967 occupation' discourse generally functions to silence any discussion of the *apartheid* nature of Zionism proper.

As argued throughout this volume, both Israel and Apartheid South Africa are manifestations of settler colonialism and embodiments of discriminatory rule. The significant difference for my purpose here is that, while in South Africa settler colonialism instituted a supremacist *minority* rule, in Palestine it ethnically cleansed the indigenous population in order to guarantee that the state it wanted to found would be Jewish in character and have a Jewish majority population: majoritarian democracy, together with its legal and constitutional framework, would enable Zionism to both implement *and* conceal the *apartheid* it set out to establish and perpetuate there.

ISRAEL'S APARTHEID AND THE FAÇADE OF DEMOCRACY

At this juncture, it is important to distinguish between de facto injustice and an inbuilt *framework* for injustice, whether explicit or implicit. It is almost a truism to say that any imagined political community will always rest on some kind of hegemonic (re)construction of history and rely on some form of manifest inequality. Similarly, quite often a form of binary – legal/illegal, moral/immoral – conceptualisation and prioritisation of certain values will dominate the horizon of the 'critical' thinking that persists in such communities. It is also true that we find colonisation and ethno-nationalism, which are both grounded in such prioritisations, in all parts of the globe – prime historical occurrences, of course, are North America and Australia.

But these are forms of de facto injustice that can be made subject to an ethical challenge, and, more specifically, to *critical* moral reflection and judgement. Ethical challenges can be mounted against any unjust social practice or dislodge any 'conventional' hegemonic ethical challenge that is found wanting. Freedom of speech and equal citizenship are paramount principles in that the premise on which they are based ensures that all citizens have an equal stake in, and have equal ownership of, the community they belong to. The framework these primordial principles constitute also carries the potential for a critical transformative and radical contestation of the collective political identification all members of the community are likely to subsume as citizens and of the boundaries of the ethnic identification they uncritically tend to accept. Thus, where such a framework is in place, de facto colonial injustice and racist laws can be challenged effectively or even annulled, and the entrenched power structures that gave rise to oppression and domination can be destabilised or even uprooted.

De facto injustice, however, should be distinguished from injustice that is *inbuilt* so as to obstruct any ethical challenge, or at best to ensure that it occurs within a clearly defined ambit. Let us look first at Apartheid South Africa as an instance of inbuilt injustice. In Apartheid South Africa, discrimination was legally and constitutionally inbuilt in order to enforce separate development. That is, separation was a constitutional cornerstone and formed the overriding principle that blocked any ethical challenge aiming to push for equality and inclusiveness. As we have seen, *apartheid* was also *explicit* in that there was no attempt to conceal its inbuilt injustice behind a façade of democracy or the equality of citizenship democracy is based on.

At first glance, there seems to be no such inbuilt *apartheid* in Israel; Israel appears to have a just constitutional framework that commits it to bringing injustices into the open and addressing them fairly. In its 1948 Declaration of Independence, does Israel not aspire to be a democracy committed to the equality of all its citizens? A *Jewish* democracy, yes, but a democracy all the same? Then, also, Israel has no laws that limit the education or possibilities of its Palestinian citizens, nor does it list certain professions they are forbidden to take up, as was the case in South Africa. Looking at Israel, you will see democratic elections and representation, occasional positive attempts at egalitarian investment in the country's '*non-Jewish*' Arab sector, and some joint Jewish/Palestinian ventures; and you will find a supreme court that prides itself on upholding a basic law of human (as opposed to Jewish) dignity and freedom.

Upon a closer look, though, central governmental investment turns out to be inherently biased in favour of the country's Jewish population, and official property law regimes and land policies push towards the 'Judaisation' of the land, meaning the transfer to Jewish citizens or institutions of lands expropriated from Palestinian ('*non-Jewish*') citizens and/or institutions, while discouraging, or even actually forbidding, *non-Jewish* Arabs from taking up residence in *Jewish* areas.[10] Many social and other benefits have purposely been made conditional upon army service so as to exclude Palestinians, who are generally barred from serving, and, of course, cannot be expected to have any great desire to serve, in the Israeli Defense Forces. It is true that those Palestinians who escaped the ethnic cleansing of 1948 and then found themselves within the borders of the newly established Jewish state were given citizenship. But that Jewish state immediately made into law British Mandate emergency regulations (issued in 1945) to place them under military rule, thus robbing its '*non-Jewish*' Arab citizens of their basic rights of expression, movement, organisation and *equality before the law*. Often portrayed as a 'fifth column', '*non-Jewish*' Arabs in Israel confront a general attitude of suspicion given the cultural and social solidarity that ties them to their fellow Palestinians in the Occupied Territories. When they expressed that solidarity at the start of the second intifada in October 2000, the state's security forces brutally suppressed their non-violent demonstrations, using snipers to shoot dead thirteen unarmed young men. The price 'non-Jewish Israelis' are asked to pay for success in bureaucratic career terms is a readiness to be seen as 'cooperative': that is, renouncing any political involvement in which, normally, they could claim a stake. Although 'non-Jewish Israelis' can vote for the Israeli parliament, the Knesset, in practice the small number of their representatives is never allowed to form part of a government coalition because that would entail 'non-Jewish' Arab voters having a say in determining the fate of the Jewish state. One of the reasons his killer gave for murdering Prime Minister Yitzhak Rabin (on 4 November 1995) was the promise Rabin had solicited from the then five 'non-Jewish' Arab Knesset members to join the bloc that enabled him to become prime minister following the 1992 elections and subsequently secure the vote on the Oslo Accords, but even Rabin had no intention of ever giving any of them a ministerial post. Similarly, it is impossible for Israelis to even imagine having a 'non-Jewish' Arab prime minister. Actually, 'non-Jewish' Arab Knesset members who openly dare to contest the very notion of a Jewish state – which they and their constituents had forced upon them – and question its democratic nature will find their freedom of speech and of association severely compromised.

Although there are some official egalitarian gestures in order to 'compensate' non-Jewish Arab citizens for the disadvantages the state subjects them to, their basic stake in the polity – not to mention their very claim to ownership of it – is fundamentally inferior to that of citizens who have passed the test that confirms their Jewishness, however arbitrary (non-Halakhic) that test might be.[11] They are treated not as part owners of the house – that is, as rightfully equal citizens of the state – but as tenants whose relatively 'generous' landlord for the time being agrees to let them stay. When wanting to move to Israel, Palestinians who wish to join relatives who are citizens of Israel face near impossible immigration criteria, while Jews from abroad and their relatives face no hurdles at all, as the Jewish state belongs to all of the Jewish people 'in perpetuity', no matter where they happen to be in the world.[12]

Distributive efforts of resources and political rights are immediately qualified in terms of 'as far as that proves possible in a Jewish state', rather than being anchored in the premise that all citizens have the same stake of political and legal equality in the polity. These and many other quotidian manifestations of inbuilt *apartheid* would automatically apply to the descendants of Palestinian refugees, were they allowed to return home to the Jewish state. *Apartheid* ideology and practice expelled their ancestors, *apartheid* ideology and practice prevent their return and *apartheid* ideology and practice blight the lives of those Palestinians who somehow did manage to return.[13]

In sum, within Israel 'proper', we find inbuilt injustice at work behind a façade of democracy. Israel's '*non-Jewish*' Arab citizens are 'allowed' a façade of representation, the seemingly democratic 'one person one vote'. At the same time, this façade is used to conceal the fact that they are denied the possibility of genuinely responding to the egalitarian challenge that concerns the fair distribution of power, rights, resources and opportunities. That is, the 'egalitarianism' they are allowed exists only as long as it does not 'harm' the Zionist premise. Constant instrumental and symbolic intimidation means that the structures of Jewish-controlled power remain firmly in place, spelling continuing entrenched oppression and domination, and, inter alia, leading to marginalisation and powerlessness as concomitant symptoms among the '*non-Jewish*' Arab population.[14] Oren Yiftachel calls a regime with such inbuilt 'creeping' *apartheid* that protects itself through a masquerade of democracy an 'ethnocracy'. Also significant is the fact that, unlike in an open *apartheid* regime, such as South Africa's, in an ethnocracy there is no explicit premise of separation. As Yiftachel argues, an ethnocratic regime could be on the way to, or moving away from, democracy. The ethnocratic case of Israel is unique in that it represents a well-disguised inbuilt *apartheid* impervious to change.[15] Rather than accepting the general dynamic view to which Yiftachel subscribes, this means that we can morally judge Israel more severely as an entrenched ethnocracy than we would do if it were an open *apartheid* system. Yiftachel may have underplayed the possibility that, in certain circumstances, where we find people harbouring collective denial (consciously or unconsciously), an ethnocracy may be as morally repugnant, if not more so, than an open *apartheid* regime.

DENIAL AND THE QUESTION OF MORAL REPUGNANCY

Does Israel's ethnocracy – that is, a democracy with an inbuilt *apartheid* bias – make it less repugnant in moral terms than the open and explicit *apartheid* regime that operated in South Africa? Differently put, if the parameters of repugnancy are considered, would the straightforward moral condemnation '*apartheid* is *apartheid*' still be helpful? After all, the 'non-Jewish' Arabs who suffer from creeping and inbuilt *apartheid* in Israel 'proper' still find themselves in a far better situation than did the blacks in Apartheid South Africa. Doesn't Israel then constitute a more just polity than Apartheid South Africa could ever have been?

The moral aversion aroused by systems of *apartheid* does not depend in the first place on whether one form of *apartheid* allows some measure of egalitarianism while another excludes it. What counts is how strong, and therefore entrenched, is the *denial* of *apartheid* and how pervasive the impunity with which it renders the affliction and suffering of its victims 'invisible', in Simone Weil's telling phrase.[16] All the more so as that denial not only prevents the open acknowledgement, honest apology and just address of the injustices of the past, but also pre-empts the conditions that should then make equal citizenship possible. There is a link between transformative potential – the plausibility of reform – and moral aversion vis-à-vis apartheid. This is because the depth of the forces that silence authentic voices of discontent, contestation and political struggle is likely to be fundamentally different in both polities. Silencing can go very deep, as the origin of silencing leads to a cyclical process in which the desperation and humiliation among those who are being silenced lead to resistance and, in turn, further violent oppression, and this tragically helps to feed an ever deeper denial on the part of the oppressor.

In an open *apartheid* regime, like that of Apartheid South Africa, *apartheid* itself was, of course, morally repugnant and there were many who continuously experienced and witnessed the brutal silencing by the regime of the African National Congress (ANC). But the ANC *existed*; it was *there*. And South Africa gradually opened up and became more susceptible to ethical challenge as sensible people on both sides of the divide were able to communicate and imagine a shared non-racial future and a shared non-racial prosperous country. André du Toit recounts how, many years before *apartheid* was finally jettisoned in 1994, the desire among key Afrikaner intellectuals and National Party politicians to survive as a flourishing minority prompted them to adopt the pragmatic openness that was to lead to the demise of *apartheid* there.[17]

In other words, because its nature was explicit, *apartheid* in South Africa harboured its own deliverance and its own reformative potential, and, in the end, contained its own collapse. My point is that when a system is explicitly morally repugnant its inherent weaknesses and the denial that conceals them are potentially more conspicuous as well. Because of the violent silencing that will seek to stifle them, challenges to explicit and open forms of inbuilt *apartheid* may be slow to mount and painful to sustain; however, since they always inhabit some openness of historical consciousness, explicit *apartheid* systems will find it difficult to shield themselves against any liberating historical unfolding of a deeper kind.

The forces of denial operating in an ethnocracy, unlike in open *apartheid*, move in the opposite direction, using, as we saw, the system's democratic elements as a façade to further entrench the already deeply rooted rationalisation of injustice. The collective unconsciousness this denial functions to underscore keeps generating opportunities for it to unite and harness reflection across the community's whole political spectrum. The democratic façade, in fact, is subservient to the forces that work to draft nearly all opinions in this way behind the ethnocratic premise, helping the hegemonic ethnocratic consensus to reinvent and consolidate itself from the inside. Again, unlike in an explicit *apartheid* system, outside pressure to shake the regime, for example by way of boycott, divestment and sanctions campaigns, will only serve to reinforce the self-preservation of the consensus. We even find that the instant alarm such campaigns tend to raise actually plays into the hands of the hegemonic mentality that nourishes this consensual denial.

Thus, the ethnocratic premise becomes embedded in a people's psyche and so constitutes an internal impediment for reflexive mirroring. The point I am making is that, in their intensity, the denial and rationalisation that characterise and contextualise a constitutional ethnocracy are crucial parameters when we want to assess the moral repugnancy of *apartheid* actions and of the racist laws and constitutions that serve to legitimise them. The intensity of the denial and rationalisation itself depends on the existential shackles characterising the mental make-up of the people who perpetrate these actions and then create the laws and constitutions to rationalise them.

Briefly put, when we try to analyse a polity that purposely provokes violence in order to entrench the system's obliviousness to ethical challenges and then uses the external moral condemnation of its actions as justification not only to totally detach itself from the prevailing historical forces but to become even more violent and impervious to any such ethical challenge, we are driven to posit an existential condition that perversely 'welcomes' external pressure in order to nourish its own historical separation. We can then also conclude that such a polity is more repugnant morally speaking than an explicit *apartheid* polity; the latter at least can still effectively and ethically question any of its given laws by participating in historical ruptures and transformations, and at one point allows for the ethical mirroring and the always reasonable chances this offers for genuine internal social struggles to emerge and for the system to disintegrate.

RATIONALISING APARTHEID: ISRAEL'S 'RIGHT TO EXIST'

Any proper response to the egalitarian challenge facing Palestine, then, would in principle rule out that *apartheid* Israel could merely be *reformed* and remain 'Israel'. With the demise of apartheid, South Africa was 'replaced' only in the weak sense of 'reform', and thus it could remain South Africa. As I outlined above, in Apartheid South Africa there was no premise that professed to make the country an *apartheid* state 'in perpetuity' in the same way as Zionism set out to do in Palestine. Existentially speaking, in South Africa the *apartheid* nature of the state was not essential and, however deep-seated, its white supremacy was capable of generating – and, in the end, did generate – the self-reflection that led to reforming, and then replacing, the *apartheid* framework.

Thus, nobody thought of – or, for that matter, condemned – deploying such phrases as 'the right of South Africa to exist as a white state' in the same manner as similar phrases are deployed in the case of Israel as the Jewish state. Tellingly, the *egalitarian* claim that Israel does not have a right to exist is always subverted by Zionists in a way that strangely turns the claim's genuine egalitarian core into some form of extremism or, preferably, anti-Semitism, while Jews who self-describe as anti-Zionists become 'self-hating' Jews. The existential sensitivity possibly at work here, however undefined, may well have something to do with the potential harm to 'Jewish existence' that somehow succeeds in deflecting criticism from the alleged main issue – Zionism. However, this same sensitivity, as we shall see, also manages to surreptitiously stage the ambit of the debate as a debate about Zionism, not about *apartheid*.

'Recognising the right of Israel to exist' has become a precondition for participating in 'moderate' political negotiations. Something is at work here that makes the expression 'existence of Israel' immediately trigger strong feelings that then prevent any challenge to its existence or any call for its replacement from taking hold in the way that they decisively succeeded in doing in the case of Apartheid South Africa.

It almost appears as if the actuality of Israel contains some elements that allow it to transcend, or lift itself above, its existence as an *apartheid* state and move beyond the unwritten *apartheid* constitution and separatist legal and political actions it has given rise to. Something is invariably challenged by the call for the replacement of *apartheid* Israel, some unconscious nerve that must not be touched. What appears to escape anti-Zionists is that any conception of the struggle against *apartheid* as one of ethno-nationalism *versus* civic nationalism – as was appropriate for, and proved successful in, South Africa – seems to hint at an existential, and thus operative, inadequacy in the case of Palestine. For anti-Zionists, any existential weight distilled from the 'right of Israel to exist' would immediately be rendered morally irrelevant. 'Why', they would ask, 'should the existential condition of the Zionists and their sympathisers *matter* to Palestinians who simply want, first, to have their land back and then to start responding to the ongoing challenge full equality of citizenship poses to the authority of law?'

It is here, I would argue, that anti-Zionism is especially naïve and its outlook found wanting. Instead, anti-Zionism should drop its 'political correctness' and connect directly to this existential condition if it wants to have a chance to make originary *apartheid* matter to those it holds captive, rather than, through an abstracted comparison with South Africa, fight its symptom, Zionism, and so again give originary *apartheid* free rein.

Anti-Zionism (as currently configured) conspires to not take seriously these troubling questions, or even to effectively ignore them. Only in this way can one explain why, for anti-Zionists, the comparison with South

Africa remains valid even in the wake of Israel's massacre in the Gaza Strip (27 December 2008 to 21 January 2009), an act of Zionist violence made even more morally repulsive by the way in which moderate and extreme Zionists and Israel's sympathising friends united behind the government's 'no-choice' rhetoric, easily prompted by the atavistically unconscious collective Jewish predicament Zionism invariably uses to 'justify' its violence. Even with the ashes in Gaza still glowing, one could hear anti-Zionists asking for sympathy with the Jewish predicament in which the establishment of the Jewish state was grounded. Exactly what kind of 'sympathy' do they have in mind?!

What is at stake in the obsessive refusal by convinced Zionists and naïve anti-Zionists alike to touch the existential nerve here? What could they possibly be trying to safeguard by letting Israel generate so much hatred against itself and run its anomalous course of violence-provoking existence – even 'to the bitter end'?[18]

Let us first look at the Zionist camp. A paradox pervades the views of 'moderate' Zionists, those who preach universal values but insist on remaining Zionists, and others, 'soft' Zionists who diagnose anti-Zionism as the core of immorality but then for various reasons refuse to act, claiming that replacing Israel by an egalitarian polity will always remain an impractical, unrealistic, 'pie-in-the-sky' idea.[19] And this paradox is symptomatic of a deeper denial. This comes to the fore when we find that leading humanists and intellectuals, who did not refrain from condemning *apartheid* in South Africa, nevertheless cling to some intuition that, they claim, calls upon them to highlight the predicament of Israel as unique. Indeed, there is much to be explored about the uniqueness of Israel's predicament if the deep denial by liberal and 'soft' Zionists counts as an authentic response. All of them rationalise partial justice, however inbuilt, as the one reasonable option; perhaps it is second best, but, for the time being, it is certainly the option one needs to hold on to. When were such arguments ever raised in the case of Apartheid South Africa? Similarly, 'soft' Zionists often stress the 'impossibility' of *apartheid* Israel giving itself up 'in one go' – that this would be too big a chunk to swallow. Would anyone have used such rationalising claims with regard to Apartheid South Africa? All these varieties on the 'moderate' Zionist spectrum claim to stake out a good enough defence by virtue of which Israel can 'justifiably' be rationalised as an ethnocracy, whether 'in perpetuity' or 'for the time being'. Never mind how immoral: Israel's 'true power and uniqueness', and thus where it differs from South Africa, lie in the scope and range of views the people represent who adopt such perverse lines of reasoning.

Joseph Massad has argued that Israel claims to have the *right* to be racist.[20] I want to paraphrase Massad's formulation somewhat by saying that Israel claims to have unique *reasons* that it considers good enough to morally rationalise the Jewish state as an *apartheid* state and that it therefore thinks it simply should take in its stride all the crimes and calamities it has inflicted and continues to inflict on the Palestinians – occupation, ethnic cleansing, dispossession, internal displacement, discrimination, and so on. Israel's 'right' to be a Jewish *apartheid* state also involves the notion that the Palestinians accept a certain kind of ulterior reasoning that reflects (as hinted at above) 'some sympathy with the cause of the Jewish people' – 'ulterior' in the same sense that the 'reasonable arrangement' that will result from this will once and for all entrench this 'right' of Israel to be an *apartheid* state, i.e., how its inbuilt *apartheid* can be rationalised as morally reasonable. Palestinians must either accept the crimes of Zionist settler colonialism or shelve all claims against it.

Massad's formulation is unique not merely because it successfully reiterates the moral inconsistency between the ways in which Israel and South Africa are treated. It points towards the self-justification of Israel's *apartheid* that is rooted in the claim of the unique historical lesson it embodies, which is itself mysteriously grounded in the being and thinking of Israeli Jews and in that of their champion friends throughout the world, Jews and non-Jews alike. 'Rightfully' responding to this lesson demands that one accepts the justification of Israel's *right* to be rationalised as a 'reasonable' ethnocracy.

Massad's formula highlights the need to ask where this ulterior justification to be immoral comes from – particularly since the entire world seems to accept and to be complicit with it. What is the origin of the denial Massad's formulation points to? What kind of challenge does it pose?

As suggested above, Israel's 'right' to be racist is grounded in the denial forged by reasons that are based on the identification and acceptance of the Jewish predicament as unique. The challenge is therefore for anti-Zionism to reconfigure itself so that it will be able to contemplate and then, crucially, find the connective tissue to the originary shackles that hold so many people unconsciously captive, in Israel and throughout the world, making them 'successful' rationalisers of Israel's right to *apartheid* in a way that trumps the more immediate critical reasons given by the conventional anti-*apartheid* or anti-Zionist struggle.

In South Africa, too, as in many other cases of colonialism, *apartheid* was justified as a matter of right. Philosophers of *apartheid* openly justified 'separate development' as valuable and significant, as a moral imperative even, and they did so on the grounds of either religious separateness of the Kuyperian neo-Calvinist kind, or the national separateness of a different *Volk*.[21] In South Africa, justification for *apartheid* was – wrongly – equated with the radical liberal justification of separate development that can be found in the contemporary moral philosophical literature.[22] Of course, such liberal claims underscored the value of diverse governance because of the respect it effectuates for the radical difference of, and for the incommensurability between, groups of people, and these claims are always made subject to equal citizenship, freedom of speech and freedom of movement between groups. Such claims could never be based on the supremacy of one dominant group determining an entrenched criterion for separation, as we find in Apartheid South Africa. This explains why the political theory that aimed to justify South Africa's *apartheid* was instantly recognised as a system of explicit racism: radical difference could not be coupled to the supremacy of one group based on the colour of their skin.

So while in South Africa there was an openly declared and justified 'right to be racist', this right is hidden and its existence denied in the case of Israel, however strongly it forms the basis for the state's discriminatory policies towards the Palestinians. Because, unlike open apartheid regimes, Israel hails itself as a democracy, 'positive' reasoning justifying separation never entered the public consciousness.

Another intriguing difference lies in the connection that ties together Jewish victimhood and Israel's justification for its racist state. Afrikaner nationalist righteousness was predicated on the notion of the new homeland being an empty space. In the case of Zionism, we have Israel Zangwill's notorious slogan describing Palestine in 1901 as a 'Land without a People for a People without a Land'.[23] Similarly, some observers of South African history portray the landing of van Riebeeck at the Cape as the capture of an empty land to which no people could claim ownership.[24] Victim mentality applied to some extent to the Afrikaners, too. Besides the immediate concern for economic survival as a minority in an age of rapid industrialisation, the Afrikaners had a strong collective memory of suffering as a group that had been colonised by both the Dutch and the British. During the Boer War, many of them were put into concentration camps, women and children included. The notion of an embedded feeling of biblical 'chosen-ness' inspired by that of the Jews had existed long before the 'Boer' could become a thesis advanced by some contemporary Afrikaner scholars. In a series of seminal critical articles, du Toit has shown this thesis to be a myth whose scope has been much exaggerated.[25]

The comparability between South Africa and Israel breaks down, however, because the victimhood grounding the justification of *apartheid* that is at stake is very different. However much they suffered,

Afrikaners were never threatened by a systematic plan for their total annihilation, as the Jews were; nobody wanted to physically destroy the 'Afrikaners' as a 'subhuman phenomenon', as the Nazis did with European Jewry. Adopting some durational sense of 'chosen-ness' is quite common and historically explicable. More crucially, it always proves to be contingent. Thus, it could not be more different from the deeply entrenched and internalised kind of separateness and supremacy that uses violence *in* history in order to self-preserve by remaining separate *from* history.

ZIONISM AND JEWISH MYTH

Meanwhile, the way in which Zionism has been using and abusing the Hebrew Bible has been admirably documented.[26] How should we approach the factual reality in which attending to the unique Jewish experience the Bible embodies serves Israel as its justification for being an *apartheid* state? Is this merely the misappropriation of a myth? Furthermore, does it help us better to grasp the forces behind the rationalisation of an *apartheid* state if we accept the debunking of the myth of the 'Jewish people' and the way it relies on the biblical account as historically accurate and if we are told that there never was a Jewish expulsion from Palestine 2,000 years ago?[27] How exactly do these forces relate to having this successfully debunked myth replaced by a differently ordered historiography? Can the contestability of a 'historical' narrative subjugate the temporality of those existential forces that condition the denial preventing the question of originary *apartheid* from being asked?

To show that Zionism rests on the abuse of a particular myth, however important, may have little to do with the existential unfolding of Zionism's separatist ideology. Moreover, and in a way that is politically crucial, the new historiography may in effect help sever potent existential connections between what it means to *be a Zionist* and what it means to *be a Jew*, thus providing the bedrock for the anti-Zionism that, however morally right, lacks existential grit.

What is the reality of that force that makes certain phenomena refuse to give up the ghost, however strong the case for their historical inaccuracy or even their historical absence? Where does the force of Zionism's self-justification or rationalisation come from? Is there perhaps some element that cannot be accounted for by the very preoccupation with the kind of time and belongingness critical historiography has contested, some quality that is potent in the case of Israel but not so in the case of South Africa?

JEWISH REACTIONS TO ZIONISM: COMMON EXISTENTIAL SHACKLES

In order to grasp the existential claim that rationalises the right of Israel to be an *apartheid* state, we need to look into the relationship between *being* a Jew and *being* a Zionist. At first sight, the claim to have the right to be an *apartheid* state seems to belong to Zionism, eschewing any link between Zionist ideology and Jewish being and thinking. There is, in fact, a long and well-known tradition of Jewish opposition to Zionism. Jews saw themselves united as a people through their connection to the Torah and God's commandments rather than as a nation consolidated through modern nationalism. Furthermore, many modern Jews – *maskilim*, who had their intellectual roots in the Jewish Enlightenment (Haskalah) movement – saw enlightened exile as something unique to the history of the Jews and as something that had to be preserved, if not cherished, and thus they were vehemently opposed to Zionism.[28]

But can we so easily say that the *apartheid* that political Zionism justifies as a matter of right is un-Jewish? After all, political Zionists ground the rationalisation of their right to be racist precisely on the historical uniqueness of the violent predicament of the Jews and their national liberation as the 'Jewish people'. I will try to show why the various Jewish reactions to Zionism either advocate or rationalise originary *apartheid* or, more crucially, why even as they oppose the *symptoms* of originary *apartheid* – Zionism – they are in effect shielding *apartheid* itself from contemplation. In a way, they are all held captive by the same existential denial, passengers on the same existential boat. I argue that certain forces – actual and self-preserving as well as self-concealing – tragically unite the four camps involved: Orthodox Jews opposed to Zionism, religious Zionists, liberal Zionists (and their non-Jewish sympathisers) and, most importantly, those who oppose Zionism as 'Jews' (as well as those non-Jews who, with truly the best intentions, support them). The thinking that connects these four camps thrown together in this existential boat involves a constant reordering of history, but it simultaneously serves to shield themselves against, and remain as other to, history. Anyone who tries to 'rock the boat' is excommunicated, marginalised, condemned or ostracised.

Self-preserving and self-concealing *apartheid* seems to have a stake in humanity – the preservation of Jewish being and thinking. And it is exactly this claim that makes Palestine such a different stakeholder for humanity compared with what South Africa ever was. It then becomes easy to see why the preservation of this stake in humanity makes the unconscious core of the objections political Zionists raise to any comparison between the two states so authentic, and renders the stance of anti-Zionists, who put the two states on a par, so inauthentic and existentially inadequate.

Let us start with the Orthodox Jews. Their opposition to modernity and to the Jewish emancipation and secularisation that brought about political Zionism stems from a deep belief in the supremacy of Jewish spirituality and history and thus in Jewish separatism. In the way it encapsulates an eschatological sense of separatism and supremacy 'to be realised', Jewish messianic history belongs to a vision of history which, for Orthodox Jews, is more primordial than the ordinary history of mankind. They are then inevitably faced with the ongoing problem of how to reconcile their participation in this ordinary history with the purpose it serves in the primordial, messianic one.

There are many different sects of Orthodox Jews, of course, and all have had to find their own way of responding to the challenges posed by secular political Zionism, especially as Zionism claimed from the start that it was undertaking its mission in the name of all Jews and for the sake of all Jews. First of all, there are the Haredim (literally 'the anxious' in Hebrew), of both Ashkenazi and Mizrahi origin, who object to Zionism for reasons of holy messianic deferral but who skilfully navigate to maintain a way of life that is based on strict Talmudic legalism, separated from the 'sinful', more secular Israeli way of life. What makes the Haredim the arch-opponents of political Zionism is the Talmudic doctrine that demands Jews remain passive in the face of, and refuse to force through, the coming of the Messiah.[29] However, to various degrees the Haredim do participate in Israeli politics and have succeeded in extracting some special and highly controversial benefits for themselves, such as exemption from the otherwise compulsory national military service. The Haredim's immediate political stance is to wait until the Jews, on the way to worldly redemption, are powerful enough to 'redeem' (read: take over) the whole of *Eretz Israel*, while ensuring that no Jewish blood is spilled in the process, even if this means acquiescence in the (temporary) evacuation of Jewish settlements in the Occupied Territories.[30]

Second, and more important for my argument, are the many hard-core religious Zionist settlers who belong to *Gush Emunim* ('bloc of the faithful'), the religious Zionist settler movement linked to the National Religious Party. The now firmly established Zionist ideology of *Gush Emunim* is in fact a nationalist adaptation – or, if you wish, a vulgarisation – of a religious movement that originally advocated a more sophisticated form of participation with Zionism for the dialectical purpose of entering into another, higher phase in history. The Jewish mystical notion of 'redemptive prophecy' that inspired this movement is based on the separation, *apartheid*, between superior Jews and inferior non-Jews. As Ravitzky and Rachlevsky have powerfully outlined, galvanised by the teachings of Rabbi Abraham Yitzhak Kook, this highly active militaristic and messianic school condemns Zionism as a corruption of Judaism, but at the same time accepts it as an essential historical phase on the way to 'redemption'. Again, for them, Zionism represents corrupt materialism that is destined to collapse after it fulfils its role in helping to conquer ('redeem') the 'Land of Israel' (*Eretz Israel*) from the non-Jews. For Kook's followers, then, Zionism signifies a perversion of everything Jewish faith stands for, especially the Judaic superior spirituality that promises to bring salvation to the whole world under the Kingdom of David that the arrival of the ultimate Messiah will re-establish. Zionism qua perversion is thus turned into a historical manifestation of the biblical story of the 'Messiah's donkey': Zionism is the donkey the interim Messiah will be riding in a historical dialectical process towards final 'redemption'. To *that end*, through dialectical thinking, Kook's followers *zealously* collaborate with 'sinful' Zionism by making the most of its fateful, because historically fleeting, nature. For them, Zionism is the means through which the 'Land of Israel' is constantly being 'sanctified'. To *that end*, they support *Gush Emunim's* highly militarised right-wing version of Zionism that encourages intense proliferation of settlements in the Occupied Territories. In line with the 'donkey' analogy, the zealous religious Zionists of *Gush Emunim* even seem 'moderate' in appearance as they share many aspects of the way of life of 'secular' and merely traditional Jews, while their dress code is similar to that of most other Israelis except for the knitted yarmulke (skullcap).[31]

Given the ulterior *apartheid* end it pursues, for *Gush Emunim* there can be no greater corruption than political Zionism. Nevertheless, the actual historical role of political Zionism is to serve as the means to that end. At the same time, for religious Zionists, for the Rav Kook followers and, more remotely, for the Haredim, there is a unique – indeed, in some sense 'fundamental' – but perverse justification for the right to have an *apartheid* state: it will be a fatefully fleeting historical phenomenon.

It is clear that Orthodox Jews do not relate to *apartheid*'s immorality towards '*non-Jewish*' Arabs in the same way as 'liberal' political Zionists, who also rationalise Zionism and the right of Israel to be an *apartheid* state. The *so-called* 'fundamentalists', those whom liberal Zionist Jews constantly strive to conceive of as 'Others', do not present reasons *for* apartheid and reasons *against* apartheid as a conflict of reasons that have to be weighed against one another, as such weighing is already an inherently modern – and thus worldly – exercise.

Although 'liberal' Zionists appear to support the need for an *apartheid* state in Israel from a very different angle than these so-called 'fundamentalist' Jews, who (as we just saw) accept Jewish supremacy more explicitly and readily and therefore do not feel the need to justify it, it is possible to detect an originary *apartheid* mentality uniting them both. Existentially, rationalising the need for a 'secular' *apartheid* state and arguing for it more explicitly in Jewish religious terms can amount to the same position. This analysis is important if we want to understand why the anti-Zionists' struggle is so different from the anti-apartheid struggle in South Africa. Attuning carefully to the trajectory Orthodox Jews cleave to, could it be that Zionism is indeed a failed, existentially suicidal, attempt to harness an essentially rootless originary *apartheid* to a national project that is destined to be ephemeral and, through self-destruction via the constant violence it provokes, eventually perhaps to wither away? Is not the ephemeral historical nature of Zionism underpinned both by the denial of liberal Zionists (whose humanist pretensions nevertheless hint at an unconscious supremacist link with their arch-opponents, the religious Zionists) and by the telling simplifications of those left-wing anti-Zionists who self-describe as 'good Jews'? Could it be, in short, that the contradictions, denials and simplifications that characterise the left in fact unite it in facilitating the unfolding of a self-concealing and self-preserving, non-nationalistic and non-territorial originary *apartheid*? Is not originary *apartheid* perfectly cloaked in the same humanist pretensions that have always constituted its main feature, whether in exile or in its incarnation as a Jewish state in Palestine?

Finally, could Zionism not be seen as a historical tool that, through its self-destructiveness, contributes to the entrenchment of originary *apartheid*? Does not originary *apartheid* hold sway precisely through the existential violence-provoking unity between liberal Zionists, those who oppose Zionism as Jews, and Orthodox Jews who oppose Zionism? And does not this violence erupt each time an attempt is made to connect to history in a normal, human way – as was done so successfully in South Africa?

NOT QUITE WALKING THE EXTRA MILE: ISRAEL'S APARTHEID AND THE COMPLICITY OF 'JEWISH' LEFT-WING ANTI-ZIONISM

In exploring the connection between the Jewish question and the Zionist question, two scholars, the late Israel Shahak and Joseph Massad, have helpfully gone quite far – although to my mind not far enough – as they have transcended the usual wider-ranging historiographical denial of this connection and have taken the issue beyond the 'current affairs' discourse. Both scholars arrive at an embryonic (and thus partial) response to the question of the extent to which Zionism, far from abusing the Jewish experience, is in fact a manifestation of Jewish being and thinking. As such, both Shahak and Massad give us a hint of the unique way in which even the seemingly most moderate left-wing Zionists tend to rationalise *apartheid*. Both arguments get nearer – although, again, arguably nowhere near enough – to asking the question of originary *apartheid*.

In his book *Jewish History, Jewish Religion*, Shahak argues that the *apartheid* of political Zionism internalised *apartheid* features that constitute central, albeit not exclusive, aspects of the Jewish faith.

Relying on his wide reading in the *Halacha*, *Mishna*, *Gmara* and *Agada*, as well as Jewish mysticism, Shahak argues that messianic thinking is linked to the segregationist thinking that is characteristic of the Jewish *Kabbala* but also draws upon the highly legalistic approach typical of central tenets of Jewish thought about sanctity and everyday life. *Apartheid* of this kind between Jews and non-Jews was advocated, for example, by such leading Jewish philosophers as Maimonides; both in his *Guide to the Perplexed,* where his philosophy interacts with Greek thought, and in his highly legalistic *Mishne Torah*, Maimonides incorporated many passages that proffer overtly racist and supremacist interpretations.[32]

Significantly, though, Shahak never says that in order to overcome Zionism one has to overcome Judaism or stop being Jewish. In other words, it is quite clear that Shahak did not aspire to essentialise Judaism as an *apartheid* faith. But he did think that the tendencies he highlights in what he called 'Jewish tribal fundamentalism' clearly informed the secular and racist Zionist ideology of Israeli Jews.

Shahak's critical message seems to be that Zionist Jews of moderate ilk could, with a bit of reflection, touch the dark forces that infuse their racism and ethno-nationalism and adopt the universal ethical tenets of Judaism, becoming in turn both anti-Zionists *and* anti-fundamentalists.[33] Anti-Zionism would need to be made capable of jettisoning the *apartheid* tenets of Judaic thought as well as the nationalistic rationalisation of the *apartheid* state that internalised those tenets.

Put another way, for Shahak, the right of Israel to exist as an *apartheid* state is implicitly in opposition to the ethical stance that can still be said to inform Judaism. Renouncing Jewish fundamentalism would herald that type of Judaism that is capable of internally cleansing any *apartheid* element and thus can progressively move from the existing ethnocracy to a non-separatist civic national existence and governance. Shahak effectively facilitates a space for ethical Judaism as he urges moderate Zionists to get rid of their supremacist *apartheid* tendencies and to stop using – or abusing – anti-Semitism and the memory of the Holocaust to nourish those tendencies. For Shahak, it is this *apartheid* righteousness, as it has survived through modernity, which fuels the Israeli claim to have the right to have an *apartheid* state while also denouncing anti-Zionism as a form of anti-Semitism or Jewish self-hatred.

Shahak's thesis represents an intriguing combination of avid scholarship and personal candour as he highlights a fundamentalist *aspect* of Jewish religion and then connects this aspect to Zionist ideology. Thus, he manages both to connect the Jewish question to the Zionist question existentially and at the same time subtly to create a space for the ethical Jewish thinking that, despite the aberration of Zionism, has succeeded in holding its own. To that extent, Shahak manages to sever the Zionist question from the Jewish question and to state unequivocally that Zionism in no way exhausts Judaism. For Shahak, then, it is still possible to be an anti-Zionist and a good Jew.

A thesis like Shahak's, isolating Jewish fundamentalism from within Jewish thought, on the one hand fully acknowledges the horrors of anti-Semitism and of the Holocaust, presenting both as extreme cases of European racism. On the other hand, it explains how violence against Jews played into the hands of this Jewish fundamentalist tendency in a way that has led modern political Zionism to mystify, if not to sanctify, anti-Semitism.

But then, of course, by creating a space for ethical Jewish thought capable of overcoming fundamentalist thinking, Shahak carefully avoids asking existential questions about the nature of 'Jewish ethics', especially whether its 'universality' does not sublimate a deep sense of separateness that also tends to assimilate anyone who becomes exposed to it. My point is that there might well not be such a space. Shahak has neutralised the need to ask deep questions about the so-called 'universality' of Jewish ethics, particularly in what way and at what price does this ethics signally help radicalise the possibility of inhabiting separateness.

One example may serve to illustrate this. Emmanuel Levinas, still one of the main champions of the radical left of today, advocated an ethics that he explicitly hailed as a Jewish contribution to a largely Greek world, and one that prioritises a relationship of obligation towards the Other, one that is based on the radical separation and exteriority that comes to us when we are face to face with Others. It is difficult to exaggerate just how pervasive the notion of the radical exteriority of the Other has become in critical 'progressive' left politics. However, here I want to limit myself to two remarks. First, arguably only an individual who feels totally 'Other' could advocate an ethics that is based on total otherness, separation and radical exteriority. Second, the Jewish state was to be a prophetic ethical state – one that would overcome exile and persecution. But, despite his ethics, Levinas has revealed a curious blind spot with regard to the wrongs committed against Palestinians by the 'sameness' of the Jewish state – a sameness his ethics is otherwise so critical of.[34]

It is perhaps Shahak's scriptural reliance that works most intensely to neutralise the need to fully ask the question of originary *apartheid*. This happens when one accepts as legitimate the thesis that it is possible to inhabit an ethical Judaism that stays aloof from the existential provocation that has led to violence against Jews, a violence that occurred *despite* the fact that many Jews belonged to the enlightened pinnacle of European culture and formed part of its ethical core. The ethical Judaism Shahak embraces also seems to transcend the existential forces as it legitimises and entrenches a discourse about 'fundamentalist' religious and political Zionism 'abusing' this violence, failing to acknowledge the common existential condition they both share.

By leaving open the possibility of severing Jewish 'fundamentalism' from Jewish 'ethics', Shahak again stops short of going all the way. He therefore fails to spot the connection between the Zionist question and the Jewish question that points to the possibility of ethical and non-fundamentalist Judaism in fact being the most sophisticated way of concealing the originary *apartheid* of Jewish being and thinking. In other words, Shahak's ethics itself becomes a camouflage for the existential process of which Zionism is an instantiation and at the service of which it operates – originary *apartheid*.

Finally, Shahak's thesis stresses that it is possible for a person to be a Jew *and* to be cleansed of all *apartheid* elements; he has in mind enlightened liberal, Marxist or post-colonialist Jews with a cosmopolitan outlook rather than a tribal *apartheid* mentality. The result of the connection Shahak makes here, but also of what he leaves open, is that he cannot fully respond to the core problem of how secular Zionists rationalise Israel as an *apartheid* state. All the same, the discourse of the intimate relationship between Jewish fundamentalism and Zionism has become the bedrock for those Jews who oppose Zionism ethically and who portray themselves as progressive, different from the 'others', the fundamentalists.

The drawback here is that some sentiment of irreducible, irredeemable 'exile', exteriority and separateness might still be lurking in the seemingly cosmopolitan secularity of those who oppose Zionism as *ethical* or – to follow Hannah Arendt – *conscious-pariah* Jews. Ethical, moderate Jews self-describe as either 'secular' – that is, allowing for a Jewish identification that is only political – or as 'mildly observant or traditional' – adopting a loosely committed observant attitude to Jewish religious laws. My argument is that it is possible for 'ethical' people who oppose Zionism *as Jews* to become complicit in the denial by ignoring the existential shackles that make up the 'how' of Zionism; and thus, in turn, they are no longer able to look more closely at themselves. The internal incoherence that arises in separating 'fundamentalist' from 'ethical' Jewish being and thinking stems from the way in which the denial complements the contradiction that informs the humanism and racism of 'moderate' Zionist Jews.

The result is that both camps on the left remain locked in a discourse that leaves the key issues untouched. The perfect song and dance of denial: on the one hand, Zionist Jews, who stick on the anti-Semitism label and attach the 'self-hating Jew' epithet to anyone who criticises their political Zionism; and, on the other hand, those individuals who oppose political Zionism as Jews, who trot out anti-Semitism and attributions of self-hatred against any voice that raises the full question of originary *apartheid*.

But being locked in an existential condition to such an extent that the outcome is a discourse of common denial again means that one can avert all suspicion that the 'left' Jewish reaction to Zionism might inadvertently assist the *apartheid* ideology, an unfolding that is no less fateful for happening unhindered. In other words, for all their good intentions, what makes some of those who oppose Zionism as Jews so very Jewish, and at the same time the unconscious protectors of Zionism, is their vehement opposition to any existential connection between the historical forces that have been provoking violence against even the most ethical of Jews, as happened in Nazi Germany, and the violence political Zionism has been provoking in Palestine. It is this collective unconscious that leads to the existential condoning of the denial that I attempt to expose, precisely by those who seem to advance the right moral argument but who do so as Jews. Again, in this way, Shahak's approximation to deep insights, together with his failure to render problematic any suggested schism between 'ethical' and 'morally repugnant' Jewish being and thinking, becomes the most sophisticated bedrock of denial. Put differently, Shahak's thesis facilitates a tellingly palatable severance of any connection between the Jewish question and the Zionist question, thereby enabling Zionists and 'enlightened' Jews to continue arguing about whether or not Zionism follows from Judaism without ever properly probing the origin of the question of *apartheid*. In this way, anti-Zionist Jews themselves become the very policing agents who ensure that the origin of denial of political Zionism will never be touched. The moment anyone attempts to look at the question of an uncritically accepted unity between them, both camps quickly and decisively close ranks and accuse that person of anti-Semitism or 'essentialism'.

Joseph Massad has tackled the same issue from a different angle.[35] The gist of Massad's thesis is that anti-Semitism and the unsuccessful and incomplete assimilation of Europe's Jews still haunt Zionist imagery, explaining Zionism's obsession with completing European Jewry's 'assimilation' in Palestine. Both factors – the persecution of the Jews in Europe and their inability to totally assimilate – drove the founders of Zionism to create 'Europe' in Palestine in such a way as to enable them to fully realise the 'European Jew' there. Alas, as it attempted to overcome both the notion and the horrific experiences of the European 'diaspora', Zionism recreated a similar imagery in Palestine by resurrecting the fear of anti-Semitism and persecution side by side with its Europeanisation of Palestine. Zionism's process of Europeanisation has meant the de-Arabization – that is, the assimilation and colonisation into this European imagery – of Israel's Arab Jews and their culture through their oppression as, and their constant relegation to the status of, second-class citizens. Furthermore, the failure to eliminate the legacy of the European diaspora and the simultaneous cultivation of a consciousness of anti-Semitism has led to a symbolic reversal that has turned Palestinians (Israel's *non-Jewish* Arabs) into 'Jews': *apartheid* persists in the very existence of the Jewish state and inhabits its very laws. In other words, the symbolic persistence of the European Jewish diaspora and anti-Semitism that is represented by Zionism ensures the persistence of the 'Palestinian' problem.

For Massad, the 'right to be an *apartheid* state' connects to the denial that stems from the grip of anti-Semitism that still haunts the world of the European phenomenon that is Zionism. Massad goes further than the scholarship of 'Jewish fundamentalism' by locating this symbolic hegemony of victimhood in the very being of *secular* Israelis (and arguably, I would add, also of all those Palestinians who adopt the discourse of being the 'last victims of the Holocaust', 'victims of the victims').

Nevertheless, existentially, by still adhering to a portrayal of anti-Zionism as an instance of European colonialism, rather than seeing this colonialism itself as an instance of originary *apartheid*, Massad's thesis arguably remains too limited in its range of application. Massad touches upon, but at the same time avoids, the Jewish question. He stops short, I believe, of exploring the nature of what both the violent experience of European Jews and their subsequent colonial acts hint at. Massad analyses a symptom, but keeps its cause out of the inquiry. He refrains from asking the question of *apartheid* that would turn the experience of European Jews into a symptom of the more originary, existential *apartheid* that pertains to the unresolved schismatic relationship of the Jews with European culture. The Europe of which Judaism attempted but failed to become an integrated part may well hint at some failure that is being recreated – as Massad does point out – in Palestine.

In other words, the violent experience of European Jews and its follow-up, the (re)creation of a violent, self-destructive national entity in Palestine, calls upon us to consider whether self-preserving originary *apartheid* may not have a positive existential stake in both the catastrophic failure to become the European Jew and the catastrophe that has been playing itself out in Palestine. For from the ashes of failure arise existential forces that are complicit in the preservation of *apartheid*. The provocation (of separation) that led to the violence in Europe might not be any different from the provocation (of *apartheid*) that, in turn, may lead to the existential demise of the Zionist project. Both are related existentially in a way that critical historiography cannot render visible.

Finally, Massad's thesis about the Jews' symbolic identification as Palestinians is *deeply* truthful. There is a continuum between the failure to be assimilated and this symbolic turning of Palestinians into Jews. The failure of the Jews to assimilate in Europe was replaced by an effort to assimilate as Europeans in Palestine. But what if such symbolic transformation also happened in Europe after all? Why should we see the historical discourse around assimilation as the assimilation *of* Jews *into* their surroundings and not, existentially, as the constant and tellingly disastrous phenomenon of assimilation *by* Jews *of* their surroundings? Arguably, Massad does not yet attune to a historicity that allows for attempts to assimilate into Jewish being and thinking all people who come into contact with Jews. There are existential reasons that Massad's diagnosis forcefully points to, but at the same time brushes aside as irrelevant, 'historically implausible' or less urgent than the more immediate connection between Zionist colonialism and the symbolic abuse of racist anti-Semitism.

Similar to Shahak, then, but in a different way, Massad stops short of going all the way. While Shahak becomes the bedrock for the scholarship and discourse that are the possible Jewish 'Other' to 'Jewish fundamentalism', which is then used to avoid the Jewish question existentially, Massad resorts to the framework of Jewish/European colonialism and thus centres on the urge to reaffirm and to build upon an uncritically accepted historiographical sense of the Jews in Europe. I argue that, in doing so, he avoids the question of the deeper non-linear historical unfolding in which Palestine might be involved.

As I see it, Massad is far too quick in suggesting that Israelis 'give up' anti-Semitism in order to foster a non-racist inclusive psyche in Palestine. Can Israelis 'give up', or indeed be forced to give up, the forces that dominate their separateness-begotten collective unconscious being and thinking about history and their otherness-from-all-others, disallowing the *ethical* awareness and sensitivity that would enable them to genuinely wonder at Jews provoking so much violence? Can Israelis just 'give up' an existential trauma whose suppression results in the self-preservation and self-concealment of originary *apartheid* as it assimilates Jewish 'ethics' and 'humanism' into the aggressive victim and 'chosen-people' mentality the trauma feeds on? Furthermore, is not the call for Israelis to 'give up' the use of anti-Semitism, to stop thinking as victims, to be and act just as other human beings – indeed, like the Afrikaners – already captive of the very being and thinking of originary *apartheid* that successfully conceals its operative forces behind such a call? Because the reactions of the left to Zionism and the way it eschews asking the Jewish question conspire in a certain way to preserve originary *apartheid*, the question arises as to whether the left itself has not been the very product of such assimilation, the tool for doing exactly that, preserving originary *apartheid*.

Furthermore, anti-Semitism is itself a racist and distorted response to Jewish originary *apartheid* as it only serves existentially to preserve that apartheid by playing into the hands of the Jewish victim mentality. Did not anti-Semitism's caricaturised and distorted response have the existential purpose of preparing for the next stage in the attempt to assimilate originary *apartheid* into the national project? As racist and militaristic anti-Semitism turns the Jewish existential condition into a mere object of hatred, it becomes a tool for the preservation of that originary *apartheid* that can never be reduced to a mere 'object', an aberration, but should rather be seen as a lingering phenomenon within Western thought. Existentially, then, the European experience of the Jews is *Jewish* in its origin, and rather than avoid exploring this, deep contemplation has to help us uncover what it was in Jewish being and thinking that provoked so much hatred against itself, precisely the kind of contemplation that both Zionists and anti-Zionists always aim to avoid or to reduce to merely a discourse of racist anti-Semitism. Summing up, both Shahak and Massad stop short of asking the question about Jewish being and thinking that would prove most illuminating – that is, the core question of its pervasive assimilating powers, its persistence and its self-concealing properties, and the way they nourish that perverse claim to have 'the *right* to be an *apartheid* state'. Both, then, seem to represent the politically correct stance that accepts the possibility of segregating the Zionist question from the Jewish question. They do not allow room for the existential inquiry into how the connection between the Jewish question and the Zionist question may help explain the violence of Zionism as an instantiation of originary *apartheid* working to preserve itself. Their gesture contributes to concealing the actuality in which originary *apartheid* violently preserves itself in a self-destructive yet 'ethical' Jewish state that is itself rationalised and justified through the experience a group of ethical people suffered at the hands of an evil desire to destroy them. In their theses, however existentially relevant, both Shahak and Massad still cause reflection to revert back to the first level of the moral, constitutional and legal comparison between Apartheid South Africa and *apartheid* Israel.

The origin of the ulterior justification of a 'right to be an *apartheid* state' has to canvass historical forces that inhabit the thinking about Zionism as *symptomatic* of, and as a *phase* in, the fateful unfolding of the Jewish condition, rather than merely as a way of *abusing* a tribal aspect – itself only part of the Jewish existential condition – in order to justify its settler colonial movement in Palestine. The challenge that vision will have to embrace – which claims that this tribal facet is somehow dispensable and can be overcome, and in turn that overcoming it will result in a de-colonised and egalitarian Palestine – must be mounted from deeper waters. Zionism is not just another instance of 'ethno-nationalism' but represents a failed attempt to control the violence provoked by originary *apartheid*, as it unconsciously seeks to preserve that *apartheid* through its own hate-provoking but ephemeral existence. The foretold failure of political Zionism is precisely the fateful success of the self-preservation of originary *apartheid*.

The denial that characterises the contradictory positions of liberal and 'soft' Zionists, as well as of those who oppose Zionism as Jews, runs very deep. Ethical moderation that nevertheless demands the right to be racist based on the uniqueness of the Jewish predicament smacks of a sense of separateness so deeply rooted that it is mysteriously but obviously capable of exerting a claim on its many (already converted) friends and sympathisers – evidently unlike South Africa at the time of apartheid – to always turn a blind eye. The obsession, when it comes to *apartheid* Israel, with arguing about Zionism but never about Jewish being and thinking ignores the possibility that Zionism is an ephemeral phenomenon – ephemeral because it is self-destructive and fatefully suicidal. The protection people bestow on it, inter alia by subscribing to the simplistic parity between Israel and South Africa, allows this self-destructiveness to work its way towards the restoration of an originary *apartheid* that knows neither borders nor boundaries. If anything, Orthodox Jews are the only ones who point to and appear to sense the existential struggle to come – a prophecy of violence to be fulfilled with all the politically correct accounts of left-wing anti-Zionism in attendance.

BY WAY OF CONCLUSION

The resounding call of the Holocaust on our being and thinking will have been in vain if the significance of the violence that *sustained* the genocide is diluted into a common humanist message *following* it. As it is, despite the unspeakable horror, the ambit that delineates contemporary Holocaust memorialisation ensures that this memory remains captive of denial – denial about how a particular way of remembering the Holocaust uniquely serves the self-preservation of originary *apartheid* by blocking the more primordial relationship between violence and memory. It is this kind of Holocaust denial that dominates left-wing responses to Zionism, both when people rationalise Israel as the Jewish state and, even more so, in the case of people who oppose it as Jews. If anything, it is not anti-Zionist Jews – whose compassion for the fate of the Palestinians is always resolutely conditioned (and thus always, somewhat bizarrely, compromised) by their failure to fully assimilate the violence into a humanist warning against the hubris of Zionism that it can overcome that violence – but moderate Zionists who, for all their secularity, provide a frank clue to the contrary: the sophisticated way in which the tribal collective unconscious provokes and utilises violence in order to self-preserve. By provocatively eschewing the contradiction between their humanist, universalist pretentions and the 'no choice' rhetoric of Zionism that makes them powerless before their tribal separateness – that is, before originary *apartheid* – moderate Zionists tell us that they unconsciously and existentially sense that the genocidal violence against the Jews that raged in Europe has had a deeply embedded stake: the unique and fateful purpose of the tribal preservation of originary *apartheid*. Put differently, fearfully grounded in the defence of 'never again', the existential denial that holds moderate Zionists captive stems from the way in which they intuit, however unconsciously and traumatically, that originary *apartheid* self-preserves through the violence it provokes. Jews against Zionism may be more sophisticated at concealing it, but the paradox both camps share is that they have heard the call to contemplation but refuse to heed it, and that they have read the sign but fail to understand it. It is on this level that this chapter calls for mindful reflection.

How deep-rooted must that provocation be, how deeply embedded that stake in self-preservation, that it fostered the unfathomably distorted notion that one could eradicate an essential phenomenon – originary *apartheid* – by killing actual human beings, as the Nazis set out to do systematically. From the tribal perspective, all-out violence against originary *apartheid* heralds unprecedented, even epochal, 'success'. That is, conceiving of this violence merely as a functional instantiation of history already denies the deeper existential stake of that which it seeks to preserve. Failing to see this means that the violence against Jews and its culmination in the Nazi genocide will also make one oblivious to the next instantiation of originary *apartheid*: the vain attempt to 'end' the violence provoked by originary *apartheid* as it self-preserves through the paradigm of the modern nation-state. True, the creation of *apartheid* Israel replaced the question of originary *apartheid* with the simpler, more 'manageable' question of Jewish colonisation, made 'palatable' by invoking the 'no choice' rhetoric of the violence the Jewish state perpetrates to rationalise the harm it embodies. Yet again, the fateful provocative fate of failure here is to ignore the fact that this violence will always succeed in pre-empting the deeper question of originary *apartheid*. Has not the phenomenon survived precisely because of the colossal ideological distortions that result from attempting either to eradicate originary *apartheid* through genocide or to 'domesticate' it within national boundaries?

In other words, the crux of this chapter lies here: that in order to fathom and not deny the origin of the violence of the Holocaust, we need to listen to the existential enormity that originated it. We need to recognise that what is at stake here has yet to be brought into language since it moves beyond any of the historical actors involved and reaches deeper than any of the immediate impulses that motivated their horrific actions. As it provokes the economy of separateness and the self-preservation which that separateness serves, this stake is irrevocably owned by the West as a whole: it unites the violence of the Holocaust with that of the Jewish state in Palestine in a common tribal economy of essential separateness.

'Can Western history and culture do without its Jews?' George Steiner has asked.[36] It cannot: the very conditions Western thought has been thrown into call for the contemplation of originary *apartheid* from the violence in Palestine and from the denial that entrenches the originary desire to be hated that moves it. We need to contemplate the Holocaust from the point of originary *apartheid*; however much it is inextricably concealed in its dialectical unfolding, originary *apartheid* created the conditions for the 'next' stage in its own self-preservation: the self-destructive, indeed existentially suicidal, Zionist state, whose existence will always be precarious and ultimately fleeting, another instantiation in the historical dialectic of the self-preservation of originary *apartheid*. Originary *apartheid* does not, indeed cannot, be made to obey statehood and it is not, cannot be, made to subject to territoriality, nor can it be halted within a sequential historical methodology that prioritises the linearity of 'before' and 'after'. Its enduring preservation is a problem owned by the West as a whole, the very West that does its utmost to ensure that it remains a non-question and that thus becomes complicit in shielding the primordial separateness and detachment from history that is originary *apartheid*'s hallmark. It needs to become possible to try to begin fathoming the Holocaust by heeding the reverberating echo of the call it has sounded for us to dare think about the existential origin of its violence and contemplate it as an inseparable part of the inner strife of Western civilisation – inseparable, that is, from the question of being in the West. The West may still need and desire its Jews 'to hate', and, as it helps to sustain that desire, the Zionist adventure may well be just a short and fatefully fleeting chapter in history. But Holocaust denial is not just the denial of events and of facts and figures. Rather, Holocaust denial consists in choosing to remain oblivious to originary *apartheid* and its collective unconscious desire to be hated – a desire captive of a mythical trauma that stems from unconsciously hating all others but that remains hidden behind the dramatic backdrop of the compassion and the infinite sense of righteousness that hinder the emergence of any reflexive form of ethics and, in turn, prevent any forgiveness towards 'Others' to manifest itself. Here we must start contemplating how to make the 'forbidden' possible, how to refuse the 'anathema' – that is, how to overcome the existential circumcision that represents the covenant of separation.

When the originary violence of the Holocaust is interpreted exclusively within the linear 'before and after' ordering of history, *that* is Holocaust denial. What *passes* for Holocaust denial and has become sacrosanct is in fact the persistent and positive essential refusal to point to the existential self-preservation of originary *apartheid* and its provocation to self-preserve. And it is this existential error that today dominates humanity's 'responsible' ethical reflection on the 'Jewish Holocaust'.

In this sense, by arguing that originary apartheid conscripts violence on the part of historical actors for its own self-preservation and then works to conceal the true effect of this violence by cloaking it in the simple racist discourse of anti-semitism, this chapter seeks to generate a different kind of existential register, one more akin to that of a Greek chorus. While fully aware that the unspeakable horror of the Nazi genocide remains unassailable, it forces us to accept that the use and abuse of the violence of the Holocaust transcends the intentionality of the historical actors who perpetrated that violence. Holocaust denial may, finally, then also mean the refusal to accept this – that is, the refusal to grasp that Nazi ideology, through an existential discourse that exclusively centred on 'racial hatred' of Jews, succeeded in thwarting the essential contemplation of originary apartheid and that it thereby served the fateful self-preservation of the collective unconscious of originary apartheid. In a chilling resonance to Massad's thesis about Zionists claiming 'the right to be racist', we can now view the architects of the Final Solution as existentially 'good Jews' and their victims as the existential 'sacrifice' ('holokauston', burnt offering) through which originary apartheid has compelled its own self-preservation. To that extent the tribal righteous detachment from suffering - even by its secular, left-wing members - fatefully encompasses the tribe's own suffering through which self-preserving originary apartheid shields its essential separate-ness. The underlying existential economy at work here – of the self-preservation of originary apartheid through its own violence-provoking existence – sums up the tragedy of the existential dynamics that this chapter has attempted to unearth.

In other words, we should not shirk from contemplating the Holocaust as showing how pervasive the power of this existential phenomenon to assimilate historical actors for the sake of its own preservation can be. That is why, beyond the irrefutable immorality of the genocide it unleashed, we must think the violence of the Holocaust in terms of being, so that, for the sake of those murdered, we can begin to grasp the existential dynamics into which both they and the perpetrators of the violence had been thrown. And we can then gradually begin to understand how exactly this 'thrown-ness' (in the sense of Heidegger's *Geworfenheit*) explains the sense in which Palestine holds a suppressed stake for the West as a whole.

Unlike South Africa and the white settlers colonising it, it is not *Zionism* that has been colonising Palestine, but originary *apartheid*. Zionism is the temporary outward foil originary *apartheid* uses to conceal itself, with, until today, Zionism's 'historical actors' guaranteeing the violence originary *apartheid* relies upon to self-preserve. Therefore, the philosophical inquiry into originary *apartheid* that is needed will have to pursue the as yet unfathomed 'is' rather than resort to what 'ought to be' in Palestine. For one thing, the self-preservation of the denial surrounding the separatist Jewish features of Zionism tells us that the existential condition that prevails in Palestine was not present in South Africa. In South Africa, after all, *apartheid* proved capable of connecting again to history and of lending itself more readily to critical historiographical analysis and moral scrutiny. By contrast, the *apartheid* of which Israel is a symptom holds such high stakes for the collective unconscious of the metaphysical and monotheistic West that the West will not even allow it to become a problem. That is, the violence in Palestine holds up a mirror to the West that the West refuses to look into. With terrifying implications, as, ultimately, the *apartheid* constituted by the *existence* of the State of Israel is more essential than the *apartheid* created on the ground by the *actions* of the State of Israel: it is the origin.

Notes

1 I would like to thank Dick Bruggeman with all my heart for his amazing empathy and sensitivity in reading, editing and commenting on the chapter.
2 For this definition, see Ran Greenstein, 'Israel–Palestine and the Apartheid Analogy: Critics, Apologists and Strategic Lessons', in this volume.

3   See H. Giliomee, *The Afrikaners: Biography of a People*, Charlottesville: Virginia University Press, 2003, Chapters 1–6.

4   For an account of the background to *apartheid* and *apartheid* ideology and detailed accounts of the legal measures of *apartheid*, see H. Giliomee and L. Schlemmer, *From Apartheid to Nation Building*, Oxford: Oxford University Press, 1989, Chapters 1–3. See also R. Omond, *The Apartheid Handbook: A Guide to South Africa's Racial Policies*, London: Penguin, 1987.

5   R. Shehadeh, *Occupier's Law: Israel and the West Bank*, Washington: Institute for Palestine Studies, 1985; E. Benvenisti, *Legal Dualism: The Absorption of the Occupied Territories into Israel*, Jerusalem: The West Bank Date Project, 1989.

6   See N. Masalha (ed.), *Catastrophe Remembered: Palestine–Israel and the Internal Refugees: Essays in Memory of Edward W. Said*, London: Zed Books, 2005.

7   See Ilan Pappé, *The Ethnic Cleansing of Palestine*, Oxford: One World Press, 2006; N. Masalha, *Expulsion of the Palestinians: The concept of 'transfer' in Zionist Political Thought, 1882–1948*, Washington, DC: Institute for Palestine Studies, 1992; B. Morris, *The Birth of the Palestinian Refugees Problem 1947–1949*, Cambridge: Cambridge University Press, 1987.

8   As a proponent of this view, see, for example, J. Carter, *Palestine: Peace Not Apartheid*, New York: Simon & Schuster, 2006. See also D. Golan-Agnon, 'The Israeli Human Rights Movement: Lessons from South Africa' in D. Downes, P. Rock, C. Chinkin and C. Gearty (eds), *Crime, Social Control and Human Rights: From Moral Panics to States of Denial*, Cullompton: Willan Publishing, 2007, pp. 270–93.

9   See, for example, H. Adam and K. Moodlay, *Seeking Mandela: Peace Making between Israelis and Palestinians*, Philadelphia: Temple University Press, 2005, Chapters 1, 2, 4.

10 See, for example, the Absentees' Property Law 1950. By 'absentees' property', the law meant land belonging to Palestinians whom the Zionist forces had expelled from the areas it had succeeded in occupying by mid-1949. Curiously, the law affected not only the more than 650,000 Palestinians who had been ethnically cleansed, but also the 150,000 or so Arabs who somehow had remained within the borders of the new State of Israel: the law defined 'absentee' in such a way that people who were very much present in Israel could still have their property declared 'absent': 'present absentee' is the Orwellian term the Israeli government created for them. Cf. David Kretzmar, *The Legal Status of the Arabs in Israel*, Boulder: Westview Press, 1987, pp. 55–60, where the author quotes a figure of 75,000 for the number of Palestinians in Israel whom the law turned into such 'present absentees'.

11 In 1970, Israel's 1950 Law of Return ('Every Jew [anywhere in the world] has the right to come to this country [Israel] as an *oleh* [immigrant]') was amended as follows: 'The rights of a Jew [anywhere in the world] under this Law ... are also vested in a child and a grandchild of a Jew, the spouse of a Jew, the spouse of a child of a Jew and the spouse of a grandchild of a Jew'.

12 'In perpetuity': cf. the Hebrew Bible, Genesis 17: 7–8, where 'God' says to 'Abraham': 'And I will establish my covenant between me and thee and thy seed after thee in their generations for an everlasting covenant, to be a God unto thee, and to thy seed after thee. And I will give unto thee, and to thy seed after thee, the lands wherein thou art a stranger, all the land of Canaan, for an everlasting possession; and I will be their God'.

13 See U. Davis, *Israel: An Apartheid State*, London: Zed Books, 1987 for illustrations of apartheid laws in Israel; see also Adalah, the Legal Center for Arab Minority Rights in Israel, for an up-to-date list of the more than sixty Israeli laws enacted since 1948 that discriminate against Palestinian citizens of Israel in all areas of life, including land and planning, education, budgets and access to state resources, prisoners and detainees, civil and political rights: http://adalah.org/eng/Israeli-Discriminatory-Law-Database.

14 Iris Marion Young, *Justice and the Politics of Difference*, Princeton: Princeton University Press, 1990, Chapters 1, 2.

15 O. Yiftachel, *Ethnocracy: Land and Identity Politics in Israel–Palestine*, Philadelphia: University of Pennsylvania Press, 2006. See also Ben-Dor and Yiftachel's response: 'Debating Israel Ethnocracy and the Challenge Of Secular Democracy', *Holy Land Studies* 6/2, 2007, pp. 177–95.

16 S. Weil, 'An Essay on Human Personality' in *Simone Weil: An Anthology*, London: Penguin Classics, 2005.

17 A. du Toit, 'Misapprehensions of the Future & Illusions of Hindsight: Some Reflections on the Significance of Intra-Afrikaner Debates to the 1980s', a paper given at the conference 'A South African Conversation on Israel and Palestine', Institute for African Studies, Columbia University, New York, 20–21 September 2002. I am grateful to S. Freedman for pointing me in this direction and to A. du Toit for providing me with a copy of his paper.

18 A notorious expression used by those Afrikaners who, during the Boer War, continued fighting the British even in the face of imminent defeat.

19 See M. Neumann, *The Case Against Israel*, London: Counterpunch Press, 2006, followed up by his 'The One-State Illusion: More Is Less', *Counterpunch*, 10 March 2008.

20 See J. Massad, 'Israel's Right to Be Racist', *Al-Ahram Weekly*, 15 May 2007.

21 For a good summary of this philosophy, see Giliomee and Schlemmer, *From Apartheid to Nation Building*, Chapter 2.

22 See J. Raz, *The Morality of Freedom*, Oxford: Clarendon Press, 1986.

23 Israel Zangwill, 'The Return to Palestine', *The New Liberal Review* 2 (1901), p. 627. As 'literally the only "way out" of the difficulty of creating a Jewish state in Palestine', Zangwill advocated an 'Arab exodus' based on 'race distribution' or a 'trek like that of the Boers from Cape Colony': I. Zangwill, *The Voice of Jerusalem*, London: William Heinemann, 1920, p. 103; see Masalha, *Expulsion of the Palestinians*, p. 13.

24 Schalk Pienaar cited in Giliomee and Schlemmer, *From Apartheid to Nation Building*, p. 42.

25 See A. du Toit, 'No Chosen People: The Myth of the Calvinist Origin of Afrikaner Nationalism and Racial Ideology', *American Historical Review* 88(4) (1983), pp. 920–52; 'Captive to the Nationalist Paradigm: Prof. F. A. van Jaarsveld and the Historical Evidence for the Afrikaner's Ideas on His Calling and Mission', *South Africa Historical Review* 16 (1984), pp. 49–80; 'Puritans in Africa? Afrikaner "Calvinism" and Kuyperian Neo-Calvinism in Late Nineteenth-Century South Africa', *Comparative Studies in Society and History* 27 (1985), pp. 209–40.

26 See M. Prior, *Zionism and the State of Israel: A moral inquiry*, London: Routledge, 1999; N. Masalha, *The Bible and Zionism: Inverted traditions, archeology and post-colonialism in Palestine-Israel*, London: Zed Books, 2007.

27 Shlomo Sand, *The Invention of the Jewish People*, London: Verso Books, 2010.

28 Y. Rabkin, *A Threat from Within: A Century of Jewish Opposition to Zionism*, London: Zed Books, 2006.

29 See I. Shahak and N. Mezevinsky, *Jewish Fundamentalism in Israel*, 2nd edition, London: Pluto Press, 2004, p. 18.

30 For an overview of the various schools, see ibid., Chapters 1–4.

31 See A. Ravitzky, *Messianism, Zionism, and Jewish Religious Radicalism*, Chicago: Chicago University Press, 1996, Chapter 4; S. Rachlevsky, *Messiah's Donkey* (Hebrew), Tel Aviv: Yediot Aharonot Press, 1998, Chapters 5, 6; the 'donkey' reference can be found in Zachariah 9: 9–10: 'Rejoice, rejoice, daughter of Zion … your king is coming to you … humble and mounted on a donkey … and his rule shall extend from the sea to the sea, from the river [Euphrates] to the ends of the earth'.

32 See I. Shahak, *Jewish History, Jewish Religion: The Weight of Three Thousand Years*, London: Pluto Press, 1994.

33 Also, Joel Kovel points to the universal ethics of the prophet, which for him runs counter to the tribal aspect of Judaism. See J. Kovel, *Overcoming Zionism*, London: Pluto Press, 2007, Chapters 1, 2.

34 See, for example, E. Levinas, *Ethics and Infinity: Conversations with Philippe Nemo*, translated by R. A. Cohen, Pittsburgh: Duquesne University Press, 1985.

35 J. Massad, 'The Persistence of the Palestinian Question' in J. Massad, *The Persistence of the Palestinian Question*, London: Routledge, 2006, pp. 166–78.

36 G. Steiner, *Errata: An Examined Life*, London: Phoenix Books, 1998, pp. 53–4, 56, 61.

PART 2

THE BOUNDARIES
OF COMPARISON

CHAPTER 4

'Visible Equality' as Confidence Trick

JONATHAN COOK

In spring 2008, Israel's most senior law officer, Attorney General Menachem Mazuz, instructed the country's Airports Authority to stop its decades-old policy of racial profiling and instead 'implement visible equality' in the screening of air passengers.[1] Mazuz's decision to intervene followed threats from human rights groups to petition the courts to end the often humiliating airport security checks of non-Jews, particularly members of Israel's community of 1.5 million Palestinian citizens.

The government had already tried to stave off pressure. Six months earlier, the Transport Minister, the hawkish former Chief of Staff Shaul Mofaz, had ordered an end to the practice of marking the luggage of non-Jews with coloured stickers to indicate various levels of supposed security threat. Palestinian citizens, including professors, businessmen and journalists, were routinely subjected to lengthy questioning, bag checks and body searches.[2] According to the Israeli daily newspaper *Ha'aretz*, Mofaz's reform was designed 'to spare these passengers embarrassment'.[3]

Although Mofaz replaced the coloured stickers with a uniform white sticker for all passengers, in practice security officials continued the racial profiling of each passenger by writing a numbered code on the white stickers. As a result, Palestinian citizens were still forced to endure humiliating treatment at the airport. Mofaz's intention had never been to end the discriminatory treatment of non-Jews; he simply wanted to lessen the bad publicity the policy was attracting by making it appear as though there was no discrimination.[4]

The Attorney General's move had no tangible effect on the policy either. Later, Israel introduced a system of barcoded stickers, making it still harder to determine that it was almost exclusively Palestinian citizens being selected for security screening. However, in 2014, after the Supreme Court repeatedly threatened to rule illegal such racial profiling – the main area in which Israel's discrimination against its Palestinian citizens was blatant rather than concealed – the government quietly ended the decades-old practice, adopting a system closer to those used in other international airports.[5] Interestingly, the decision to simply drop the extra security procedures for Palestinian citizens raised doubts about whether the routine harassment of Palestinian citizens had ever had a security rationale.[6]

'Visible equality' – the appearance of equality, as opposed to real or substantive equality – neatly encapsulates Israel's approach towards its one in five citizens who are Palestinian, the vestiges of the Palestinian people, most of whom were expelled from their homeland during the 1948 war. In this respect, Israel has been extremely careful not to follow in the footsteps of Apartheid South Africa, where the overarching policy of discrimination against non-whites was flaunted both legally and administratively. Except in its separate and unequal treatment of non-Jews at the airport, in the main Israel has avoided wherever possible publicly discriminating against its Palestinian citizens. (When officials admit historic discrimination, it is usually characterised as security-related, an unfortunate by-product of Israel's larger conflict with the Palestinian people.)

Instead, Israel has implemented a policy of covert, or veiled, discrimination that is in some regards as damaging to the individual and communal interests of the country's Palestinians as apartheid was to South Africa's black population. This difference in the 'visibility' of the discrimination practised by these two states has been possible mainly because Palestinian citizens in Israel are a minority, even if a significant one, whereas blacks constituted an overwhelming majority in Apartheid South Africa. Israel has, therefore, been able to project an image of itself as a democracy, rather than as an apartheid regime, in ways that would have been implausible had they been tried by the former South African state.

Nonetheless, there are strong grounds for arguing that Palestinian citizens are subjected to an apartheid system inside Israel, even if it is one that does not precisely mimic the South African model. By 'apartheid', I mean the largely separate treatment of populations, based on ethnic or racial criteria, inside a single territory enforced through law, state procedures and official practice. The primary goal of such separate treatment is to allow one group to control the state's chief resources to the detriment of the other group. Separate park benches and segregation on buses – the 'petty apartheid' that South Africa was famous for[7] – are not necessary for a political and legal system to have an apartheid character. South African apartheid took this distinctive form because of the country's particular circumstances: a small white minority faced with a large black majority. In other circumstances, such as in Israel, where the privileged group comprises a decisive majority after waging an earlier ethnic cleansing campaign, the features of petty apartheid have not been needed.

Strict segregation between Jews and Palestinians in Israel exists in the main realms of national life: citizenship rights, constitutional protection, political representation, recognition of diaspora interference, land and planning laws, education, employment, and law enforcement. The various laws governing these aspects of life are mutually supporting and reinforcing, as we shall see, and have allowed the Jewish population to control the country's resources, principally land and water, for its own benefit.

DEGRADED CITIZENSHIP

The notion of citizenship is particularly complicated in Israel – and for good reason. Two important laws define citizenship: the Law of Return (1950) and the Citizenship Law (1952), each law creating a different and unequal class of citizenship based on national belonging. The Law of Return gives all Jews everywhere the automatic right to come to Israel and become citizens. By contrast, the Citizenship Law, while conferring citizenship on those Palestinians who remained inside Israel in 1948, imposes severe restrictions on extending the same rights to other non-Jews. In particular, it ensures that the 750,000 Palestinian refugees from the 1948 war and their millions of descendants are denied the right ever to return to their homes and claim Israeli citizenship. These two laws together are designed to ensure that Israel remains a Jewish state in perpetuity: the Citizenship Law denies Palestinian citizens the right to bring exiled family members to Israel, while the Law of Return guarantees precisely this right, and more, to Jewish citizens of Israel.

In short, Palestinian citizens, unlike Jewish citizens, have no possibility of family unification or of helping relatives to immigrate. The sole loophole – a Palestinian citizen was entitled to bring to Israel a Palestinian spouse who was not a citizen and eventually gain him or her citizenship – was closed by an amendment to the Citizenship Law in 2003.[8]

These two laws create a hierarchy of citizenship based on ethnic belonging in an additional sense. Strangely, Israeli law does not recognise the nationality of 'Israeli', instead treating citizenship and nationality as entirely separate and independent categories of belonging.[9] Formally, every Israeli, whether Jew or Palestinian, shares a common Israeli citizenship, while, conversely, none is entitled to an Israeli nationality – thereby upholding the principle of visible equality. Instead, the state selects each citizen's nationality from a list of more than 130 possibilities that include Jewish, Arab, Hebrew, Samaritan, Russian and Assyrian.[10]

The reason for this peculiar legal distinction between citizenship and nationality is simple: Israel is defined as 'the state of the Jews', not the state of Israelis. Were an Israeli nationality recognised by law, the main consequence would be the ending of legal recognition of special national rights for Jews and its replacement with national rights for Israelis – or, to put it another way, equality for all citizens, the definition of a liberal democratic state. By creating a distinction between the nationalities of Jewish and Palestinian citizens, the state can privilege Jewish nationals over non-Jewish nationals.

The privileging of Jewish nationality in law ensures the maintenance of Israel as a Jewish state in three ways. First, as we have seen, Jews who are not Israeli citizens – that is, Jews in the diaspora – are eligible for the privileges of automatic citizenship enshrined in the Law of Return. Second, international Zionist organisations such as the Jewish National Fund and the Jewish Agency, as the presumed moral and legal representatives of diaspora Jews, enjoy quasi-governmental status to promote the interests of world Jewry inside Israel rather than the interests of all Israeli citizens. And third, Palestinian citizens have no legal grounds for appealing against the exclusive national rights enjoyed by Jews or for demanding their own national rights, such as a right of return for their Palestinian relatives.

In other words, the state has understood that an Israeli nationality would entail two consequences harmful to a Jewish state: the denial of automatic citizenship rights to diaspora Jews, and the equalisation of rights between all citizens, whether Palestinian or Jew. It would spell instant death for Israel as a Jewish state, in both a legal and a demographic sense. Instead, Israel's current citizenship laws put Palestinian citizens in an invidious position. On the one hand, they are denied the right to identify as Palestinians or exercise communal rights as members of a distinct national group, whether in culture, language or education. On the other, they are denied the right to identify meaningfully as Israelis because they are not Jewish. It is not simply that they are second-class citizens, like blacks in the US or Ethiopians in Israel: it is that in a legal sense they do not really belong to their country at all. They are more like long-term temporary guest workers.

In this regard, their situation can be said to be worse than that of blacks in Apartheid South Africa. Azmi Bishara, a former Palestinian member of the Israeli parliament, has observed that South African apartheid, unlike the Israeli version, 'took place within a framework of political unity. The racist regime saw blacks as part of the system, an ingredient of the whole. The whites created a racist hierarchy within the unity'.[11]

The Supreme Court has refused to uphold an Israeli nationality. Most famously, in 1971 Judge Shimon Agranat ruled that such a demand for recognition was not legitimate because it embodied what he called a 'separatist' approach.[12] Separatist from what? From the rest of world Jewry, who are seen in Israeli law to be the sovereign people of Israel.

Finally, it should be noted that, even within Israel's Palestinian population, there are gradations of citizenship. The most significant concerns a group called the 'present absentees' – an Orwellian term for those internally displaced in 1948. They are considered both present in Israel but permanently absent from their homes. There are no precise figures for the number of present absentees, but these refugees and their descendants are believed to comprise a quarter of today's Palestinian minority, more than 300,000 citizens. They have been denied the right ever to reclaim land or property they owned before the 1948 war, which was transferred to a state official known as the Custodian of Absentee Property. Descendants of the present absentees are permanently denied a right to claim their parents' property, in effect inheriting the parents' degraded form of citizenship.[13]

LACK OF CONSTITUTIONAL PROTECTION

In the Declaration of Independence, the document that established Israel on 14 May 1948, the founders of the Jewish state promised to 'uphold the full social and political equality of all its citizens, without distinction of religion, race, or sex'.[14] In addition, the drafting of a constitution – presumably to anchor the principle of equality in law – was supposed to be completed within a few months. That goal was officially abandoned in June 1950, and instead Israel's legislators began formulating a set of basic laws that were intended one day to form the basis of a constitution. Today there are eleven basic laws, but still no constitution.[15]

In 1992, under pressure after signing various international human rights standards, Israel passed a piece of legislation, the Basic Law on Human Dignity and Freedom, that is often considered to be the country's equivalent of a bill of rights. Notably, however, this law does not enshrine basic constitutional protections, such as equality, freedom of expression, freedom from religious coercion and the rights of the individual before the courts. In fact, a principle contrary to equality was established: Israel was defined as a Jewish state, thereby formally codifying the privileged status of its Jewish citizens. While opposition to secular human rights by the influential community of the ultra-Orthodox Jewish religious fundamentalists doubtless played a part in the way the basic law was formulated, this is far from the whole story.

Enshrining the principle of equality in a foundational piece of legislation would also have reversed the thrust of decades of policies conferring privileges on Jews only. It would have begun unravelling the distinction between Jewish and Palestinian citizenship we have already noted. As long as equality is not one of the pillars of Israeli legal principle, then Palestinian citizens have no grounds for seeking redress in the Supreme Court for the legally sanctioned discrimination they suffer.

One Palestinian academic in Israel, Yousef Jabareen, has noted what he calls the 'remarkable normative duality' in Israeli law. On the one hand, unlike petty apartheid in South Africa, Israel formally bans discrimination on the grounds of race or national belonging in relation, for example, to employment and entry to public places. On the other, however, it expressly institutionalises inequality between Jewish and

Palestinian citizens in the major areas of national life.[16] This legal and intellectual contortion is necessary to solve the conundrum of Israel's self-definition as a 'Jewish and democratic' state and to maintain the idea of visible equality. The legal group Adalah has identified more than fifty laws that explicitly enshrine inequality between Jewish and Palestinian citizens, including in the way the state defines itself, state symbols, immigration, citizenship, political participation, land, culture, religion, state budgeting and more.[17] We shall consider some of these laws in subsequent sections.

The important point to note here, however, is that the inequality referred to above is not de facto discrimination, or discrimination as a result of bias by officials in implementing and enforcing laws designed to promote equality. Palestinian citizens suffer this kind of de facto discrimination too, of course, as do ethnic minorities in most liberal democratic or binational states. De facto discrimination is one of the reasons why Palestinian communities are at the bottom of every socio-economic index in Israel. This kind of discrimination, both historic and current, explains in part the fact that Palestinian citizens have lower incomes, higher unemployment, greater poverty, more inadequate municipal infrastructure, shorter life expectancy, higher infant mortality, greater school drop-out rates, and so on.

But Palestinian citizens must also contend with a far more damaging de jure discrimination: that is, inequality that is the goal of Israeli legislation, and which it is the job of state officials to implement. This kind of inequality cannot be appealed against in the courts precisely because it is intentional, as was inequality between blacks and whites in Apartheid South Africa.

Nonetheless, this de jure discrimination is better veiled than its South African equivalent because Israel has conferred on all citizens, whether Jew or Palestinian, the same individual rights. This ostensible equality, however, has been fatally undermined by creating a body of laws that ignores Israel's binational reality and assigns collective rights to one national group only: Jews. These collective rights, for Jews, always take priority over the individual rights available to all Israelis, ensuring that, in a contest of rights, Palestinian citizens invariably lose out. When members of the Palestinian minority try to challenge discrimination in the courts, they are confronted by a judge who is ready to uphold their individual rights (under the democratic component of the state's self-definition) but who is not willing to recognise that the discrimination flows from the privileged status of Jews enjoying collective rights as citizens of a self-defined Jewish state. We shall consider how this works in more detail in the section on land.

The lack of constitutional protection for Palestinian citizens against official discrimination is further exacerbated by the continuing existence of a state of emergency in Israel, which has been renewed annually since 1948. According to the dovish politician Yossi Beilin, in upholding the state of emergency for six decades, Israel is 'embarrassing and childish. There is no other country like it in the democratic world'.[18]

But in reality far more depends on the state of emergency continuing than Beilin suggests. Not least, it breathes life into a set of draconian emergency regulations first promulgated by the British during the Mandate. Were the state of emergency to be ended, as the Israeli scholar Uri Davis has pointed out, the office of the Custodian of Absentee Property – the Israeli official responsible for safekeeping property confiscated from Palestinian refugees – would be disbanded. In law, the property belonging to the Palestinian refugees would then have to be returned.[19]

The state of emergency also maintains the validity of a host of other emergency regulations, such as the Jurisdiction Law, which allows for administrative detentions, and the Terrorism Prevention Order, which is the basis for declaring groups terrorist organisations. Although these laws can be used against Jewish citizens (and in extreme circumstances are), their main purpose is to free the hands of the security services when dealing with Palestinian citizens, with little or no oversight from the civil courts. The Shin Bet, the domestic security agency, is the main beneficiary of these laws, exploiting their powers to crush even legitimate forms of dissent. For example, the Shin Bet can shut down newspapers whose opinions the government disapproves of, and it can interfere in the Palestinian education system, both blocking the appointment of teachers known to have expressed political views and recruiting informers from among the pupils.

The Shin Bet has also declared that it is entitled to use the emergency laws to protect Israel from its own democratically elected representatives. In 2007, for example, the Shin Bet sought the prosecution of Knesset member Azmi Bishara, ostensibly for spying for Hizbullah during Israel's attack on Lebanon a year earlier. As a result, he was forced into exile. However, the Shin Bet's real goal appeared to be to neutralise his campaign to reform Israel into a democratic state. In the words of the Prime Minister's Office, the Shin Bet is empowered to protect Israel from anyone 'working toward changing the basic values of the state by obviating its democratic or Jewish character'.[20] In its view, it is entitled to use its powers 'even if such activity is sanctioned by the law'.[21]

DENIAL OF POLITICAL PARTICIPATION

Despite Israel's self-definition as an ethnic state, most observers assume it is a normal democracy for the simple reason that its Palestinian citizens have the vote. However, this has been an easy generosity for a state in which, after most of the native Palestinian population were expelled six decades ago, there is a clear Jewish majority. In one indication of how irrelevant universal suffrage has been in ensuring meaningful representation for the Palestinian minority, Israel allowed its Palestinian citizens to vote in parliamentary elections right from the creation of the state, even though they were subject to martial law until 1966.[22] One Palestinian academic in Israel, Asad Ghanem, has called the minority's political participation 'completely symbolic'.[23] Certainly, it is a necessary component of Israel's policy of creating 'visible equality' for its Palestinian citizens.

Two factors ensure that political power in Israel is retained solely in Jewish hands and used exclusively for the benefit of the Jewish population.

The first is that the country's independent Palestinian parties, including the one small Jewish and Palestinian coexistence party, have been excluded from every government coalition and every major decision-making body in Israel's history. Even when Yitzhak Rabin needed the support of the Palestinian parties to push through the Oslo diplomatic process in the early 1990s, he refused to let them join the coalition. Instead, they were relegated to membership of what became known as the 'blocking majority'. That offered them access to some parliamentary committees from which they had previously been barred, but even this small concession provoked fierce criticism from many Jewish politicians. In contrast, small Jewish parties of religious fundamentalists or openly fascistic groups have been regularly invited into such coalitions.[24]

Israel's leading Zionist parties have also been opposed to allowing Palestinians, even 'loyal' ones belonging to their own factions, to wield the power of a government ministry. The first Palestinian minister, Ghaleb Majadele of the Labor Party, took up the marginal portfolio of Science, Culture and Sport in 2007.[25] Even then his appointment caused widespread protest. The policy of excluding the Palestinian minority's representatives from the democratic process is seen as entirely legitimate by the wider Jewish electorate. Because Israel ensures that Jewish political, social and economic concerns are entirely separate from Palestinian concerns, there are no shared interests on which Israelis could vote; instead, they vote tribally.

The second factor is that all the political parties contesting national elections are required to operate within a political framework that is an entirely Jewish, Zionist one. The late Israeli sociologist Baruch Kimmerling noted:

A vote for an 'Arab party' is in fact lost because generally a law passed with a majority based on such votes, or a government based on their support, is considered illegitimate. This derives from the constitutional definition of the state as 'Jewish and democratic'.[26]

More than this, however, Israel's self-definition as a 'Jewish and democratic state' means that Palestinian parties are skating close to illegality when they campaign for Israel's democratisation by ending its Jewish character. The constant threat of disqualification, and prosecution, hangs over the minority's politicians. This has been an effective way to rein in free speech and silence dissent. In the years following the outbreak of the second intifada, Israel launched investigations of all of its Palestinian MKs (members of the Knesset), regularly accusing them of incitement or sedition when they promoted their political platforms.[27] The country's two most senior and influential Arab leaders, Azmi Bishara of the National Democratic Assembly and Sheikh Raed Salah of the Islamic Movement, were both hounded relentlessly by the security services. They were also prosecuted in cases that largely collapsed because of a lack of evidence but which did grave damage to their reputations and that of Palestinian citizens generally.[28]

Despite the Palestinian minority's total exclusion from political influence, the climate is growing ever more hostile to their representatives. This trend has been particularly evident since the Palestinian, non-Zionist parties began demanding Israel's reform from a Jewish state to 'a state of all its citizens', or a liberal democracy. In the 2003 Knesset election, two Palestinian candidates and one party, that of Azmi Bishara, were banned from standing by the Central Election Committee, a body dominated by the main Zionist parties. The disqualifications were made possible by a May 2002 amendment to the Basic Law on the Knesset that outlaws candidates and parties that 'deny the existence of the State of Israel as a Jewish and democratic state'. The disqualifications were overturned at the last minute by an enlarged panel of the Supreme

Court, although only by a wafer-thin majority.[29] So far, the courts have continued to block attempts to disqualify non-Zionist parties and their candidates made at every subsequent election.[30]

As a result, right-wing Jewish MKs have been seeking to bypass the court, whose justices appear to regard themselves as the guardians of the principle of 'visible equality'. Following the election of a right-wing government under Benjamin Netanyahu, a raft of bills tried to limit the role of non-Zionist parties. At the time of writing, they included legislation to require Palestinian MKs to swear an oath of loyalty to Israel as a 'Jewish and democratic state' and to make possible the revocation of citizenship for disloyalty. The latter bill, proposed by the Interior Minister Eli Yishai, was intended to target two Palestinian MKs, Azmi Bishara and Haneen Zoabi.[31] Bishara had been forced into exile in 2007 after being accused of spying for Hizbullah, though no evidence was produced; Zoabi had been stripped of her parliamentary privileges, possibly as a prelude to trial, for participating in an aid flotilla to Gaza in May 2010. Both were members of the National Democratic Assembly Party, which has led the campaign to democratise Israel.

In contrast to the Palestinian minority's exclusion from the corridors of power, diaspora Jews (who do not have Israeli citizenship) have strong representation inside the political system and in state agencies through various international Zionist bodies: chiefly the Jewish Agency and the Jewish National Fund inside Israel, and the World Zionist Organisation in the Occupied Territories. These bodies have a keen influence on the decision-making process relating to two key apartheid issues inside Israel: the immigration and settlement of Jews in Israel (and the West Bank); and the confiscation of Palestinian land for exclusive use by Jews. Although these Zionist organisations enjoy a quasi-governmental status, none is subject to Israel's anti-discrimination legislation (itself rarely enforced). According to their charters, these organisations represent the interests of world Jewry, not Israel's population, and can therefore entirely ignore the Palestinian minority in their decisions. The particularly insidious role of the Jewish National Fund in relation to land policies will be considered in the next section.

LAND, PLANNING AND SEGREGATION

The distinctive civic, legal and political edifice of the Jewish state considered so far is not accidental. There is a reason why Palestinians have been excluded from true citizenship in their own state, subjected to a raft of discriminatory laws designed to keep them separate and weak, and denied participation in the political process. The goal has been to ensure that the native Palestinian population inside Israel, and the millions of Palestinians living in exile to whom they are connected, are in no position to resist their dispossession as individuals or as a national group. And the most important resource taken from them, as with other colonised peoples, has been territory. If any single Israeli policy demonstrates the apartheid nature of the Jewish state, it is its approach to land.

Most of the land belonging to Palestinians was seized during the 1948 war, after 80 per cent of the Palestinian population inside the Jewish state's borders were expelled in an ethnic cleansing campaign.[32] The substantial land holdings of the Palestinians who became Israeli citizens was taken on various pretexts. The most significant measure applied to the quarter of the Palestinian population in Israel who were classed as internal refugees, or 'present absentees', and thereby stripped of the rights to their homes and property. The Absentee Property Law of 1950 affected all the refugees, both those in exile and those with Israeli citizenship. Much of this land was to be found in more than 500 Palestinian villages that were destroyed in the aftermath of the war. The lands of the destroyed villages were either used for the building of exclusive Jewish communities or buried under the foliage of national forestation programmes overseen by the Jewish National Fund.

But that still left significant areas of Israel to which some 120 surviving Palestinian communities and their inhabitants held the title deeds. Israel devised various strategies to seize this land too, leaving the Palestinian minority with little more than the land on which their communities were built. Today, less than 3 per cent of Israel's territory is either municipal land belonging to Palestinian communities or privately owned by individual Palestinians. Almost all of the rest has been 'Judaised', or made Jewish. Some 80 per cent is owned by the state, a further 13 per cent belongs to the Jewish National Fund (most of it transferred to the Fund by the government in the early 1950s),[33] and the final 4 per cent is owned privately by wealthy Jews or by religious institutions, chiefly the Greek Orthodox church.

In short, 93 per cent of land inside Israel has been nationalised, not for the benefit of Israeli citizens but for the Jewish people worldwide (again underscoring the significance of Israel's distinction between citizenship and nationality). Traditionally, this land has not been sold, either to Jews or to Palestinians, but leased by the state. In this way, it has been held permanently in trust for the Jewish people. Or, as Ariel Sharon explained in 2002, Palestinian citizens – 'Israeli Arabs', as he called them – had 'rights in the land' whereas 'all rights over the Land of Israel are Jewish rights'.[34] According to this view, Palestinian citizens were merely tenants, temporary or otherwise, while the Jewish people were the landlords of Israel.

Apartheid South Africa also prevented its disadvantaged ethnic population from having access to most of the country's land. It did so through legislation such as the Group Areas Act of 1950 and by creating a series of sham black homelands known as Bantustans. In the Bantustans, the black population was forced to claim citizenship and could thus be deprived of its right to live inside the far larger area of South Africa – some 87 per cent – designated for whites. (The Bantustans also solved the 'visible equality' problem for Apartheid South Africa of simply denying blacks the vote. Instead, they were offered the vote, but only in their Bantustans.)

According to the historian Gabriel Piterberg, Israel's wholesale nationalisation of Palestinian land for the benefit of the Jewish people was given 'the guise of a huge land transaction that the state had conducted with itself'.[35] It was achieved in four stages: first, the use of various military and legal pretexts for confiscating Palestinian land; second, the transfer of this land to Jewish communities as part of a 'Judaisation' programme; third, the containment of Palestinian communities within tightly delimited boundaries so that they could not encroach on Judaised territory; and finally, the establishment of an administrative system to ensure that Palestinians would never regain rights to their property, as well as the creation of admissions committees to deny Palestinians any chance of ever residing in Jewish communities. The last stage has been implemented with particular care so as not to jeopardise the official policy of 'visible equality'. The result, nonetheless, has been a strict enforcement of geographic segregation between Israel's Palestinian and Jewish communities in almost all areas of the country.[36]

The goals of 'Judaisation' were explained in typically blunt manner by Ariel Sharon in 1977 when he was Agriculture Minister. Referring to the Palestinians' demographic domination of the Galilee, he warned that 'the region is again the Galilee of the gentiles [that is, Palestinians]. I've begun intensive activity ... to prevent control of state lands by foreigners'.[37] His views were echoed in 1986 by the National Council for Planning and Building as it issued its master plan for the northern district, which includes the Galilee: 'The taking control of [the region] by Arab elements is a fact that the State of Israel is not dealing with as it should and this will cause distress for future generations'. The aim of the master plan, it added, was 'preserving the lands of the nation and Judaizing the Galilee'.[38]

The initial stages of Judaisation – confiscating Palestinian land and transferring it to Jewish communities – were largely achieved during the eighteen years of the military government (1948–66). In this period,

Israel devised a range of laws, in addition to the Absentee Property Law, to make the wholesale confiscation of Palestinian land possible. The most important were declaring Palestinian areas 'closed military zones' and requisitioning Palestinian agricultural land on the grounds that it had been judged 'fallow'.[39] Palestinian citizens had little hope of resisting such confiscation because they were strictly confined to their communities, requiring permits from the military governor to move about.

A further justification for land confiscation was introduced as the military government was nearing its end, with the passage of the Planning and Building Law in 1965. This legislation detailed every location in the country where a community had been recognised by the newly established planning authorities. These planning bodies, staffed by Jews, refused to approve the establishment of any new Palestinian towns or villages, making natural expansion impossible, and tightly confined the permitted development area of Palestinian communities, justifying a harsh policy of enforcing house demolitions against Palestinian citizens. Today, tens of thousands of Palestinian-owned homes and buildings are subject to demolition orders.[40] Jewish communities, particularly the expansive rural cooperative communities of the *kibbutzim* and *moshavim*, were treated indulgently and often allowed to encroach on the land of their Palestinian neighbours.

In addition, the Planning and Building Law recognised only 124 Palestinian communities, thereby 'unrecognising' dozens more – mainly Bedouin villages in the Negev and the Galilee – that predated Israel's creation. The inhabitants of these unrecognised villages have been effectively criminalised: public companies are banned from supplying their homes with water, sewerage and electricity services; no schools or medical clinics are allowed, however large the village; and all homes inside the community are subject to automatic demolition orders. The goal is to make conditions unbearable for the residents so that they will move off their land and into overcrowded but recognised Palestinian communities. The state can then expropriate their land and property.

As a result, as many as 100,000 Bedouin in the Negev have relocated to 'planned townships', deprived communities at the bottom of every socio-economic index. But as many again have refused to move. Today, nearly a tenth of the Palestinian minority live in appalling conditions in unrecognised villages, under the constant threat of house demolition.

Having expropriated most of the Palestinian population's land, and having tightly contained their communities through the enforcement of discriminatory planning regulations, Israeli officials then turned to the international Zionist organisations to enforce a strict residential segregation between Jews and Palestinians. According to the Jewish National Fund's charter, only Jews are allowed to live on its land – most of the inhabited land in Israel, it should be noted. The Fund and the Jewish Agency also oversee admission committees vetting candidates to join the majority of the 700 or so rural Jewish communities that control most of the nationalised land in Israel, thereby ensuring that all applications from Palestinian citizens are blocked. In this way, a rigid geographic separation in the living spaces of Jews and Palestinians – a form of apartheid – has been maintained, with Palestinian citizens confined to their ghetto communities.

Again, the courts have threatened, in the name of 'visible equality', to end such communal segregation. In 2000, the Supreme Court ordered that an application from a Palestinian family, the Kaadans, to live in the Jewish community of Katzir must be reconsidered, after the admissions committee had turned the family down. Katzir continued rejecting the Kaadans on the grounds that they failed a test of 'social suitability' – until the courts again intervened.

With hundreds of exclusively Jewish communities fearing that more Palestinian families might flee their overcrowded villages and apply for residency, evasive action was taken on two fronts. First, Jewish communities in heavily Palestinian-populated areas introduced a requirement that candidates swear loyalty to various Zionist principles as part of the application process. And second, a law was passed in

2011 to give legal standing to the assessment by admissions committees of a candidate's 'social suitability'. Tellingly, the law – while justifying discrimination – upheld the principle of 'visible equality' by stating that the committees 'may not refuse a candidate only on the basis of race, religion, sex, nationality or disability'.[41] The law was upheld by the Supreme Court in 2014.[42]

One other noteworthy change was the decision in 2009 by the Netanyahu government to force through the parliament a reform of Israel's land laws, against the furious opposition of most of the Zionist parties. Netanyahu, apparently influenced as much by neoliberal principles as by Zionism, introduced a land privatisation programme to allow Israeli Jews to buy their own homes.[43] The long-term impact of the reform was unclear at the time of writing. Safeguards were in place to ensure that those without Israeli citizenship would be ineligible to buy and own land. In addition, most of the land for sale was expected to be in rural communities that are subject to admissions committees and therefore bar Palestinian citizens. Human rights groups were concerned that much of the land sold off would be Palestinian refugee property, thereby further complicating the issue of how the refugees, both those in exile and those with Israeli citizenship, might receive restitution in a future peace agreement.

SEPARATE EDUCATION SYSTEMS

Underpinning policies designed to exclude Palestinian citizens from Israel's national life and hamper their attempts at interacting with Jewish citizens has been the development of a separate and much inferior Arab education system. Paradoxically, Israel has often justified separate schooling for Palestinian and Jewish children on the grounds that the minority's language and culture can best be protected in this way – another pillar of its 'visible equality' policy. That argument might be persuasive had Israel invested in Arab education. Instead, the minority's schools have always been a pale shadow of Jewish schools, with severe shortages of teachers, classrooms and books, and government interference in the development of the curriculum to marginalise Arab culture and deny a Palestinian identity. In this way, the Palestinian minority has been kept weak and isolated, out of view of the international community, and unable to resist the theft of its land.

A Central Bureau of Statistics survey from 2001 revealed the extent of the starkly different funding of Arab and Jewish education. It found that, aside from teachers' salaries, the money set aside for the education of each Arab student was less than a quarter of that for a Jewish student in a secular state school. The differential was even higher when the comparison was with a Jewish student in a state religious school: he or she received twelve times more than the Arab student.[44] Underfunding on such a scale explains the depressing picture in Arab schools. The *Ha'aretz* newspaper noted in 2005: 'There is still a shortage of 1,500–1,700 classrooms, 4,000 trained teachers, computers, laboratories and gyms'.[45] A report by Human Rights Watch in 2001 identified continuing and systematic discrimination against Arab schools in resources in all areas: bigger class sizes; fewer and inferior textbooks; reliance on inadequate, temporary and sometimes dangerous buildings; a widespread lack of kindergartens, vocational programmes and remedial classes; and a virtually non-existent special education programme for disabled children.[46]

The curriculum in Arab schools also deprives pupils of the chance to understand their history and develop a national identity, and appears to have been developed to encourage high drop-out rates. The literature curriculum has not been updated since 1981, and most major figures in Arabic and Palestinian literature, such as the poet Mahmoud Darwish, are banned (although Darwish can be taught, even if he rarely is, in Jewish schools). Referring to the exclusion from the Arab curriculum of world classics such as Shakespeare and Kafka, Dr Mahmud Ghanayim, Head of Arabic Language at Tel Aviv University, suggested that it signalled 'the government's attempt to create an Arab student who is not open to the world'.[47]

Attempts by liberal Education Ministers to temper the staunchly Zionist tone of the history curriculum have resulted in uproar, and have usually produced no significant change. In 2007, Yuli Tamir's decision to allow textbooks in Arab schools to mention the fact that Palestinians referred to their dispossession in 1948 as the Nakba, or 'Catastrophe', was widely condemned.[48] The textbook was withdrawn by her successor, Gideon Saar, in 2009.[49] Meanwhile, an investigation by *Ha'aretz* in 2004 showed that, although technically it is possible for Arab schools to teach some Palestinian history, they almost never do because the Education Ministry has not made the relevant textbooks available.[50] A law was passed in 2011 that denies funding to any public institution, including schools, that commemorates the Nakba. A petition to the Supreme Court was rejected a year later.[51]

The careful manipulation of the curriculum by Jewish officials is mirrored by the keen interest of the domestic security service, the Shin Bet, in controlling the educational environment in Arab schools. It has long been an open secret that the Shin Bet recruits spies from among both Arab teachers and pupils, and that all teaching appointments are vetted by a Shin Bet official in the Education Department. As one former head teacher observed: 'In fact, the better you do as a teacher in an Arab school, the more tainted you become in the eyes of the other teachers and the pupils'.[52]

However, successive governments denied any interference by the Shin Bet. This deception slowly unravelled. In 2004, a senior official told *Ha'aretz*: 'The Shin Bet not only determined and intervened in the appointment of principals and teachers, but even decided who the custodians and janitors that clean the bathrooms in the Arab schools would be'.[53] A year later, the head of the Education Ministry, Ronit Tirosh, promised that the Shin Bet official in her department would leave his post and that future appointments would be made according to professional criteria.[54] However, the apparent change of approach probably reflected an assessment by the Shin Bet that, after its interference in the education system had become public knowledge, a policy of damage limitation was needed to resurrect the impression of 'visible equality'. All indications were that appointments were continuing to be vetted.

Although higher education is not segregated, it has been an effective arena for marginalising intellectuals and leaders among the Palestinian minority and encouraging them to emigrate. In the state's early decades, access to university was all but impossible for most Palestinian youngsters, however bright, with as many as 90 per cent who took their matriculation exams failing. When families could afford to, they sent their children to study abroad. Scholarships available from the Communist Party, the only non-Zionist party allowed for many years, meant that the most likely destinations for many were universities in the Soviet bloc. Statistics from the mid-1970s show that, by that stage, some 18,000 Palestinian citizens had left the country, many presumably to study, and had never returned.[55]

Despite years of intensive lobbying, no public university has been established in a Palestinian community, not even in the city of Nazareth. None of the existing universities teaches in Arabic – the main languages of instruction are Hebrew and English – one of several disadvantages Palestinian students face when competing with Jewish colleagues. Fewer than 1 per cent of academic staff are Palestinian.[56] Even though Palestinians of university age are a quarter of that age group, they comprise only 8 per cent of the student body. A 2009 report by Dirasat, a Nazareth-based non-governmental organisation, revealed that 5,400 students – or a third of all Palestinian students from Israel – were studying in Jordan, mostly because of the difficulties they faced in the Israeli higher education system.[57]

These obstacles include the greater weighting given in the matriculation exams to Hebrew over Arabic; the use of psychometric tests that favour fluent English speakers (a third language for Palestinian students); and the cultural bias in the same tests towards Western culture. The intentional aspect of such discrimination was revealed in 2003 when the psychometric tests were briefly dropped to help what were referred to as 'weaker' sections of society. That apparently did not include Palestinian students. When the Committee of University Heads heard that the number of Palestinians gaining entry to university had risen sharply after the test's ending, the tests were immediately reinstated. The university heads justified their decision on the grounds that 'the admission of one population [Palestinians] comes at the expense of the other [Jews]'.[58]

Once in higher education, Palestinian students face a series of additional problems, including receiving official recognition for their student organisations. Instead, Palestinians must rely on the main student organisation, dominated by the Jewish student body, to represent their interests. Protests on campus, particularly at Haifa University, where the largest number of Palestinian youth study, must be licensed, a measure to prevent Palestinian student dissent. Students violating this rule can be suspended or expelled, or have their degrees withheld.[59]

Palestinian students must endure not only a heavily Zionist-slanted curriculum but also the racism of senior staff, sanctioned by their universities. Leading Israeli academics, including David Bukay and Arnon Soffer at Haifa University and Raphael Israeli at Hebrew University in Jerusalem, regularly give voice to racist opinions, including in the classroom, without fear of disciplinary action. One Israeli, who was called to give 'expert' testimony on behalf of the state in a trial in 2004, observed that the Arab mentality was composed of 'a sense of victimization', 'pathological anti-Semitism' and 'a tendency to live in a world of illusions'.[60] Bukay, who lectures in political science at Haifa, has written a number of derogatory books on the 'Arab mind'. A typical statement in one, apparently similar to comments he makes in the classroom, is: 'There is no condemnation, no regret, no problem of conscience among Arabs and Muslims, anywhere, in any social stratum, of any social position'.[61]

A JEWISH ECONOMY

The other major resource colonised peoples have to offer apart from land is their labour. That was certainly the case in Apartheid South Africa, which exploited the black majority as a labour force while depriving it of political power. Israel has been far more ambivalent about the need to exploit the labour of its Palestinian minority.

In accordance with the principle of 'visible equality', Palestinian citizens are protected from discrimination in the workplace by legislation, including the Employment Service Law (1959) and the Equality of Opportunity at Work Law (1988). A Commission for Equal Opportunity at Work was established in 2007.[62] These formal protections, however, have been largely negated by Zionist practice. Since Israel's establishment, Palestinian citizens have had to contend with much more deeply rooted Zionist ideas such as 'Hebrew labour' and 'redemption of the land' – principles that expected of Israeli Jews that they purify themselves of their weak diaspora nature through settling and working the land themselves.

Israel has had to partially compromise on these 'ideals', given the reality that nearly a fifth of the population was Palestinian even after the 1948 ethnic cleansing campaign. Nonetheless, it has largely succeeded in marginalising and ghettoising the Palestinian labour force. In the state's early years, the minority lost its traditional agricultural way of life as its lands were confiscated for Jewish settlement. Palestinian citizens were rapidly converted into landless casual labourers, entirely dependent on a 'Jewish economy'. Most men now work in construction, agriculture, quarrying and unskilled service industries, while unemployment among Palestinian women has reached levels of about 80 per cent, far higher than in neighbouring Arab states.[63] Most professionals among the minority, such as doctors and lawyers, are restricted to working inside their own communities.

Enforcing this segregated employment structure have been official public institutions, state monopolies and the government itself. The most important is the Histadrut, the trade union federation and, peculiarly, also one of the country's biggest employers. It has worked relentlessly to exclude the Palestinian minority from a voice in workers' issues over many decades. In the tradition of 'Hebrew labour', the Histadrut refused Palestinian citizens membership until 1959, a decade after Israel's establishment, and even then they had to participate in a separate 'Arab department' in the union.

In the zero-sum politics of ethnic labour relations inside Israel, the Histadrut has rarely lobbied on behalf of Palestinian workers or considered their interests when they have collided with those of Jewish workers. The federation, for example, supported the imposition of severe movement restrictions on the minority at the time of the military government as a way to prevent Palestinian workers competing for jobs.[64] And, when a million Russians arrived in Israel in the 1990s following the collapse of the Soviet Union, the Histadrut turned a blind eye as businesses and government bodies fired Palestinian workers, including doctors, to make room for the recent immigrants.

The Histadrut runs some of Israel's biggest firms and, until the 1990s and a wave of privatisations, had diverse concerns, including a newspaper, the country's largest bank, a construction firm, the national bus company Egged, and a dairy production company. In the late 1970s, even though the Histadrut was the second largest employer in the country after the government and at the height of its power, there was not a single Histadrut-owned firm or factory in a Palestinian community, nor were there any Palestinian managers in its 600 industries.[65]

Shmuel Toledano, a former adviser on Arab affairs to the prime minister, observed in 1977: 'All the economic positions in this country are filled by Jews, the Jews control all the banks, all the corporations.

In politics and the Histadrut, they have all the power'.[66] Things have barely improved since. Almost no industry has been established in Palestinian communities, both because of a lack of space following land confiscations by the state and because the government has encouraged businesses to locate in Jewish areas through special development grants.

Asad Ghanem of Haifa University has noted that, over time, many Palestinian villages have grown to the point where technically they are considered towns but they continue to lack any economic base. 'These conditions underline the near total subordination of the Arab economy to the Jewish economy'.[67] The average monthly income for a Palestinian family is today about 60 per cent of that of a Jewish family, even though a Palestinian family is typically larger than a Jewish one.[68] A predictable consequence is that poverty rates are also far higher. Every other Palestinian citizen is classified as poor, compared with less than a fifth of Israeli Jews; and 60 per cent of all Palestinian children are living below the poverty line, compared with a quarter of Jewish children.[69]

The state bureaucracy has treated the Palestinian minority little better than the Histadrut has done. Despite the passage of legislation in 2000 requiring affirmative action in the civil service, only 6 per cent of the country's 57,000 civil servants were reported to be Palestinian in 2010, and almost all worked in ministries that need separate sections dealing with the Palestinian minority, such as education and health.[70] A report by the Civil Service Commission the same year revealed that the Finance Ministry had only three Palestinian citizens on its staff of 743, while the Foreign Ministry employed seven out of a staff of nearly 1,000. Most were in low-level positions or recruited from among the small but loyal Druze population.[71]

The under-representation is even worse in the state monopolies, such as the telecoms company Bezeq and the Israeli Electricity Corporation. Nachman Tal, a former senior adviser in the 'Arab section' of the domestic security service, the Shin Bet, reported that in 2004 there were only six Palestinian citizens among the 13,000 staff of the electricity company.[72] The Bank of Israel, after threats of legal action, finally recruited a single Palestinian employee to its staff of 800 in 2007.[73] And Palestinian workers are almost never employed in Israel's vast 'security-related' public industries, such as the Rafael armaments factories, the El Al national carrier and the water company Mekorot. Because of these low recruitment levels, some 15,000 Palestinian graduates were reported to be either unemployed or working outside their profession, typically as low-paid teachers.[74]

CRUSHING RESISTANCE

Israel has intermittently inflicted a shocking and lethal assault on its Palestinian minority. In what looks suspiciously like a pattern, such outrages have occurred once in each generation – in 1956, 1976 and 2000 – suggesting that their purpose is to teach a general lesson to Palestinian citizens: to remind them that their citizenship is provisional, or that civil protest against their inferior status will not be tolerated, or that emigration may be the wiser course. Certainly, the quick resort to violence by the state against unarmed citizens, not unlike the army's cruel behaviour in the West Bank and Gaza, has sent a powerful message to the minority that ultimately its status in the eyes of the Jewish state is little different from that of the Palestinians under occupation.

The first major act of brutality occurred in 1956 when a brigade of soldiers was ordered to set up unannounced checkpoints at the entrances to several villages close by the West Bank. According to their orders, they were supposed to enforce a curfew 'without sentimentality' and 'make no arrests'. Some forty-nine workers returning to the village of Kafr Qassem were executed, including seven children. A trial found several officers guilty, although all soon received pardons, and the commander who ordered the killings was fined one penny.[75] Credible evidence suggests that the curfew was imposed on the villages – in an area known as the Little Triangle, hugging the north-west edge of the West Bank – as part of preparations for the expulsion of tens of thousands of Palestinian citizens into what was then Jordanian-controlled territory under cover of the Suez War.[76]

In the same year, 1956, a wave of bomb scares began in Palestinian communities. One explosion in the village of Sandaleh killed fourteen schoolchildren. Over two years, nearly 1,000 such bomb alerts were recorded by the police.[77] Given the isolation of Palestinian communities during this period of the military government, it is difficult to regard this wave of attacks as anything but centrally organised. Certainly, it reinforced the impression among Palestinian citizens that they were not welcome.

The Kafr Qassem massacre occurred when there were severe restrictions on Palestinian citizens' freedom of movement and right to organise protests. Since then, the state's ability to intimidate and silence the minority has been compromised by a need to maintain its policy of 'visible equality'. However, two lethal assaults by the security services against large civil protests have reminded the Palestinian minority of the devalued nature of its citizenship.

On 30 March 1976, the minority called its first ever one-day general strike to protest against a new wave of land confiscations in the Galilee. In particular, the three neighbouring villages of Sakhnin, Deir Hanna and Arrabeh had been served with orders that large swathes of their agricultural land – land that had been declared a 'closed military zone' to create a firing range decades before – were to be seized as part of the Judaisation programme. The prime minister of the day, Yitzhak Rabin, ordered the army to enforce a general curfew on Palestinian communities, and sent the army into the three villages at the centre of the confrontation. The use of the army, rather than the police, was a clear signal that the authorities still regarded the minority as an enemy rather than as proper citizens. The military government may have ended but the mentality behind it remained unchanged. During the course of the strike, the army opened fire on demonstrators in Arrabeh and Sakhnin, killing six of them. The anniversary of the deaths is commemorated by Palestinians as Land Day.

There were echoes of both Kafr Qassem and Land Day in the events of October 2000, at the start of the second intifada, when the police entered Palestinian towns and villages in northern Israel. They were ordered to use extreme force to crush protests being held in solidarity with Palestinians in the Occupied Territories. Some thirteen unarmed demonstrators were shot dead and hundreds more injured when the police opened fire with rubber bullets and live ammunition. A lengthy state inquiry revealed evidence of a shoot-to-kill policy but failed to identify the policemen who had carried out the killings. Evidence also pointed to the possibility that prior approval for the shootings had been given by the prime minister, Ehud Barak, although this avenue was not pursued.[78] The inquiry recommended that the police investigations unit, which had stopped its hunt for the suspected policemen early on, restart its work. However, after a series of evasions, the unit finally announced in early 2008 that no charges would be pressed against any policemen.[79] One of the officers involved, Benzi Sau, was repeatedly promoted despite a recommendation to the contrary from the inquiry.[80]

DEMOGRAPHY AND ETHNIC CLEANSING

The key policy debate in Israel – though one till now conducted mainly behind closed doors – is whether the apartheid system of rule over the Palestinian minority can be maintained without considering again some form of ethnic cleansing, or 'transfer', possibly through an imposed peace agreement. Central to this debate is the question of whether it is possible to maintain the illusion of 'visible equality' – the idea of Israel as a 'Jewish and democratic' state – in the face of an ever larger Palestinian minority and its increasingly noisy refusal to accept its lack of meaningful citizenship. As the campaign for Israel's reform into a 'state of all its citizens' has grown, so has the labelling of the largely quiescent Palestinian minority as a 'demographic time bomb' and a 'fifth column'. The higher birth rate of Israel's Palestinian population is seen not only as a security issue but also as an 'existential' threat to the Jewish state.

After the 1948 war, during which 80 per cent of the Palestinian population living within the borders of the new state were expelled, the issue of demography – and the need to maintain a Jewish majority – lost some of its urgency. During the second intifada, however, concern about the country's demographic trends reached fever pitch again, prompted by an apparent loss of new sources of Jewish immigration, Palestinian citizens' continued higher birth rates, and fears about the minority's campaign for Israel's democratisation.

When the Herzliya Conference, an annual security convention, was launched in late 2000, its main theme was the threat posed by the growth of the Palestinian minority and its connections to Palestinians in the Occupied Territories. From this conference new kinds of legislative assault on the citizenship of Palestinians emerged. As we have noted, in 2003 the government amended the 1952 Citizenship Law to bar Palestinian citizens from bringing to Israel a spouse from the West Bank or Gaza. Officials feared such marriages might allow a right of return for Palestinian refugees 'through the backdoor'.[81]

It was not surprising that opinion polls soon found similar demographic worries among the Jewish public. A survey in 2003 showed that 57 per cent thought Palestinian citizens should be encouraged to emigrate, through inducements or force.[82] In a follow-up poll in 2006, the figure had risen to 62 per cent.[83] In another survey that year, 68 per cent of Israeli Jews said that they did not want to live next to a Palestinian citizen.[84] These racist views have been encouraged by leading journalists, academics and politicians of all persuasions, fearful that the presence of a growing Palestinian minority will one day destroy the state's Jewishness.

Leading the charge in promoting 'transfer' has been Israel's far-right, particularly Avigdor Lieberman, a Moldovan immigrant and leader of the Yisrael Beiteinu Party. Lieberman, once director-general of the Likud Party and Netanyahu's foreign minister, has been promoting a 'Separation of Nations' policy, whereby mutual transfers of territory ensure that Jewish settlers in the Occupied Territories are included inside an expanded Israeli state, but as many Palestinians as possible are relocated to what he calls a future Palestinian state – although, like most Israelis, he appears to mean by statehood no more than a patchwork of ghettos in the West Bank and a besieged prison in Gaza. He has recruited influential allies in Washington to his cause, including former US Secretary of State Henry Kissinger.[85]

In putting forward his proposal, Lieberman has exhumed the idea of transfer from the dark recesses of Zionism, freeing Israeli politicians to speak about it openly, especially as part of what may be presented as a potential 'peace agreement' with the Palestinians of the Occupied Territories. In particular, he has made respectable the idea of transferring the Little Triangle, a small area of Israeli territory close to the West Bank and densely populated with 250,000 Palestinian citizens, to a future Palestinian state. He has also campaigned for Palestinian citizens to be required to sign a loyalty oath, not to their country but to Israel as a Jewish state. Those refusing would presumably be expelled.

On a trip to the US in 2006, Lieberman explained his vision of conditional Israeli citizenship to American Jewish leaders at the Saban Center for Middle East Policy in Washington: 'He who is not ready to recognise Israel as a Jewish and Zionist state cannot be a citizen of the country'.[86] A consensus appears to be forming behind the Lieberman approach. In 2007, as Israel's foreign minister, Tzipi Livni observed that a Palestinian state would be the 'answer' to Israel's Palestinian citizens: 'They cannot ask for the declaration of a Palestinian state while working against the nature of the State of Israel as home unto the Jewish people'.[87] Benjamin Netanyahu contributed his own dimension to this process by repeatedly demanding in 2010 and again in late 2013 and early 2014 that the Palestinian leadership recognise Israel as 'the state of the Jewish people' as a precondition for talks on Palestinian statehood.[88] In 2014, Netanyahu also threw his support behind a new basic law that would define Israel as the nation-state of the Jewish people, formalising and consolidating the existing situation for the Palestinian minority.[89]

CONCLUSION

The exclusion of Israel's Palestinian minority from meaningful citizenship and political influence, as well as legislation codifying inequality based on ethnic belonging, has made possible the systematic theft of Palestinian land. Israel has largely thwarted the threat of the Palestinian minority, effectively resisting its dispossession by stifling the emergence of a middle class, from which intellectuals and a national leadership might emerge, and by demonstrating its determination to exercise force ruthlessly. Instead, insofar as it has been able, Israel has ensured that most of the Palestinian population is deprived of a decent education and reliable employment, that fault lines within the minority are exaggerated and manipulated, and that Palestinian citizens are isolated from Jewish citizens so that there is no danger that intimate relationships – the basis for solidarity – might develop.

In all these ways, Israel's policies have strong echoes of the policies pursued by South Africa's apartheid regime. The key difference, as we have noted several times, is the fact that South Africa was faced with a black majority while Israel has to deal with a Palestinian minority. This has provided Israel with the space to create an illusory democratic image – the promotion of 'visible equality' rather than real equality. As a result, unlike South Africa, which always struggled to persuade the world that its apartheid regime was democratic, Israel has been far more successful in shielding the structure of its political and legal system from view.

Notes

1   'Mazuz Moves to Limit Racial Profiling at Ben-Gurion Airport', *Ha'aretz*, 6 April 2008.
2   See, for example, 'Arab Editor Opts Out of the Katsav Trip after Airport Flap', *Ha'aretz*, 17 February 2004.
3   'Colored Tags for Arabs' Luggage at Ben Gurion Airport Discontinued', *Ha'aretz*, 7 August 2007.
4   Among the damaging revelations were testimonies from Palestinian citizens about their treatment contained in a report, *Suspected Citizens*, by the Arab Association for Human Rights, published in December 2006.
5   'After Years of Humiliation, Israeli Arabs Say Getting Better Treatment at Airport', *Ha'aretz*, 26 March 2014. However, the airport authorities stepped up their checks on non-Jewish passengers and political dissidents arriving at Ben Gurion airport, and continued harassment of Palestinian citizens using the El Al airline at overseas airports.
6   The Shin Bet may have felt that racial profiling was costing too much in bad publicity, given the increasingly limited benefits. Historically, the checks were less about security than used as ways both to intimidate Palestinian citizens wanting to travel internationally, maintaining them as an inward-looking, 'backward' minority, and to gather information on the minority (similar to the collaboration system). In an increasingly globalised, connected world – one with satellite TV, email and Internet, as well as sophisticated state-organised surveillance – these aims had become largely redundant.
7   I have borrowed the term 'petty apartheid' from the Israeli scholar Uri Davis.
8   For more on the implementation of this law, see my book *Blood and Religion: The Unmasking of the Jewish and Democratic State*, London: Pluto Press, 2006, Chapter 3.
9   The Citizenship Law is also translated as the Nationality Law, a confusion possible given that the same Hebrew word embraces both concepts.
10 'So This Jew, Arab, Georgian and Samaritan Go to Court', *Ha'aretz*, 28 December 2003.
11 'A Short History of Apartheid', *Al-Ahram Weekly*, 8 January 2004.
12 Marwan Dalal, 'Imagined Citizenship', *Adalah's Newsletter*, Vol. 12, April 2005.
13 Uri Davis, *Apartheid Israel*, London: Zed Books, 2003, p. 100.
14 Walter Lacquer and Barry Rubin (eds), *The Israel-Arab Reader*, New York: Penguin, 2001, pp. 82–3.
15 For more on the problems of drafting a constitution, see my article 'Israeli Constitutional Committee Faces Double Bind', *Middle East Report* 231 (Summer 2004).

16 See www.adalah.org/en/law/index.

17 See www.adalah.org/en/content/view/7771.

18 'An Alarm Clock That Never Stops', *Ha'aretz*, 4 June 2007.

19 Davis, *Apartheid Israel*, p. 126.

20 'PMO to Balad: We Will Thwart Anti-Israel Activity Even if Legal', *Ha'aretz*, 17 March 2007.

21 'Democracy for Jews Only', *Ha'aretz*, 30 May 2007.

22 For accounts of this period, see two books: Sabri Jiryis, *The Arabs in Israel*, New York: Monthly Review Press, 1976; Fouzi el-Asmar, *To Be an Arab in Israel*, London: Frances Pinter, 1975.

23 Susan Nathan, *The Other Side of Israel*, London: HarperCollins, 2005, p. 246.

24 In recent times, religious fundamentalist parties have included Shas and United Torah Judaism, and fascistic parties Moledet and Yisrael Beiteinu.

25 'Cabinet Okays Appointment of Majadele as First Arab Minister', *Ha'aretz*, 28 January 2007.

26 Baruch Kimmerling, 'Religion, Nationalism and Democracy in Israel', *Constellations* 6(3) (1999), p. 360.

27 *Silencing Dissent*, Nazareth: Arab Association for Human Rights, 2002.

28 In late 2001, Bishara was charged over a trip he made to Syria, for which he had diplomatic immunity, and a speech in which he suggested that Palestinians under occupation could learn from Hizbullah's resistance to the occupation of South Lebanon. Both charges were ultimately rejected by the courts. Bishara was later accused of treason, for helping Hizbullah during the 2006 Lebanon war, while he was out of the country; he has not returned. No evidence against him had been produced. Salah, arrested in May 2003, faced an array of charges that he had funded terrorist organisations in the Occupied Territories. During his lengthy trial, almost all of the charges were dropped and the state arranged a plea bargain. Salah admitted funnelling funds to organisations proscribed by Israel, mainly Islamic charities helping orphans and widows. Salah, however, maintains that he had authorisation from the security services for the donations he made.

29 'Court: MKs Tibi, Bishara and Far-Right Activist Marzel Can Run', *Ha'aretz*, 11 January 2003.

30 'High Court Overturns Decision: Zoabi and Marzel Can Run in Election', *Ha'aretz*, 18 February 2015.

31 'Knesset to Mull Bill Revoking Citizenship from People Convicted of Disloyalty', *Ha'aretz*, 11 October 2010.

32 See Ilan Pappé, *The Ethnic Cleansing of Palestine*, Oxford: Oneworld, 2006.

33 Hussein Abu Hussein and Fiona McKay, *Access Denied*, London: Zed Books, 2003, pp. 152–3.
34 Quoted in Nimr Sultany, *Israel and the Palestinian Minority: 2004*, Haifa: Mada, 2005, p. 34.
35 'Erasures', *New Left Review*, July–August 2001.
36 This policy of segregation is strictly enforced in rural areas, mainly through the admissions committees. However, it is under threat in some Jewish new towns established in Palestinian areas. In particular, the Jewish towns of Upper Nazareth and Karmiel, built in the midst of large Palestinian communities to fragment and contain them, are struggling to prevent homes being sold to Palestinians fleeing the overcrowding of their ghettos. Israel and the Zionist organisations are currently struggling to find a way both to maintain 'visible equality' and to deny Palestinian citizens access to these towns. See 'In Watershed, Israel Deems Land-Use Rules of Zionist Icon "Discriminatory"', *Forward*, 4 February 2005.
37 Ian Lustick, *The Arabs in Israel*, Austin: University of Texas Press, 1980, pp. 317–18.
38 *Adalah's Newsletter*, Vol. 43, December 2007.
39 Jiryis, *The Arabs in Israel*, Chapter 4.
40 The report of the Gazit Committee in 2000 found some 30,000 illegal 'structures' in Palestinian communities, mostly because of a lack of master plans to legalise them. Abu Hussein and McKay, *Access Denied*, p. 270.
41 'Knesset panel okays bill letting small communities bar Arabs', *Ha'aretz*, 28 October 2010.
42 'High Court Upholds Residential Screening Law, Enabling Jewish Villages to Keep Arabs Out', *Ha'aretz*, 18 September 2014.
43 'High Court challenges ILA land to homeowners ad campaign', *Jerusalem Post*, 10 July 2007.
44 'Report: Haredi School Spending Twice as Much per Pupil as State Schools', *Ha'aretz*, 6 August 2005.
45 'Shin Bet Will No Longer Scrutinize Arab Educators', *Ha'aretz*, 6 January 2005.
46 *Second Class: Discrimination against Palestinian Arab Children in Israel's Schools*, New York: Human Rights Watch, 2001.
47 'The Palestinian Literature Vanished on the Way to the Classroom', *Ha'aretz*, 25 May 2004.
48 'Education Ministry Approves Text Referring to 1948 as "Nakba"', *Ha'aretz*, 22 July 2007.
49 'Sa'ar Drops "Nakba" from Arab Textbooks', *Jerusalem Post*, 30 August 2009.

50 'The Palestinian literature vanished'.

51 'High Court Rejects Petition against "Nakba Law"', *Jerusalem Post*, 5 January 2012.

52 Nathan, *The Other Side of Israel*, p. 89.

53 'The Palestinian literature vanished'.

54 'Shin Bet will no longer scrutinize'.

55 Lustick, *The Arabs in Israel*, p. 280n.

56 'Know Thy Neighbor – but Don't Hire Him', *Ha'aretz*, 12 July 2001.

57 'Israel's Arab Students Are crossing to Jordan', *The National*, 9 April 2009.

58 'Numerus Clausus', *Ha'aretz*, 16 December 2003.

59 See, for example, 'Haifa U. Suspends Students for Protesting', *Ha'aretz*, 1 November 2001; 'Student Union Bans Arab Activity on Campus, Citing Pro-Terror Stand', *Ha'aretz*, 12 April 2002.

60 Sultany, *Israel and the Palestinian Minority*, p. 102.

61 'In the Name of Truth', *Ha'aretz*, 28 April 2005.

62 Yousef Jabareen, *An Equal Constitution for All?*, Haifa: Mossawa, 2007, p. 26. Revealingly, Commissioner Tziona Koenig-Yair in a lengthy interview with *Ha'aretz* about her work failed to mention discrimination towards Arab citizens, focusing exclusively on general discrimination against women. 'Are women still suffering workplace discrimination?', *Ha'aretz*, 9 June 2010.

63 'Why Do Fewer Arab Women Have Jobs in Israel Than in Saudi Arabia?', *Ha'aretz*, 23 November 2009.

64 Jiryis, *The Arabs in Israel*, pp. 219–21.

65 Lustick, *The Arabs in Israel*, pp. 96–7.

66 Ibid., p. 263.

67 Asad Ghanem (ed.), *Civic Developments Among the Palestinians in Israel*, Cairo: Ibn Khaldun, 2006, pp. 20–1.

68 Ibid., p. 17.

69 'Government Report: 1.65 Million Israelis Living below Poverty Line', *Ha'aretz*, 5 September 2007.

70 'MK Tibi: Arabs' Representation in Civil Service Shameful', *Ynet*, 15 August 2010.

71 'Arabs and Druze Represent Only 5% of Civil Servants', *Ha'aretz*, 25 May 2004.

72 'Even the Shin Bet Is against Discrimination', *Ha'aretz*, 25 May 2004.

73 'Bank of Israel Has 1 Arab Employee', *Ynet*, 10 April 2007.

74 'Hi-Tech Underclass', *Jerusalem Post*, 1 January 2010.

75 Jiryis, *The Arabs in Israel*, Chapter 6.

76 Nur Masalha, *A Land without a People*, London: Faber and Faber, 1997, pp. 21–33.

77 Jiryis, *The Arabs in Israel*, p. 155.

78 For more on the Or Commission that investigated these events, see my book *Blood and Religion*, Chapters 1 and 2.

79 'AG: No Charges over 13 Deaths in October Riots', *Ha'aretz*, 28 January 2008; my article 'Impunity on both Sides of the Green Line', *MERIP Online*, 23 November 2005.

80 'Senior Police Officer Promoted against Or Cmte. Conclusions', *Ha'aretz*, 25 May 2006.

81 Cook, *Blood and Religion*, pp. 125–33.

82 'The Democracy Index: Major Findings 2003', Israel Democracy Institute: www.idi.org.il/sites/english/PublicationsCatalog/Pages/The_2003_Israeli_Democracy_Index/Publications_Catalog_7735.aspx.

83 'Poll: 62% Want Arab Emigration', *Ynet*, 9 May 2006.

84 'Poll: Israeli Jews Shun Arabs', *Ynet*, 22 March 2006.

85 'A New Opening for Mideast Peace', *Washington Post*, 3 December 2004.

86 'Lieberman: The Unfaithful Cannot Be Citizens', *Ynet*, 10 December 2006.

87 'FM Livni: Palestinian State Should Satisfy Israeli Arab National Desires', *Israel Insider*, 18 November 2007.

88 'Gov't Prepares "Contingency Plans" if Direct Talks Blow Up', *Jerusalem Post*, 22 September 2010.

89 'Netanyahu Pushes to Define Israel as Nation State of Jewish People Only', *Guardian*, 4 May 2014.

CHAPTER 5

Apartheid, Israel and Palestinian Statehood

LEILA FARSAKH

Hegel remarks somewhere that all facts and personages of great importance in world history, occur as it were, twice. He forgot to add: the first time as a tragedy, the second as farce.

K. Marx, 'The Eighteenth Brumaire of Louis Bonaparte', 1852, p. 1

INTRODUCTION

The comparison between Apartheid South Africa and the Israeli–Palestinian conflict has often been made, but it has gained a particular vigour since the eruption of Al-Aqsa Intifada in 2000. Israeli policy of checkpoints, closure and permits, its construction of the separation barrier in the West Bank since 2002, and its latest siege and war against Gaza in December 2008 have made many activists and academics argue that Israel is to all intents and purposes an apartheid state. The call by the World Conference against Racism in Durban, South Africa, in 2001 to end the Israeli brand of apartheid, the mushrooming of anti-Israel apartheid weeks on numerous American and European university campuses since 2004, and the Palestinian civil society call for boycott, divestment and sanctions (BDS) against Israel since 2003 are just a few examples of the most vocal and visible forms of political activism that seek to emphasise the apartheid nature of Israel's policy towards the Palestinians.[1]

161

On the other hand, many continue to contest the validity and usefulness of the apartheid analogy in Israel. Those who abhor the comparison argue that Israel is different to Apartheid South Africa insofar as it is a democracy that was created to be a safe haven for the Jewish people after the horror of the Holocaust. It is a state that provides its Arab minority with citizenship rights, which, while incomplete, are more than what the indigenous population in South Africa was ever given before or during apartheid. Opponents of the apartheid analogy have also long argued that Israel and Apartheid South Africa are economically and demographically different. Israel has not been demographically dominated by the natives nor labour-dependent on the indigenous population in the way that white South Africa was. Just as importantly, Israel is a state whose creation was supported internationally ever since United Nations (UN) Resolution 181 was adopted in 1947, and which was officially recognised by the Palestinian leadership itself as having a right to exist, as confirmed by the Palestine Liberation Organization (PLO) declarations in 1988 and again in 1993 with the Oslo peace accords.

The aim of this chapter is to provide a more in-depth examination of the apartheid analogy. It seeks to understand the utility of using the term 'apartheid' to describe the Israeli colonisation project in Palestine. It argues that the answer lies in understanding the notion of 'separate development' that was so central to apartheid, just as it was to Israel, and the way it played itself out in each case. As has been explained elsewhere by numerous authors, what has made the comparison between Apartheid South Africa and Israel attractive is the colonial foundation of both states.[2] Both Apartheid South Africa and the Zionist project in Palestine were concerned with land expropriation and exclusive territorial control. Both were based on European settlers appropriating already inhabited land, expelling the indigenous population, and depriving them of equal political rights within their polity. During the 1948 war, Israel expelled two-thirds of the Palestinian population from their homes; ever since, they have kept 93 per cent of the land under official state control. In 1913, the white South African government displaced and confined the indigenous black population to only 7.6 per cent of the land. However, many have argued that the comparison between Apartheid South Africa and Israel also stops at the point of this colonial history because of the different economic and demographic strategies that each state adopted.

In this chapter, I beg to differ. I build on the work of Uri Davis and Oren Yiftachel, among others, who have argued that Israel is an apartheid state, even if it did not spell it out as clearly and vocally as the National Party did in South Africa. Uri Davis has maintained that Israel's legal discrimination against Palestinians inside Israel in land, economic and citizenship rights makes it an apartheid state. Oren Yiftachel talks about Israeli 'creeping apartheid', showing how Israeli politics of land distribution, urban planning and economic development in the Negev and southern Israel have dis-appropriated Palestinian land and segregated the Palestinian citizens into impoverished and de facto politically excluded areas. He, as much as Davis, refuses to distinguish Israeli policy towards Palestinian citizens from those directed towards people in the West Bank and Gaza. They see it as part and parcel of Israeli colonialism and its aim to absorb Palestinian land while excluding Palestinians from any meaningful equal political rights.[3]

Here, however, I focus on Israeli politics towards the Palestinian project of statehood in the West Bank and Gaza. I argue that, although Israel never intended to be an apartheid state in the way that South Africa officially was, it established a de facto apartheid, and specifically a Bantustan, reality in the West Bank and Gaza. By focusing in particular on the response of settler states to indigenous people's struggle for political rights, I show how both Apartheid South Africa and Israel created, paradoxically, similar political structures that sought to 'resolve' the question of the indigenous population's political rights without compromising the settlers' political and economic supremacy.

This is best illustrated in the way in which the Oslo peace process fragmented the Palestinian quest for an independent state by providing them with an autonomy that is not much different from what the Bantustans offered the black South Africans during the apartheid era. Understanding the fundamental Bantustan character of the Palestinian autonomy is necessary in any attempt to explain the evolution of the Israeli–Palestinian conflict and its prospects.

The first part of the chapter explains the specificity of the apartheid regime and its applicability to Israeli policy towards the Palestinians. It focuses on a key construct of the apartheid era, the Bantustans; these were political constructs providing the indigenous population with self-rule under the colonial power's supervision. The second part analyses the Oslo peace process and the extent to which the autonomy it provided to the Palestinians in the West Bank and Gaza is a revised version of a Bantustan construct. The third part focuses on the economic predicaments of the Bantustans and their implication for the future of the conflict.

APARTHEID AND BANTUSTANS

'Apartheid' is an Afrikaans word for 'separateness'. It was a legally sanctioned system of segregation installed by the South African National Party government in 1948 as a means to preserve white supremacy in South Africa. It institutionalised and strengthened economic, social and political segregation between the white settlers and the native black population imposed since colonial times, and which many considered under threat as a result of economic and political development taking place in South Africa from the 1940s onwards.[4] White economic growth and supremacy since the establishment of the modern South African Union in 1911 rested on the domination of less than 18 per cent of the population, which was white, over the native Africans and Indians, who represented 82 per cent of the population. It relied on the supply of cheap black labour to the mines, cities and white agricultural land, and the fact that black workers were not allowed to compete economically with white labour. This was made possible by restricting the Africans to the native reserves, which, by 1936, comprised 13.8 per cent of South Africa's land, and by regulating their mobility through pass laws. The South African National Party believed that the system of segregation installed since 1911 was coming under threat in the 1940s as a result of South Africa's growing industrialisation and growing demands for workers in the cities and mines. This meant that many employers were turning a blind eye to illegal African workers and more Africans were being illegally urbanised and taking up semi-skilled jobs in white areas.[5] The supporters of the National Party were also concerned about increasingly vocal and organised African opposition to segregation and the demand for equal political rights in the 1940s.[6]

The ideological premise of apartheid was based on the concept of 'separate development'. It rested on the idea that races are and must remain separate, since each had and needs to maintain its own political, economic, social and cultural institutions. It relied on three key institutional pillars. The first was the rationalisation and institution-alisation of racial segregation. The Group Area Act of 1950 and other legislation classified South Africans into racial groups (black, white, coloured and Indian) and enforced residential segregation by means of forced removals to the reserves, which were redefined as Bantustans or native 'homelands'. Between 1960 and 1980, the white government forcibly displaced over 2 million people from urban areas and into the reserves. The proportion of the African population living in white areas dropped from 60 per cent in 1960 to 46 per cent in 1980 as a result of forced displacement.[7] White state legislation also categorised the indigenous population into various Bantu, or tribal, groups. It refused to treat them as a single ethnic or cultural, let alone political, entity, as African political activists of the African National Congress (ANC) and Pan Africanist Congress (PAC) insisted.[8]

The second pillar of apartheid was the implementation of more stringent control measures on African labour and mobility. The Native Act of 1952, among other laws, scrapped local varieties of passes and introduced a single standard document called a reference book; for the first time, women had to carry this document, as well as all men above sixteen years of age. This new system of control helped the state manage more directly African labour flows to urban workplaces.

The Bantustans

Third and perhaps most importantly, apartheid was based on the idea of *separate political* development for whites and for the indigenous population. The 1951 Bantu Authorities Act and the Promotion of Bantu Self-Government Act in 1959 institutionalised the residential and political separation of the natives from the whites. They sought to resolve the question of Africans' political rights by disenfranchising them from any voting rights[9] in white South Africa and by giving them self-rule in ten Bantustans or homelands. These were demarcated within the 13.8 per cent of the land area that had been allocated to the reserves since 1936. The apartheid architects argued that the indigenous people were ten separate 'nations', with their own languages, cultures and traditions and their own political territorial space. In 1960, Prime Minister Verwoerd stated that the government's intention was 'for the natives people [to have] in their areas the same benefits in every way as for the whites in their areas – including eventual sovereign independence'.[10] The Transkei was chosen to be the first homeland to exercise self-rule and eventual independence, as it was considered the most ethnically homogeneous and economically better endowed.[11]

Within the Bantustans, the white government defined self-rule for the indigenous population by reviving and reformulating tribal institutions, which it maintained were the main vehicle for African political representation. A tribal chief was also appointed to each Bantustan by the white government and made accountable to it. The chief was given more executive and financial power than traditional tribal leaders had, thereby eroding the tradition of having the tribal leader be the first among equals. The nominated tribal chief ruled with an elected local legislative assembly, with whom he shared civilian and functional jurisdiction over the native population in his specific Bantustan. The Bantu local government was able to levy taxes and manage the local economy. It was also allowed to have a local police force, whose activities were coordinated and supervised by the white security apparatus. However, Bantu legislative assembly bills had to be approved by the government of Pretoria. The source of authority and scope of jurisdiction of the Bantustan's parliament did not emanate simply from the indigenous population; rather, it depended on decrees and acts passed by the South African government or parliament.

Economically, the apartheid regime sought to enhance the ability of the Bantustans to regulate and subsidise the cost of reproduction of the African labour supply to the white areas. In this respect, it did not seek to eliminate labour migration to white areas but rather to improve the ability of the reserves to absorb the unemployed and poor population that had no place in the white capitalist system.[12] This was to be done by improving agricultural production along capitalist lines and away from subsistence farming, through the introduction of border industrial zones that would attract white capital while employing indigenous labour, and through financial aid supplied by the white government.[13]

In 1974, after over fifteen years of self-rule in the Bantustans, the white South African legislature proclaimed Bantu homeland citizenship. In 1976, it declared four out of the ten Bantustans sovereign independent states, including the Transkei.[14] The ANC, however, never accepted this 'independence', nor the notion of the separateness of African nationhood. It declared the Bantustans to be puppets in the hands of the apartheid regime. The international community, moreover, never recognised the South African Bantustans as sovereign entities.[15]

ISRAEL'S 'CREEPING APARTHEID'

In order to understand the extent to which Israel is an apartheid state, the key point is to analyse the Israeli notion of 'separateness' and the extent to which it has succeeded in legitimising it in a way that South Africa never could.

Like the Afrikaners and most other settler colonial projects, Israel was also attached to the notion of its separateness from the indigenous population. It was particularly obsessed with territorial appropriation and separateness in the same way as the Afrikaners were, claiming a right to a pure ethnic state. Unlike the Afrikaners, though, Israel framed this quest in nationalist rather than racial terms. Moreover, it endeavoured to ensure a Jewish demographic majority that whites never obtained in South Africa. During the Nakba that led to Israel's creation in 1948, Israel ethnically cleansed two-thirds of the Palestinians from their land, allowing only 160,000 to remain.[16] It kept the latter under military control until 1966, after which it gave them Israeli citizenship, but these Palestinian citizens of Israel never represented more than 20 per cent of the total Israeli population. After the 1967 war and Israel's territorial conquest of more Palestinian and Arab land, it decided not to annex the West Bank and Gaza Strip in order not to endanger the Jewish character of the Zionist state.[17] Palestinians in the West Bank and Gaza were treated as a stateless occupied population whose destiny was to be resolved through diplomatic negotiations with Israel's Arab neighbours.[18]

The economic structure of the Israeli–Palestinian conflict has also protected the notion of Israeli 'separateness' and mitigated against its comparability with the apartheid structure of domination. As argued already by Shafir, among others, what has prevented Israel from becoming an apartheid state has been its ability to avoid an economic dependence on the indigenous population. Zionist settlers before the creation of the State of Israel advanced the notion of Jewish labour, which sought to protect it from competition from cheaper Arab workers. Indeed, before 1948, less than 35 per cent of the labour force in the Jewish economy of Mandate Palestine was Arab. After 1948, Arab labour in the Israeli economy did not represent more than 20 per cent of the total workforce. After 1967, when Israel occupied the West Bank and Gaza, Palestinian labour from the Occupied Territories was absorbed within the construction and agricultural sectors. However, Palestinians did not represent more than between 7 and 9 per cent of the total labour force working inside Israel.[19] In other words, Israel's strategy of control and domination over the land and people differed from that used by Apartheid South Africa.

Another factor that has made the apartheid analogy difficult in the case of Israel has been the Palestinian response to its claim of separateness. The indigenous people's response to the colonial settler project in South Africa and Palestine were different. In the case of Israel–Palestine, they framed it in nationalist terms, whereas in South Africa it was defined in terms of a struggle for equal political rights. The Palestinian National Movement emphasised the national Arab character of Palestine. It claimed the right of return and the destruction of Israel as a colonial entity, while calling for the creation of a secular democratic state for all Christians, Muslims and Jews in Palestine. However, by 1974, the PLO called for the creation of a separate Palestinian state on any piece of liberated land of Palestine. In 1988, the Palestinian leadership acknowledged Israel's right to exist and by 1993 initiated the Oslo peace process with Israel to end the occupation of the West Bank and Gaza. With the Oslo peace process, the PLO gave up any claim to 78 per cent of historical Palestine and to any thought of citizenship rights within Israel. In other words, the Palestinian leadership de facto accepted, rather than challenged, Israel's colonial reality and claim to separateness. By contrast, the ANC in South Africa, which became the main political voice of the natives, refused the Afrikaners' notion of separate development and the concept of distinct African nations within South Africa.[20] Although the leaders of the Bantustans and many of their followers maintained that separation from the white regime was the only way to achieve African social, economic and political mobility and independence, the ANC insisted on the abolition of apartheid and the achievement of equal citizenship rights – not national rights – within the whole of South Africa.

Moreover, it has been difficult to define Israel historically as an apartheid state because of the way in which the international community has responded to its claim of separateness. Unlike in South Africa, where the international community opposed apartheid and the concept of territorial separation through the creation of Bantustans, in the case of the Arab–Israeli conflict it supported Israel's creation in 1947, with UN Resolution 181. This resolution enshrined the notion of territorial partition as a solution to the conflict, as it called for a two-state solution as the only peaceful outcome. UN Security Council Resolution 242, following the 1967 war, which became the basis for all peace negotiations between Israel and its neighbours, protected Jewish Zionist nationalist claims and called for the return of land in exchange for peace. The 2003 Quartet Roadmap clearly stated that the creation of a Palestinian state in the West Bank and Gaza is the only solution that will end the Israeli–Palestinian conflict.

However, the particularity of the Israeli apartheid model lies in Israel's attempt to legitimise its notion of 'separateness' in the eyes of the population it colonised and expelled as much as in the opinion of the international community. It is most evident in Israel's refusal to allow the Palestinians to achieve a viable state on 22 per cent, let alone 43 per cent, of their historical land, as the partition plan in UN Resolution 181 stipulated. Although Israel strived and succeeded, until 1993, in following a colonial trajectory that was different economically and demographically from the one followed by Apartheid South Africa, it ultimately adopted tools and mechanisms used by the South African apartheid regime. Since 1993 in particular, beginning with the Oslo process, Israel has sought to resolve the question of the indigenous population's political and economic rights by confining them in territorially fragmented areas that are unviable economically and politically. They are not different in structure from the native self-ruled Bantustans during the era of Apartheid South Africa.

PALESTINIAN BANTUSTANS: OSLO AND PALESTINIAN SELF-DETERMINATION

The Oslo peace agreements, signed in 1993 and 1995, ushered in a new era in Israeli–Palestinian relations. They provided the first official Israeli recognition of the existence of a Palestinian question and of the PLO as the representative of the Palestinian people. Their aim was to devolve Israeli rule over the West Bank and Gaza to an elected Palestinian authority. The PLO had hoped that the Oslo peace process would lay the groundwork for establishing a state on part of historical Palestine – namely in the West Bank and Gaza – in return for its recognition of Israel's right to exist. In principle, the Oslo agreements were supposed to be temporary peace agreements until a final status agreement was signed by Israel and the PLO. They were also meant to provide Palestinians with more than simply autonomy. At least, this was the point of view of the international community and the Palestinian negotiators.

However, whatever the declared intentions of the Oslo peace agreements might have been, they did not prepare the Palestinians for independence from Israel. Rather, they set the stage for a new form of Israeli domination over the Palestinians that endured long after the suspension of the peace negotiations in 2000, with the eruption of Al-Aqsa Intifada. The Oslo peace agreements created an apartheid regime of control and emptied the concept of a Palestinian state of any content by de facto containing those living in the West Bank and Gaza in unviable Bantustans. The 'Bantustanisation' of the West Bank and Gaza Strip over the past twenty years has been the outcome of the way in which the Oslo process dealt with the question of the transfer of authority from Israel to the Palestinians, the issue of territorial separation and the question of population and labour movements.

Transfer of authority

The Oslo Accords give the Palestinians political autonomy, as manifested in the establishment of an elected Palestinian authority, the devolution of Israeli rule over Palestinian civilian affairs and the establishment of Palestinian security forces. However, they do not guarantee the creation of an independent sovereign Palestinian state. The accords' legal structure puts the Palestinian entity in a similar position to South African Bantustans under the apartheid regime, in four main ways.

First, Oslo failed to guarantee the end of Israel's occupation and its withdrawal from the West Bank and the Gaza Strip. As in the South African Bantustans, Oslo emphasised a gradual approach to self-rule, dealing first with Gaza-Jericho and then transferring functional and civilian jurisdiction to the rest of the West Bank. It separated the final status issues from the interim issues, without committing to a clear aim for the negotiations or to Palestinian unilateral claims to the West Bank and Gaza.

Second, the Oslo process did not make the native electorate the *only* source of authority for the Palestinian entity. Although the Oslo agreements called for the establishment of a Palestinian national council and presidency, elected democratically by the Palestinian people, the jurisdiction of these elected institutions did not stem only from the national electorate. Rather, it remained dependent on the Israeli military authority in the West Bank and Gaza Strip together with the Israeli civil administration, neither of which were dismantled. The military government, like the commissioner general in the case of South Africa, delegated to the newly elected Palestinian/native council the jurisdiction that the latter was supposed to have.[21] This included a series of territorial, civilian and legal jurisdictions that were defined by Israel. The elected Palestinian council and the Palestinian National

Authority (PNA) were given mainly civilian, or functional, jurisdiction over 93 per cent of the Palestinian population living in the West Bank and the Gaza Strip. They were not given full territorial jurisdiction, nor bestowed with any sovereign identity, a fact facilitated by the exclusion of the issues of borders, Israeli settlements, Jerusalem and sovereignty from the prerogatives of the Oslo agreement.[22]

Third, Oslo did not affirm the superiority of international law over the Israeli law that has been governing the occupied Palestinian territories since 1967. There was no mention of UN General Assembly Resolution 181, which provides the international legitimacy for an Arab state in historical Palestine, nor of the Geneva Conventions, nor of the other UN resolutions affirming Palestinian rights to self-determination.[23] UN Security Council Resolutions 242 and 336 were the only UN resolutions referred to in the accords, but these have been typically silent on the subject of Palestinian rights to statehood, or on the size and boundaries of the Occupied Territories. They refer to the Palestinians as refugees needing a humanitarian solution. Their silence with regard to Palestinian national rights has made it easy for Israel to impose its own interpretation of these rights, especially as there was no role for the international community to supervise or monitor the process. In the case of South Africa, the international community never accepted the 'sovereign status' of the Bantustans nor of apartheid. Rather, in 1973, the UN General Assembly adopted Resolution 3068, which defined the International Convention on the Suppression and Punishment of the Crime of Apartheid.

Fourth, the Oslo agreements focused on establishing an infrastructure of close cooperation between the Israeli and Palestinian parties for the transfer of civilian and security responsibilities, as was the case with the transfer of authority from the white South African government to the Bantustans. While the Palestinians were given the upper hand in running their civilian and security affairs in areas under their control, they still had to coordinate with the Israeli authorities via joint Israeli–Palestinian committees. These committees were created in every field, from water to economic affairs and health, and, most importantly, to security matters. One of the first things that the Declaration of Principles (DOP or Oslo I) and the Interim Agreement (Oslo II) called for was the establishment of a Palestinian police force that would ensure public order and would cooperate closely with the Israeli side on security issues.[24] However, Israel continued to have the upper hand in security matters. This type of security cooperation was also fostered between the white government and South Africa's Bantustans.[25]

'Bantustanisation' of Palestinian land

Territorially, the Oslo agreements facilitated the 'Bantustanisation' of the West Bank and the Gaza Strip by institutionalising the fragmentation of the area and consolidating Israel's claim to it. Before 1993, Israel had already expropriated and enclosed militarily about 36 to 39 per cent of the West Bank land, and it kept direct control over the whole of the Occupied Territories. Although Oslo promised to maintain the territorial integrity of the West Bank and the Gaza Strip (DOP article VI), it did not specify how this integrity could be maintained. As is well known, the Oslo Accords divided the West Bank and the Gaza Strip into three zones – A, B and C. Although in principle the PNA was supposed to control most of the West Bank and the Gaza Strip by 1996, the reality was that it had only territorial and civilian jurisdiction over less than 19 per cent of the West Bank by July 2000 (area A). Palestinian jurisdiction remained fragmented and excluded from 59 per cent of the West Bank (excluding East Jerusalem) and 30 per cent of the Gaza Strip (area C).

The fragmentation of the West Bank and the Gaza Strip was consolidated by the presence of Israeli settlements, a phenomenon that was not central to the South African apartheid system but was fundamental to the process of Palestinian 'Bantustanisation'. In 1993, a total of 196,000 settlers lived in 145 settlements dispersed all over the West Bank, including East Jerusalem, and Gaza. The Oslo Accords did not reverse this fragmentation but rather institutionalised it. They explicitly recognised sole Israeli jurisdiction over Israeli settlements and settlers, from both a territorial and a functional point of view.[26] Furthermore, Oslo did not ensure that settlements would not expand in the interim period. Between 1993 and 2000, over seventy-two settlement outposts were built and the settler population (including in East Jerusalem) increased by two-thirds, reaching a total of 375,000.[27] Israel built over 250 miles of bypass roads and an average of 2,500 new houses per year in the settlements over the same period.[28] This expansion shattered the Palestinian territorial contiguity in the West Bank and the Gaza Strip. After the eruption of Al-Aqsa Intifada, settlement construction continued unabated, growing by over 5 per cent per annum in East Jerusalem and the West Bank. Another 130,000 settlers moved to the Occupied Territories between 2000 and 2013, increasing the settler population to a total of 560,000 by the end of 2013.

The 'Bantustanisation' was also consolidated by the way in which the Oslo agreement legitimised Israel's claim over the lands of the West Bank and Gaza Strip. Article XI.c of Oslo II states that only Israel territorially controls area C. Article 16.3 of Protocol III clearly states: 'The Palestinian Council shall respect the legal rights of Israelis (including corporations owned by Israelis) relating to Government and absentee land located in areas under the territorial jurisdiction of the Council'. Articles 12, 22 and 27 from Protocol III confirm this right with regard to all other lands (including bypass roads). In other words, the PNA accepted Israel's claim over Palestinian land, even over land that lies in area A.

Just as importantly, the Oslo process set the stage for separating the West Bank from the Gaza Strip and for treating territorial claims in each differently. The Oslo Accords talk about Israeli *withdrawal* from the Gaza Strip and Jericho but only about *redeployment* from the rest of the West Bank.[29] The difference in terms is important, since withdrawal implies an end to the occupation while redeployment entitles Israel to reinstall itself in any area whenever it deems it necessary. Since 1990, Israel has demarcated borders with the Gaza Strip more clearly than with the West Bank,[30] facilitating the transformation of the former into a de facto demarcated Bantustan. Israel's disengagement from Gaza in 2004 has simply confirmed this transformation. It pointed out the economic and political instability of Gaza and its complete dependence on Israel's mercy. Since 2006, Gaza has been under siege from Israel and the international community for its election of the Hamas government.

Last but not least, Israel consolidated its fragmentation of Palestinian land with its construction of the separation barrier inside the West Bank from June 2002 onwards. This wall, which is not being built along the 1948 armistice Green Line, will be 703 kilometres long, and 20 per cent of the wall will be 8 metres high. It will incorporate 11.8 per cent of West Bank land inside Israel and displace an estimated 110,000 Palestinians who live in the area between the wall and the armistice Green Line. By 2012, 62 per cent of the wall had been built.[31] Upon completion, it will have established an Israeli unilaterally defined border that violates the 1967 boundaries and leaves the Palestinians with control over less than 53 per cent of the West Bank.[32] Although the International Court of Justice and the Israeli Supreme Court ruled against the route of the wall, its construction has not stopped.

The 'Bantustanisation' of people's movement

The 'Bantustanisation' of the West Bank and the Gaza Strip is intrinsically bound up with the way in which the Oslo process institutionalised Israel's control of Palestinian population movement. Palestinian labour continued to need the Israeli economy but found it increasingly difficult to access it as a result of the permit and closure policy.[33] Between 1993 and 2000, Israel imposed over 484 days of closure, which locked the Palestinians in over sixty-three enclaves and stalled any attempt to grow domestically or to rely on non-Israeli markets to absorb its growing labour force. After October 2000, over 770 checkpoints were placed in the West Bank and the Gaza Strip; these prevented Palestinians from moving for work within the West Bank or inside Israel.[34]

After April 2002, Israel turned many of the checkpoints into permanent security terminals, large concrete buildings guarded by private security guards and army personnel that regulate the movement of the Palestinian population from one area to another. It also cut the Occupied Territories into eight main districts that Palestinians could not exit without holding a permit or using their own car.[35] These made the Palestinian areas into de facto Bantustans, given municipal and local government authority, but totally at the mercy of Israeli checkpoints and permit policies as well as its military interventions.

The Oslo process institutionalised the closure and permits system as the regulatory mechanism for controlling Palestinian movement. Article IX of the Protocol of Redeployment and Security Arrangements in Oslo II clearly stated that Israel alone has the right to close its crossing points, prohibit or limit the entry of persons into its areas, and determine the mode of entry of people into its areas (including area C). With regard to the permit system, Oslo made it more analogous to the South African pass law system, even if its origins were different. While in Apartheid South Africa the pass system was central to ensure the control and supply of cheap labour to the South African economy, in Israel and Palestine it was introduced primarily for security reasons. The Protocol on Civil Affairs specifies that permits are the only documents that allow a Palestinian to enter any Israeli-defined areas (article 11.2). These include permits for businessmen and workers who are employed in the settlements as well as in Israel. Negotiated and implemented by security officials, rather than by politicians or economists, the Protocol on Civil Affairs determined people's movement not according to the economic interests of both sides, but rather by what the military establishment in Israel defines as 'security' (article 11). The articulation of the permit system, together with the pattern of Israel's territorial control and Palestinian demographic expansion, inevitably transformed the West Bank and the Gaza Strip into de facto fragmented, unsustainable population 'reservations'.

The Bantustans' economies

Economically, the Oslo peace agreements, just like apartheid, reformulated rather than ended the native people's dependency on the colonial economy. The Palestinian economy before Oslo was service-oriented and dependent on employment in the Israeli economy. Some 35 to 40 per cent of workers from Gaza and 32 to 36 per cent of workers from the West Bank were working in Israeli areas between 1982 and 1992.[36] The economies of the South African reserves were also dependent on black migration to white industrial areas, as well as on subsistence farming in white areas. In the case of Transkei in South Africa, over 60 per cent of the workers were migrant workers. The share of agriculture in the South African Bantustans' gross domestic product (GDP) was less than 11 per cent in 1985, compared with 16 per cent in the West Bank in 1992.[37]

The Oslo Interim Agreement, in its Economic Protocol preamble, promised to 'lay the groundwork for strengthening the economic base of the Palestinian side and for exercising its right of economic decision making in accordance with its own development plans and priorities'.[38] As with Apartheid South Africa's plan for the Bantustans, the colonial state sought to enhance the productive capability of the natives in their own areas, even if it was for different purposes. In the case of South Africa, economic growth in the Bantustans was necessary to help subsidise the cost of black labour production needed in white areas. This was not a concern for Israel, where workers from the Occupied Territories constituted no more than 7 per cent of the total workforce and 35 per cent of all those employed in the construction sector.[39] Rather, Israel's aim was for economic prosperity in the Palestinian autonomous areas to reduce Palestinian labour migration to Israel. It was meant to foster the peace process. As in the case of South Africa, economic growth in the Palestinian areas was meant to alleviate indigenous poverty and prevent it from spilling into white areas.[40]

In both the Palestinian and the South African case, economic growth in the Bantustans depended on four interrelated strategies. First, it relied on the creation and expansion of a native public sector that would manage the native economy. The PNA, like the Bantu authority in the homelands, was given the right to define the economic strategy for its areas, to establish a monetary authority and investment boards in its area, and to hire administrators and a police force to take care of law and order. The PNA became a major employer, absorbing 30 per cent of the total workforce in Gaza and 20 to 24 per cent of that in the West Bank between 1994 and 2006.[41] In the Transkei and other Bantustans of South Africa, public employment absorbed 20 per cent of the domestic workforce.[42] The security forces remained the largest sector in this regard, as they represented over 50 per cent of all those employed in the public sector.[43]

Second, Oslo, as much as apartheid, fostered dependent trade relations between the native and settler economies. The Bantustans in South Africa continued to trade with the white areas, according to permit and pass regulations, while Israel and the PLO signed a customs union agreement that allowed the Palestinians to trade a few permitted items with third countries. Oslo also made Israel transfer to the Palestinians revenues from goods destined for the West Bank and Gaza, upholding the same principles that the custom union had established between Pretoria and the homelands, but under an economic formula that was far less generous.[44] However, despite these concessions, Israel remained the largest importing and exporting markets for Palestinian goods (90 per cent and 70 per cent respectively of Palestinian imports and exports). Meanwhile, customs revenues became a considerable form of leverage in the hands of Israel, since it withheld them whenever it deemed it necessary. Customs revenues represented as much as 70 per cent of the PNA's fiscal budget and as much as 20 per cent of the Palestinian gross national product (GNP). In 1996, and more frequently after Al-Aqsa Intifada, Israel withheld these revenues in the name of security and until it deemed that the PNA had done enough to stop attacks against Israel.[45]

Third, industrial zones were suggested as a major panacea to the economic problems of the Bantustans. These were viewed as an excellent opportunity to attract capital into the Bantustans as well as to generate local employment that in turn would reduce the propensity for migration to white areas. These industrial zones were also planned along the borders between the West Bank and Israel. In the case of South Africa, each of the ten Bantustans had one or more of these industrial zones built at their borders with white areas, as well as a number of mines excavated within them.[46] In the case of the West Bank, three industrial zones were planned together with two in the Gaza Strip. In 2008, another seven were suggested as a means to alleviate unemployment.[47] So far, however, these have failed to generate much employment since their growth depends on their goods having free access to Israel and the outside world. Israel has limited trade from outside the territories since 2000.

Fourth, aid and foreign investment were considered central to economic growth in the Bantustans, both in the case of South Africa and in the Palestinian areas. The difference between the two cases was the *source* of this aid. In South Africa, the white government was the main supplier of aid to the Bantustans, which was used mainly to help cover their fiscal deficit and generate rural and industrial reforms. In the case of the PNA, no aid came from Israel. Instead, it came from the international community, which committed to financially advise and help the Palestinian economy, through the World Bank and the International Monetary Fund, to lay the foundation for an independent state. An average of $850 million a year in aid was injected into the Palestinian economy between 1995 and 2000, and over $1 billion a year since 2001. This amounted to nearly a quarter of the Palestinian GDP. Since 2001, aid has helped ease the fiscal deficit that the Palestinian economy has continued to accumulate.[48]

The result of these structural economic changes, however, was not a reduction in poverty, let alone development. Poverty in the South African Bantustans actually increased by 25 per cent between 1965 and 1985, largely as a result of the failure of agricultural land to feed the growing population and the limited capacity of industrial zones to grow and absorb labour. The South African Bantustan economies also remained dependent on migration to white areas, which in 1980 still absorbed 50 per cent of the Transkei workforce. Poverty also increased in the Palestinian Occupied Territories after Oslo, largely as a result of Israel's closure policy, which prevented Palestinian goods and labour from moving within the Palestinian territories as well as outside them. It remained much more acute in the Gaza Strip than in the West Bank, largely because the borders remained more porous with Israel in the case of the latter. In 1996, poverty touched 46 per cent of the population in the Gaza Strip, increasing to 79 per cent in 2007. In the West Bank, the figures were 23 per cent and 45 per cent respectively.[49] In 2014, it was still at 45 per cent in the Gaza Strip and 16 per cent in the West Bank.[50] Meanwhile, both in the South African Bantustans and in the West Bank and Gaza Strip, private sector development relied on alliances with the public sector, which became increasingly corrupt and inefficient.

CONCLUSION: THE WAR ON GAZA AND ITS AFTERMATH

The violence of Al-Aqsa Intifada and Israel's response to it have made many supporters of the apartheid analogy argue that what Israel is creating is worse than what the apartheid regime in South Africa ever established. Both the level of destruction that Israel has inflicted on the Palestinians and its continuous infringement and fragmentation of their land have put the Palestinian territories today in a worse position than the South African Bantustans were ever in, especially given Israel's wars on Gaza since December 2008.[51] The level of assault on Gaza, and the depth of the siege in an area with a population of 1.8 million, was not seen in South Africa's Bantustans. The cost of the damage inflicted on the Gaza Strip as a result of Israel's wars in 2012 and 2014 was estimated at over $2 billion each time, which is the size of the Strip's GDP.[52]

Palestinian areas have indeed been made far smaller territorially and economically unviable, despite all the international aid the PNA has received. The Gaza Strip has been cut off from the rest of the world since 2006 and has split politically from the West Bank after the Hamas takeover in June 2007. It has become more like an open-air prison than a project of state building.

What has been particularly difficult for the apartheid analogy is the failure of Palestinian resistance during the intifada to challenge the Israeli structure of domination in the way in which the anti-apartheid movement was able to challenge the white government. This is largely because Israel has remained economically independent of the Palestinians in a way that South Africa never was with regard to black labour. Since Oslo, the Israeli economy has prospered while the Palestinian economy has plummeted. Israel's GDP has more than tripled over the past twenty years and its per capita income grew by over 5 per cent a year between 1994 and 2000 and by over 4 per cent since 2002. Less than 1 per cent of its labour force came from the West Bank and unemployment was at less than 9 per cent between 1997 and 2007. Meanwhile, the latest Israeli war on the Gaza Strip has destroyed whatever remained of the Palestinian economic activity there. Even before the war, the Gaza economy was declared to have nearly collapsed, 56 per cent of the population were food insecure and over 34 per cent unemployed. According to the latest World Bank report, the manufacturing sector is 98 per cent inactive, banking has shrunk drastically and the private sector has been destroyed. All we talk about now in Gaza is 'tunnel economics', the economics of the informal sector smuggling through Egypt, and of monopoly thugs unaccountable to the law. The situation in the West Bank is not much better, even if the economy has not yet fallen into the hands of informal agents, with unemployment at 40 per cent in Jenin and around 26 per cent in Ramallah. Real GDP per capita income of Palestinians today is 30 per cent lower than it was in 1999.[53]

Just as alarming is the international position towards Israeli policy and Palestinian resistance. This resistance has become particularly difficult in an international context defined in terms of the post-9/11 'War on Terror' rather than in terms of people's right to self-determination, as it was in the 1960s and 1970s. Unlike the situation in South Africa, the international community failed to support the Palestinian national struggle against Israel after 1993 and especially so after 2000. It failed to hold Israel to account for its obligation to retreat from the Occupied Territories, to freeze and dismantle Israeli settlements in the West Bank, or to stop the war on Gaza. Above all, it failed to accept the Palestinian democratic election of Hamas in 2006 and punished it for this choice by cutting aid. It considered Hamas a terrorist organisation rather than a legitimate Palestinian political force to be dealt with. The fragmentation of the Palestinian national movement has only contributed to its weakness and de facto to Israel's immunity.

However, it is important to remember that the ANC also had its internal crises in the 1970s and that it took the international community several decades to support the ANC freedom charter that it produced in 1955. What is clear today is that the Palestinian national movement is at a major turning point and the question is what direction it will take. The developments of the past twenty years have clearly buried all viable possibilities for a Palestinian state. They have shown once again the impossibility of a viable territorial separation in the Israeli–Palestinian conflict and, at the same time, Israel's inability to end the conflict. The increasingly vocal Palestinian grassroots organisations calling for the end of Israeli apartheid suggests new peaceful methods of resistance. The growing movement calling for a one-state solution is reviving old ideas about how best to resolve the Israeli–Palestinian conflict. While it is still too early to see how great an impact this grassroots movement will have on the present Palestinian leadership or on the creation of new leaders, its momentum is growing. Probably its biggest asset is the fact that the two-state solution was tried and failed, and that Israel is more clearly than ever an apartheid state.

Notes

1   Nancy Murray, 'Dynamics of Resistance: The Apartheid Analogy', *Electronic Journal of Middle Eastern Studies* 8 (Spring 2008), pp. 132–48. See also the Palestinian NGOs statement, made during the World Conference against Racism in Durban, South Africa, August/September 2001, calling for an end to Israel's brand of apartheid: see www.lawsociety.org/apartheid/palngo.html.
2   Leila Farsakh, 'Independence, Canton or Bantustans: Wither the Palestinian State?', *Middle East Journal* 59(2) (Spring 2005), pp. 230–45.
3   Uri Davis, *Apartheid Israel: Possibilities for the Struggle Within*, New York: Zed Books, 2003; Oren Yiftachel, *Ethnocracy: Land and Identity Politics in Israel–Palestine*, Philadelphia: University of Pennsylvania Press, 2006.
4   Deborah Posel, *The Making of Apartheid 1948–1961: Conflict and Compromise*, Oxford: Clarendon Press, 1997.
5   White agricultural farmers were also worried that South Africa's industrialisation was taking away cheap black labour as workers preferred to work in cities than on their farms. Cities typically paid better wages than agricultural employment. See Posel, *The Making of Apartheid*; Harold Wolpe (ed.), *The Articulation of Modes of Production*, London: Routledge and Kegan Paul, 1980.
6   Gwendolen M. Carter, Thomas Karis and Newell M. Stultz, *South Africa's Transkei: The Politics Of Domestic Colonialism*, Evanston: Northwestern University Press, 1967.
7   Bill Freund, 'Forced Resettlement and the Political Economy of South Africa', *Review of African Political Economy* 29 (July 1984), pp. 49–63.
8   Carter, Karis and Stultz, *South Africa's Transkei*, pp. 13–17.
9   As early as 1936, legislation was passed that removed Africans in the Cape Province from the common voting roll, allowing them only to vote indirectly

for three white representatives to the House of Assembly. This right was later rescinded with the Bantu Citizenship Act in 1970, as natives were completely disenfranchised from potential claims to South African citizenship.

10   James Addison, *Apartheid*, London: Batsford, 1990, p. 9.

11   See also Carter, Karis and Stultz, *South Africa's Transkei*; Christopher Hills, *Bantustans: The Fragmentation of South Africa*, London: Institute of Race Relations, 1964.

12   Maurice Legassick and Harold Wolpe, 'The Bantustans and Capital Accumulation in South Africa', *Review of African Political Economy* 7 (1976), pp. 87–107.

13   Hills, *Bantustans*, pp. 21–36.

14   The other three are Bophuthatswana (1977), Venda (1979) and Ciskei (1981).

15   Barbara Rogers, *Divide and Rule: South Africa's Bantustans*, London: International Defence and Aid Fund, 1976.

16   See Ilan Pappé, *The Ethnic Cleansing of Palestine*, London and New York: Oneworld, 2006.

17   Some 40 per cent of the total population under Israel's control in the aftermath of the Six-Day War was Palestinian.

18   Leila Farsakh, *Palestinian Labour Migration to Israel: Labour, Land and Occupation*, London: Routledge, 2005.

19   Gershon Shafir, *Land, Labour and the Origins of the Israeli–Palestinian Conflict, 1883–1914*, Cambridge: Cambridge University Press, 1989; Farsakh, 'Independence, Cantons or Bantustans', pp. 123–34.

20   See Carter, Karis and Stultz, *South Africa's Transkei*, pp. 13–17.

21   See articles 1.1 and 15.4 of Chapter 1 of the *Israeli–Palestinian Interim Agreement on the West Bank and the Gaza Strip*, 28 September 1995 (Oslo II).

22   See article V of the *Israeli–Palestinian Declaration of Principles on Interim Self-Government Authority*, Washington, 13 September 1993 (DOP or Oslo I).

23   See http://domino.un.org/unispal.nsf.

24   Articles VII and XII in DOP and article XIII in Chapter 2, Oslo II.

25   Carter, Karis and Shultz, *South Africa's Transkei*.

26   Articles IA, XVII and XVIII in Protocol IV of Oslo II.

27   FMEP, *Report on Israeli Settlements in the Occupied Territories*, Vol. 11/6, Vol. 12/1, Vol. 13/6, Washington, DC: Foundation for Middle East Peace, 2001, 2002, 2003.

28   Israeli Central Bureau of Statistics, *Statistical Abstract of Israel*, 1995, 1998, 2002, Tables 2.7, 22.5, 22.12.

29   See article II of the Cairo Agreement, 4 May 1994, and article X, Chapter 2 of Oslo II.

30 By establishing the Eretz checkpoint in Gaza and controlling all border crossing.

31 B'Tselem: www.btselem.org/english/Separation_Barrier/Statistics.asp.

32 See UN OCHA, *The Humanitarian Impact of the West Bank Barrier on Palestinian Communities*, New York: United Nations Office for the Coordination of Humanitarian Affairs, 2008, p. 5.

33 Work in the Israeli economy was key to keeping unemployment rates at less than 7 per cent in the West Bank and Gaza Strip between 1970 and 1993, and for sustaining a labour force growing at more than 4 per cent per annum. See Leila Farsakh, 'Palestinian Labor Flows to Israel: A Finished Story?', *Journal of Palestine Studies* 32(1) (Autumn 2002), pp. 13–27.

34 See World Bank, *Twenty-Seven Months Intifada, Closure and Palestinian Economic Crisis: An Assessment*, Washington, DC: World Bank, 2003, p. xi.

35 See ARIJ, *The Israeli Security Zone Make Up 45.25% of the West Bank, Including 158 Israeli Colonies*, Jerusalem: Applied Research Institute Jerusalem, 2002: www.poica.org/casestudies/security-zones/.

36 Farsakh, *Palestinian Labour Migration to Israel*, pp. 80–4

37 A. Lemon, *Apartheid in Transition*, London: Gower, 1987, pp. 171–3; World Bank, *Developing the Occupied Territories: An Investment in Peace*, Washington, DC: World Bank, 1993, Vol. 4, pp. 22–5.

38 See preamble to the Economic Protocol, Interim Agreement (Oslo II).

39 Farsakh, *Palestinian Labour Migration to Israel*, p. 88.

40 See Hills, *Bantustans*; Roger Southall, *South Africa's Transkei: The Political Economy of an Independent Bantustan*,London: Heinemann, 1986, for arguments about the economic rationale for the Bantustans. See also Shomon Perez, *The New Middle East*, New York: Holt, 1993, for arguments on the need for economic prosperity in the West Bank and Gaza.

41 MAS, *The Economic Monitor, 1994–2000*, Ramallah: Palestine Economic Policy Institute, 2001, p. 165.

42 See also Abnash Kaur, *South Africa and Bantustans*, Delhi: Kalinga Publications, pp. 33–7.

43 S. Fischer, A. Alonso-Gamo and U. E. Von Allman, 'Economic Developments in the West Bank and Gaza Strip since Oslo', *Economic Journal* 111(472) (2001), pp. 254–75.

44 This customs union agreement was different to the one South Africa signed with Lesotho and Botswana, insofar as it was based on a macro, rather than a micro data formula for revenue sharing. This meant that it was less generous to the Palestinian economy than in the case of Lesotho and Botswana. See Mona Jawhary, *The Palestinian–Israeli Trade Arrangements: Searching for Fair Revenue-Sharing*, Ramallah: MAS, 1995.

45 World Bank, *Four Years: Intifada, Closures and Palestinian Economic Crisis: An Assessment*, Washington, DC: World Bank, 2004.

46 See Kaur, *South Africa and Bantustans*; Southall, *South Africa's Transkei*.

47 See Hugh Tomlinson, 'Seven New Industrial Zones Proposed for West Bank', MEED, 17 December 2008.

48 UNCTAD, *Palestinian War Torn Economy: Aid, Development and State Formation*, Geneva: United Nations Conference on Trade and Development, 2006.

49 World Bank, *Palestinian Economic Prospects: Aid, Access and Reform. Economic Monitoring Report to the Ad Hoc Liaison Committee*, Washington, DC: World Bank, 2008.

50 World Bank, *Economic Monitoring Report to the Ad Hoc Liaison Committee*, Washington, DC: World Bank, 2014.

51 Ronnie Kasrils, 'Who Said Nearly 50 Years Ago That Israel Was Not an Apartheid State?', *Media Monitors Network*, 17 March 2009.

52 World Bank, *Economic Monitoring Report to the Ad Hoc Liaison Committee*.

53 World Bank, *Palestinian Economic Prospects*; PCBS.

PART 3
NUANCED COMPARISONS

CHAPTER 6

Femicide in Apartheid: The Parallel Interplay between Racism and Sexism in South Africa and Palestine–Israel

ANTHONY LÖWSTEDT[1]

Femicide is the intentional targeting of girls and women with lethal force because they are girls and women. It is a global phenomenon and a symptom of sexism, which manifests itself in different manners in different cultures, and sometimes in very similar ways in very different cultures. In Western countries, femicide today is usually called a 'crime of passion' or 'domestic violence', general terms that may also include 'viricide', in which men and boys are killed because they are men and boys. 'Gendercide' is the common term for femicide and viricide. In total, viricide is possibly a more common occurrence than femicide, even when non-combatant victims alone are considered. Throughout history, it has not been uncommon for conquerors to take women, especially young women, as slaves, or to simply let women go, while exterminating non-combatant men, especially men of 'battle age', among a conquered population.[2]

In both viricide and femicide, however, most of the killers are men. In many cultures, moreover, femicide takes place in systematic forms virtually unaccompanied by viricide: examples include female infanticide, which occurs in India and China today, or *sati* (Hindu widow burnings), female genital mutilation (mainly in north-east

Africa), 'witch' burnings (mainly in Europe and Africa south of the Sahara), 'honour killings' (mainly in south-west Asia), maternal mortality (making girls or women pregnant when they are too young and/or too weak to survive childbirth), or rape-murder, which takes place everywhere, but in systematic form especially in conflict zones.[3]

The predominant indigenous forms of femicide in South Africa and Palestine – 'witch' burnings and 'honour' murders (usually called 'honour killings') respectively – are as different on the surface as any other two varieties of femicide, but they share many deep structure similarities, as this chapter aims to show. In my view, both South Africa under white domination and white rule and modern Israel–Palestine are apartheid societies in a wide, generic sense and in the sense of international law. This means that an invading racial group has conquered a territory (outright or through takeover from earlier foreign occupiers, such as the Israelis from the British), subjugated an indigenous majority, stolen most of the land and repopulated it with immigrant or invader settlers, and continuously discriminated against the indigenous racial group in various ways. Many indigenous people have been ethnically cleansed in the process – that is, either exterminated or driven out of their country. Bantustans, 'reserves' or 'homelands', scattered pockets of the land least desired by the invaders and their descendants, have been created by the invader group to contain the least wanted strata of the remaining indigenous population to provide a reserve pool of very cheap labour for the racial elite, for example for the whites in South Africa and for the Jews in Israel–Palestine, or for this elite to avoid perpetrating total genocide (out of a sense of pity or for moral or international legal reasons or fear of retaliation), or due to military inability, or as a combination of these factors.[4]

I will attempt to demonstrate that apartheid's racial elites have at least two things to gain from the practice of femicide within the apartheid victim communities, and that the former therefore consciously or unconsciously either promote or at least accept it.

First and foremost, indigenous femicide can be seen as an asset in the divide-and-rule strategies of the apartheid elites. The Palestinian preoccupation with morals, from courting and sexual morals to the ethics of punishment, prevention and protection, keeps the genders from dealing with the apartheid oppression and liberation from it. There is rage, fear, heartbreak and suspicion between the genders and between the generations. And so much of the energy of indigenous passion, resentment, aggression and violence, even lethal violence, that could be directed against the apartheid elites is therefore spent on domestic issues instead.

Relating to this, Israel uses Palestinian collaborators about whom it knows what other Palestinians must not know: that is, honour- and shame-related information, sometimes gathered in cruel and illegal ways from Palestinian minors in Israeli prisons and under Israeli detention. As we will see, Palestinians will even kill each other in order to control the flow of this kind of social information, which is very important to Palestinian society at present. I am not aware to what extent, if any, this kind of indigenous femicide took place in Apartheid South Africa. It is quite possible that Israel has thus brought a new divide-and-rule mechanism into the phenomenon of apartheid, one of infiltration and racist sabotage of the indigenous population by means of prompting, enabling or threatening femicide.

Secondly, indigenous femicide can be used by apartheid elites as a pseudo-argument for the backwardness of the indigenous culture, and, a fortiori, for the superiority of the new elite culture. ('Those barbarians do not deserve the vote, or a state of their own. They need to be treated like animals or children, at least until they become civilised'.) From early times onwards, both South African whites and Zionist Jews saw themselves as spreading civilisation in the countries they invaded. And those invasions received some of their excuses on these grounds.[5]

There is, however, also a third aspect of femicide under apartheid which must be seen as a drawback from the point of view of the apartheid elites. By keeping its young women in near-constant fear of falling victim to indigenous femicide, the predominantly male leadership of the oppressed indigenous majority is able to ensure early marriage of most women and, consequently, very high birth rates, with which it may eventually gain decisive military or electoral strength.[6] Indeed, continuous and steep black population growth has even been considered as the main reason behind the demise of South African apartheid.[7] In the absence of social security and pensions for the elderly oppressed people, and in the presence of a high death rate of young men from the apartheid conflicts, a high birth rate is, of course, also something welcome in victim families, if only for family economic reasons. Therefore this aspect cannot be reduced to merely a patriarchal scheme. Moreover, having children has become one of the few ways with which indigenous women and men can do something against the ongoing ethnic cleansing of their home country without necessarily being punished personally (by the invaders and their descendants) for it, although, of course, many are, especially through one of the many forms of collective punishment[8] perpetrated by the apartheid elites. Nevertheless, the price of exponential population growth is high. Women and girls are severely oppressed and sometimes murdered, and the overall economy and the natural environment also suffer severely from the pressures of population explosions of the victimised, racialised group under apartheid.[9]

Furthermore, the apartheid perpetrators are just as sexist, and they are racist, too. Through racist citizenship and immigration laws and practices, as well as their own means of unnaturally raising birth rates, they try to compete demographically against the racial majority with their own population explosions. And so, additional pressures upon the apartheid victims accumulate. The result is a vicious spiral of rising population density, more competition over dwindling resources, especially over land and water, and increasing violence.

Indigenous femicide is thus a two-edged sword for both apartheid elites and apartheid victims. The (much higher) death tolls in the conventional apartheid conflict, in which men are the principal victims – more than twelve times higher for members of the indigenous majority[10] – reveal that two bad aspects against one 'good' aspect for the apartheid victims may be considered less devastating for the victimised racial group (rather than a hundred against one or a hundred against three body counts, as in the winter 2008–09 and summer 2014 conventional flare-ups in Gaza[11]). This strategic, or game-theoretical, consideration may be one of the main reasons why indigenous femicide still takes place among Palestinians.

'WITCH' BURNINGS

From the beginning of the nineteenth century, 'witch' burnings among blacks were recorded in South African history. Mostly, however, 'witches' were punished with less final means than death. Their property was confiscated and/or they were deported. During the nineteenth century, executions took place especially in the eastern part of the country, where the once mighty Xhosa and Zulu and other cultures and groups were facing cultural and physical extinction due to the onslaught of white military, settler and missionary presence.[12]

Towards the end of apartheid, the persecution of 'witches' reached near-epidemic proportions in the north of the country, where the Venda, Pedi, Tsonga, Sotho and other cultures came under intensified fire from the whites. From 1985, 'witch' burnings started to spread rapidly in these and other rural parts of South Africa. The situation reached a climax in 1990, the year Nelson Mandela was freed after twenty-seven years in jail.[13] The killings have subsided since 1994, partly due to the reinstatement of traditional chieftains, who were previously often seen as collaborators with the apartheid regime but who had also seen to it that witch burnings would not become epidemics. The indirect influence of apartheid, however, reaches further than that. The absence of competitive demographic growth in particular, it will be argued below, is another main reason why 'witch' burnings are now taking place less frequently in South Africa, and beyond.

Indigenous women targeted for femicide are targeted as if they were the apartheid enemy. A common modern execution method for 'witches' in South Africa is the same as that used for collaborators with the apartheid regime: the so-called 'necklacing', in which a car tyre is placed around the neck of the victim and set alight, burning the victim to a slow and painful death.[14]

The South African 'witch' burnings mostly victimise middle-aged women, but many young women and many men are also found 'guilty' and executed. Numbers are unknown, since many killings go unreported. Women are targeted at an estimated ratio of between four and five to one, so that this is possibly a less gendered form of institutional murder than 'honour' murders. As with Palestinian and Israeli acts of demographic war, the concept of 'culture' was often used by lawyers in order to defend perpetrators against the charge of murdering people, mainly innocent women, in this way.[15]

'HONOUR' MURDERS

Reliable, exact numbers of 'honour' murders are equally hard to obtain, for the same reasons that apply to femicide in South Africa. The murders often go unreported as such and there is a high level of local solidarity with the perpetrators. Still, informed guesses are often made. The United Nations estimates that there are around 5,000 'honour' murders annually worldwide. Nadera Shalhoub-Kevorkian, one of the most famous campaigners against femicide in Palestine, mentions 234 cases of possible femicide between 1996 and 1998 that the Palestinian Attorney General had closed by classifying the cause of death as 'fate and destiny', alongside twenty-eight cases of 'murder' and eleven cases of death 'for which the cause of death or the killer is "Unknown"'.[16] This adds up to 245 possible 'honour' murders carried out with practical impunity.

Some of the twenty-eight convicted murderers, however, received very light sentences, such as two months in prison plus a fine.[17] According to information cited by Gendercide Watch, twenty-three 'honour' murders took place in the Occupied Palestinian Territories in 1999.[18] Kawther Salam, the Palestinian journalist, says that things got much worse after the outbreak of the second intifada a year later. In June 2007, she wrote:

> Over [one] hundred young women and girls were killed by their families during the last few months in Palestine because of perceived slights at the honor of their families. Many hundreds have been killed during the last two years. As the situation in Palestine has deteriorated, these murders of women by their own families have increased dramatically.[19]

As in South Africa, it appears that femicide gets worse, in terms of the death toll, along with the conventional apartheid conflict. But it also appears as if the two kinds of killings are relatively independent. Otherwise, femicide would not still be taking place in South Africa today, and 'honour' murders would not have taken place in Palestine prior to the modern State of Israel.

Catherine Warrick explains the meaning of 'honour' in Arab culture in the following way:

> The concept of honor (sharaf) has to do with social standing on the basis of moral behavior; men's honor is intimately connected to the sexual chastity of their female relatives. Thus a woman's or girl's bad conduct would not only embarrass her family but would impugn the honor of the entire family, particularly the men, who have the right and duty of defending this honor.[20]

However, 'honour', 'bad conduct' and 'witchcraft' are such elastic concepts that 'femicide' becomes a preferable theoretical *and* descriptive term, among both Palestinians and South Africans. 'Honour' and 'witchcraft' are basically excuses for men (and many women) to enforce patriarchy, or to use patriarchy in order to carry out acts for personal gain. For instance, one South African man borrowed money from his aunt and then did not want to pay her back. After lightning had struck her village, he accused her of witchcraft and influenced the villagers to threaten her with execution if she ever set foot in the village again, so that he would not have to pay back his debt at all.[21] Similarly, Palestinian girls and young women have been murdered in the name of 'honour' for merely chatting with men, for smoking in public, for unsubstantiated rumours and gossip, and even for being raped.[22]

Shalhoub-Kevorkian warns against the danger of perpetuating orientalist myths in this regard:

> Naming femicide as 'crimes of passion' in the West and 'crimes of honor' in the East is one reflection of the discriminatory constructions of frames of analyses, which build a simplistic system that hides the intersectionality among political, economic, cultural, and gender factors.[23]

Femicide is one of the two central subjects of this article, and although it takes on different guises in different parts of the world, it is a global phenomenon, whereby a single theory, as yet absent, could go a long way towards bringing about its eradication.

Honour will not disappear. In any event, honour is more than what is contained in the Warrick quote above. Honour is, among other things, tied to the idea of virtue and to the very idea of what is good. It is an individual matter as well as a kind of glue which can bind individuals together into a good and strong community. Yet, 'honour' also destroys lives – both female and male lives – in other ways than apartheid- and demographic warfare-fuelled killings do. If the concept of honour could be somehow de-stratified and de-gendered, either to the degree that both rights and duties can be made equal for all male and female members of the community, or so that duties are rigorously increased with increasing rights (as in the ancient Egyptian notion of 'vertical solidarity'[24]), at the same time ensuring that betrayal be punished equally for male and female members of the community, then, in my opinion, it would also be welcome to continue its role as a central value or make a promising return to central values. Because honour is also about loyalty and respect.

In an article that deals with 'honour' murders in Pakistan, Jordan and Palestine–Israel, Gendercide Watch mentions three levels of responsibility for the killings: the murderers themselves, usually male relatives of the victims; the state authorities, which do not do enough to legislate against, investigate or punish 'honour killings'; and 'societal' factors – in particular, women who support and abet such crimes.[25] Other such factors, however, are left unmentioned.

My argument below is that apartheid societies such as South Africa and Palestine–Israel are characterised by demographic competition, within which femicide is exacerbated, and that part of the responsibility for femicide should therefore be shouldered by the racial minority elites, who created apartheid societies, who implement and practise apartheid, who initiated the demographic race, and who keep the initiative throughout most of that race. For them, femicide and domestic violence (violence within the family) serve the purposes of dividing the resistance of the indigenous racialised majority against apartheid as well as providing an excuse for the subjugation of an entire nation. They also produce a resource and a basis for the apartheid armies for recruiting collaborators within the subjugated racial majority in times of enhanced armed conflict. Every indigenous family is more or less divided due to this violence or the threat of it, and thus it serves elite purposes; it serves apartheid purposes. I am not arguing, however, that apartheid causes femicide. It is merely a factor among others. The relationship between (processes of) apartheid and femicide is one of complex correlation rather than causation.

The most important difference between femicide in South Africa and Palestine–Israel is perhaps the age of the victims. They are much younger in the current case of apartheid. But this difference is merely a gradual one, which changes from day to day. It does not make any difference at all with regard to the essence of apartheid.

THE DEMOGRAPHIC WAR

At the same time as the white-run state and white civil society pressured black women not to have children at all, for example by handing out masses of contraceptives among blacks, and even punished them directly for having children and generally ignored the health needs of the black population,[26] the black resistance movement pressured the very same women to maximise their number of children instead. The latter was known as the 'Making Soldiers' campaign.

> All those opposing the wishes of the young men [who usually led the resistance in rural areas] were reminded that it was every woman's obligation to give birth to new 'soldiers', in order to replace those warriors killed in the liberation struggle. The idiom of the adolescents referred to these patriotic efforts as 'operation production' … it was forbidden for the girls to use contraceptives.[27]

People (mostly women) within the liberation movement who opposed this strategy or simply preferred other means of liberation were often accused of witchcraft, as were many women who were perceived as collaborating with the white authorities in other ways. The usual punishment for witchcraft as well as for collaboration with the apartheid enemy, especially towards the end of the struggle, was death.[28] This was a sophisticated, targeted form of femicide, unlike, for example, female infanticide or female genital mutilation, which are indiscriminate, blanket forms of femicide and violence against women. In South

Africa, as well as in Palestinian communities, the women who refuse or are unlikely to play along with the patriarchal game of demographic war are targeted, or 'protected' from the targets by indigenous agents of patriarchy. In both cases, there are femicidal mechanisms already in place that can be used to eliminate those who challenge patriarchy relatively easily. The indigenous patriarchy expects all indigenous girls and women to conform to the pattern of marrying early and raising large numbers of children. Those who do not are not automatically targeted, but if they are suspected of influencing other girls and women to question or reject the pattern, they might be targeted. Again, apartheid is the backdrop without which this particular brutalisation of South Africa and Palestine–Israel becomes less understandable from a social scientific perspective.

The main weapons in the demographic war between Israeli Jews and (all) Palestinians are racist immigration laws and practices, ensuring a high rate of Jewish immigration to Israel and its illegal settlements in the Occupied Palestinian Territories, coupled with ethnic cleansing policies and practices against Palestinians on the one hand, and a high 'natural' Palestinian birth rate on the other.[29] The 'Law of Return', a so-called 'Basic Law' in Israel, which has no constitution, allows any Jew who so wishes to become a citizen of Israel. It is also used to exclude millions of non-Jews from the country and from the territories that the country has captured, especially Palestinians who own land in Israel or the Occupied Palestinian Territories that have been confiscated by Israel (or by Jewish settlers), and to whom compensation is owed by Israel according to international law.[30]

The total fertility rate in the Gaza Strip in 2008 was 5.19 children born to each woman. In the West Bank it was 3.31. Israel had a fertility rate of 2.77 in the same year. All of these are higher than the world average.[31] But the fertility rate of Palestinians with Israeli citizenship, around 20 per cent of Israel's entire population, is almost twice as high as that of Israeli Jews.[32] Like white South Africans, Israeli Jews are barely replacing themselves with offspring, despite the high fertility of many Orthodox families. The increase in the Jewish population of Israel and the Occupied Palestinian Territories is mainly due to immigrants, the vast majority of whom are Jews or become Jews through marriage and/or conversion. Arab immigrants, like the numerous black migrant labourers in Apartheid South Africa, are granted citizenship only in extremely exceptional circumstances, sometimes if they have collaborated with or spied for Israel.

However, the current fertility rates are not as extreme as only a decade and a half ago. Between 1991 and 1995, Gaza's fertility rate was 7.73 children per woman, the highest in the world.[33] Since then, Gazans have been anxiously awaiting and expecting the formation of an independent Palestinian state, which would make demographic competition with Jews superfluous. That is one explanation for the drop by almost a third. Another factor is the increasingly desperate situation in Gaza with regard to health, due to overcrowding as well as the effects of the embargo, closure, siege and the practical imprisonment of the whole Gazan population, along with the recurrent massacres of Gazans by Israel. A third factor is the increasing education and urbanisation of women, which leads to a larger share of women in the workforce and fewer children for that reason.[34]

The demographic competition, or the demographic war, is fought by Israel in very similar, but not identical, ways to those used by Apartheid South Africa. Aside from racist citizenship and immigration policies nearly identical to Israel's, South Africa outlawed interracial marriage and even 'intimacy' between members of different races. Israel has achieved the same results without real state agencies, since only religious marriage is recognised by the state; and religious authorities, whether Jewish, Muslim or Christian, refuse to marry members of different religious communities. This artificial barrier between the racial groups is therefore equivalent to Apartheid South Africa. If reality does not correspond with the apartheid ideal of racial purity, it is so much worse for reality in the apartheid state. Even though it is not a state, the Palestinian National Authority (PNA) has, deplorably, not yet recognised 'mixed' marriage either. It must therefore carry some responsibility, though much less than Israel since the latter is larger, much more powerful and has existed much longer than the PNA, for artificially separating groups that desperately need to engage in peaceful ways with each other, and on equal terms with each other.

Israel has the most racist governmental immigration policy in the world today, basing access to rights and privileges on legislation and policies referring to the 'Law of Return' and the 'Jewish character' of the State of Israel and of all of its most privileged citizens and citizenship applicants. It also spends considerable resources on getting Jews (and other non-Arabs) to immigrate to Israel and to Israeli-occupied territories. This overall policy, which is also supported by influential and wealthy non-governmental agencies and organisations, such as the World Zionist Organization, the World Jewish Congress and several important US lobby groups, is intimately related to the fact that Israel is the only country in the world without internationally declared borders, and it is also the only country in the world that is by (its own) law the home of a racial group, the Jews, rather than the home of its citizens. And so the immigration policy is correlated with Israel's ongoing territorial expansion, its racist state, and a slow but relentless policy of ethnic cleansing, of expulsion and killings of Palestinians, as well as with Palestinian resistance against these policies.[35]

Israel's elites want a higher Jewish fertility rate. For this reason, Israel has the highest relative in vitro fertilisation rate in the world and the largest number of fertilisation clinics per capita in the world, and it is the only state in the world that fully subsidises fertilisation treatment.[36] Moreover, no other country allows wives or life partners to have sperm removed from a deceased man without prior written consent.[37]

The Israel Council for Demography (ICD), which comprises top Israeli gynaecologists, public figures, lawyers, scientists and physicians, seeks to 'encourage the Jewish women of Israel – and only them – to increase their child bearing, a project which, if we judge from the activity of the previous council, will also attempt to stop abortions', according to journalist Gideon Levy. '[M]ethods to increase the Jewish fertility rate and prevent abortions' and 'techniques to encourage abortions and reduce the birthrate among Arab women' were both to be 'at the center of the committee's discussions' in 2002.[38] Another commentator, Will Youmans, remarked that: 'This obsession is binary and inverse: they want more Jews and less Palestinians'. Moreover, the ICD encourages all-Jewish pregnancies by offering tax breaks, 'housing benefits and other government grants', as well as further discouraging mixed marriages (as if they were not already discouraged enough, i.e., made practically impossible, except for some people who marry abroad).[39] Similar to the ICD in its goals is EFRAT, an organisation calling for an end to abortions for Jewish women, and Jewish women alone, in Israel. In 2005, it was an organisation endorsed and supported by the then Israeli president, Moshe Katzav, as well as by the then former prime minister, Benyamin Netanyahu.[40] The apartheid and ethnic cleansing machine that is Israel consists of state as well as non-state actors.

Both the Israeli government and the Ramallah-based nationalist Palestinian In'ash El-Usra Society promised social aid to families with more than ten children during the 1970s. The director and founder of In'ash El-Usra, the late Sameeha Khalil, was jailed by the Israeli army six times in the first quarter century of the organisation's history but she was never charged with any offence. Apparently, she thought that she might have been persecuted because of being related to a Palestinian militant.[41] But her persecution should perhaps be related instead to the demographic war. Israel gave up its similar scheme of prompting and rewarding the Jewish repopulation of Palestine only after its prime minister, Golda Meir, was shocked to find out that Arab families in Israel had been the main beneficiaries of the programme during its pilot phases.[42]

The pressure is on Jewish Israeli women to have children for the (perceived) sake of their race, but they are much better off than their Palestinian counterparts in this regard. They are encouraged, expected and pressured to give birth, but at a much higher average age than Palestinian women are. Whereas Palestinian women are often expected to get married and have children already in their teens, Jewish Israeli women are typically allowed to live their own lives, to educate themselves and embark on professional careers, until that pressure starts making itself felt when the women are already into their thirties. Moreover, unwed or single Jewish Israeli mothers are not stigmatised as are their Palestinian counterparts. Finally, two-thirds of the global Jewish population may still be persuaded, enticed or pressured to become Israeli citizens. Racist immigration laws are much more efficient in Israel than they were in South Africa. And there are many additional non-Arabs who become Jews, too, through conversion. Thus, in terms of this sexist pressure, Jewish Israeli women are usually treated with silk gloves compared with Palestinian women, and even compared with white women in South Africa, who were excluded from most types of higher education and formal employment except secretarial and clerical work and nursing under apartheid. White women were supposed to stay at home and raise ever larger new generations of the master race, and were expected to do so by the apartheid elites.[43]

Rapid and competitive population growth becomes normal in apartheid, causing increasingly severe conflicts over resources and space. Both the people, including the invading settlers, their descendants and the regular immigrants, and the environment suffer tremendously under the strain. But, of course, the people who suffer the most are the indigenous. As with the initial invasion and all subsequent physical violence, the *basic* blame for the population race and its grave consequences must be placed squarely with the oppressive racial minority elites. Azmi Bishara, a Palestinian with Israeli citizenship, summarised the problem in terms of Israeli culpability and Palestinian lack of refusal to be drawn into the demographic war, and, therefore, of (unevenly) shared responsibility for the demographic warfare:

> Some Arabs and Palestinians have internalised the logic of Zionist demographic scare tactics to the extent that they see the slur of 'demographic bomb' [a common and typically dehumanising Israeli reference to unborn Palestinians] as something good. They boast of the Palestinian woman's womb, for lack of anything better to boast. Is this what our unified strategy has come to? Aside from the primitiveness and backwardness of regarding women as wombs the demographic factor is not, in itself, conducive to righteousness. It embraces a racist vision that is not driven towards just solutions. Racism is the basic motive for separation.[44]

Let us keep our concepts well defined, however, in this context. Palestinians, and other populations victimised by apartheid, may be guilty of a separatist vision, and even of racism, against the racial elite. But only the latter are guilty of separate*ness*, of apartheid.

SOLIDARITY WITHIN THE RACIAL ELITE

In an apartheid society, the racialised elite is strongly unified, as opposed to the oppressed, indigenous racialised majority. The only notable exception is the Anglo-Boer War (1899–1902). But it is a qualified exception. The British who fought the Boers were not (yet) South Africans; they were British citizens and British imperialists and colonialists. They were not looking to assume power in the independent Boer republics. They were looking to incorporate these lands into the fast-growing British Empire. In retrospect, it is quite a feat that the two largest groups of whites, armed to the teeth and with seemingly insatiable appetites for privilege and wealth, fought each other only once during nearly three and a half centuries of white domination and rule in South Africa. The parallel assassinations of the South African and Israeli prime ministers, Hendrik Verwoerd (1966) and Yitzhak Rabin (1995), were carried out by very genocidally inclined extremists, who thought apartheid was not anti-indigenous enough.

Aside from these minor exceptions, however, a minority of whites dominated South Africa in solidarity with each other, all the while considering blacks their main enemies. Similarly, during more than sixty years of apartheid in Israel, no serious strife or civil war has erupted between different groups of Jews. They disagree about many things but all the political parties in government are united in opposition to Arabs or Palestinians, whose land they took, and against whom they discriminate vigorously.

DIVIDE AND RULE

Apartheid elites have, on the other hand, engineered deep divisions and even civil wars between groups belonging to the conquered indigenous racial majority. The South African war between African National Congress (ANC) and Inkatha during the early 1990s was the bloodiest conflict within South Africa's borders during apartheid in the narrow sense (1948–94).[45] It was prompted by political difference: at this point in time, the ANC stood for armed resistance against apartheid and liberation of the whole country while Inkatha advocated negotiation and cooperation with the white elites and for achieving Bantustan independence. There was also an ethnic divide: the ANC was led and mainly followed by Xhosa, Inkatha by Zulus. Lastly, the divide was territorial: Xhosaland, divided by the whites into several Bantustans separated by white-held land, was generally pro-ANC, while Zululand (a single political entity, yet geographically divided by the apartheid elites into twenty-nine major and forty-one minor Bantustan fragments) was largely pro-Inkatha.[46] With the aid of the international community, especially with the aid of the USA, Israel has achieved a similar kind of conflict and division between Hamas and Gaza on the one hand, and Fatah and the remaining Palestinian fragments of the West Bank on the other.[47]

But these are engineered conflicts. They may go on for years, but hardly for decades. The oppressed racial groups have far too much in common to go on fighting each other.

The divisive role of sexism is a much more persistent feature in the conflicts between members of the indigenous majority under apartheid conditions. In South Africa, femicide has survived apartheid (and neoliberalism, as the prominent Egyptian feminist Nawal El Saadawi might say[48]). Not only is apartheid a sexist strategy, however; sexism is an apartheid strategy, too.

Israeli secret services pick many Palestinian collaborators out of the Palestinians who otherwise could be outed with real or imagined, shameful, past improprieties, either their own or those of family members.[49] For some time, the Israeli secret government agencies, police and army have been recruiting minors, people twelve to eighteen years old, for collaboration, especially among the thousands of Palestinians it has held and still holds as prisoners.[50] According to Mohammed Al-Haj Yahyah of Hebrew University in Jerusalem, collaborators are also 'recruited outside detention centers, e.g. through jobs in settlements, work in Israel or through other collaborators'. Not all of them are recruited with 'honour'-related extortion. Some are offered money, shortened jail sentences, similar services for family members, and other kinds of incentives. Others are subjected to torture and to other kinds of pressure or threat designed to make Palestinians change sides in the conflict.[51] An additional variety of the military use of Palestinian children by Israel is to force them to serve as human shields for soldiers and for the notorious 'border guards'.[52]

An example of the former, provided by Defence for Children International, a global human rights group, is the case of Iyad, a seventeen-year-old boy from the West Bank city of Ramallah who was shown photographs of his sister in sexual positions with another

Palestinian, a collaborator, by the Israeli authorities. The authorities threatened to 'release the pictures in Ramallah' unless Iyad became a collaborator. He was later arrested by Palestinian security forces while planting a bomb inside a Palestinian activist's car.[53]

Considered together, femicide and political infighting are easily the main crimes of indigenous victim populations in apartheid societies. There are also murders of different degree (i.e., 'first-degree murder' and so on) of the members of apartheid elites, but the numbers of these murders are dwarfed by the numbers of intra-indigenous murders.

Israeli law treats sixteen- and seventeen-year-old Palestinians as adults, although Israeli Jews are still children until they are eighteen years old. It even allows Palestinian twelve-year-olds from the Occupied Palestinian Territories, although they are officially categorised as 'juveniles', to be tried as adults. For example, under Israeli Military Order 378, twelve- to fifteen-year-old Palestinian children may be sentenced to up to ten years in prison:

> for throwing a stone at a stationary object such as the Wall, and twenty years for throwing a stone at a moving vehicle ... Similarly, they are subject to a prison sentence of ten years for participating in a protest march or an unauthorised political meeting in contravention of Military Order No. 101.[54]

The Public Committee Against Torture in Israel has protested against and challenged in court different forms of psychological torture by the Israeli General Security Services (GSS), including:

> the arrest and exploitation of innocent family members of the detainees under interrogation, for the purpose of applying additional pressure to force a confession or obtain information. In some cases the GSS has informed prisoners, either falsely or accurately, that their relatives are also being tortured.[55]

Not only confessions and information, however, are obtained in this manner, but, as we have seen, active and lethal collaboration, too. To sum up: one way in which Israel profits from the 'honour' murder system is in the depiction of Palestinians and Palestinian society as 'primitive' and 'brutish', thus providing an excuse for Israeli un- and anti-democratic military rule and numerous other cruel policies against the subjugated indigenous population. Another, as we have seen, is the use of sensitive information about people's sex lives and the creation of it in order to recruit secret collaborators among Palestinians: that is, as a method of coercion into collaboration. In related ways, the system of 'honour' murders generally serves Israeli divide-and-rule strategies against a potentially overwhelming Palestinian majority of nearly two to every Israeli Jew. This is perhaps its most important use from the strategic Zionist perspective. It splits every Palestinian family, at least potentially, down the middle.

There are also ways in which Israel slashes Palestinian families *across* the middle: that is, into generations. For instance, Palestinians with Israeli citizenship and East Jerusalemites sometimes find themselves prohibited from living at home with their children due to Israeli efforts to de-Arabize the country by means of bureaucracy. Their only way of living with their children then is to emigrate.[56] In addition to fragmenting the Palestinian nation into separated geographic entities – into different religions or different political parties, or into groups with different citizenship status (or none at all) – Israel is systematically splitting up Palestinian families as well, vertically (into sexes) as well as horizontally (into generations).

Moreover, the Israeli apartheid system of oppression and decimation of Palestinians is a root cause of poverty and despair, driving Palestinians into activities such as collaboration, extortion rackets or prostitution. And since this oppression and decimation is carried out with full impunity although it flagrantly violates international law, Israelis have as yet had nothing to lose directly from using the Palestinian 'honour' murder system for its military purposes, especially in order to break Palestinian resistance against Israeli apartheid. The losses in terms of early marriage of Palestinian women and enhanced birth rates is only a long-term potential loss for the Israeli elites, who can and often do revert to other methods of limiting and shrinking the size of the Palestinian population, the relative growth of which may, however, in the end be the prevailing force in the demographic war. Israelis and Israeli agencies using Palestinian femicide for divide-and-rule purposes may at times even be unaware of the disadvantages for the Zionist project, in terms of the demographic war, of encouraging Palestinian femicide.

WHAT TO DO WITH ALL THAT AGGRESSION

White males made sure that black women remained dependent on black male incomes in Apartheid South Africa, because their own meagre incomes could not support their families. This meant that the black males could come home from their demeaning jobs and experiences at the end of the day, or the end of the year for millions of mine and other migrant workers who saw their families only once a year, and dump their aggressions and frustrations on them rather than attempt to overthrow the existing social and political order.[57] Steve Biko described the point as follows:

> transport conditions are appalling, trains are overcrowded all the time, taxis that they use are overcrowded, the whole travelling situation is dangerous, and by the time a guy gets to work he has really been through a mill; he gets to work, there is no peace either at work, his boss sits on him to eke out of him even the last effort in order to boost up production. This is the common experience of the black man. When he gets back from work through the same process of travelling conditions, he can only take out his anger on his family which is the last defence that he has.[58]

Obviously, indigenous men are less likely to rebel – a very desperate measure considering the advanced state of military technology in the hands of the racial elite – if they have someone correspondingly powerless to terrorise in turn. An equivalent end result applies to Palestinians:

> The historical oppression that Palestinians have faced has brought about a community need to protect the inner domain from external infiltration … In addition, the violence of occupation has deprived Palestinian men and women of a safe and secure lifestyle. The more Palestinian men have suffered at the hands of the Israeli occupiers (e.g. beatings, incarceration, humiliation), the more they have been prone to vent their anger and feelings of helplessness and inferiority on women. All these factors have increased the prevalence of femicide.[59]

It is here that a divide-and-rule policy, an indispensable tool in the hands of a dominant and belligerent self-racialised minority, turns out to be most useful and most deleterious to the oppressed, and also racialised, majority. Splitting an oppressed indigenous ethnic majority along geographical, ethnic or political lines may appear in history books as well as in mainstream mass media to be the most significant and important strategy of the invader minority, yet splitting it vertically within every family, within every clan, within every village, surely has a far more profound effect.

CULTURAL IDENTITY AND FEMICIDE

Is the Israeli-Palestinian conflict really secondary? Is patriarchy the real enemy? It is indeed a real enemy of the actual and potential victims of 'honour' murders, but their death toll, though substantial, is dwarfed by the direct Palestinian death toll from the conflict with Israel. And female Palestinian lives would have been saved from femicide if it were not for Israeli apartheid.[60] Israeli apartheid is the main enemy of all Palestinians, and even of all Israeli Jews – some of them more than others, of course. Apartheid is a crime against humanity under international law, it dehumanises people on both sides, and it is a disgrace that it is so intense and so violent in the midst of our international community, which has acted and legislated against it to an extent that can only be matched by action and legislation against genocide, ethnic cleansing, slavery, forced population transfer, torture, human trafficking, arbitrary imprisonment, rape, sexual crimes and forced disappearance, all or almost all of which are currently being suffered, along with apartheid, by Palestinian women. Unfortunately, gendercide is not yet legally a crime against humanity as such.[61]

But isn't there a danger of attacking Palestinian culture, which is itself under an appalling threat of extinction under Israeli apartheid, when one attacks femicide, which is part of Palestinian culture? I do not believe so. Palestinian culture is permeated by solidarity and concern for collective well-being, which are more essential Palestinian values. The reason why Palestinians have not (yet) experienced mass starvation as the blacks in southern Africa did as a result of apartheid warfare is not due to Israel at all. Palestinians will share their last piece of bread if given a chance. Perhaps I am mistaking traditional Arab hospitality for these values, but to me they are central Palestinian values, which I believe *demand* an end to femicide. All cultures contain contradictions, and Palestinian culture, like any other, cannot stop evolving or changing, even if it is under threat of extinction.[62] And, in my opinion, an end to femicide can only be seen as a good development – even more beneficial, for instance, than a reconciliation between Hamas and Fatah.

It is often among Palestinian refugees outside Historic Palestine, refugees who have a right to return home under international law but are prevented from doing so by Israel, that the danger of cultural genocide is greatest. And here we also find staunch resistance to any change in the 'honour' system. Especially in Lebanese refugee camps – where Palestinians are treated worse than anywhere else, except in the Israeli-occupied territories – 'honour' is defended strictly, even by women. In Jordan, Palestinian refugees and their descendants make up the majority of the entire population, and 'honour' murders also take place there.[63]

Israeli apartheid is partly responsible for femicide and for additional social problems far beyond the borders of the apartheid territory itself. Similarly, 'witch' burnings have taken place not only in South Africa but also in Zimbabwe, Congo, Malawi, Tanzania, Kenya and elsewhere in recent history – and still do so today.[64]

Yet Palestinians are not as threatened by cultural genocide as most black South Africans were. The example of language, a central element of culture, shows that Palestinians are in fact relatively lucky in cultural regards. Even if there are some Palestinians in Israel who are losing their Arabic in favour of Hebrew and English, they are still surrounded by hundreds of millions of Arabic speakers in the wider realm.

Linguistic (and physical) genocide took place in South Africa, on the other hand, soon after the whites arrived, when many Khoisan languages became or were made extinct. A handful of survivors of this entire phylum of languages (one of only four indigenous phyla in all of Africa) are still spoken today, but they are all on the verge of disappearing. None of the liberated South Africa's eleven official languages is a Khoisan language.[65]

'Honour' murders are older than both Islam and Christianity, and their removal, one might argue, could threaten the entire Arab culture. Yet slavery is an old tradition, too, and we have legislated against it and prosecuted it all over the world. (But we have not wiped it out, neither in the traditional sense nor as contract or wage slavery nor as human trafficking.) Age alone does not make cultural traits acceptable or desirable. Finally, as Shalhoub-Kevorkian says: '[F]emicide … is not about culture but, rather, is part of a sociopolitical and economic legacy that reflects a hidden machinery of oppression'.[66] That machinery appears in especially destructive forms in apartheid societies. Perhaps there is nowhere that femicide is as destructive as it is under apartheid.

If, indeed, femicide were essentially culture or tradition, it would be much harder to get rid of it than it really is. Femicide is mainly about power and politics. And, of course, it is used as an excuse for others than Israel to extend their power into Arab and Muslim communities today. Shalhoub-Kevorkian continues:

> situating the analyses of women's status in the Arab world within the polarity of preserving the traditional manner versus accepting Western colonized culture not only does not contribute to our understanding of femicide but may also hinder future change. Rather there is a need to ask how we can propose change that challenges oppressive practices and mores while safeguarding those practices that promote female development.[67]

It should be clear to anyone that military occupation, theft of land and racist discrimination are not practices that promote Arab female development.

FEMICIDE AS A CONSEQUENCE OF DE-SECULARISATION IN APARTHEID SOCIETIES

It has been pointed out that the national liberation struggle *paradoxically* led to an increase in femicide in Palestine.[68] It is a paradox since women are part of the struggle as supporters and fighters, and the struggle is essentially about rights, about claiming and receiving equal rights. In a rights-imbued culture, the liberation of women from patriarchy should be part of the liberation of the nation. Women and girls suffer the oppression and exploitation at least as much as men do. They are equal partners in the project of liberation, although there is usually a division of labour, through which most of the battlefield losses are male.[69]

Yet, despite these strong arguments in favour of ending indigenous femicide, its frequency appears to increase with the intensification of the struggle against apartheid.

This apparent paradox can be at least partly explained with de-secularisation as a common trend in apartheid societies. The invaders' culture becomes de-secularised to a large extent because the invaders feel guilty and construct mechanisms of a divine will that allows their crimes to take place. This can be observed both with the Dutch Reformed Church in South Africa and with similar uses by religious Zionists of the same passages of the Bible (among others, Exodus and the Book of Joshua) in favour of ethnic cleansing and genocide of the indigenous (Canaanite) population in what was to become 'their' Promised Land. In the present case of apartheid, this 'Promised Land' was Israel for a short while, then Palestine for a long time, and has now been Israel again for a short while.[70] And if genocide becomes an easier responsibility to bear, then femicide and other kinds of homicide and crimes against humanity do as well.

The indigenous culture becomes de-secularised for a totally different reason: because it finds itself on the verge of suffering cultural (including linguistic) genocide under apartheid. Thus, defence of the home becomes much more than just a territorial defence or defence of natural and human resources. It also becomes a defence of language, religion and other central cultural traditions.[71] Along with the game-theoretical calculation mentioned above, this is another main reason why femicide continues in apartheid and post-apartheid (or epiapartheid) societies such as Palestine–Israel and South Africa respectively. It is hard to make any major changes in Palestinian or even in black South African cultures at present. They are under fire.

But this also becomes an excuse for patriarchal purposes. A more secular culture, especially among perpetrators of apartheid, is likely to bring down the number of femicides, but that is not the important point in this context. Rather, true liberation from apartheid, taking class and gender as well as race into account – that is, true respect for human rights – will end femicide.

HOW TO END FEMICIDE IN SOUTH AFRICA

South Africa's entire education system is still suffering from heavy apartheid legacies, and schools are necessary for nurturing critical thinking, which is necessary to end 'witch' hunts. Economic apartheid, in particular, is still making sure that black children receive inferior education. However, it is not just apartheid that should be blamed. Neoliberal economic structures, which have barely done anything to raise employment levels in the country since liberation, are also ensuring that the poor stay poor and uneducated.[72]

Moreover, apartheid perpetrators have hardly been punished. Only a few lower-level police assassins have been convicted, but none of the apartheid bosses: no police chief, no soldier, no politician, no minister, no businessman, no media mogul has ever been convicted of apartheid. There is still a culture of crime with impunity that has lingered since apartheid. And if you can get away with a crime against humanity in South Africa, without even losing any of your ill-gained riches, then what does that tell the country's lesser criminals, including the perpetrators of femicide? White domination, exploitation, discrimination and violence against blacks in South Africa went on uninterrupted for 350 years. It cost fewer human lives within the country's borders than the Israeli version of apartheid during what I call apartheid in the narrow sense (1948–94), but more lives if one counts the victims of South African-induced wars outside the country during that time, and all of these killings, hundreds of thousands of killings, were carried out with full impunity.[73] South African apartheid was also closer to (and included more) slavery than Palestinian hardship until very late in the game. Nevertheless, compared with the indigenous South Africans, Palestinians have suffered an even greater loss of land (in relative terms) and are facing even more refined methods of torture, limitations on their freedom of movement, entrenched support from the superpowers of the day, media manipulation and control, and upgraded weaponry.[74]

Since apartheid became a crime against humanity only towards the very end of the South African apartheid regime, a condition that changed the international legal context in a positive direction, it is to be hoped that the shortcomings and mistakes of the South African liberation will not be repeated in Israel–Palestine. Apartheid should have been criminalised more in South Africa, and there should be counter-measures to the ravages of neoliberal reforms that are now an added burden in addition to the crime against humanity that is still suffered in numerous ways, mainly by the indigenous population.

HOW TO END FEMICIDE IN PALESTINE AND ISRAEL

Although the formal end to apartheid has yet to yield an end to femicide in South Africa, 'witch' burnings would probably have been a great deal more prevalent if political apartheid were still there. Unfortunately, the same scenario may well materialise in Israel–Palestine: if apartheid ends there, 'honour' murders seem likely to continue, though with less frequency.[75] But the future has not been written. And an end to Israeli apartheid will at least radically bring down the death toll from femicide in Palestine and the Palestinian diaspora, as has been the case with South Africa. A consistent human rights policy, more consistent than in South Africa, may even end femicide along with apartheid in Israel–Palestine. At least, international law has developed far beyond the situation in 1994. Since then, both apartheid and femicide have become crimes that are more difficult to defend.

Yet, Israel has made sure that human rights have never become an agenda item, let alone a priority, in Israeli–Palestinian negotiations, unless, of course, the rights of Israeli Jews alone are involved. And the Palestine Liberation Organization (PLO) has acquiesced with this disastrous process.[76] However, it must be added that negotiations have been on terms and conditions that have mostly been determined and set by Israel from the very outset. Israel has argued from a position of political, military, diplomatic and economic strength at each stage of negotiations. Avi Shlaim, the Israeli historian, has shown that military strength has been, and still is, the linchpin of any Israeli negotiations with Arabs. This is the infamous Israeli 'Iron Wall' doctrine. Israel has either waged war with Arabs, including Palestinians, or negotiated from a position of military strength.[77] Only Israel, therefore, has really been able to make inclusive human rights – the rights of Palestinians as well as of Jews, and of women as well as of men – a priority or even an agenda item in negotiations, and it has chosen, very consciously, not to do so.

It should also be borne in mind that there are pseudo-solutions to the problems investigated here, which may appear to improve the situation but in fact create new problems or end up being counterproductive. Legally limiting the number of children allowed in a family, as in overpopulated present-day China, is simply an instance of barking up the wrong tree. Women have reproductive rights, and they are basic human rights. Although Gaza is even more densely populated than (all of) China, if a Gazan woman really wants seven children, then having them must be up to her, and not the decision of any man or any group of men or other women. To let Palestinian refugees 'return' only to areas presently under PNA rule is another pseudo-solution. These Bantustans are already overcrowded and they have unacceptably high unemployment rates, like the former South African Bantustans today. Most of the refugees or their immediate ancestors were driven out of what is today Israel and therefore that is the only place to which they can return in the true sense of the word, and to which they must be allowed to return with dignity – and not only because of international law, which demands the Palestinian right of return (UN General Assembly Resolution 194). With any other ultimate destination than anywhere in Historic Palestine, rather than just 10 per cent of it, the use of the word 'return' would be hypocrisy. Playing down Israeli responsibilities in order to direct all blame to Palestinian families and the PNA to end femicide is yet another pseudo-solution. But so is the opposite 'strategy': to play down Palestinian responsibilities. Therefore, I do not see any priority among the various levels of responsibility for Palestinian femicide. This may seem a pessimistic conclusion, as there is seemingly no simple solution. There is no logical or practical single place in which to start attacking Palestinian femicide. But, at least, there is a solution. It is known as human rights.

Furthermore, attacking apartheid – a crime against humanity that involves grave violations of most human rights – is going to be beneficial in the struggle against femicide, especially if it is a balanced attack that takes into consideration all kinds of human rights violations as parts of the problem. It is here that boycotts, divestment and sanctions against Israel and its supporters can and do play eminent, if not decisive, roles in the liberation from apartheid, as they did in South Africa, and also in ending the demographic war, and therefore possibly also in ending femicide.[78] An intensification of the armed struggle, on the other hand, may lead to an increase in femicide, as it did in South Africa during the last two decades of the struggle against apartheid there. But this is not necessarily the case. There is no iron law of history that determines that a single further instance of femicide, viricide or any other form of homicide has to take place, whether within or across the two sides of the apartheid divide. A rights-imbued culture has yet to dominate the Israeli–Palestinian context, but it certainly does not lie outside the realm of the possible. That is why the overall comparison with the South African context is so inspiring, as Desmond Tutu has argued.[79]

CONCLUSION

Femicide under apartheid, for example the 'witch' burnings in South Africa or the 'honour' murders in Israel–Palestine, are symptoms and responsibilities of indigenous patriarchies. But, in both cases, they are severely exacerbated by the demographic warfare that is initiated and by the racism, oppression, divide-and-rule strategies and torture techniques that are legalised and implemented by the invading racial minority elites and their racial minority elite descendants. Therefore, some of the responsibility must be placed with these apartheid elites.

Indigenous women and girls are at the bottom of the apartheid ladder of violence. In Apartheid South Africa, housekeepers, cleaners, domestic servants and nannies were some of the most used, abused and exploited professionals.[80] Domestic workers, most of them black and female, normally had to face oppression, violence and humiliation from white men, *and* white women, *and* black men, sometimes on a daily basis. But let us never forget the remaining agency in indigenous women suffering under apartheid. Miriam Makeba, herself a former domestic worker, Winnie Madikizela-Mandela and countless other women, even some white and Jewish women (such as Marion Sparg and Ruth First), played key roles in bringing down South African apartheid and in establishing a human rights culture and constitution in its place. Liberation, in fact, would not have come about without the agency of indigenous women. The same will be true of Palestinian women with regard to Israeli apartheid, with figures such as Nadera Shalhoub-Kevorkian and Fadwa Tuqan, to name just two. They are, so far, also among the many unsung heroes of the struggle. There will be Jewish women with them too,[81] but not enough, not for a while yet.

Notes

1   I would like to thank Alana Kazykhan, Kim Cooper, Kawther Salam, Benjamin Fasching-Grey, Husam Madhoun, Patricia Löwstedt, Ilan Pappé, Dima Khalidi, Natasha Khalidi, Caitlin Spencer Martinez, Judith Forshaw, Ramalakshmi Lakshmanan and Andra Goran for research assistance and helpful comments on various drafts of this paper, which is dedicated to the memory of Sibusiso Mazibuko, and to his family, Morongoa Machete, and their son, Kagiso.

2   A recent example is the Srebrenica massacre in Bosnia in 1995, when
    Bosnian Serb army and militia units murdered an estimated 7,000 to 10,000
    Bosnian Muslim male captives, aged twelve to seventy-seven, while a similar
    number of female captives were spared. See Adam Jones, 'Case Study: The
    Srebrenica Massacre, July 1995', Gendercide Watch: www.gendercide.org/
    case_srebrenica.html. In South Africa, six times more men than women
    were killed during the period investigated by the Truth and Reconciliation
    Commission, 1960–94. Aside from being the main victims of armed group
    conflict, males are also the main victims of corporal punishment, and of
    violent crimes against individuals resulting in serious physical injury and/
    or death. Men are more likely to be the victims of many further forms of
    violence, including some forms of ostracism, at least sometimes instigated
    by women. In particular, the failure to 'live up' to male stereotypes, such as
    refusing to fight or do military service, is often punished harshly, sometimes
    with death. Legal punishment of perpetrators of sexual assault is actually
    more severe if the victim is female than male under most jurisdictions today.
    The crime is also often more likely to remain unreported if the victim is a
    boy and not a girl. See David Benatar, 'The Second Sexism', *Social Theory
    and Practice* 29(2) (April 2003). Patriarchy victimises both women and men;
    nevertheless, in my view, female human beings are the main victims of
    sexism. Although they have a longer life expectancy than males, the content
    of that life is still often essentially one of discrimination and subservience.
    In feudal society, the landlords were supposed to defend the land with their
    lives, while living through most of their days off the labour of others. It was
    not all that different from the lots of men and women today.

3   Jill Radford and Diana E. H. Russell, *Femicide: The Politics of Woman Killing*,
    New York: Twayne Publishers, 1992; Diana E. H. Russell and Roberta
    Harmes (eds), *Femicide in Global Perspective*, New York: Teachers College
    Press, 2001; Gendercide Watch: www.gendercide.org.

4   Hazem Jamjoum, 'Not an Analogy: Israel and the Crime of Apartheid',
    Electronic Intifada, 3 April 2009: http://electronicintifada.net/v2/article10440.
    shtml; Ben White, *Israeli Apartheid: A Beginner's Guide*, London: Pluto,
    2009; Edward S. Herman, 'Israeli Apartheid and Terrorism', *ZMag*, May
    1994, republished in *Al-Bushra*: www.al-bushra.org/apartheid/herman.
    html; Flore de Préneuf, 'Israel's Apartheid: 1, 2, 3', *Al-Bushra*, 3 November
    2000: www.al-bushra.org/apartheid/apartheid1.htm; Ilan Pappé, *The Ethnic
    Cleansing of Palestine*, Oxford: Oneworld, 2006; Adam Jones, *Crimes against
    Humanity: A Beginner's Guide*, Oxford: Oneworld, 2008, pp. 143 ff. A more
    detailed definition of apartheid is proposed in Chapter I.7 in Anthony

Löwstedt, *Apartheid – Ancient, Past and Present: Gross Racist Human Rights Violations in Graeco-Roman Egypt, South Africa, and Israel–Palestine*, Vienna: Gesellschaft für Phänomenologie und kritische Anthropologie, 2014, pp. 98–103: http://gesphka.files.wordpress.com/2014/09/apartheid-2014.pdf. For reasons of brevity I am not including it in this chapter.

5   Steve Biko, *I Write What I Like: A Selection of His Writings*, Johannesburg: Picador Africa, 2004 (1978), p. 20; Leonard Thompson, *A History of South Africa*, New Haven: Yale University Press, 1990, p. 135; Anonymous, 'Palestine: "femicide" on the rise', InfoSud Human Rights Tribune, 8 March 2007: www.infosud.org/Palestine-Femicide-on-the-rise,1240; Ronnie Kasrils, 'Who Said Nearly 50 Years Ago That Israel Was an Apartheid State?', *Links: International Journal of Socialist Renewal*, 17 March 2009: http://links.org. au/node/960; Avi Shlaim, *The Iron Wall: Israel and the Arab World*, London: Penguin, 2001 (2000), pp. 4 ff. Not all femicide in apartheid is indigenous. For example, the rape and murder of Palestinian women by Jews took place in the war of 1948–49 but seems to have subsided since then. See Pappé, *The Ethnic Cleansing of Palestine*, pp. 208–11; Ari Shavit, 'Survival of the Fittest? An Interview with Benny Morris', *CounterPunch*, 16 January 2004: www. counterpunch.org/shavit01162004.html. Rape-murder and other kinds of violence against black women by white men took place throughout the era of white supremacist rule in South Africa, and have continued since, although there has been a lesser degree of impunity following the end of apartheid. See Rashida Manjoo, *The South African Truth and Reconciliation Commission: A Model for Gender Justice?*, draft document, Geneva: United Nations Research Institute for Social Development, 2004: www.unrisd. org/unrisd/website/document.nsf/ab82a6805797760f80256b4f005da1ab/ f2177ff8c83e0bb4c125723400591907/$FILE/Manjoo.pdf.

6   An additional kind of revolutionary change prompted by population growth of the oppressed indigenous majority was the economic need to offer higher education to South African blacks from the 1970s onwards. As the white population dwindled, blacks were increasingly needed in managerial and skilled occupations in the capitalist industrialist economy. Such jobs had been monopolised by whites before, but now universities had to be built for blacks since they had not been allowed to study at universities (with a few exceptions) up to this point. So, during the 1970s and 1980s, universities for blacks were built, but built to be worse than universities for whites. The racially segregated system of education showed once more how costly apartheid is compared with other social systems. However, the new economic situation also led to more interaction between blacks and whites

at work, and may thus have contributed to the relatively peaceful resolution of South Africa's apartheid problem. See John Iliffe, *Africans: The History of a Continent*, Cambridge: Cambridge University Press, 1995, pp. 281 f.; John Reader, *Africa: A Biography of the Continent*, London: Penguin, 1998 (1997), p. 674. At present there are no such openings to dependencies between Jews and Arabs in Israel–Palestine. Israel has not disengaged from Gaza, as it claims, but it has largely disengaged from Palestinian labour, although the current import of globalisation migrants from all over the world is much costlier to the Israeli economy than a docile Palestinian underclass would be. See Löwstedt, *Apartheid – Ancient, Past and Present*, Chapter II.5.3.

7   Iliffe, *Africans*, p. 271. According to Iliffe, the most basic 'underlying historical process' from 1886 (the discovery of gold in the Witwatersrand, which initiated rapid industrialisation) until the end of apartheid in South Africa a century later was demographic growth. During that time, the country's total population grew from about 3 or 4 million to 39 million. (Palestine–Israel's population has also increased roughly tenfold in the last century, which is two and a half times higher than the average global population growth.) At the 'root' of the many factors that contributed to the downfall of white political supremacy, he writes, was population growth. By this he means both overall growth and the equally dramatic relative growth and decline of the black and white racial groups respectively. The white population share shrank from 21 per cent of the entire South African population in 1951 to 13.7 per cent in 1995, and then further to under 10 per cent today. I believe, however, that Iliffe makes too much of demographic change. In my opinion, domestic and foreign resistance to South African apartheid should also be considered as important factors.

8   On Israel's massive, systematic, diversified, continuous, methodical, sometimes robotic, collective punishment against Palestinians, see Juliana Fredman, 'Collective punishment on the West Bank: dialysis, checkpoints and a Palestinian Madonna', *CounterPunch*, 26 August 2003: www.counterpunch.org/fredman08262003.html; Alain Gresh, 'War Crimes: Israel's Offensive against Peace', *Le Monde Diplomatique*, July 2006: http://mondediplo.com/2006/06/19palestine; Ali Abunimah, 'The Vigilante State: Collective Punishment and Collective Impunity in Israel', *Palestine Center Information Brief No. 164*, 18 July 2008: www.thejerusalemfund.org/ht/display/ContentDetails/i/2247/pid/2254. On sporadic collective punishment of Israelis by Palestinians, see Bradley Burston, 'The Qassam as Ccollective Punishment', *Ha'aretz*, 25 January 2008: www.haaretz.com/the-qassam-as-collective-punishment-1.237931.

9 See Robert Ross, *A Concise History of South Africa*, Cambridge: Cambridge University Press, 1999, pp. 144 ff. In this chapter, entitled 'The Costs of Apartheid', Ross goes into some detail with regard to the damage, for example about how previously lush and agriculturally valuable areas, especially in the Bantustans, have been turned into treeless near-deserts due to the South African elites' apartheid policies. But he does not explore the causal factors in much detail and does not mention the competitive demographic growth unique to apartheid, i.e., he does not appear to consider demographic warfare a factor in environmental deterioration.

10 Löwstedt, *Apartheid – Ancient, Past and Present*, Chapters I.1.2, I.1.3

11 In February 2009, the death toll resulting directly from that 'Gaza War' was 1,440 Palestinians, mostly civilians, according to Palestinian medical sources, and thirteen Israelis (three civilians and ten soldiers), some of whom were killed by 'friendly' (Israeli) fire. Liz O'Neill, 'Catholic Relief Services to Aid 28,000 in Gaza and the West Bank', Catholic Relief Services, 19 February 2009, Reuters Alertnet: www.crs.org/newsroom/releases/release.cfm?id=1664. Israel put the Palestinian death toll at 1,300 but apparently ignores those who died from their wounds after the ceasefire. See Ethan Bronner, 'Soldiers' Accounts of Gaza Killings Raise Furor in Israel', *New York Times*, 20 March 2009. In the Gaza War of 2014, death statistics were more balanced, but not much – 2,205 Palestinians against seventy-one Israelis and one foreign national. See UN Office for the Coordination of Humanitarian Affairs (OCHA), 'Gaza Crisis: Facts and Figures', 15 October 2014: www.ochaopt.org/content.aspx?id=1010361.

12 Tlou Makhura, 'Missionary and African Perspectives on the Politics of Witchcraft among the Xhosa and Zulu Communities in the 19th century Cape and Natal/Zululand', draft paper, Wits Interdisciplinary Research Seminar, 15 September 2003.

13 Johannes Harnischfeger, 'Witchcraft and the State in South Africa', paper presented at 'Afrocentrism and Eurocentrism on the eve of the 21st Century: African Studies in a World Context', International Conference in Celebration of the 70th Birthday of Professor A. B. Davidson, Moscow, 2000: www.africana.ru/biblio/afrocentrism/12_Harnischfeger.htm.

14 Nancy Scheper-Hughes, 'Children without Childhoods', *New Internationalist*, March 1995: www.newint.org/issue265/children.htm. In some cases, 'witch' burnings were prepared or accompanied with *toyi-toyi*, in other circumstances an expressive and moving war dance and a masterpiece of non-violent intimidation that was also used in confrontations with the 'system', i.e., with the white police and army forces. See Bill Keller, 'Apartheid's Grisly

Aftermath: "Witch Burning"', *New York Times*, 18 September 1994. Similarly, the 'honour' murder by Hamas militants of the Palestinian girl Yusra Al Azami in her fiancé's car at a Gaza beach on 10 April 2005, with the official Hamas justification of 'moral reasons and the fight against corruption', was a planned action by the militant group. Many gunmen were in the Hamas car, as if it were a militant operation against Israelis or collaborators. Khaled Al Haroub, 'The Murder of a Girl Due to Moral Reasons', *Al Hayat*, 28 April 2005, republished in *Miftah*, 29 April 2005: www.miftah.org/Display. cfm?DocId=7313&CategoryId=5.

15   Hallie Ludsin, 'What South Africa's Treatment of Witchcraft Says for the Future of Its Customary Law', *Berkeley Journal of International Law* 21 (2003), pp. 62–110.

16   Nadera Shalhoub-Kevorkian, 'Re-Examining Femicide: Breaking the Silence and Crossing "Scientific" Borders', *Journal of Women in Culture and Society* 28(2) (2002), p. 583; Nadera Shalhoub-Kevorkian, 'Femicide and the Palestinian Criminal Justice System: Seeds of Change in the Context of State Building?', *Law & Society Review* 36 (2002), p. 587 (quote).

17   Shalhoub-Kevorkian, 'Femicide and the Palestinian Criminal Justice System', p. 588. Jordanian law allows for such lenient treatment of murderers if 'honour' is involved, and Jordanian law is applied by the Palestinian National Authority. (Jordan ruled the West Bank from 1948 to 1967.)

18   Adam Jones, 'Case Study: "Honour" Killings and Blood Feuds', Gendercide Watch, 20 January 2008: www.gendercide.org/case_honour.html.

19   Kawther Salam, 'Who Won Gaza: Dahlan-US-Israel or Hamas?', *The Daily Life of Kawther Salam*, 18 June 2007: www.kawther.info/K20070618A.html. See also Anonymous, 'Palestine: "Femicide" on the Rise'.

20   Catherine Warrick, 'The Vanishing Victim: Criminal Law and Gender in Jordan', *Law & Society Review* 39(2) (June 2005), p. 322.

21   The woman's own family was destroyed by the incident that took place in 1990. See Adam Jones, 'Case Study: The European Witch-Hunts, *c.* 1450–1750, and Witch-Hunts Today', Gendercide Watch: www.gendercide.org/case_witchhunts.html.

22   Shalhoub-Kevorkian, 'Femicide and the Palestinian Criminal Justice System', pp. 577 ff.; Anonymous, 'Honor Killing: Killing of Women on the Basis of Family Honor', *Palestinian Human Rights Monitor* 6(4) (August 2002): www.mefacts.com/cached.asp?x_id=11685; Donald Macintyre, 'Hamas Admits Its Gunmen Shot Betrothed Woman in "Honour Killing"', *Independent*, 13 April 2005; Soraya Sarhaddi Nelson, 'Mother Kills Raped Daughter to Restore "Honor"', Knight Ridder Newspapers, 17 November 2003.

23 Shalhoub-Kevorkian, 'Re-Examining Femicide', p. 590. On orientalism, see
    Edward W. Said, *Orientalism*, New York: Vintage, 1979 (1978); Ziauddin
    Sardar, *Orientalism*, Buckingham and Philadelphia: Open University Press,
    1999.
24 Jan Assmann, *Ma'at, Gerechtigkeit und Unsterblichkeit im Alten Ägypten*,
    Munich: Beck, 1995 (1990), pp. 92–121, 245–51; Jan Assmann, *Stein und
    Zeit, Mensch und Gesellschaft im alten Ägypten*, Munich: Fink, 1991, p. 177.
    Sociologist Pierre Bourdieu wrote: 'The ethos of honour is fundamentally
    opposed to a universal and formal morality which affirms the equality in
    dignity of all men and consequently the equality of their rights and duties.
    Not only do the rules imposed upon men differ from those imposed upon
    women, and the duties towards men differ from those towards women, but
    also the dictates of honour, directly applied to the individual case and varying
    according to the situation, are in no way capable of being made universal'
    ('The Sentiment of Honour in Kabyle Society', translated by Philip Sherrard,
    in John G. Peristiany (ed.), *Honour and Shame: The values of Mediterranean
    Society*, London: Weidenfeld & Nicolson, 1966, pp. 191–241; quoted in James
    Bowman, *Honor: A History*, New York: Encounter Books, 2006, p. 15). But
    an essence of respect and loyalty can often be found in honour, and that is
    what, in my opinion, must not disappear from what is left of the honour
    culture, which has in fact been the norm in human history. The honour
    culture is still active in most of the world, but it is now being challenged
    dramatically by egalitarian movements, especially with regard to rights, but
    also with regard to the whole concept of honour. According to Bowman,
    Honor, p. 309, these movements also include 'fantasies' such as 'Hollywood's
    international liberalism [which] can imagine no revival of heroism on behalf
    of any less inclusive entity than humanity itself'. Bowman, who mainly
    wants national honour (patriotism), military honour and chivalry revitalised,
    in order to protect (US) men and women against terrorists as well as urban
    gang culture (pp. 322 f.), believes a 'new inequality' is necessary to revive
    honour (pp. 311 ff.), one that is based on more respect for politicians, judges
    and soldiers (p. 314) but, apparently, one that is preferably without women
    in the roles of secretary of state or defence (pp. 321 f.). I disagree, and I find
    it puzzling that anti-feminist and right-wing Westerners claim women's
    rights as their own domain and achievement. Honour is perhaps tied to
    meritocratic society, but it can still be based on respect and loyalty instead of
    military honour and patriotism, so that vertical and horizontal solidarity may
    still harmonise, on global as well as local scales. And, on the global scale, I
    believe, the most chivalrous thing men can do for women is simply to accept

and respect them as human beings with equal rights.

25 Jones, 'Case Study: "Honour" Killings and Blood Feuds'. Women are also
substantially involved in other forms of femicide, such as female genital
mutilation. It should be added that it is also civil society's, as well as the state
authorities', responsibility to tackle the problem with additional preventive
measures and to provide more and better protection for victims. See
Anushree Tripathi and Supriya Yadav, 'For the Sake of Honour: But Whose
Honour? "Honour Crimes" against Women', *Asia-Pacific Journal* 2 (2004),
pp. 76 f.

26 Iliffe remarks on the dramatic relative demographic change: 'The change took
place despite white immigration and feverish official attempts to encourage
large families among whites and contraception among Africans [blacks] –
in 1991 South Africa had twice as many family planning clinics as health
clinics' (Iliffe, *Africans*, p. 281). As late as 1978, there was only one medical
doctor per 44,000 blacks but one per 400 whites. With this as a measure,
the racially segregated healthcare for whites was 110 times better than that for
blacks. In direct correlation with this, the infant mortality rate at the time
was 2.7 per cent for whites, 20 per cent for urban blacks and a staggering
40 per cent for rural blacks. Nearly one in two rural black South African
babies thus died at birth or soon afterwards. (More recently, Afghanistan
had the highest infant mortality rate in the world, more than a quarter –
257 out of 1,000 – of babies born alive did not survive long. See Stephanie
Nebehay, 'Afghanistan Is World's Worst Place to Be Born: UN', Reuters,
20 November 2009.) A quarter of all black infants who survived birth in
Apartheid South Africa, moreover, suffered malnutrition or stunted growth.
After giving birth in hospitals, black women were routinely discharged
immediately, on the same day or the same night, and forced to take the next
bus home, sometimes in the middle of the night, and sometimes even if
there were no buses at all. Furthermore, 'Black women were injected with
the controversial contraceptive Depo Provera, often without their consent,
counseling, or being given another birth control option. White women
weren't even told about Depo Provera. Factories coerced black women to be
injected' (Anonymous, *Human Rights and Health: The Legacy of Apartheid:
Patterns of Human Rights Violations*, Washington, DC: American Association
for the Advancement of Science, 1998; see also Anonymous, 'S. African Truth
Hearings Inspire Poverty Hearings', Reuters, 4 March 1998). This was not
random violence, or due to personal racism. Indigenous women and their
children were intentionally targeted by the oppressive racial minority as
obstacles to the repopulation and socio-economic policies of the apartheid

elites. It was systematic violence, perpetrated by the state, the 'public' servants and 'civil' society, all of them partners in crime. That, and some of the democratic trappings of Apartheid South Africa (elections and freedom of expression, though only for whites) and of Israel (elections and freedom of expression, though only for racially, demographically and historically filtered citizens) is why I prefer to analyse apartheid societies rather than apartheid states.

27 Harnischfeger, 'Witchcraft and the State in South Africa'. See also Ross, *A Concise History of South Africa*, pp. 175 ff.
28 Harnischfeger, 'Witchcraft and the state in South Africa'.
29 Janet Abu-Lughod, 'The Demographic War for Palestine', *The Link* 19(5) (December 1986), republished in *Americans for Middle East Understanding* (AMEU): www.ameu.org/The-Link/Archives/The-Demographic-War-for-Palestine.aspx; Rhoda Ann Kanaaneh, *Birthing the Nation: Strategies of Palestinian Women in Israel*, California Series in Public Anthropology 2, Berkeley and Los Angeles: University of California Press, 2002. Abu-Lughod points out that Israeli Jews in particular, but also Palestinians, have used violence to change demographics and to encourage members of the other race to leave the country and (for Palestinians) to stop further invasion and immigration of Jews by this means of intimidation. The mainstream strategy of Palestinians, however, remains the one of appeal to international law and to the moral fibre of the global community, and of implementing 'soft' pressure, i.e., boycotts, divestment and sanctions (see note 78 below). Palestinian resistance thus remains overwhelmingly non-violent, although this has so far proven to be very costly and of very little benefit to the Palestinians.
30 Although a democratic constitution, 'guaranteeing all persons equal and non-discriminatory rights in civil, political, economic and religious matters and the enjoyment of human rights and fundamental freedoms' (UN Plan of Partition, Article 10) was a prerequisite, UN General Assembly Resolution 181 (II), for international recognition of Israel after its foundation over six decades ago, Israel has so far rather arrogantly refused to come up with any constitution at all. See Uri Davis, *Apartheid Israel: Possibilities for the struggle Within*, London: Zed Books, 2003, pp. 65 ff.
31 Central Intelligence Agency (USA), 'The World Factbook', February 2009: www.cia.gov/library/publications/download/download-2009/. Caution: this is the website of an official US spy agency and a warfare unit of the greatest military machine the world has ever seen (or not seen), which should be consulted with particular scepticism since the USA has and has

had many stakes in keeping alive both apartheid and genocidal societies, including itself, throughout its history. On US aid for the South African apartheid regime, see Peter Kornbluh (ed.), *Conflicting Missions: Secret Cuban Documents On History of Africa Involvement*, National Security Archive Electronic Briefing Book No. 67, Washington, DC: George Washington University, 2002: www.gwu.edu/~nsarchiv/NSAEBB/NSAEBB67/; Howard H. French, 'How America helped Savimbi and Apartheid South Africa', *New African*, June 2002, p. 7 (first published in *New York Times*, 1 April 2002); William Blum, 'The Men Who Sent Mandela to Jail', *New African*, October 2002; William Blum, 'Voting for Apartheid at the UN', *New African*, February 2003. On US aid for Israel, unparalleled in the history of bilateral aid, see John J. Mearsheimer and Stephen M. Walt, *The Israel Lobby and U.S. Foreign Policy*, New York: Farrar, Straus & Giroux, 2007. I have, unfortunately, been unable to corroborate the CIA's demographic figures.

32 Davis, *Apartheid Israel*, p. 211.

33 Philippe Fargues, 'Fertility as a Weapon in the Palestinian–Israeli Conflict', Population Council news release, 26 October 2000, on Philippe Fargues, 'Protracted National Conflict and Fertility Change: Palestinians and Israelis in the twentieth century', *Population and Development Review* 26(3) (September 2000), pp. 441–82: www.jstor.org/discover/10.2307/172315?sid=21105695838761&uid=2&uid=3737528&uid=4. The highest rate in the world in 2008 was in Mali, with 7.34 births per woman, i.e., lower than Gaza's birth rate thirteen years earlier. See Central Intelligence Agency (USA), 'The World Factbook: Rank Order – Total Fertility Rate', 17 February 2009: www.cia.gov/library/publications/download/download-2009/ (see also note 31 above).

34 Abdullah Khayat, 'A Problem for Palestine: Gaza's Birthrate highest in Middle East', *Washington Report on Middle East Affairs*, January 1994: www.wrmea.org/1994-january/demographics-a-problem-for-palestine-gaza-s-birthrate-highest-in-middle-east.html.

35 See Davis, *Apartheid Israel*, pp. 62 f., 91–108; and, for example, David Landy, '90 Inca Israeli-Jews: Recruiting for the Demographic War', *Race and Class*, April 2003. Yossi Alpher, an Israeli intellectual and former adviser to Ehud Barak, the former Israeli prime minister, has pointed out that most Israelis now prefer 'demographic solutions' to the Israeli–Palestinian conflict – including forced expulsions of Palestinians and the creation of isolated Palestinian Bantustans – to 'geographic solutions', i.e., to continued Israeli territorial expansion with different degrees of incorporation of conquered populations. This marks a departure from earlier predominant modes of

strategic apartheid thought in Israel, in which the two kinds of 'solution' were more often seen as mutually reinforcing each other. It also means that the demographic aspect of the Israeli–Palestinian conflict is gaining in importance and urgency, even in comparison with the conventional armed conflict. See Yossi Alpher, 'Demography Tops Territory in New Strategic Calculus', *Forward*, 7 January 2005. On ethnic cleansing, see Pappé, *The Ethnic Cleansing of Palestine*; Gideon Levy, 'Erasing the Past in Israel', *Ha'aretz*, 5 June 2005, republished in *Miftah*, 6 June 2005: www.miftah.org/Display.cfm?DocId=7626&CategoryId=5. On the power of Zionist lobby groups, especially the American Israel Public Action Committee (AIPAC), see M. Shahid Alam, 'Israel's Proxy War?', Media Monitors Network, 19 February 2003: www.mediamonitors.net/mshahidalam1.html. According to Alam, Israel instigated a proxy apartheid war against Arab nationalism in Iraq, which is not fought by Israeli soldiers at all. If true, or to the extent that it is claimed to be true, it is a kind of war that has been waged only by global superpowers until now. Perhaps a country that is one of the top five nuclear weapons powers (Anonymous, 'Factbox: Facts and Fears on Israel's Suspected Nuclear Arms', Reuters, 4 July 2004), the biggest recipient of bilateral aid ever (Joel Kovel, *Overcoming Zionism: Creating a Single Democratic State in Israel–Palestine*, London: Pluto, 2007, p. 131), and one of the top four arms dealers in the world (Naomi Klein, *The Shock Doctrine: The Rise of Disaster Capitalism*, London: Penguin, 2008 (2007), p. 436) should be called a global superpower, although in both size and population it is smaller than Hong Kong. On the current Iraq War as a proxy war by Israel and the Israel lobby in the USA, see also Mearsheimer and Walt, *The Israel Lobby and U.S. Foreign Policy*, pp. 229 ff.

36 Susan Martha Kahn, *Reproducing Jews: A Cultural Account of Assisted Conception in Israel*, Durham: Duke University Press, 2000. (Incidentally, the preferred sperm donors in Israel are Aryan-looking or Ashkenazy, blue-eyed men.) In a thoughtful review of this book, the reviewer, Galina Vromen, describes four factors commonly held responsible for Israel leading the world statistics in these matters: 'the belief held by rabbis that children born to unmarried women are considered legitimate and full Jews; the common perception among both religious and secular Jews in Israel that it is worse to be childless than to be a single mother; the social and financial support the country gives to single-parent families; and – least discussed but certainly not the least important – the fear that the Jews will be vastly outnumbered by Arabs as reflected in demographic trends'. One could easily draw the conclusion that the last factor is in fact the most important one, and,

moreover, that the reviewer would agree with this judgement. See Galina Vromen, 'Pro-Natal, Par Excellence', *Ha'aretz*, 20 July 2001: www.haaretz. com/culture/books/pro-natal-par-excellence-1.64584.

37 Anonymous, 'Israel to Let Wives Harvest Dead Husbands' Sperm', Reuters, 13 November 2003.

38 Gideon Levy, 'Wombs in the Service of the State', *Ha'aretz*, 9 September 2002: www.haaretz.com/print-edition/opinion/wombs-in-the-service-of-the-state-1.34696, quoted in Omar Barghouti, 'On Refugees, Creativity and Ethics: Commemorating the Second Anniversary of the Intifada', *ZNet*, 28 September 2002: http://zcomm.org/znetarticle/on-refugees-creativity-and-ethics-by-omar-barghouti.

39 Will Youmans, 'Understanding the Existential Threat: Israel's Demographic Obsession', *CounterPunch*, 7 December 2002: www.counterpunch.org/youmans1207.html.

40 Nigel Parry, 'Haaretz.com Runs Ad Discouraging Jewish Abortions as "Only Solution" to Arab Population Growth', *Electronic Intifada*, 7 December 2005: http://electronicintifada.net/v2/article4333.shtml.

41 Elizabeth W. Fernea, *In Search of Islamic Feminism: One Woman's Global Journey*, New York: Doubleday, 1998, p. 353. In'ash El-Usra today provides assistance to orphans, political prisoners, needy children and students as well as providing a kindergarten and a day-care centre (see www.inash.org).

42 Salim Tamari, 'Demographic Nationalism: False Assumptions and Inevitable Truths', *Bitter Lemons*, 4 July 2005: www.bitterlemons.org/previous/bl040705ed23.html#pal2.

43 Sisonke Msimang, 'Affirmative Action in the New South Africa: The Politics Of Representation, Law and Equity', *Women in Action* 1–2 (2000), republished in *Isis International*: www.isiswomen.org/index. php?option=com_content&view=article&id=612:affirmative-action-in-the-new-south-africa-the-politics-of-representation-law-and-equity&catid=129&Itemid=452; Kahn, *Reproducing Jews*; Vromen, 'Pro-natal, par excellence'.

44 Azmi Bishara, 'A Short History of Apartheid', *Arabic Media Internet Network*, 8 January 2004, republished in *If Americans Knew*: www.ifamericansknew. org/cur_sit/apartheid.html. See also Shalhoub-Kevorkian, 'Re-Examining Femicide'; Ghassan Khatib, 'Demography Negates Democracy', *Bitter Lemons*, 4 July 2005, republished in *Miftah*, 5 July 2005: www.miftah.org/ Display.cfm?DocId=7860&CategoryId=5. The same (mild) accusation of racism should be directed at the indigenous patriarchal South African elites who contributed considerably to the demographic explosion in South Africa.

45 Nelson Mandela, *Long Walk to Freedom: The Autobiography of Nelson*

Mandela, Boston: Back Bay Books and Little, Brown and Company, 1995 (1994), pp. 587 ff.

46 Leonard Thompson, *A History of South Africa*, New Haven: Yale University Press, 1990, pp. 191 ff.; Alan Lester, *From Colonization to Democracy: A New Historical Geography of South Africa*, London and New York: Tauris Academic Studies, 1996, pp. 126 ff.; Biko, *I Write What I Like*, p. 143.

47 Tanya Reinhart, 'The Hamas Government Should Be Recognized', *ZNet*, 1 June 2006: http://zcomm.org/znetarticle/the-hamas-government-should-be-recognized-by-tanya-reinhart/.

48 Nawal El Saadawi, *The Nawal El Saadawi Reader*, London: Zed Books, 1997, p. 67.

49 Chris McGreal, 'Web of Betrayal, Blackmail and Sex That Killed Two Lovers Who Turned Informer', *Guardian*, 3 June 2006: www.guardian.co.uk/world/2006/jun/03/israel; Anonymous, 'An In-Depth Look into the Dossier on Collaborators: Palestinian Security Official: We Arrested 30 Collaborators in Two Months', *Qudsway*, 2004 (Arabic): www.qudsway.com/akhbar/arshiv/2004/4-2004/b/report-4&19&16642.htm (accessed 12 July 2006).

50 B'Tselem, The Israeli Information Center for Human Rights in the Occupied Territories, 'Statistics on Palestinian Minors in the Custody of the Israeli Security Forces', March 2015: www.btselem.org/english/Statistics/Minors_in_Custody.asp. During the last fifteen years hundreds of minors from the Occupied Palestinian Territories have been held by Israel at almost all times, only very rarely dipping below 200 children. See also 'Israel: Palestinian Children Still Being Tortured in Israeli Prisons', OMCT Appeal, World Organisation Against Torture, 3 July 2001: www.omct.org/index.php?id=&lang=eng&actualPageNumber=56&articleSet=Appeal&articleId=933.

51 Mohammed Yahyah, 'Psychological Effects of the Problem on Children and Ways to Address It' in DCI, *Dealing with Alleged Child Collaborators in the Occupied Palestinian Territory in the Spirit of the Convention on the Rights of the Child*, Ramallah: Defence for Children International (DCI) – Palestine Section, 2005: http://reliefweb.int/sites/reliefweb.int/files/resources/67B866DFD36D4FDA4925701F00097B2E-dcips-opt-20apr.pdf. Since 2003, at the very latest, the US and British armed forces have used torture techniques and 'intelligence strategies' against Arabs based on very similar principles, for example in Baghdad's infamous Abu Ghraib prison and elsewhere. See Brian Whitaker, 'Its Best Use Is as a Doorstop', *Guardian*, 27 May 2004: www.theguardian.com/world/2004/may/24/worlddispatch.usa; Jason Leopold, 'British Authorities Probing New Claims Soldiers Tortured,

Raped Iraqi Prisoners', *Truthout*, 14 November 2009: www.truthout.org/topstories/111409jl02.

52 Amir Givol, Neta Rotem and Sergeiy Sandler, *The New Profile Report on Child Recruitment in Israel*, New Profile: The Movement to Demilitarize Israeli Society, 2004: http://newprofile.org/english/node/249. Moreover, Israelis – especially the illegal settlers on Palestinian land but also via the state's indirect recruitment of Jewish Israeli children in Israel as soldiers-to-be – and Palestinians both use children of their *own* race for military purposes (ibid., pp. 5 ff.).

53 Jihad Anton Shomaly, *Use of Children in the Occupied Palestinian Territories*, Ramallah: Defence for Children International (DCI) – Palestine Section, 2004, p. 35: www.essex.ac.uk/armedcon/story_id/000205.pdf. In a DCI field survey of forty former child prisoners, twenty-five respondents reported that they were asked or pressured to be collaborators for the Israeli occupation. The 'pressure' also included severe physical and psychological torture (ibid., pp. 31 f.).

54 Virginia Tilley (ed.), *Occupation, Colonialism, Apartheid? A Re-Assessment of Israel's Practices in the Occupied Palestinian Territories under international law*, Cape Town: Human Sciences Research Council of South Africa, 2009, p. 114, republished in *Electronic Intifada*: http://electronicintifada.net/downloads/pdf/090608-hsrc.pdf. Israeli Military Order 132 is the main piece of racist legislation Israel uses to grant itself the right to try Arab children as adults. 'The generally accepted definition of a child under Article 1 of the Convention on the Rights of the Child is "every human being below the age of 18 years", with which Israel complies in relation to Israeli children … Israel does not accept the applicability of the Convention on the Right of the Child in the OPT [Occupied Palestinian Territories]' (ibid., p. 188).

55 Tilley, *Occupation, Colonialism, Apartheid?*, p. 182. Israel also carries out other kinds of targeted collective punishment of family members of alleged Palestinian criminals, such as home demolitions. See the Israeli Committee Against House Demolitions (www.icahd.org).

56 Tilley, *Occupation, Colonialism, Apartheid?*, pp. 207 ff.

57 Ross, *A Concise History of South Africa*, p. 159.

58 Biko, *I Write What I Like*, p. 112.

59 Shalhoub-Kevorkian, 'Re-Examining Femicide', p. 584.

60 I am not implying here that racism is universally more destructive than sexism. Rather, sex, race and class should be considered as at least potentially equal with regard to both destructive intent and intensity. See Angela Y. Davis, *Women, Race and Class*, New York: Random House, 1983; Angela Y.

Davis, 'Foreword' in Chela Sandoval, *Methodology of the Oppressed*, Theory
Out of Bounds Vol. 18, Minneapolis and London: University of Minnesota
Press, 2000, p. xi; bell hooks, 'Intersections: Race, Sex and Class, Counter-
Racisms: Constructions, Interactions, Interventions', symposium held at the
University of Vienna, 14–15 November 1997: www.univie.ac.at/Geschichte/
GEGEN-RASSISMEN/aehook.html.

61 Jones, *Crimes against Humanity*.

62 Shalhoub-Kevorkian, 'Re-Examining Femicide', p. 583; Anthony Löwstedt,
Kultur oder Evolution? Eine Anthropologische Philosophie, Frankfurt am Main:
Lang, 1995.

63 Rosemary Sayigh, 'Researching Gender in a Palestinian Camp: Political,
Theoretical and Methodological Problems' in Deniz Kandiyoti (ed.),
Gendering the Middle East: Emerging Perspectives, London: I. B. Tauris, 1996
(reprinted 2007), p. 148. Warrick ('The Vanishing Victim', p. 325) quotes
sources saying that honour murders take place especially among Palestinians
in Jordan but cautions that this is according to Jordanian non-experts. She
also hints that class may play a role here, as Jordanians generally hold most of
the political power in the country. Shalhoub-Kevorkian certainly also holds
economic class to be related to femicide in the Israeli-occupied West Bank:
'most "crimes of honor" that have come to my attention are committed in
poor areas' ('Re-Examining Femicide', p. 597).

64 Jones, 'Case Study: The European Witch-Hunts'. The African witch hunts
have so far yet to reach the European proportions of 1450–1750, when
100,000 to 110,000 were put on trial and 40,000 to 60,000 people (20 to
25 per cent of whom were men) were executed for witchcraft, according to
information quoted by Jones. See also C. Warren Hollister, J. Sears McGee
and Gale Stokes, *The West Transformed: A History of Western Civilization*, Fort
Worth: Harcourt College Publishers, 2000, pp. 618–21, who prefer the higher
of the first two estimates and base their 33 per cent male casualty figure on
data from Eastern European, where, according to them, sometimes more
men than women were killed for being 'witches'.

65 See note 71 below.

66 Shalhoub-Kevorkian, 'Re-Examining Femicide', p. 582.

67 Ibid., p. 601. See Göran Therborn, 'NATO's Demographer', *New Left Review*
56, March–April 2009: http://newleftreview.org/II/56/goran-therborn-nato-s-
demographer. Therborn's review of Gunnar Heinsohn's *Söhne und Weltmacht:
Terror im Aufstieg und Fall der Nationen* (Munich: Piper, 2008) discusses
Heinsohn's far-right, neo-fascist (yet painfully familiar since the crusades)

fear-mongering over population growth in African and Arab countries, a much welcomed, though seriously mistaken, geopolitical interpretation of demographic development for Israeli and NATO or other Western coalition designs for warfare against angry, young, Muslim men.

68 Deniz Kandiyoti, 'Contemporary Feminist Scholarship and Middle East Studies' in Kandiyoti, *Gendering the Middle East*, p. 9; Shalhoub-Kevorkian, 'Re-Examining Femicide', p. 592.

69 Anthony Löwstedt, 'The Main Victims in the Israeli–Palestinian Demographic War Are Palestinian Women', *Miftah*, 14 May 2005: www.miftah.org/Display.cfm?DocId=7435&CategoryId=5.

70 Löwstedt, *Apartheid – Ancient, Past and Present*, Chapter II.9.2-3; Shlomo Sand, *The Invention of the Land of Israel: From Holy Land to Homeland*, London and New York: Verso, 2012. South Africa did experience some secularisation during the twentieth century, but I believe that it was a very rare event in apartheid history and not at all due to South African developments but to global ones against which both South African traditionalist and de-secularising forces were powerless. I have failed to detect any significant counter-current to de-secularisation during Israel's modern history, or any during nearly 1,000 years of apartheid in late antiquity Egypt (see note 75 below).

71 Like gendercide, cultural and linguistic genocide are also not (yet) crimes against humanity, mainly due to obstacles presented by a small number of countries led by the USA and Israel. See Unescopress, 'General Conference Adopts Convention on the Protection and Promotion of the Diversity of Cultural Expressions, October 20, 2005', Press Release No. 2005-128: http://portal.unesco.org/en/ev.php-URL_ID=30298&URL_DO=DO_TOPIC&URL_SECTION=201.html (only the USA and Israel voted against this convention, which, of course, must apply in those countries nonetheless); Löwstedt, *Apartheid – Ancient, Past and present*, Chapter III.6. At the time of writing, more than half of the world's languages are threatened by extinction. On average, one language vanishes every two weeks. This is almost certainly unprecedented in human history. Analysts mainly consider the spread of commercialism and consumerism and, secondly, the spread of English as the main factors behind what is perhaps the greatest threat to cultural diversity ever. But there are many additional factors, such as US- and UK-driven cultural imperialism, oligopolistic and centralist developments in communications businesses and technology, a dynamic of sharp population increases of already large populations, and the spread of French, Arabic and Chinese, to name but a few. Terralingua, 'UNHCHR Submission on

Linguistic Rights in Education, Submitted May 15, 1998, to the XVI Session of the Working Group on Indigenous Populations of the United Nations Centre for Human Rights, Geneva, July 27–31, 1998', UN Document E/CN.4/Sub.2/ AC.4/1998/2; Francesco Capotorti, *Study of the Rights of Persons Belonging to Ethnic, Religious and Linguistic Minorities*, New York: United Nations, 1979, p. 37; Tove Skutnabb-Kangas, *Linguistic Genocide in Education: Worldwide Diversity or Human Rights?*, Mahwah, New Jersey: Lawrence Erlbaum, 2000. A selection of chapters from the book are available at www.columbia.edu/cu/ cser/issp/files/bibliography2013/Skutnabb-Kangas%20LinguisticGenocide%20 v-xiii%2065I-668pdf.pdf. See also Robert Philippson, *Linguistic Imperialism Continued*, Hyderabad: Orient BlackSwan, 2009; Cees Hamelink, 'Confronting Cultural Rights', *Media Development*, 58(4) (2001), pp. 44–7: http://41.89.26.5/cgi-bin/koha/opac-search.pl?q=au:HAMELINK,%20 Cees%20J; Will Dunham, 'Australia Top "Hot Spot" for Vanishing Languages', Reuters, 18 September 2007; Anthony Löwstedt, 'Rights versus Diversity? The Accelerated Extinction of Languages and Cultures as an Aspect of Current Globalization Trends', *International Review for Information Ethics* 7 (09/2007): www.i-r-i-e.net/inhalt/007/21-loewstedt.pdf.

72 Pusch Commey, 'South Africa: Economic Apartheid Lives On!', *New African*, November 2009; Pusch Commey, 'South Africa: The Triumph of the African Spirit', *New African*, February 2003; Trevor Ngwane, 'Sparks in the Township', *New Left Review* 22 (July–August 2003): http://newleftreview.org/ II/22/trevor-ngwane-sparks-in-the-township.

73 And when the body count includes all white-induced killings in areas under white rule since 1652, then the difference becomes huge in absolute numbers. Here, we are well into the millions, whereas the total Palestinian–Israeli or even Arab–Israeli death tolls are 'only' in the hundreds of thousands. See Löwstedt, *Apartheid – Ancient, Past and Present*, Chapters II.1.2, II.1.3.

74 Löwstedt, *Apartheid – Ancient, Past and Present*; Anthony Löwstedt, 'Comparing Israeli Oppression with South African Apartheid', *Palestine Report* 12(4) (13 July 2005). In this article, I argue that South African and Israeli apartheid are difficult to rank due to the reasons mentioned but that comparisons should not be ruled out. With more knowledge, a scientific way of measuring or gauging apartheid intensity can be made possible.

75 'Honour' murders have been taking place in the region since before Christianity, and they are carried out in Christian as well as Muslim families. Femicide has also lingered long after the demise of other apartheid states, including Egypt, after Greek and Roman rule from 332 BCE to 642 CE (female genital mutilation, in Christian as well as Muslim families), Palestine

since the crusader kingdom of 1099–1291 ('honour' murders), Guatemala after
Spanish and Spanish-descendant rule from 1523 to 1996 (rape-murder), and
Zimbabwe under white rule (Rhodesia) in 1965–80 ('witch' burnings). See
Löwstedt, *Apartheid – Ancient, Past and Present*, Chapters I.1.4, II.1.1, II.2.1.

76 Hanan Ashrawi, *This Side of Peace: A Personal Account*, New York: Simon
& Schuster, 1995, pp. 292 f.; Mazin Qumsiyeh, 'Geneva understandings
Promote a Failing Apartheid Solution', *Boykot Israel*, 2 December 2003:
www.boykotisrael.dk/geneva_understandings_promote_a_.htm; Amnesty
International, 'Statement to UN Commission on Human Rights. Agenda
Item 8: Question of the Violation of Human Rights in the Occupied Arab
Territories, Including Palestine, 58th session, 18 March – 26 April 2002',
26 March 2002: www.amnesty.org/en/documents/MDE15/027/2002/en/.

77 Shlaim, *The Iron Wall*.

78 BDS Movement, 'Final Declaration and Action Plan of the Bilbao Initiative',
4 November 2008: www.bdsmovement.net/2008/final-declaration-and-
action-plan-of-the-bilbao-initiative-213. This is a ten-point plan for
transnational civil society action for justice in Palestine, which refers to
'apartheid' five times, calls for phased and flexible boycotts, divestment
and sanctions (BDS) against the Israeli state and Israeli business, i.e., against
the political, military and economic elites of apartheid Israel and
its supporters. See also Neve Gordon, 'Boycott Israel', *Los Angeles Times*,
20 August 2009: www.latimes.com/news/opinion/commentary/la-oe-
gordon20-2009aug20,0,1126906.story. This paragraph should not be
interpreted as meaning that apartheid can or should be defeated before
anything is done against femicide. On the contrary: the two struggles are
intimately related and defeating either one of these crimes will make it much
easier to defeat the other.

79 Desmond Tutu, 'Realizing God's Dream for the Holy Land', *Boston Globe*,
26 October 2007: www.boston.com/news/globe/editorial_opinion/oped/
articles/2007/10/26/realizing_gods_dream_for_the_holy_land/?page=full.

80 Msimang, 'Affirmative Action in the New South Africa'.

81 For instance, the courageous Women in Black (www.womeninblack.org),
Machsom Watch (www.machsomwatch.org), or the many hundreds of Israeli
conscientious objectors, who prefer prison to more or less criminal military
service with impunity. In Israel, all Jewish women, with a few exceptions, are
conscripted to do military service along with men, although for two years
instead of three. See New Profile: The Movement for the Demilitarization of
Israeli Society: www.newprofile.org/english/.

CHAPTER 7

The Many Faces of Protest: A Comparative Analysis of Protest Groups in Israel and South Africa

AMNEH BADRAN

PREFACE

While Apartheid South Africa and Zionist Israel share similar political systems which allowed for the development of similar civil societies (ethnically based, mainly exclusive, limited and weak), in both instances protest evolved over the years to support different political platforms and also played different roles. The majority of protest groups in the two dominant societies adopted liberal political views; however, these differed substantively. By the mid-1980s, the majority of white South Africans had accepted the African National Congress's (ANC's) platform of an inclusive, non-racial, united and democratic South Africa, and had joined the struggle for 'one person one vote' and equality, based on a bill of rights that would protect all equally before the law, although the latter fell short in terms of defining social equality and justice. Most Israeli protest groups support a territorial compromise, based on division and separation, within the framework of a 'two-state solution' formula. They believe in the ideology in power – that is, Zionism – and are committed to a Jewish state; thus they seek a settlement that protects the existing system and structure of power vis-à-vis the Palestinians. Their commitment to equality and justice founders in the presence of their ideological beliefs, including their allegiance to the Jewish state and its security. Thus, their position towards and role in the national consensus have differed from those of the white protest groups.

To verify the foregoing, this chapter is arranged in four sections. The first introduces and explains a number of concepts and variables that are relevant to this particular research. The second discusses the politics and roles of the different categories of white South African groups, and gives brief examples. The politics and roles of the different categories of Israeli (Jewish) protest groups are explained in section three, again with a few brief examples, while the fourth and concluding section sheds light on the similarities and the differences between the two cases.

It is important here to highlight the period covered by the research. For Apartheid South Africa, this was the 1980s and the early 1990s, until the apartheid system was formally dismantled in 1994. In the case of Zionist Israel, the period researched extended from the beginning of the first intifada in 1987 to the signing of the Geneva Initiative in 2003 during the second intifada.[1]

INTRODUCTION

This introduction explains a number of concepts and variables relevant to this chapter. First, when speaking about the politics of protest groups, it should be made clear that this entails specifying whether they are liberal or leftist, and where they stand on the continuum of inclusivity versus exclusivity. As to protest groups' political platforms, they are based on the politics adopted in the first place by the different protest groups. They manifest their positions in more detail. They expose their ideas and activities in more concrete ways. With regard to the roles of protest groups, they are meant to examine whether the political ideas, discourse and activities of groups are effective: 1) in altering the overriding consensus among the dominant societies towards a peace-enabling direction that could make a difference when the conditions and balance of power are right; and 2) on checking how far they alter this direction: that is, whether they move towards a rights-based inclusive peace or promote compromise that benefits the dominant side. The second conceptual issue is my choice of the term 'protest groups', rather than 'peace groups' or any other expression. There are three reasons for this. First, in both cases, different groups or organisations protested against their governments' policies or strategies towards the dominated side, advocating different kinds of peace and ways to reach it. Second, the protest groups themselves in both cases did not use a common label. The Israeli groups chose to label themselves 'peace groups' while South African white groups referred to themselves as 'anti-apartheid groups'.[2] The third reason, which is of no less importance, is that the word 'peace' has many meanings: in the Palestinian–Israeli context, it has been misused and/or overused to such an extent that it is difficult to refer to it in a positive or neutral way. Some would even describe it as a contaminated word. Thus, I felt that it was important to have a term that was sufficiently neutral and that could be used to refer to both cases with ease. The term 'protest' meets this function.

The third issue relates to independent and intermediate variables that in both cases affected the political realm of protest by influencing the course of action or the pathways of the dependent variables. The dependent variables, which are the focus of this chapter, are the politics and roles of protest groups, while in both cases the independent variable is the political system. This research argues that neither political system represents democratic systems. The criterion used is that of compatibility with civic nationalism or civic public culture,[3] which is a prerequisite to an inclusive democracy that protects liberties and represents and serves all its citizens equally. On the political continuum of inclusivity versus exclusivity, inclusive democracy contrasts totalitarian and authoritarian systems and other systems that adopt exclusive ethnic nationalism.

Both examined states adopted the latter, and consequently developed restricted or exclusive 'democracies' or a masters' 'democracy'[4] for the ethnic group in power. By their very nature, they were unable to incorporate the values, laws and procedures of inclusive nationalism, or, in other words, that of civic citizenship of a liberal democracy.

To preserve an exclusive or masters' 'democracy', both systems developed centralised political systems where the state built an interlocking relationship with the different societal spheres under its hegemony.[5] This can be explained as follows:

> The state exercise/d hegemony over the different spheres and both states continue/d, to a great extent, to control the moral order through corporatist regimes that manifest/ed themselves in the politics of national consensus. Consequently, both developed ethnically-based, mainly exclusive, limited and weak civil societies … both civil societies were part and parcel of the national effort of nation and state building, and later of state protection. In the case of Israel, the majority of civil organisations still represent arms for the government or subcontractors to the state … Hence, for both civil societies, issues of inclusivity, independency, equality and citizenship constitute/d challenges.[6]

As far as the intermediate variables are concerned, they affect the environment in which the focal variables function and therefore influence their positions and modes of behaviour.[7] To a significant extent, they determine the different pathways taken by the different dependent variables and, as such, produce variations in the outcomes of the two cases. They include external factors and 'objective' realities. They can be organised into three groupings: changes at the international level, for example the fall of the Berlin Wall; the visions and strategies of the resistance movements in both conflict areas – the Palestine Liberation Organization (PLO) and the ANC and their respective successes and failures; and, finally, a number of internal factors, some of which are products of strategic policies undertaken by both ethnic states in shaping their strategic interests and relations with the dominated side.

Among the latter are the demographic balance[8] and the economic relations[9] that both political systems developed vis-à-vis the Other. The different evolved demographic realities and economic relationships in the two cases affected the political environment of protest, and in both instances influenced the politics and roles of the protest groups. Also, state legitimacy[10] and support given by neighbouring states to the respective resistance movements constituted other examples of intermediate variables, which had different impacts. The legitimacy status of the South African political system is not equivalent to that of Israel, and the ANC's support from neighbouring African states is not equivalent to that received by the PLO from Arab states.[11] Many of the latter, directly or indirectly, recognised Zionist Israel, while some even signed peace treaties and normalised relations with it. This was not the case with Apartheid South Africa.

Finally, there is another intermediate variable that should not be forgotten. This involves changes at the international level. Compared with the white South Africans, the Zionists have enjoyed a great advantage in shaping the policies of the hegemonic powers (the UK and later the US).

In terms of numbers, it is important to note that protest groups constituted a minority in both civil societies.

THE POLITICS AND ROLES OF WHITE SOUTH AFRICAN PROTEST GROUPS AND INDIVIDUAL ACTIVISM

For the purposes of researching this issue, I classified white protest groups into categories; this helps in unfolding the details of the different components of the protest arena and revealing the political strands within this milieu, and also shows how each contributed to the anti-apartheid struggle. Based on their politics, political platforms and relationship with the ideology in power, the groups were classified in two major categories, each of which was divided into two sub-categories (see Table 7.1). The first major category is what I describe as white liberal protest organisations or groups, and its sub-categories are mainstream liberal groups and progressive liberal groups. The second major category is that of white individuals in black-run leftist resistance groups. Its sub-categories are mainstream left and radical left groups. This categorisation reflects the groups' politics during the 1980s, when major shifts occurred, especially towards a political centre in which the non-racial, inclusive politics of the public arm of the ANC, the United Democratic Front (UDF), became dominant.

Table 7.1. Categorisation of white protest groups

Liberal white protest groups	1. Mainstream groups
	2. Progressive groups
Whites in (black-run) leftist groups	1. Mainstream left
	2. Radical left

This classification shows the political spectrum within which white protest groups and individuals[12] worked. It is important to note that lines between categories and sub-categories were not clear-cut but were sometimes blurred; however, there were certain beliefs, principles and values that were typical of each category.

Liberal protest organisations and groups

At the outset, it is important to clarify what is meant here by 'liberal', 'mainstream' and 'progressive'. In the context of South Africa, the liberal organisations are those that, historically, held political views similar or close to those of the Progressive Party or the Progressive Federal Party. They were gradualists who sought change by process, and who adopted policies and strategies that fitted within the legal framework of the political system. Until the 1980s, many of them did not commit themselves to a clear end result. Since they were well connected with the free market business community, they were skilful in marketing their positions at the international level; in addition, they favoured a decentralised system where government intervention was limited. They stressed individual empowerment and self-reliance instead of persistent government intervention and state transfers to the poor, which they believed would disempower the poor and leave them dependent.[13] While certain values were important for the liberals, they still argued for 'case uniqueness': that is, the uniqueness of the case of South Africa. They were also keen to address cultural differences that could be used as a justification for some sort of separation within the framework of a federation.

By the early 1980s, a shift had occurred in the positions of the liberal groups. Jill Wentzel[14] defined the liberals as pragmatists who believed in parliamentary democracy, free speech, individual rights and liberties, non-racialism, the rule of law and non-violent change.[15] She argued that, by the mid-1980s, liberalism in South Africa had begun to slide, and cited as an obvious indicator the resignations of Dr Frederick Van Zyl Slabbert and Dr Alex Boraine from the Progressive Party and their publicly stated view that opposition from within the parliament had no further role to play in effecting change within South Africa.[16] They found refuge instead in the civil society sphere, by establishing the Institute for a Democratic Alternative for South Africa (IDASA) and opening direct contact with the ANC.

The shift in the views of many liberals and liberal organisations led to a chasm among the liberals, which is recognised and reflected in the categories presented in this chapter. The mainstream organisations are those that retained the old viewpoints, positions and strategies, and which subsequently decreased in number. The progressive organisations are those that challenged some of the old views, positions and strategies, and either adopted or came closer (in varying degrees) to the platform of the Freedom Charter that had been launched by the ANC and other congresses in 1955. They moved towards support for majority rule (for example, Black Sash,[17] IDASA,[18] FFF,[19] ECC[20] and NUSAS[21]) and a form of social democracy instead of liberal democracy, thereby opening the door for talks about talks and a compromise on South Africa's economic policies. Voices that did not support violent means of resistance, but understood why blacks had resorted to them, also appeared among them. Many became affiliated with the UDF or worked closely with it. Thus, in this context, progressiveness was associated with coming closer to the politics of the oppressed (the mainstream left) and with finding common ground to enable them to work together in the struggle against apartheid and for an inclusive non-racial democracy of 'one person one vote'. The mainstream groups continued to be associated with the historical views, stands and strategies of the liberals, such as the Progressive Party, the South African Institute of Race Relations (SAIRR) and the Urban Foundation.[22] The latter was a business group that opposed apartheid but stood firm in protecting free market policies and the business interests of the whites.

The SAIRR was among the organisations that continued to represent the old liberal mainstream. Having reviewed its publications (including its famous annual survey of race relations), read articles by director John Kane-Berman, and interviewed a research staff member, Frans Cronje, I conclude that the Institute continued to hold the old liberal ethos. It had been a liberal multiracial organisation in which whites always played the dominant role. Being multiracial gave it significance, compared with others who saw themselves as non-racial or anti-racial. Multiracialism gives significant weight to racial differences; non-racialism recognises the four races in South Africa but seeks unity; while anti-racism does not accept the concept of race.[23]

The SAIRR claimed to be neutral and apolitical while aiming to disseminate factual data. It played a major role in disseminating information about the situation in South Africa through its annual survey, which was considered by many – nationally and internationally – to be a document of great importance in terms of following up what was happening in Apartheid South Africa. Along with others, the survey sensitised international bodies and challenged government reports and analyses of the situation, although it did not challenge the national consensus at the level of revoking the system altogether. It continued to argue for change from within through gradualism and pragmatism, and as such it failed to address the system of structured violence inflicted by the apartheid policies. It even leaned towards the government in arguing how to make the presence of the state security forces in the townships 'accepted there as protectors of the peace and guardians of legitimate authority'[24] at a time when it was no secret that the South African police did not have clean hands with regard to violence.

As laid down by its director, John Kane-Berman, SAIRR's vision for power sharing stressed gradualism and no commitment to 'one person one vote' democracy. In his ten-point peace package, he argued that:

> Once the principle of power sharing is accepted, the precise form it would take, and detailed formula for the make up of the country and of Parliament, would all be matters for negotiation, along with appropriate measures to protect cultural and language rights, religious freedoms, the rule of law, civil liberties and so on.[25]

As for progressive liberal organisations, the main principles that brought together groups belonging to this sub-category were: being against apartheid, support for non-racialism, acceptance of 'one person one vote' (majority rule), the rule of law and the need for a bill of rights to protect citizens' civil and political rights, the belief that whites had a place in a new South Africa run by the ANC, opposition to the imposition of emergency law, no commitment to capitalism per se, but a commitment to non-violent protest and to a negotiated settlement.

Some organisations emphasised some of these principles more than others did. Some supported sanctions while others chose not to take a position. Most did not support violent resistance but showed an understanding of why it had been employed by the black majority. Sheena Dunkan of Black Sash said: 'I don't approve of violence but I understand why people resort to it'.[26] Some were more vocal than others, but even so they became the Charterists compared with the rest of the liberals, and were also referred to as progressive liberals. Among the main groups who fitted within this sub-category were the National Union of South African Students (NUSAS), Black Sash, the End Conscription Campaign (ECC), the Five Freedom Forum (FFF), the IDASA, the Christian Institute for Southern Africa (CISA), the Centre for Inter-group Studies/Centre for Conflict Resolution (CCR), the Cape Town Democrats, Christian Youth Workers (Christian Socialists) and the Civil Rights League, among many others. However, a major example was Black Sash.

Black Sash is an organisation of liberal women that was established in 1955 and is an example of a group that moved from the cradle of mainstream liberalism to 'militant' or 'radical' political positions (in the view of the 'old' liberals), or to progressive liberalism (as seen by those on the left). It shifted from silent protest about violations of human rights to the provision of legal services. It linked its research and political statements to its fieldwork and managed to build a credible voice as an anti-apartheid protest group and as one struggling for social democracy.[27] In his first speech after being released in 1990, Nelson Mandela referred to Black Sash as 'the conscience of white South Africa'.[28]

During the 1980s, Black Sash worked closely with the black-led UDF. Its activities reflected its clear political stands and principles, and it aimed to exert pressure for regime change and in shaping an alternative future. Its principles included a commitment to justice (by refusing to accept apartheid and its policies as an ideology or a system), respect for human rights and the rule of law, and political as well as other freedoms. Sheena Dunkan also stressed Black Sash's commitment to the five freedoms of the FFF: 'freedom from want, freedom from fear, freedom of speech and association, freedom of conscience, and freedom from discrimination'.[29] Equality for Black Sash meant equal rights, not income, which was what the rule of law was about.[30]

With regard to the issue of violence, Black Sash challenged the apartheid government: 'South Africans must remember that their fellow South Africans have been driven to armed struggle by the institutionalized violence of apartheid. The only way to end violence is to establish justice and the rule of law'.[31] In the same press release, Black Sash stressed that the government's military raids beyond the country's borders violated international law. In another statement, it equated the apartheid government's policies with those of Nazi Germany:

> leadership training in schools, community education programmes which are compulsory for civil servants, evangelical outreach, [are] all redolent of Nazi Germany in the 1930s, of 20th century Russia ... [These] are the weapons of the South African state in its attempt to destroy the image of the enemy – communism – which it created in the first place. There is no enemy. There are only people who want freedom to decide their own future.[32]

If these principles are compared with those of Women in Black or of Bat Shalom, two leading Israeli women's organisations, there is no doubt that those of the Black Sash were more daring and challenging to the system.

It can be argued that Black Sash played a significant role in raising public awareness of the suffering of the majority, both locally and internationally. It provided factual information and services and, as noted above, presented political stands that challenged those of the government and the mainstream liberals. It associated itself with the struggle of the oppressed, and contributed to undermining the ideology of apartheid and shaping the alternative. It broke the prevailing national consensus not only in society but also among the mainstream liberals. It was actively present in the networks between white groups and in the white–black network, which in turn contributed to the provision of a space between whites and blacks that could be bridged and strengthened cooperative efforts in the framework of the UDF political platform. In choosing this path, Black Sash, with others, created a gulf within the old liberal cluster and weakened it. Finally, it is important to mention that Black Sash was involved in second-track diplomacy meetings, which were considered by many as talks about talks to prepare the ground for official negotiations on the basis of inclusivity, non-racialism and majority rule. The principles that shaped the parameters of the 'settlement to be' were discussed in greater detail in many of the second-track diplomacy meetings that were held in the second half of the 1980s, such as the Dakar and Lusaka meetings.

Whites in leftist (black-run) resistance groups

The number of whites, groups and individuals who chose to follow this path was limited, but certainly constituted more than a handful. Some chose the mainstream leftist groups while others joined the radical leftist groups. Those who favoured the mainstream leftist sub-category joined the ANC, the South African Communist Party (SACP) and/or the UDF. In many cases, prominent figures chose this path, revoking the communitarian 'tribal' consensus, and some even joined the military wings of the ANC and the SACP.

The UDF, as the public arm of the ANC, managed to reach out to the white protest organisations and had white affiliates that included groups such as the Cape Democrats, NUSAS, the Johannesburg Democratic Action Committee (JODAC) and the youth congresses.[33] It also had white members in their personal capacity, most of whom were members of the banned ANC and SACP. The UDF included people from the whole political spectrum who agreed with its general political programme and also offered an inclusive platform that enabled its members, affiliates and close partners to use the phrase 'our country South Africa', as can be found in the writings of the UDF, IDASA, FFF, ECC, Black Sash, NUSAS and the Cape Democrats. Peaceful and 'legal' means of protest were used. Different organisations had different degrees of closeness with the ANC, and, eventually, in terms of political views, objectives and strategies, the lines between progressive liberals and mainstream leftist groups often became blurred.[34] Coordinated work became the norm, and, as the white members and affiliates came closer to the politics of the UDF or ANC, they played an important role in dividing the broad white consensus and fracturing the white community, leaving it without one voice.[35] As a result, a powerful new voice of non-racialism, inclusive of whites but against racism and the system, began to develop. In terms of numbers, the presence of whites was disproportionately small, but they played an important symbolic role – to show that a 'rainbow nation' was possible.[36]

Others who joined the banned ANC and the SACP trod a risky path that cost some of them their lives, such as Ruth First, or that led to permanent injury, as in the case of Judge Albie Sachs. Such individuals were driven mainly by moral and/or ideological beliefs, and by joining the ANC they exercised different forms of resistance. Hunter estimates the number of whites who had a direct connection with the ANC at 5,000 countrywide.[37] It is a small number but an impressive one when compared with the case of Israel. In terms of role and importance, Phyllis Naidoo, a veteran Indian member of the SACP, stressed that, while the number of whites was minimal, their contribution was significant.[38] This point of view complements that of many who emphasised that white participation sent a message to the black majority that there were whites who opposed apartheid and took risks in protesting against it and in supporting the struggle of the oppressed. This message contributed not only to the validity of the notions of non-racialism and inclusivity, on which the final agreement was based, but also to the idea of reconciliation.

The second sub-category is that of the tiny group of white radical leftists. The radical left or the ultra-left continued to be entrenched within the socialist agenda, and was critical of both the mainstream and progressive liberals and the mainstream left. Radical leftists perceived the liberals as a patronising elite, seeking self-interest and unable to address racial or class exploitation, and simultaneously regarded the mainstream left as not radical enough and ready to compromise. They did not accept the mainstream left's policy of pragmatism, arguing that it was part of a policy of compromise that would end in a sell-out. They considered the 'two stages theory' of a national political liberation that would be followed by an economic revolution to be misleading, and looked at it from a conspiracy theory point of view, arguing that it was possible to defeat the apartheid system totally without any such compromise. The political settlement was viewed as an elitist deal that would lead to a neoliberal political system,[39] a democracy that was a product of political power being ceded by South Africa's whites to the ANC in return for the ANC accepting that (mainly white-run) capitalism would continue.[40]

These radical leftists refused to follow the path of the SACP, but could not galvanise sufficient public support for their views. Some associated them with the Trotskyists. They were always a tiny group, with few whites among them, and historically have been considered as marginal and non-influential.

THE POLITICS AND ROLES OF ISRAELI (JEWISH) PROTEST GROUPS AND INDIVIDUAL ACTIVISM

Using the same criteria applied to the case of South Africa, Israeli protest groups and individual activism were categorised. On the basis of their politics, political platform and relations with the ideology in power, they are classified into three major categories (see Table 7.2). First is the liberal Zionist protest category, which is divided into two sub-categories: the mainstream Zionist groups and the critical Zionist groups. Second are the leftist protest groups, which include the non-Zionist and the anti-Zionist groupings. The third category refers to Israelis who have joined the PLO in their personal capacities.

Table 7.2. Classification of Israeli protest groups

Liberal Zionist protest groups	1. Mainstream Zionist groups
	2. Critical Zionist groups
Leftist protest groups	1. Non-Zionist groups
	2. Anti-Zionist groups
Israelis who joined the PLO	A dozen individuals

The liberal Zionist protest groups

These groups are often referred to as the left, and less often as liberal groups. Groups that belong to this category are certainly not leftist and are not liberals in the full sense of the word, since they do not adopt socialist or communist doctrines, nor do they unconditionally adopt human rights principles. They are also spoken of as the left because of their location on the political map compared with the right and centre. However, in this chapter they are referred to as liberals because of their support for the free market economy, their focus on human rights (unless they endanger the security of the Jewish state), and the fact that there is a left that holds a leftist political and socio-economic agenda.

Mainstream Zionist protest groups

Members belonging to this sub-category share the following views. Israel is a legitimate entity. 'The war of 1948 was a fair one. It was either me or you'.[41] The war of 1967 was a just war of defence, and the problem was with the occupation of 1967. Peace is possible through a territorial compromise. Israel has to negotiate from a position of strength. A two-state solution with adequate security arrangements is the answer to protecting the state's national interests and making peace (but only since the 1990s). According to Jeff Halper, groups belonging to this category believe that 'we are on opposite sides with the Palestinians, "us and them, my interest versus your interest"'.[42] The two historical narratives are irreconcilable. Palestinians need to show good intentions towards Israel – to prove that they want peace. Israel's image is a concern and the mainstream Zionist groups defend it. They are close to the Labor Party's politics and it is thus difficult for them to protest against a Labor government. They refuse calls not to serve in the army. Strategic ambiguity in their positions is the norm. Finally, they consider the national consensus[43] as the limit that, if broken, loses them their credibility and constituency. Therefore, they act from within that consensus.

These groups also share a number of characteristics. First, they suffer from 'first day syndrome'.[44] In the event that there is a military campaign – for example a war, transfer or attack – 'on the first day, Israeli progressives line up behind their government, believe its excuses, support and defend its actions. Only after some time … weeks or months … [do] they begin to recover and to return to a position of opposition',[45] but this will be only on a tactical level.[46] They are the closest among the different protest groups to the security ethos, and many of their leading members are ex-security or army personnel, members or ex-members of the Knesset, or have served in government posts or held positions in Zionist parties. Most are Ashkenazim, middle class, and well educated.

Members of this sub-category are supporters of the Meretz Party and the Labor left, along with a few who are members of the Shinui party. However, many groups belong to this sub-category, and they differ in their political focus and strategies. A few have developed (specific) joint peace plans, as in the case of the Geneva Initiative and the Ayalon–Nusseibeh plan, whereas others have chosen not to do so, or have adopted broad political parameters for a future settlement. While most organise joint projects with the Palestinians, they stop short of addressing the existing structure of power between the occupied and the occupier. Groups that belong to this sub-category include Peace Now, the Economic Cooperation Foundation, the Peres Center for Peace, the Israeli side of the Geneva Initiative, Four Mothers, the Council for Peace and Security, the Arik Institute, the Israeli side of the Ayalon–Nusseibeh plan, the Israeli side of the People's Peace Campaign, and so on. Among these groups, the oldest, the most recognised (both nationally and internationally), the one most capable of mobilising, and therefore the most visible, is Peace Now.

The national Israeli Jewish peace movement, Peace Now, was founded in 1978 during the Israeli–Egyptian negotiations; it has had no Palestinian member in the core group. Its approach is to wait until something dramatic happens and then respond. As a gradualist, it acts on a sporadic basis and holds ambiguous positions. Tsali Reshef, a spokesperson, explained why this approach was adopted when he described Peace Now as 'a mood and not a movement',[47] while Galia Golan talks of reading public opinion and asking 'What is the mood today?'[48] Its core leadership decides what will preserve the national interest and fit within the national consensus. Until 1988, a year after the first intifada had erupted, Peace Now's political positions were perpetuated by the prevailing Zionist tendencies to demean or deny the existence and rights of the Palestinians as a nation; thus, autonomy in cooperation with Jordan was the acceptable option proposed.[49]

During the first intifada, Peace Now made cosmetic changes to its previous positions, but only after the PLO had publicly accepted United Nations (UN) Resolution 242 (indirectly recognising Israel and limiting Palestinian land rights to those areas occupied in 1967 – that is, 22 per cent of mandatory Palestine) and after Arafat had renounced terrorism. The new position adopted the calls of leftists for negotiations with the PLO, but fell short in terms of political substance. It was far from advocating a two-state solution based on the principle of equality between sovereign nations. It used phrases such as 'Palestinian national existence' instead of 'Palestinian national self-determination', while Jerusalem was referred to as the undivided capital of Israel, where expression would be given to the Islamic and Christian holy places and to the national affinities of the Arab inhabitants.[50] The Palestinian right to self-determination was later accepted by Peace Now within the framework of the right of both sides to self-determination in '*Eretz Israel*', and of guarantees for Israeli security.

As far as the Oslo period (1993–2000) is concerned, Peace Now supported the Oslo Accords uncritically. It can be argued that this was for two reasons: 1) because it had contributed to shaping them through second-track diplomacy meetings; and 2) because one of its principles was to support *any* agreement with which the Israeli and Palestinian leaderships concurred. Peace Now perceived negotiations as fair game: the party that does better in the negotiations obtains the better result. There was no argument about certain principles – such as international legality or universal precepts – that needed to be adhered to in order to achieve peace. The notion of 'support our government and get the most out of it'[51] was the norm. As human rights violations in the Occupied Palestinian Territories (OPT) increased, Yossi Sarid (Meretz leader and a frequent speaker in Peace Now rallies) argued that: 'If we have to cut some corners of human rights to get a settlement, let it be a necessary evil that we will fix later'.[52] In the same vein, Uri Avnery quoted Sarid, in Yitzhak Rabin's time, as saying during negotiations: 'We must twist the arm of Arafat, but without breaking it'.[53] In terms of activities, Peace Now, as a mobilisation and activist group, adopted a low profile. It redirected its attention towards new types of activities that were regarded as suitable during a peace process; these included watching and reporting on settlement expansion and 'outposts', and running dialogue meetings through people-to-people programmes. It was therefore criticised for 'going to sleep' during a critical period. It neither confronted nor mobilised the Israeli public against the policies of their government in the OPT and/or in the negotiations.

With the beginning of the second intifada in 2000, Peace Now suffered from the 'first day syndrome', which this time turned into a long 'first day'. As a low-profile mobilisation protest group, Peace Now effectively disappeared from view, and it was almost two years before it acted visibly and organised a mass demonstration. It adopted Prime Minister Barak's arguments that the Palestinian leadership had rejected Israel's generous offer at Camp David, that the Palestinians did not want peace, that Arafat had orchestrated the second intifada, that there was no longer a partner for peace, and that heavy-handed force was the means to address the Palestinian intifada or 'violence'. These components developed a new national political consensus that Peace Now members then accepted, some vocally and others in silence.

After that period, Peace Now became heavily involved in two joint Israeli–Palestinian initiatives, the People's Peace Campaign, which was later replaced by the Ayalon–Nusseibeh peace plan,[54] and the Geneva Initiative.[55] Both of these aimed to find a partner and a peace plan. It was as if the Palestinian side, through semi-formal groups, had to prove its eligibility, and then Peace Now would campaign on the basis that a partner existed. This had also happened in the first intifada, when the PLO had to accept certain conditions in order to be approved as a valid partner. Both initiatives come within the level of second-track diplomacy negotiations, and both also bring together mostly mainstream Fatah members with mainstream 'liberal' Zionists. This differs from the case of South Africa, where the UDF was partnered with the progressive liberals, not the mainstream liberals. The UDF functioned with those who were ready to come close to, or to accept, its platform and work with it on the dismantling of apartheid as an ideology and a political system, and who accepted international law as a term of reference. This has not happened with either of these two Israeli initiatives.

Critical liberal Zionist groups

Groups that belong to this category are distinguished from the mainstream liberal organisations by the fact that they are Zionists – but critical Zionists compared with the mainstream ones. The critical Zionist groups are keen to preserve the ideological consensus, but they challenge the political consensus to the extent that the mainstream groups have labelled them as radical 'leftists'. They represent an array of political positions on the left of the mainstream liberals. Those on *their* left are the non-Zionists and the anti-Zionists. Compared with the mainstream groups, the political positions of organisations such as Gush Shalom are clearer. Some of them bluntly challenge part of the security ethos – Yesh Gvul and New Profile, for example – while others focus on solidarity and human rights-oriented activities. The latter group includes Ta'yaush, Bat Shalom, the Coalition of Women for Peace and Machsom Watch. The majority are issue-oriented. Those that choose to make political stands propose a better deal for the Palestinians as part of the two-state formula. However, an approach of constructive ambiguity is adopted – for example by Bat Shalom – albeit to different degrees. Many reject a boycott of Israel, while some support a selective boycott.

They share some concerns and characteristics. They are concerned about the soul of the Jewish people, since occupation is perceived as 'killing both sides'. They worry about democracy and the long-term security of Israel. They advocate a compromise but are ready to move further in recognising Palestinian rights and demands. The gap is narrower between the historical narrative they adopt and that of the Palestinian side, compared with the gap between the Palestinians and the mainstream Zionists. Even though some disappear during crises because of the 'first day syndrome', they come back to activism more quickly than mainstream groups. Some lose faith that they can bring about change by working inside Israel and therefore invest more in advocacy work at the international level. Many of them challenge state strategies such as the Wall, unilateralism, disengagement plans, the assassination of Palestinian activists, the siege of Gaza, and the war against Lebanon in 2006. Few make links between the occupation of 1967 and the war, and the eviction of the majority of Palestinians in 1948. The problem is occupation, but although some are ready to acknowledge certain mistakes on the part of the state before the occupation of 1967, they do not question state legitimacy, since the latter touches the ideological consensus and they do not challenge this. Some believe that their role is to prepare the ground for Peace Now to take new issues to the public, 'a small wheel that could move a bigger wheel'.[56] They are, to different degrees, ahead of mainstream liberals on the path towards universal principles.

Protest groups that belong to this sub-category are those mentioned above plus the following: Women in Black, Refuseniks, the Israeli side of the Palestinian–Israeli Joint Action Committee, the Israeli Committee Against House Demolitions (ICAHD),[57] Courage to Refuse, the Committee for Israeli–Palestinian Dialogue,[58] Campus LoShotek,[59] and so on. This sub-category is home to the largest number of active Israeli protest groups.

Gush Shalom is one of the oldest and most visible groups. Its political stance lies in the middle of the continuum of those that belong to this sub-category, where some choose to take position (or positions) and others do not. It was established in 1993 by a group of protesters who, in late 1992, had spent forty-five days opposite the Israeli prime minister's office protesting about the expulsion of 415 Islamist activists. 'During the debates in the tents, and in view of the silence of other peace groups, some of the protestors decided that a new Israeli peace movement was needed. They defined themselves as "more peace-oriented than Peace Now"'.[60]

Gush Shalom did not reject or fully support the Oslo Accords, but maintained an ambivalent position. While it read the mutual recognition of Israel vis-à-vis the PLO as a great step towards influencing the Israeli public, it nevertheless analysed it as a bad agreement, criticising the fact that it did not mention the ultimate aim and arguing that this would make the interim stages lose their meaning.[61] Being vocal about Oslo's tragic flaws did not stop Gush Shalom, shortly after the signing of the Oslo Accords, from requesting that Israeli activists support it and concentrate on lobbying within Israeli society and the Israeli government to ensure that the minimum obligations already agreed to by Israel were carried out.[62] Later during the Oslo period, Gush Shalom became very critical of the government's policies in the OPT and of the way it had handled the negotiations. In 1995, Uri Avnery accused Rabin of not negotiating in good faith, arguing that by delaying the implementation of the Declaration of Principles, the Israeli government was building 'facts on the ground': expansion of settlements, especially in Jerusalem, and closure and other measures that paved the way for an envisioned solution of an archipelago of enclaves, for example.[63] In that respect, it was far ahead of Peace Now.

During the second intifada, Gush Shalom criticised Barak for the failure of the Camp David negotiations, and Avnery in particular blamed Barak for delivering a devastating blow to the Israeli 'peace movement', describing him as a 'peace criminal'.[64] It was a blow that pushed the Israeli public to the right. In terms of political stands, Gush Shalom continued to be driven by a belief in a practical political programme for solving the conflict.[65] This programme would adopt a two-state solution based, as claimed, on equality and mutual respect, and would strive for maximum cooperation.[66] In this programme, perceived equality would be achieved through commitment to a Jewish state and the dictation of the balance of power, which did not allow for international law to be respected, the latter being considered a 'non-basis': 'It has a very low standing in Israel ... no one takes UN resolutions seriously ... we accept international law if we make a separation between the conventions and the resolutions'.[67]

Nevertheless, the compromise and 'practical' deal that Gush Shalom proposes to the Palestinians is better than that of the mainstream liberal groups. The Palestinian 'historical compromise'[68] is acceptable to Gush Shalom, in contrast to the territorial compromise proposed by the mainstream Zionists, as a basis from which to negotiate. However, for Gush Shalom, the historical compromise requires a number of compromises from the Palestinians with regard to, for example, the right of return, Jerusalem, and the sovereignty of the future state, which, according to Gush Shalom, has to be demilitarised.

Being more vocal, critical and active in solidarity with the Palestinians, Gush Shalom found itself being awarded the label of a radical movement by the mainstream liberals. While those on its left accuse it of undermining the values of equality and justice, Yehudith Harel, a former member of Gush Shalom, argues that equality has been treated on the level of slogans, and justice has been limited to support for the two-state solution.[69] Uri Davis praises its work on the 1967 occupation and settlements,[70] but accuses Gush Shalom – and Avnery in particular, because of his role in the war of 1948 – of perpetuating the Nakba by failing to engage in self-critical analysis of the war crimes that were committed then, and of later betraying the rights of the refugees and their descendants.[71]

Finally, it could be argued that Gush Shalom managed to send a message of solidarity to the Palestinians and reached out to civil society groups in the international arena. It also managed to develop a more advanced political discourse vis-à-vis the political consensus, although not the ideological consensus, if it is to be compared with Peace Now. However, both groups failed to address the existing asymmetry of power between the settler-ethnic state and the indigenous population, the Palestinians. Both are committed to Zionism and have protected the existing power structure of the exclusive and occupying Jewish state.

Leftist protest organisations and groups

Groups that belong to this category are described as leftists because they share some or all of the following political characteristics. Some oppose Zionism and the state's consequent policies from a Marxist ideological conviction or because they refute all ideologies. Others are ready to address the state's responsibility for the eviction of Palestinian refugees, the Nakba, by which they challenge the essence of the ideological consensus of the state. Groups that belong to this category are the Alternative Information Centre (AIC), Matzpen, Shararah,[72] the Anarchists, Zochrot, Neturei Karta[73] and the Movement against Israeli Apartheid in Palestine.[74] A few academics, journalists and writers are also active in this sub-category. These groups represent and can mobilise smaller numbers than the critical Zionists, who in turn represent and can mobilise smaller numbers than the mainstream Zionists. The activists among this category are numbered in the dozens. They are labelled as self-hating Jews, lunatics, marginal, ineffective or irrelevant. Some of the anti-Zionists have chosen to leave Israel as an act of protest and live abroad, such as Shimon Tzabar, who died in London in 2006.

Over the years, the leftists, except for a handful, have not crossed the national divide to the extent of joining the Palestinian resistance, including the armed struggle, as happened in the case of South Africa, where white members, especially from the SACP, chose to do so. Therefore, there has been no development of a joint front for an inclusive struggle and solution.[75]

While values of equality and justice and issues relating to colonialism, Zionism, racism, the Nakba and the validity of international law have largely been absent, marginal or discussed on a limited scale only by the different liberal Zionist groups, these have been very much a focal point in the leftist political discourse and vision for peace. The leftists stand for universal values and a human rights-based approach to solving the conflict. The AIC, which was established in 1984, is a good example of this. During the first intifada, the AIC was very active both in terms of providing information about the situation on the ground, and in its involvement in solidarity activities and the provision of an alternative political analysis. It also provided a space for joint encounters, sometimes initiating contacts.[76] Later, the Oslo Accords created a political split within the AIC. While all agreed that it was a bad agreement, some saw their role as being to denounce it because nothing good would come out of it, whereas others thought that it might create a dynamic that could lead to the end of occupation, and therefore their role was to push it further.[77] Later, as Oslo was dictated to by the side with power, the AIC insisted on a rights-based approach, in contrast to the compromise approach of the 'liberal' Zionists. It became very critical of the Oslo Accords and the dynamics of the Zionist liberal protest groups, a position similar to that of Gush Shalom. The second intifada was seen by the AIC as an inevitable result of the failure of the Oslo Accords.

The AIC views itself as an anti-Zionist organisation that is part of the anti-globalisation and the anti-capitalist or anti-imperialist movements.[78] It rejects Zionism because it encompasses a negation of the Other, the Palestinians, which necessarily means ethnic cleansing sooner or later.[79] Thus, it considers Israel a racist colonial state, and seeks to develop a joint Palestinian–Israeli agenda in the struggle for justice, freedom and equality. It supports a two-state solution as a phasic one, but one that adheres to the right of return. A secular state for all its citizens is the second phase, a long-term joint project.[80] This secular democratic solution sets aside socialism until the appropriate conditions emerge. Comparing it with the South African case, the Israeli leftists are seen to have a three-stage plan, the first phase of which starts with the division of historical Palestine: this position differs from that of the leftists in South Africa.

In terms of its role, the AIC has succeeded in preserving a space in which the two sides can meet and search for a possible future, develop an alternative leftist discourse, and reach out to and galvanise support among like-minded groups in the international arena. It continues to represent a political perspective on behalf of anti-Zionist Israeli activists, who, I believe, number between 100 and 200 individuals.

Israeli individuals who joined the PLO

While many white South Africans joined the ANC and the SACP, as noted above, only a handful of Israelis have joined the PLO. There were two individuals who publicly joined the Fatah movement, while around a dozen were charged with, or accused of, membership in PLO factions such as the Democratic Front for the Liberation of Palestine and the Popular Front for the Liberation of Palestine. The two who joined Fatah – and still belong to the movement – are Uri Davis and Ilan Halevi. Uri Davis joined the PLO out of anti-Zionist convictions and has been a member of Fatah and the Palestine National Council (PNC) since 1984. He is critical of the Oslo Accords and the PLO for not developing an anti-Zionist democratic alternative to Zionism.[81] He also believes that it is easier to correct the PLO/PNC than the apartheid Israeli regime. Ilan Halevi takes a different view, arguing that Israel is not an apartheid state like South Africa.[82] A former member of Matzpen, he states that for pragmatic reasons he has been a Fatah member since 1973.[83] Active in Fatah, he worked at the Palestinian Ministry of Foreign Affairs, and supported the Geneva Initiative until he died.

Israeli protest groups and second track diplomacy

Before concluding this section, it is important to highlight very briefly the fact that the different Israeli protest groups were involved in second-track diplomacy. The anti-Zionist and the non-Zionist groups represented by the Israeli Communist Party started these encounters after the war of 1967. Later, as the PLO became interested in reaching out to the Zionists, the latter took over the 'business' from the leftists. These meetings culminated in the secret talks of Oslo, which became formal, and later in the Ayalon–Nusseibeh plan and the Geneva Initiative, which were agreed upon after the eruption of the second intifada in 2000. Anyone following the development of such meetings can argue that the politics of the mainstream liberal Zionists overtook those of the critical liberal Zionists. As such, the parameters for a settlement, as they stand at present, to a great extent have been shaped by, and reflect, the politics of the mainstream Zionist groups, and particularly Peace Now. These parameters, which were negotiated with leading Palestinian activists and semi-officials, lag far behind those agreed upon in the case of South Africa. They accommodate the ideology in power and the existing exclusive system. They stress that the settlement should be based on the two-state formula that entails division of land, a separation of peoples, and a kind of Palestinian state that is subject to conditions. Nor do they hold Israel accountable for the Nakba or for subsequent injustices to which the Palestinian people have been subjected.

CONCLUSION: THE SIMILARITIES AND DIFFERENCES BETWEEN THE TWO PROTEST CASES

This chapter shows how two similar political systems that produced similar civil societies developed fairly dissimilar protest groups in terms of their political platforms and roles. As discussed earlier, this was linked to the intermediate variables that are located between the two exclusive systems and the outcomes of protest groups; in both cases they changed the pathways taken by the majority of protest groups. Changes at international level, the visions and strategies of both resistance movements, demography, economic relations between the dominant and the dominated side in both cases, support received by the ANC and the PLO from neighbouring countries, the legitimacy of both ideologies in power, along with other variables, all contributed to different political discourses of protest, to different positions and subsequently to different roles.

In the case of Apartheid South Africa, all protest groups, both liberal and leftist, stood against apartheid, as an ideology and an exclusive system, and undermined it. Even so, they differed over the future alternative and on strategies to reach the end result. By the early 1980s, the rift that had occurred between the liberal groups brought most of them closer to the politics of the UDF, the public arm of the ANC. Many adopted the UDF's platform and joined the struggle for a united, non-racial, democratic South Africa. The more hesitant, gradualist and pragmatic mainstream liberals lost their leading role, and it was the progressive liberals who became active participants in the struggle for the move towards a 'rainbow nation', where all are equal in the eyes of the law. Thus they contributed to altering the dominant consensus from that of separation to that of inclusive peace, where both sides would benefit from a compromise between the political and the economic.

There were thousands of whites who joined the leftist (black-run) mainstream and radical groups, and some paid with their lives for the struggle. They sent a strong message to the blacks that they were equal participants in the resistance and they contributed to the success of the ANC-led coalition and later to the idea of reconciliation.

In the case of Zionist Israel, the intermediate variables did not exert pressure on the dominant side, as had occurred in the case of Apartheid South Africa. The change that the liberals have been ready to take on board has remained rather cosmetic and perpetuates the existing structure of power. The mainstream Zionist liberal groups, under the leadership of Peace Now, continue to be dominant. The critical Zionists have been labelled by the mainstream groups as radical leftists, while the leftists are called lunatics or self-hating Jews. Over the years, Israeli mainstream liberal groups, which are close to the Labor and Meretz parties, have argued the need for a compromise based on the division of Palestine and a settlement that Israel would reach from a position of strength, one that would protect its Jewish nature and its security. Such a settlement would entail Palestinian compromise over land occupied in 1967, the right of return, Jerusalem, and its sovereignty over the future entity. The critical Zionist groups have dared to challenge publicly the government's policies and strategies and, unlike the mainstream groups, are ready to recognise aspects of the Palestinian narrative. They are also ready to propose a better deal for the Palestinians as part of a two-state formula. Thus, many of the groups that belong to this category challenge the political consensus, even though, like the mainstream Zionist groups, they continue to abide by the ideological consensus. Both are still far from seeking to alter the dominant national consensus to that of a just and inclusive peace. They promote a compromise that protects the ideology and system in power and that benefits the dominant group.

The Israeli leftist groups are very limited in size and outreach. They remain marginal but have survived over the years as advocates for a human rights-based solution. Their core principles continue to be commitment to international law and the values of equality, justice and anti-racism. They advocate an inclusive settlement, a one-state solution that could follow a first phase settlement of two states. They must still meet the big challenges that lie ahead of them in order to become effective players in altering the Israeli national consensus towards a peace between equals, which both sides will benefit from equally.

Notes

1   The choice of period of study for the two cases was based on the following factors: analogies can be made between the two periods of the two cases; there was an increase in protest activities (cooperation across the divide, mobilisation, provision of services for the oppressed, and so on); the number of protest groups increased; these were considered as periods of transition for political change; during the periods of study, secret and open, formal and informal negotiations were held; strife and tension among and across the divided communities reached unprecedented levels in comparison with previous periods; and these were described as periods of 'peace industry' in the Israeli–Palestinian case and 'change industry' in Apartheid South Africa.

2   This labelling reflected different models of protest. Since the majority of Israeli groups are Zionist, they not only stood for Zionism but also avoided naming themselves as anti-occupation groups. As Zionists, they believe in the idea of '*Eretz Israel*' but are ready to accept a territorial compromise in exchange for peace. Thus, it could be argued that being for peace is more

neutral and less demanding; in addition, peace can have different meanings. They also support division and separation along national lines and, as such, protest activism has not been able to take the form of an inclusive struggle and the conflict has been addressed in a piecemeal fashion. The opposite was true in the South African case, where the struggle was founded on the negation of the ideology in power and the quest to build an inclusive alternative. The grand vision was clear and a joint struggle took place for a united non-racial and democratic South Africa.

3 Anthony D. Smith, *The Nations in History: Historiographical Debates about Ethnicity and Nationalism*, Cambridge: Polity Press, 2000, pp. 15–20.

4 Kenneth P. Vickery, '"Herrenvolk" Democracy and Egalitarianism in South Africa and the US South', *Comparative Studies in Society and History* 16(3) (June 1974), pp. 309–28. Vickery argues that 'masters' democracy' is a Herrenvolk democracy. It is a regime 'democratic for the master race but tyrannical for the subordinate groups'. It is authoritarian vis-à-vis the Other but can be very egalitarian towards its own group.

5 Amneh Badran, 'Civil Society and Peace-Building in Ethnic-National States: A Comparative Study of Israeli/Jewish Protest Groups Today and White Protest Groups in South Africa under Apartheid', unpublished PhD thesis, University of Exeter, 2007, p. 163.

6 Ibid., p. 163.

7 Paul Pennings, Hans Keman and Jan Kleinnijenhuis, *Doing Research in Political Science: An Introduction to Comparative Methods and Statistics*, 2nd edition, London: Sage, 2006, p. 35.

8 In the case of Apartheid South Africa, the apartheid political system, like its predecessor, ran a 'masters' democracy' in which an ethnic minority governed the majority. In the case of Zionist Israel, the Zionist movement aimed for a Jewish ethnic state in which the Jews would be the majority. Different schemes were therefore implemented to transfer the indigenous population (the Palestinians), and to a great extent they have succeeded in achieving this aim. Since its establishment in 1948, Israel has run a 'masters' democracy' vis-à-vis a minority of Palestinian citizens. Following the conquest of the rest of mandatory Palestine in 1967, the State of Israel did not grant citizenship status to the Palestinian population there but left them stateless under its military occupation.

9 The relationship of economic interdependency in the case of South Africa prepared the ground for a different outcome (an inclusive settlement) from that in the Palestinian–Israeli conflict, where Palestinian economic dependency has contributed to a different political discourse. A majority of

Israeli protest groups continue to play a significant role in forming opinions in favour of ideas that promote separation.

10 From an early stage, the South African political system lost its claim to be a legitimate democratic system, and its establishment on the basis of race and its exercising of extensive discriminatory laws and policies more or less doomed it to worldwide condemnation. This has not been the case with Zionist Israel. Israel has managed to promote itself as a Jewish liberal democracy, or even as the only democracy in the backward Middle East. Its ethnically based nationalist ideology, its exclusive 'democratic' system, and subsequently its discriminatory laws and policies towards the Palestinians have received little attention over the decades. Only in the past ten years or so have some critical voices begun to question the notions of exclusivity built into its ethnic political system that have promoted a 'masters' democracy'.

11 Ebrahim Ebrahim is Senior Adviser (political and economic) to the current Deputy President (June 2004) of South Africa. He spoke at the Jericho International Conference 'The Palestinian–Israeli Conflict: Future Prospects for an Agreed-Upon Solution', 3–4 June 2004. I refer to his presentation and to a personal interview with him.

12 It is important to note that whites who joined the struggle against apartheid in their personal capacities by joining the ANC and/or the SACP have not been given sufficient attention in existing scholarly studies. They have either been neglected or mentioned only briefly in a way that has not shown their role in the struggle.

13 See the Helen Suzman Foundation: http://hsf.org.za/about-us/mission (accessed 9 May 2006).

14 Jill Wentzel is a solid believer in liberalism and an ex-activist in the Black Sash protest group who opposed the shift in Black Sash positions. She is also a close friend of the South African Institute of Race Relations.

15 Jill Wentzel, *The Liberal Slideaway*, Johannesburg: South African Institute of Race Relations, 1995, p. vii.

16 Colin Knox and Padraic Quirk, *Peace Building in Northern Ireland, Israel and South Africa: Transition, Transformation and Reconciliation*, Basingstoke: Palgrave Macmillan, 2000, p. 167.

17 Based on an interview with Sheena Dunkan, president of Black Sash in the 1980s and a current member of the Black Sash board of trustees, Johannesburg, 24 February 2006.

18 Based on an interview with David Schmidt, a former staff member of IDASA, Cape Town, 9 March 2006.

19 Raymond Louw (ed.), *Four Days in Lusaka: Whites in a Changing Society June 29–July 2, 1989*, Johannesburg: Five Freedoms Forum, 1989, pp. 39–54.

20 Based on an interview with Sue Briton, a founder member of the End Conscription Campaign, Durban, 28 February 2006.

21 Based on an interview with Dr Jon Hyslop at the University of Witwatersrand, Johannesburg, 20 February 2006.

22 Based on an interview with Frans Cronje, a researcher at the SAIRR, Johannesburg, 23 February 2006.

23 Based on an interview with Na'eem Jeenah, head of the anti-censorship programme at the Freedom of Expression Institute, Johannesburg, 23 February 2006.

24 In a press statement on political violence issued by the SAIRR to the South African Press Association on 11 July 1985.

25 John Kane-Berman, 'Ten-Point Peace Package', *Financial Mail*, 26 July 1985 (article written in his capacity as a director of the SAIRR).

26 Interview with Sheena Dunkan.

27 *Black Sash 1955–2005: The Golden Jubilee Report*, Cape Town: Black Sash, 2005, pp. 1–8.

28 Ibid., p. 7.

29 Mike Oliver, Cavin Evans and Gael Neke, 'The Role Of Whites in a Changing Society' in Louw, *Four Days in Lusaka*, back cover.

30 Interview with Sheena Dunkan.

31 Press release issued by Black Sash, 15 December 1982. Carol Archibald, *Records of the Black Sash: 1955–1995*, Historical and Literary Papers 24, Johannesburg: Library, University of the Witwatersrand.

32 Press release signed by Sheena Dunkan in July 1987. Archibald, *Records of the Black Sash*, note 29.

33 Oliver, Evans and Neke, 'The Role Of Whites in a Changing Society', p. 51.

34 Interview with Dr Caroline White, an English-speaking activist in the United Women organisation and Black Sash in the 1980s and a lecturer at the University of Natal from 1997 to 2000, London, 29 January 2006.

35 Interview with Na'eem Jeenah, Head of the Anti-censorship Programme at the Freedom of Expression Institute, Johannesburg, 23 February 2006.

36 Based on an interview with Dr Keith Cottschalk, Head of the Department of Political Studies, University of the Western Cape, 8 March 2006.

37 Based on an interview with Roland Hunter, Johannesburg, 22 February 2006. Hunter is at present the Director of Revenue in the Department of Finance and Economic Development in the City of Johannesburg.

38 Interview with Phyllis Naidoo, an Indian veteran member of the South African Communist Party, Durban, 2 March 2006.

39 Patrick Pond, *Elite Transition: From Apartheid to Neo-Liberalism in South Africa*, Scottsville: Natal University Press, 2000, especially the introduction and first two chapters.

40 'Chasing the rainbow: a survey of South Africa', *The Economist*, 8 April 2006, p. 8.

41 Based on interviews with Dror Etkes (Coordinator of Settlements Watch at Peace Now) and Uri Avnery of Gush Shalom, 20 June 2005 and 28 September 2005 respectively.

42 Based on an interview with Jeff Halper, Coordinator of ICAHD, Jerusalem, 30 August 2004.

43 In the Israeli context, the *national consensus* has two levels: the ideological and the political. The *ideological consensus* is the primary level of consensus, and is based on the Zionist ethos of the right of the Jewish people (from everywhere) to a national, secure home in '*Eretz Israel*', i.e., Palestine, which is manifested in a democratic Jewish state that holds the values envisioned by the prophets of Israel. This is the common premise that unites the right, the centre and the 'left' or liberals. It is Zionism that binds the 'peace' people with the ultra-nationalists. The *political consensus* is based on the ideological level of the national consensus. The political consensus has clear principles, stands and viewpoints. However, it is not static and can sometimes be temporary. For example, the consensus has changed with regard to the existence of a Palestinian nation. After decades of a consensus of denial, the Palestinian people have become recognised as a nation. Another example is the principle of a two-state solution, which has become part of the present Israeli political lexicon, whereas it was a very marginal or a non-existent notion twenty years ago. Finally, the consensus about the availability of a partner has also shifted, from Jordan as the acceptable partner, to a local leadership that could be a partner, to the PLO as a partner, and finally to there being no partner.

44 Michael Warschawski quoting Jamal Zahalka in Maxine Kaufmann Nunn (ed.), *The Non Co-Operation with Specific Laws: Creative Resistance; Anecdotes of Non-Violent Action by Israel-Based Groups*, Jerusalem: Alternative Information Center, 1993, p. 100.

45 Ibid., p. 100.

46 It is important to note that Peace Now stood firmly behind the government of Israel in its war on Lebanon in 2006.

47 Reuven Kaminer, *The Politics of Protest: The Israeli Peace Movement and the Palestinian Intifada*, Eastbourne: Sussex Academic Press, 1996, p. 98.

48 Interview with Galia Golan, a member of the decision-making core group in Peace Now, Jerusalem, 6 July 2005.

49 Jan Demarest Abu Shakrah, 'Israeli Peace Forces: Can They Change Israel's Direction?', photocopied article is in my possession, p. 26. Abu Shakrah is a researcher and a human rights specialist.

50 Kaminer, *The Politics of Protest*, p. 113.

51 Based on an interview with Yehudith Harel, Jerusalem, 8 August 2005. Harel is a veteran Israeli peace activist. An ex-member of Peace Now who moved to Gush Shalom, she eventually become a supporter of a one-state solution.

52 Interview with Rabbi Arik Asherman of Rabbis for Human Rights, who referred to Sarid's view on human rights in the mid-1990s.

53 Uri Avnery, 'Is Oslo Dead?', *Palestine-Israel Journal* 5 (Winter 1995), p. 27.

54 The Ayalon–Nusseibeh proposed peace plan (2002) is an outcome of informal negotiations between Ami Ayalon, the former Israeli General Security Service Chief (Shin Bet) and Dr Sari Nusseibeh, a prominent member of the Fatah movement. They agreed on a broad framework for reaching a political settlement to the Israeli–Palestinian conflict. It is based on the two-state formula while considering the security concerns of Israel as a Jewish state.

55 The Geneva Initiative was launched in Geneva in 2003. It is the first detailed proposed plan to reach a settlement for the Israeli–Palestinian conflict. Leading members of the Meretz Party and Peace Now, from the Israeli side, and leading members from the Fatah movement and Fida Party, from the Palestinian side, negotiated this informal plan.

56 Based on an interview with Uri Avnery, leader of Gush Shalom, Tel Aviv, 28 September 2005.

57 ICAHD is located on the edge of the left in this sub-category.

58 This was founded by Israelis of oriental origin, the Sephardim.

59 This group is similar to the campus-based student organisations that were established during the first intifada and later disappeared.

60 Amneh Badran, *Zionist Israel and Apartheid South Africa: Civil Society and Peace-Building In Ethnic-National States*, Abingdon: Routledge, 2010, p. 152.

61 Based on an interview with Uri Avnery, leader of Gush Shalom, Tel Aviv, 28 September 2005.

62 Yossi Schwartz, 'The Israeli Left between the Al-Aqsa Intifada and the Road Map' in Yasser Akawi, Gabriel Angelone and Lisa Nessan (eds),

From Communal Strife to Global Struggle: Justice for the Palestinian People, Jerusalem: Alternative Information Centre, 2004, p. 23.

63 Avnery, 'Is Oslo Dead?', p. 30.
64 Interview with Uri Avnery.
65 Interview with Uri Avnery.
66 A pamphlet by Gush Shalom entitled: 'Truth against Truth – a Completely Different Look at the Israeli–Palestinian Conflict', 2003, p. 28.
67 Interview with Uri Avnery.
68 Historical compromise means, in this context, the Palestinian acceptance of having a Palestinian state on the land occupied in 1967, which consists of 22 per cent of mandatory Palestine. The remaining 78 per cent is already under the control of the State of Israel, and has been so since 1948.
69 Interview with Yehudith Harel.
70 Based on an interview with Dr Uri Davis (by telephone), 20 August 2006.
71 Uri Davis, *Apartheid Israel: Possibilities for the Struggle Within*, London: Zed Books, 2003, p. 148.
72 Shararah, the Spark, is no longer active as a group. In the 1980s it had close ties with the Democratic Front for the Liberation of Palestine and was harassed by the Israeli government, which imprisoned a number of its members.
73 I acknowledge that the Neturei Karta religious group is not by any means leftist; however, it shares one leftist political position by being anti-Zionist. There is no other case like it, so rather than leaving it out, I chose to mention it in this category.
74 The Movement against Israeli Apartheid in Palestine is not yet active but it has a website. It is registered in England and expects to start working in two to three years when financial resources are available and the political environment is conducive. Based on an interview with Uri Davis: www.mediamonitors.net/uridavis2.html.
75 One can argue that there were several reasons for this. First, it was due to the position of the Israeli Communist Party (Hadash), which did not question Israel's legitimacy and was among the first to advocate a two-state solution. From the 1950s onwards, it gave weight to a discourse of compromise and pragmatism as being the correct approach, one that the 'liberals' in fact adopted some decades later. Second, the framework of a two-state solution along national lines eventually won over the united secular state framework that the PLO had espoused at some point. Third, there has been little readiness among the leftists to cross national lines and join the struggle of the Other: this would entail a much higher price than that of being ostracised.

They have continued to work from within the law and there have been very few exceptional cases. Fourth is the historical context in which Israel has managed to ignore the existence of the Palestinians and the Palestinian cause. It took the PLO decades to bring the Palestinian question back to life. Finally, Israeli denials about a long period of Palestinian existence and their rights, divisions along nationality and cultural lines between Jews and Palestinians, and the asymmetry of power have contributed to producing an environment that favours separate work. Hence, Moshe Machover refers to Azmi Bishara's comment that: 'You work with your public and I work on mine'. (Based on an interview with Professor Moshe Machover, who was involved in such meetings, London, 23 August 2006.)

76 Interview with Michael Warschawski, AIC, Jerusalem, 22 July 2005.
77 Interview with Michael Warschawski, 22 July 2005.
78 Interview with Michael Warschawski, Jerusalem, 1 March 2005.
79 Interview with Michael Warschawski, 1 March 2005.
80 Based on an interview with Nassar Ibrahim, coordinator of *Ru'ya Ukhra* and co-editor of *News from Within*: both magazines are published by the AIC (an Israeli–Palestinian anti-Zionist organisation), Beit Sahour, Palestine, 11 June 2005.
81 Interview with Uri Davis.
82 Based on an interview with Ilan Halevi, an Israeli Jewish member of the Fatah movement, Ramallah, 17 September 2005.
83 Interview with Ilan Halevi.

PART 4

FUTURE MODELS AND PERSPECTIVES

CHAPTER 8

The Inevitable Impossible: South African Experience and a Single State

STEVEN FRIEDMAN

Attracting ribald laughter at an academic conference is not usually a source of pride. But being laughed at for declaring in mid-1987 that a negotiated end to apartheid was possible is an exception.

The delegates at the South African sociology conference who found the idea of a negotiated settlement so amusing only two and a half years before it began to become a reality were reflecting the mainstream view that an accommodation between the white minority and black majority was impossible. For years, scholarship and common wisdom insisted that blacks and whites could not share a political space in peace.[1] The struggle for the end of apartheid seemed to be 'necessarily a zero-sum game'[2] in which white rule would endure or be violently overthrown: either way, a common society was not possible. In the 1980s, the intense violent conflict between the apartheid government and the black-led resistance, accompanied by apocalyptic government statements urging a 'total strategy' to counter the 'total onslaught' of the anti-apartheid forces,[3] seemed only to confirm the prognosis, rendering any claims to the contrary utopian.

We now know that this society seemingly locked in endless conflict was on the verge of a negotiated transition to a common political order. And that, while relations between the races that were once in conflict have not been easy in South Africa after apartheid, a single democratic state has not threatened the physical safety, or indeed the lifestyles, of the formerly governing whites.

South Africa is mentioned regularly in the Middle East debate. While some Zionists find the comparison threatening,[4] it is sometimes seen as an inspiration by those seeking an end to the conflict. This chapter does not propose the South African experience as a recipe for the Middle East. It is, rather, concerned with showing how aspects of South Africa's recent history may demonstrate that a state shared by Israelis and Palestinians is not a utopian dream, but both a possibility and the only viable way to resolve the conflict. It seeks to show that what seems fantastic and 'impossible' can come to appear as the only realistic option by examining how the leadership of Afrikaner nationalism came to see a democratic state as a better guarantor of their interests than domination through separation.

ELITE PARALLELS: AFRIKANER NATIONALISM AND ZIONISM

Equating Zionism and Afrikaner nationalism is controversial. But there are commonalities. Both insist that the survival of a group can be secured only by a state defined in ethnic or cultural terms. They are both 'ethno-nationalist movements geared to the objective of establishing nation-states in sovereign control of exclusive national territories'.[5] And if some Zionists find the parallel disturbing, Afrikaner nationalists embraced it, drawing analogies between the Jews and the Afrikaners as 'people of God' in a hostile environment.[6]

Both, therefore, see a sovereign nation-state and 'exclusive national territory' as essential to safety. The causes of the Jewish need for security are too well known to require repetition – for Afrikaner nationalism, statehood was a protection against British colonialism and the black majority. The use by the British of concentration camps to intern Afrikaner women and children during the South African war at the turn of the twentieth century was a poignant parallel with the Jewish experience – and tales of beleaguered Afrikaner pioneers surrounded by aggressive black tribesmen offered a resonance with Zionist references to the early pioneer period.

Zionists continue to insist that only an ethnic state can insure against the perils facing Jewry – physical annihilation or cultural death through assimilation. In this view, a 'two-state solution' to the Middle East conflict is the limit of the possible since a single state is a recipe for national suicide. As a response to American Jewish scholar Tony Judt's criticism of an ethnic state[7] had it: 'Sixty years after the attempt to wipe out the Jewish people in Europe, after which the countries of the world were kind enough to allow Holocaust survivors to build a national home for themselves, along comes a historian … and proposes that the Jews commit suicide'.[8] The Zionist mainstream remains firmly within a paradigm which insists that: 'If the goal of the sovereign nation-state cannot be … maintained then … there is *no future*'.[9] The Afrikaner nationalist leadership concluded, by contrast, that there is a future without ethnic control of a state. How did this occur?

THE UNWORKABLE DREAM

The Afrikaner nationalist elite did not reconsider its reliance on an ethnic state in a flash of revelation. It did so, very reluctantly, after a lengthy process in which repeated attempts were made to shore up racial rule in the face of pressures on the apartheid system.[10]

These can be divided into three related categories: first, 'objective constraints' – structural flaws within the system that, even in the absence of overt opposition, began to render it less workable. Thus, from the late 1960s, the economy began to run out of skilled white labour. Black workers were needed for the skilled posts from which they had been barred,[11] giving them a bargaining power that they used to challenge racial domination. The second category was contradictory goals – its leaders pursued aims that contradicted each other and threatened the system's workability. A key example was the system of ethnic 'homelands' or 'Bantustans' for black people. Apartheid was buttressed by an ideology and strategy which assumed that black demands for political rights could be deflected by creating black 'self-governing' or 'independent' ethnic territories. The key goal was to entrench white power in the remaining 87 per cent of the country. The goals proved contradictory. The Bantustans could not become self-governing in practice because they then might become centres of independent black power, threatening white control. They also needed land and resources if they were to enjoy even notional viability. But the white electorate's needs took priority and so they received far less than they were said to need. While segregated 'homelands' could never have satisfied black aspirations, the contradictions ensured that they could not even attain the minimum standard of viability that the system's architects set for themselves.

Inevitably, the system also faced 'subjective' constraints, prompted by human agency. The most important was black resistance. This dates from the beginnings of white domination but the crucial period began with the Durban strikes of 1973[12] and, three years later, the revolt against Afrikaans education in the Soweto township, which began months of urban rebellion.[13] Both were watersheds because they prompted reforms as well as repression, suggesting that the balance of power between minority rulers and the voteless majority had changed, albeit imperceptibly. The system was also subjected to sustained and growing international pressure, which limited the options of its rulers and created levers for the resistance. The international campaign against apartheid is well known and details need not be repeated here. It sharply influenced the strategies of apartheid's rulers.[14]

These pressures prompted a retreat from apartheid that took almost two decades and followed a distinct pattern. The Afrikaner nationalist leadership responded by seeking to concede enough to ward off the pressures but not enough to threaten the system. It would repeatedly shift ground, in effect defining aspects of apartheid as 'marginal' and therefore dispensable so that the 'core', white political rule, would be preserved. But, because minority ethnic rule was untenable, the retreat served only to expose the core, not insulate it. In 1985, the core was breached when the principle of black participation in national politics was accepted, albeit under strictures which ensured that white power would remain intact.[15] This moved to a stress on 'power sharing' in which white and black leadership would enjoy an equal say despite the latter's overwhelming majority: this was a further retreat, demanding for whites a veto, but not the right to decide alone. Within four years, majority rule was conceded.[16]

For some, this was a 'surrender' by a weak white leadership[17] that could have negotiated a bargain retaining a veto for the white minority. This assumed that apartheid could have been reformed on terms which would leave whites holding onto power derived purely from their racial origins and out of proportion with their numbers – ironically, precisely this view was held by left critics of the government who feared that it could use reform to strengthen its hold on power.[18] But white rule did not end because of a strategic miscalculation or failure of nerve. The system could not survive without reform – but it could not survive reform. Once the retreat began, as it had to do in the face of pressures, the system could only erode. Thus, when this interviewer asked an official why he and his colleagues had not ejected black people from the 'white cities' in which their sojourn was meant to be temporary, he replied: 'We tried – again and again and again. But they kept on coming back'.[19] In much the same way, repeated attempts to build a wall around white rule foundered on black resistance.

Once Afrikaner nationalist leadership acknowledged that black demands for participation had to be accommodated in some form, it implicitly accepted that what black people felt mattered and that constitutional change was therefore subject to black approval – which could not be obtained for a system that left whites at least half in charge simply by virtue of their whiteness. The result was that every reform, every 'refinement', did not entrench minority power – it reduced options for coercion and opened new spaces for resistance. While this did not, at the time of the negotiated settlement, threaten to overthrow white power by military means, it combined with international pressure to raise the costs of maintaining the system and therefore to erode the will to preserve it.

The retreat was speeded by aspects of Afrikaner nationalist ideology and political culture. Apartheid was applied in a particularly harsh fashion because Afrikaner nationalism was guided by assumptions that, ironically, also helped its leaders see the inevitability of change. Some colonisers in Africa were comfortable with the idea that the colonised could be absorbed into their culture as 'second- or third-class' – French or Portuguese – citizens. Or, in the British style, they could be admitted under sufferance if they adopted 'standards of civilisation' set by the coloniser. Afrikaner political culture, presumably because it was forged in a struggle against (British) colonisation, could not accommodate second-class citizenship – one was either part of the polity or one was not. Black people could not, therefore, be absorbed; they could only be excluded from the political community and, in aspiration if not in reality, the economy.[20] But once the system began its retreat, this obstacle to change became an asset because apartheid's architects were aware of the contradiction between accepting that black people have a permanent right to live in 'white' South Africa but not granting them the right to vote there.[21]

Perhaps as a result, key sections of the Afrikaner nationalist elite redefined the preconditions for Afrikaner survival – as reform proceeded, exclusive ethnic control of the state was no longer deemed necessary. The result was the growing acceptability of a 'post-national future for Afrikaners'.[22] While intellectual and ethical considerations played a role in this conversion, it was also related to the change in

Afrikaner circumstances: rising education levels and increased wealth meant that continued prosperity and the private spaces and institutions that money could buy offered an alternate survival route. An increasing tendency towards cosmopolitanism among the elite also made it possible to conceive *in extremis* of a life lived in comfort and security beyond South Africa's borders. To most, the idea that it was possible to live elsewhere provided an option which had not existed when a necessary condition for Afrikaner identity was held to be residence in Africa. The vast majority would remain, under more than tolerable conditions, within South Africa. But the knowledge that a life elsewhere was possible induced a source of security.

As the retreat from apartheid gathered pace, the system's unacceptability to black and international opinion meant that what was intended as a strategy to shore up white rule became a means of ensuring its orderly and relatively peaceful demise. The architects of reform could not preserve white rule. But they ensured that it would end with far less bloodshed and cost than would have been entailed by clinging to the system to its end. Far from giving the country away, reform reduced the costs to the minority of apartheid's end and made a future without control of the state a possibility – and, for most, a very comfortable one.

Negotiating the terms

Afrikaner nationalist leaders were able to recognise before the costs of an ethnic state became intolerable that they would need to give way to a shared polity. They were far less perceptive in their negotiation of the terms of the transition to it.

Their negotiating strategy was built on the premise that a white veto on change enforced by the constitution could become acceptable to local black and international opinion.[23] This failed to see that the core objection to apartheid was that whites acquired power by virtue of their race and that a racial veto would be seen to perpetuate this, in the eyes not only of black South Africans but of the Reagan administration.[24] And it distracted attention from proposals that might have more realistically sought to preserve minority interests.

This pattern was repeated in other aspects of the negotiations. Government proposals repeatedly endorsed options such as radical devolution to racially segregated suburbs, which were rejected because they seemed to preserve racial decision-making. Less obviously, the government's preference for a closed list proportional electoral system, based on a misreading of likely electoral outcomes, ensured an arrangement that significantly reduced the influence of minority parties.[25]

By overestimating the 'saleability' of modified white rule to their negotiating partners and other key influences on the process, the Afrikaner nationalist negotiators missed opportunities to influence the post-apartheid order in ways that might have better protected their constituency.

LESSONS FOR THE MIDDLE EAST

What lessons does this experience hold for Israeli Jews?

The most obvious is that Zionism now faces what Afrikaner nationalism faced – significant pressure to reform. While the 'objective' pressure of dependence on Palestinian labour is absent, other forms of resistance may be effective. Thus the existence of a large diaspora on which Zionism depends could become a source of weakness as pressure for boycott, divestment and sanctions grows. It is not inconceivable that, as this pressure mounts, the United States will use its influence to demand a settlement on Palestinian terms. Given the depth of Israeli dependence on the US, of course, this could become a decisive lever for change.

In this context, the 'two-state solution' becomes analogous to reform apartheid, the attempt by the Afrikaner nationalist elite to change apartheid while retaining the core principle of ethnic rule. Both seek to make concessions to pressure on the ethnic state to preserve its essence – in this case, a Jewish state, albeit within reduced borders. In the Middle East, as in South Africa, the key question is whether it is possible to envisage pressures for change being accommodated while preserving the Zionist core of an explicitly Jewish state.

Unrealistic realism

It is extremely difficult to imagine a two-state solution that could achieve this. If a separate state is to address the aspirations of Palestinians, it would need to be economically viable – even apartheid's visionary planners insisted that the black 'homelands' could not defuse opposition to minority rule unless they had the resources to address the material needs of 'their people'.[26] In the Middle East, this would entail, among other measures, substantial development cooperation, engaging time and skills as well as money, and Palestinian access to Israeli labour markets and other institutions – apartheid shows that separate institutions in resource-poor territories ensure continued poverty and discontent. It would require Israeli acknowledgement that the fate of Jews and Palestinians are intertwined – even if the Israeli electorate were to consider the (possibly violent) removal of some 500,000 settlers on envisaged Palestinian land a price worth paying, or if, even more unlikely, the settlers were persuaded to move voluntarily. A viable Palestinian state is possible only if Israelis recognise their interdependence with their neighbours and this is reciprocated. But, if the two sides became aware of their common destiny to cooperate in building a Palestinian state, with all the sacrifices and difficulties this is likely to entail, why the need to separate? If South African experience is a guide, a single state requires less acknowledgement of interdependence than a shared polity, because, in the latter, the material disadvantage of the group seeking to escape what it sees as bondage is partly compensated for by the attainment of political rights in a single polity. The fact that post-apartheid South Africa must still contend with high levels of inequality and black poverty[27] is a blemish on its achievements. But the willingness of the poor to accept gradual change in their conditions is far greater than under apartheid.[28] And addressing poverty and deprivation within a single economy is far less costly than seeking to develop a new economy in a separate geographic space.

Like the apartheid reforms, therefore, a Palestinian state is likely not to deflect pressure on Israel as an ethnic state, but to increase its intensity since it is almost inevitable that this state would experience high levels of poverty, which its residents would compare unfavourably to the relative affluence of their Israeli neighbours. Rather than a key to peace for Jewish Israel, it is likely to become a place where young Palestinians seethe with resentment at conditions that will be blamed by ethno-nationalists on the other side of the divide on Palestinian leaders who 'settled for crumbs'. That the Palestinian state will become a base for more tragic violence seems far more likely than that it will become a buffer.

In another analogy with South Africa, the two-state solution is likely to find itself beset with contradictions as Israeli governments try to square the circle of meeting the needs of their Jewish electorate for land and resources while somehow ensuring that a Palestinian state is affluent enough to prevent it becoming a dire security threat.

Rethinking security

Given these strategic realities, is it possible to envisage a rethinking of Jewish security analogous to the Afrikaner nationalist reassessment that questioned the need for an ethnic state?

Recent history has offered little support for the contention that an ethnic state is the most likely source of Jewish security. Political Zionists saw a Jewish state as an antidote to anti-Semitism. They had more in mind than the notion that, if Jews possessed a territory and army, they would protect themselves. Rather, they believed that a Jewish state would make anti-Jewish prejudice disappear. Some were

Western European Jews who had held high hopes of assimilating into mainstream society and had, in their view, been rebuffed.[29] They became convinced that, deep down, the non-Jew would always despise the Jew as long as the Jew lacked a state: after years without a state, Jews had become degraded and servile and so unworthy of respect. They would recover their dignity and the respect of others only when, like everyone else, they acquired a state.

But the antidote to prejudice became its cause, a process analysed by the historian David Biale.[30] He shows that mainstream Zionism became dominated by an 'ideology of survival' that saw the state not as an antidote to anti-Semitism but its target, surrounded by enemies – not only the states around it that refused to recognise it and made war on it, but much international opinion too. Contrary to the Zionist promise, the state did not cure anti-Semitism; it attracted it. If political pressure on Zionism grows, this irony may well ensure that many more Jews come to see an ethnic state as a liability rather than a form of insurance.

Equally importantly, Biale offers a reading of Jewish history that, perhaps unwittingly, undermines the equation of Jewish security and autonomy with statehood. He shows first that Jewish powerlessness in the diaspora was often relative – in many cases, Jews governed their own communities. And Jewish statehood was never as autonomous as ethnic nationalists believe: on the contrary, it invariably relied on the support of a world power.[31]

This pattern continues. It is tragically evident that Jews are physically far safer in the liberal democracies from which ethnic nationalism is meant to protect them than in a Jewish state: Jews are far more likely to face physical attack in Sderot or even Tel Aviv than in Washington, DC or London. Despite the Zionist portrayal of liberal democracies as Weimars waiting for the inevitable Third Reich, in most cases Jews have lived in safety in these societies for centuries. By contrast, the ethnic state has faced constant insecurity. Second, Israel depends for its survival on another state, the United States.[32] This highlights a contradiction at the heart of the political Zionist notion of Jewish security: if the goodwill of non-Jews is a broken reed, an ethnic state dependent on non-Jewish protection is a source of perpetual insecurity since its protector may turn on it at any moment. If, on the contrary, the goodwill of the US is assured, then at least some non-Jews can be relied upon to protect Jews, and so a rationale for ethnic statehood falls away.

Ethnic nationalist statehood has not delivered to Jews the safety and autonomy it promised – it could be argued that it has offered less than Afrikaner nationalism, since, in the heyday of apartheid, its beneficiaries lived in a blissful albeit myopic tranquillity that Israeli Jews have never enjoyed. It is, therefore, hardly inconceivable to imagine Jewish Israeli leaders reassessing their notions of security in ways that would begin to see a liberal democratic shared state as a surer source of Jewish security than an ethnic nationalist polity.

AN ALTERNATIVE OF THE MIND – AND HEART?

The South African settlement was partly possible because an intellectual alternative to ethnic nationalism was available to its Afrikaner nationalist elite, in the form of a strand of white liberalism, which initially had few Afrikaner adherents but was well known enough to become a resource when needed. There were also exemplars within 'Afrikanerdom', such as the clergyman Beyers Naudé, who was hounded out of the Dutch Reformed Church because of his opposition to apartheid. As pressure for change grew, a vigorous debate redefined Afrikaner identity.[33] This hastened change and was available after democracy was established, making adaptation to it easier. It was possible only because intellectual and moral alternatives existed on which the debate could draw.

This makes it significant that an alternative Jewish tradition does exist that could help to prepare Jews for a shared future not premised on ethnic nationalism. At present, it is small and in need of much development. But the same could be said of Afrikaner dissent under apartheid. That there are traditions available to Jews which point beyond ethnic nationalism may make both the advent of a shared state and its success more likely.

While a Jewish identity with the territory on which Israel is sited is very old, *political* Zionism, with its stress on an ethnic state as a precondition for Jewish survival, is only about 100 years old.[34] And, until the Nazi terror, it was hardly a majority position. For some strains of Orthodox Judaism it was an unconscionable apostasy.[35] Reform Judaism and Jewish socialists also rejected it. Political Zionists were also subjected to scorn by cultural and spiritual Zionists who supported the revival of Jewish nationhood but did not endorse the creation of an ethnic state.[36]

The claim that Zionism is the 'national liberation movement' of the Jewish people[37] is based on the frequent references to the Promised Land in the Bible and in Jewish tradition. But it is not clear that this is an exhortation to a political programme. Some Jews – a handful today, but probably the majority for much of the last 2,000 years – identify the Jewish aspiration for a homeland with the coming of the Messiah.[38] While this may seem like quaint folklore, it can be understood in a way that makes an ethical point: since the age of Messiah is for some Jews a time in which society will be sustained by human harmony rather than coercion,[39] a Jewish state will become ethically possible only when violence no longer rules human affairs – a Utopian aspiration that illustrates the incompatibility of ethnic statehood with ethical principle.

Political Zionism could also be seen as a denial, not an affirmation, of Jewish identity. Zionists often describe their Jewish critics as consumed with 'self-hatred': people who would rather not be Jewish and who express this by condemning the state that expresses Jewish peoplehood. But the scholar Daniel Boyarin invites us to think of political Zionism as self-hatred.[40] For some 1,800 years, he argues, Jews, because they had neither a state nor an army, created a value system in which violence and power were seen as expressions of barbarism.[41] The Jew, unable to fight, relied on the intellect and spirit. Assimilated Jews in Western Europe –

chief among them the founder of political Zionism, Theodor Herzl, and his intellectual ally Sigmund Freud – rejected this because they longed to be like the non-Jews around them. They concluded that the only way to be like everyone else – and thus fully endorse the values of the non-Jewish world – was to acquire a state and an army. In this view, it is ethnic nationalism, not opposition to it, which rejects Jewish identity.

These examples offer only a brief glimpse of how Jewish tradition can be interpreted to sustain an attempt to build Jewish survival in the Middle East on shared statehood rather than an ethnic state. They suffice, however, to show that moral and cultural resources do exist that could come to support a journey beyond ethnic nationalism.

CONCLUSION: READING THE SIGNS

This brief discussion of the ways in which the South African experience may point the way to a viable shared future for Jews and Palestinians in the Middle East has consciously sought not to offer a 'South African model'. Besides the danger of romanticising South Africa's transition and of assuming equivalences with the Middle East, it is questionable whether there is any such thing as a 'South African model'. The process described here was as much a result of ad hoc adaptation to a fluid reality than the outcome of a conscious set of strategies. There is no South African recipe that can be applied neatly to the Middle East.

But the South African experience does hold lessons for the Middle East. It shows, firstly, that the creation of an ethnic state in a multi-ethnic environment will inevitably create pressures as those at whose expense it is established reject their exclusion. These pressures cannot be deflected by force; they can only be accommodated by reform. But, while the reformers invariably hope, once they begin their task, to retain the ethnic nature of the state, they learn, often amid great conflict, that it is not the detail of the ethnic state but its essence that has prompted the pressure; the only way to resolve the conflict created by the pressure is to negotiate the end of the ethnic state and to replace it with an order that offers them, as a group and as individuals, the best guarantee of a life lived in liberty, justice and security.

The core of the Middle East problem is the insistence that Jews can survive only in an ethnic state. The creation of a Palestinian state alongside Israel is an attempt, albeit a well-meaning one in many cases, to preserve the problem. The South African experience suggests that the attempt cannot ensure Jewish security – on the contrary, it is likely to pose new threats to it. The replacement of the ethnic state by one shared by Israelis and Palestinians, built on mutual guarantees, is the only route to a peaceful Jewish life in the region.

But those who established the ethnic state are not doomed to be bystanders, observing the unfolding of a reality they are powerless to change. South Africa shows, too, that how the transition to an order beyond the ethnic state occurs, and the terms on which it is negotiated, will do much to determine reality after the switch. The sooner the ethnic state's leadership recognises reality and begins to plan for it, and the more it is able to develop a strategy for safeguarding its core values and interests based on a realistic appraisal of the difference between legitimate concern and unwarranted privilege, the more security is it likely to ensure. It is to this agenda – to framing proposals that safeguard Jewish interests in a shared state but which are plausible because they take into account Palestinian concerns – that the concern for Jewish security must turn.

Notes

1 For a review of pessimistic prognoses, see Timothy Sisk, *Democratization in South Africa: The Elusive Social Contract*, Princeton: Princeton University Press, 1995. See also Marina Ottaway, *South Africa: The Struggle for a New Order*, Washington, DC: Brookings Institution, 1993.

2 Sisk, *Democratization in South Africa*, p. 7.

3 For an account of this period, see Martin Murray, *South Africa: Time of Agony, Time of Destiny: The Upsurge of Popular Protest*, London: Verso, 1987.

For analysis of the strategies that underpinned the events, see Phillip Frankel, Noam Pines and Mark Swilling (eds), *State, Resistance and Change in South Africa*, London: Croom Helm, 1988.

4   See Ehud Olmert's warning that: 'More and more Palestinians are uninterested in a negotiated, two-state solution, because they want to change the essence of the conflict from an Algerian paradigm to a South African one. From a struggle against "occupation" in their parlance, to a struggle for one-man-one-vote'. David Landau, 'Maximum Jews, Minimum Palestinians', *Ha'aretz*, 13 November 2003.

5   André du Toit, 'Misapprehensions of the Future And Illusions of Hindsight: Some Reflections on the Significance of Intra-Afrikaner Debates to the 1980s', paper delivered at 'A South African Conversation on Israel and Palestine', Institute for African Studies, Columbia University, 20–21 September 2002.

6   For sources and a critique see André du Toit, 'No Chosen People: The Myth of the Calvinist Origins of Afrikaner Nationalism and Racial Ideology', *American Historical Review* 88(4) (1983), pp. 920–52; 'Captive to the Nationalist Paradigm: Prof. F. A. van Jaarsveld and the Historical Evidence for the Afrikaner's Ideas on his Calling and Mission', *South African Historical Journal* 16(1) (1984), pp. 49–80; 'Puritans in Africa? Afrikaner "Calvinism" and Kuyperian neo-Calvinism in Late Nineteenth Century South Africa', *Comparative Studies in Society and History* 27(2) (1985), pp. 209–40.

7   Tony Judt, 'Israel: An Alternative Future', *New York Review of Books*, 23 October 2003.

8   Yoel Esteron, 'Who's in Favor of Annihilating Israel?', *Ha'aretz*, 28 November 2003.

9   Du Toit, 'Misapprehensions of the Future and Illusions of Hindsight', p. 3, emphasis in original.

10 The analysis in this section is based on Steven Friedman, *Understanding Reform*, Johannesburg: SA Institute of Race Relations, 1986; *Reform Revisited*, Johannesburg: SA Institute of Race Relations, 1987.

11 See, for example, T. R. H. Davenport, *South Africa: A Modern History*, Johannesburg: Macmillan, 1987; Alf Stadler, *The Political Economy of Modern South Africa*, Cape Town: David Phillip, 1987.

12 Institute for Industrial Education, *The Durban Strikes, 1973*, Durban: Institute for Industrial Education, 1974.

13 John Kane-Berman, *Soweto: Black Revolt, White Reaction*, Johannesburg, Ravan, 1978.

14 Friedman, *Understanding Reform*; Steven Friedman (ed.), *The Long Journey: South Africa's Quest for a Negotiated Settlement*, Johannesburg, Ravan, 1993.

15 For the concessions that followed this, see Steven Friedman, *The Shapers of Things to Come?: National Party Choices in the South African Ttransition*, Johannesburg: Centre for Policy Studies, 1992.

16 See Doreen Atkinson, 'Brokering a Miracle?: The Multi-Party Negotiating Forum' in Steven Friedman and Doreen Atkinson (eds), *The Small Miracle: South Africa's Negotiated Settlement*, Johannesburg: Ravan, 1995, pp. 13–43.

17 Cabinet minister and former National Party negotiator Tertius Delport is said to have grabbed former president F. W. de Klerk by the shirt front, yelling 'What have you done? You've given South Africa away' when de Klerk announced the terms of the constitutional settlement. Patti Waldmeir, *Anatomy of a Miracle: The End of Apartheid and the Birth of the New South Africa*, Harmondsworth: Penguin, 1997, p. 232.

18 See Sheena Duncan quoted in *Financial Mail*, 25 January 1980, and cited in Hein Marais, *South Africa: Limits to Change: The Political Economy of Transition*, Cape Town, London and New York: UCT Press and Zed Books, 1998, and Karen Jochelson, 'Reform, Repression and Resistance in South Africa: A Case Study of Alexandra Township, 1979–1989', *Journal of Southern African Studies* 16(1) (March 1990), p. 1.

19 Unpublished research, 1987, Urban Foundation archives.

20 Douglas Pierce, *Post-Apartheid South Africa: Lessons from Brazil's 'Nova Republica'*, Johannesburg: Centre for Policy Studies, 1992.

21 In an interview during the 1980s, a government minister explained that abolishing controls on black movement to the cities necessarily meant that black people could no longer be denied a say in national government because people had a right to vote where they lived. The notion that the right to live somewhere also entailed the right to vote would have sounded very odd to an ideologue of French, Portuguese or British colonialism.

22 Du Toit, 'Misapprehensions of the Future And Illusions of Hindsight'.

23 Friedman, *The Shapers of Things to Come?*

24 The administration official responsible for Africa, Herman Cohen, declared during 1992 that ethnic vetoes were unacceptable to the US. Herman J. Cohen, 'The Current Situation: Statement Before the Sub-Committee on Africa of the House Foreign Affairs Committee, Washington, DC, 23/7/1992', *US Department of State Dispatch* 3(30) (27 July 1992).

25 Steven Friedman, 'Too little knowledge is a dangerous thing: South Africa's bargained transition, democratic prospects and John Rawls's veil of ignorance', *Politikon* 25(1) (June 1998), pp. 57–80.

26 The 1956 Tomlinson Commission report purported to spell out the costs of providing economically workable black 'homelands'. As noted above, its proposals were never implemented. Hermann Giliomee and Lawrence

Schlemmer, *From Apartheid to Nation-Building*, Cape Town: Oxford University Press, 1989, p. 55.

27 See, for example, Haroon Bhorat, *The Post-Apartheid Challenge: Labour Demand Trends in the South African Labour Market, 1995–1999*, Working Paper 03/82, Cape Town: Development Policy Research Unit, University of Cape Town, 2003; Haroon Bhorat, 'Labour Market Challenges in the Post-Apartheid South Africa', unpublished paper presented at Colloquium on Poverty, Cape Town, 1 October 2003.

28 For black responses to continued poverty and inequality in a democratic South Africa, see Craig Charney, *Voices of a New Democracy: African expectations in the new South Africa*, Johannesburg: Centre for Policy Studies, 1995.

29 The resultant psychology has been sketched by Daniel Boyarin, *Unheroic Conduct: The Rise of Heterosexuality and the invention of the Jewish Man*, Berkeley: University of California Press, 1997.

30 David Biale, *Power and Powerlessness in Jewish History*, New York: Shocken, 1986.

31 Ibid,, pp. 10–33.

32 Ibid, p. 170.

33 Du Toit, 'Misapprehensions of the Future and Illusions of Hindsight'.

34 *Business Day*, 6 September 2001.

35 Aviezer Ravitzky, *Messianism, Zionism and Jewish Religious Radicalism*, Chicago and London: University of Chicago Press, 1996.

36 See the discussion of Simon Dubnow and Ahad-Ha'am in Gilbert S. Rosenthal, 'The Clash of Modern Ideologies in Judaism' in Raphael Jospe and Stanley M. Wagner (eds), *Great Schisms in Jewish History*, New York: University of Denver and Ktav Publishing House, 1981, pp. 235–48.

37 Barry A. Kosmin, Jacqueline Goldberg, Milton Shain and Shirley Bruk, *Jews of the 'New South Africa': Highlights of the 1998 National Survey of South African Jews*, London and Cape Town: Institute for Jewish Policy Research in association with the Kaplan Centre, University of Cape Town, 1999, p. 15.

38 Ravitzky, *Messianism, Zionism and Jewish Religious Radicalism*.

39 Emmanuel Levinas, 'Messianic Texts' in *Difficult Freedom: Essays on Judaism*, translated by Sean Hand, Baltimore: Johns Hopkins University Press, 1990, pp. 59–98.

40 Boyarin, *Unheroic Conduct*, in particular pp. 271–312.

41 There are echoes of this argument in the view of the philosopher Franz Rosenzweig, who argued that Jews were 'outside history'. Franz Rosenzweig, *The Star of Redemption*, translated by William W. Hallo, South Bend: University of Notre Dame Press, 1985.

CHAPTER 9

Redefining the Conflict in Israel–Palestine: The Tricky Question of Sovereignty

VIRGINIA TILLEY

Scholars arguing for similarities between the policies of Israel in the Occupied Palestinian Territories and those of South Africa during apartheid invariably confront protests that the two cases are not sufficiently homologous to justify this comparison.[1] Even when they are made in bad faith, merely to deflect study of the question, such challenges must be addressed, and counter-arguments have not only expanded the discussion but sometimes suggest whole new models for understanding it. For instance, it is sometimes argued that the conflict in Israel–Palestine is not truly racial in character, so any accusation of its involving apartheid – which international law has established as involving 'racial groups' – is specious or at best misguided. The first response is direct: to clarify that local constructions of 'Jewish' and 'Arab' in this context have indeed obtained racial qualities, and that formulations of 'racial discrimination' in international law therefore do include the Israeli–Palestinian conflict, such that the case can be opened to scrutiny for policies of apartheid. More importantly, this deeper theoretical work has begun to redefine the conflict itself, altering our perspectives and insights into its true nature and illuminating more viable paths to its resolution.

One protest that is especially productive in this way is the objection that the two cases are not homologous regarding the dominant state's sovereignty. Intuitively, apartheid was universally denounced as a morally loathsome system of racial domination because it was imposed by the government of a sovereign state (South Africa) over part of its own population, people who by all contemporary international norms and standards have the right to full citizenship and equal treatment under state law and yet were denied this right solely on the basis of race. By contrast, Israel is not the recognised sovereign in the Occupied Palestinian Territories (OPT, including East Jerusalem, the West Bank and Gaza Strip); it is considered by most authorities to be a belligerent occupier of them.[2] Israel itself – although holding the OPT under its exclusive control for nearly half a century – has not formally annexed the West Bank or East Jerusalem, and certainly abjures any claim to the Gaza Strip, while recognising no other state to have any sovereign authority over them and claiming that they are therefore only 'disputed' territories. This status would seem to alter the international human rights law that applies by excluding laws regarding rights to citizenship and to the same civil rights enjoyed by citizens of the occupying power, such as democratic representation to its legislature. Even under international humanitarian law (especially the Fourth Geneva Convention), protected persons in Occupied Territories are not nationals of the occupying power; to make them citizens could even be seen as violating their rights. Hence, even if Israel's practices regarding the Palestinian population in the OPT are identified as racist, the Israeli government arguably still cannot be guilty of the crime of apartheid regarding people who are not Israeli citizens, are not supposed to be, and are living in territory that is not part of the State of Israel.

The third element of this argument fails for one simple reason: the presumption that a state can be held culpable of apartheid only regarding the population within its formal sovereign territory is simply incorrect, as established by the precedent of Apartheid South Africa's governance of Namibia. This point is addressed below in order to set it aside. But the first two elements move into questions that are more subtle, even sensitive, yet compelled by conditions that have held now for nearly half a century. The most obvious is massive and still-expanding Israeli settlement in East Jerusalem and the West Bank, an infrastructure that has grown so vast, expensive and destructive of any future Palestinian state as to suggest strongly Israel's aim to annex much of these territories permanently (an aim confirmed, not least, by the Israeli government's regular public statements of intent to do so).[3] This policy has been denounced, externally and internally within Israel, as an obstacle to peace. But considering settlement growth together with the package of Israel's policies in the OPT – including appropriation of natural resources such as aquifers, construction of extensive civilian infrastructure throughout the territory, agricultural and industrial development totalling hundreds of billions of dollars and seamless integration of all this into Israel's economy and society – the current landscape reveals a larger picture: that Israel is enjoying full sovereignty throughout the OPT in all but name and can administer and dispose of the territory as it wills. The only notable way in which Israel is not sovereign is in its immunity from the human rights obligations that would apply if it were recognised to be so.

Thus, we find the current dilemma facing the international community, especially in considering the moribund 'peace process', manifesting as a seeming paradox. The belief that Israel is not the rightful sovereign in the OPT has supported conclusions that the only lawful, effective and morally legitimate solution to the conflict is Israel's withdrawal to permit the formation of a Palestinian state. This position is firmly based on several principles of international law: not least, the inadmissibility of acquiring territory by force (as Israel seized the OPT in the Six-Day War of 1967) and the right of peoples to self-determination (translated here as the Palestinian people's right to an independent Palestinian state). From this perspective, compelling Israel's withdrawal from the OPT is now the first responsibility of the international community: hence the current international diplomatic trend to recognise the 'State of Palestine', with 136 states having done so at the time of writing. But as Israel remains immune to pressure and its hold on the OPT has only consolidated more with every passing month since 1967, this principled stance has, in practice, left the Palestinian population in an unintended trap. For as long as Israel is not legally sovereign in the OPT *and not supposed to be*, Israel is in practice absolved from providing citizenship and related equal rights to the OPT's population. As it stands, Israel's policies in the OPT violate several important human rights norms as well as multiple provisions of international humanitarian law. But as long as diplomacy holds that the Palestinians' political rights are ultimately to be satisfied in some mythical state of the future rather than by the state governing their lives, Israel's practices toward Palestinians in the OPT manifest in international law and diplomacy as discrete violations, or even, under the Oslo Accords, as rightly providing for some measure of Palestinian 'interim' self-governance. Although this situation has certainly raised international protest about Israel's behaviour, it has gleaned nothing like the international stigma that would accrue to a fully fledged apartheid regime. Yet the very same policies that Israel now practices in the OPT – most graphically its draconian physical separation of the Jewish and Palestinian populations through physical walls, checkpoints and pass laws – would clearly manifest as an apartheid regime if Israel were recognised as the territory's formal sovereign.

In sum, it is precisely Israel's lack of formal sovereignty that, to date, has enabled Israel to preserve its hold on the territory, by creating a slack and feckless environment regarding the dual legal system that enables the expansion of Jewish settlements and inflicts such misery on the Palestinian population. In other words, the fact that Israel *does not* hold formal sovereignty is the key condition that allows it to evade its own existential Scylla and Charybdis: on one side, international opprobrium for maintaining an openly apartheid regime; and, on the other, the ruinous consequences for Jewish statehood of enfranchising such a large non-Jewish population.

This chapter therefore opens the sensitive question of whether the hitherto incontestable premise underlying this impasse – Israel's lack of sovereignty – must now be reconsidered. The question necessarily resonates beyond the present case to the ways in which related international law and norms operate more generally. International law requires that states negotiate with other parties in good faith about matters under negotiation – natural resources, trade, security, and so forth – but no law or norm clearly addresses good faith regarding sovereignty itself: for example, where a state is deceptively abjuring an open claim of sovereignty in order to avoid the legal obligations or consequences that would pertain to that sovereignty. In such a case, what are the obligations of the international community? Should the state simply be held accountable, as a foreign power, to withdraw? Certainly, on principle the answer must be yes, but what if doing so fails to address the real needs of a population that for decades must endure foreign rule by a foreign power that has no intention of withdrawing, that international politics cannot compel to withdraw, and that further indicates in word and deed its intention to eliminate permanently any possibility of viable independent statehood and self-determination for the territory's indigenous population? At what point should that 'foreign' power be held accountable for legal responsibilities that accrue with sovereignty, such as providing citizenship and equal rights to its entire territorial population? Historically, in other cases the international community has responded by insisting on this, as discussed below. But even if such an approach is sometimes appropriate, or simply so pragmatic as to seem necessary, according to what criteria should it be made?

The following discussion explores these questions as they apply to Israel–Palestine. First, reviewing basic concepts regarding sovereignty, then considering how these norms have interplayed historically with the special phenomenon of settler colonialism, establishes that the international community has in fact often endorsed the sovereignty of a 'foreign' power over territory acquired by conquest. Comparison with the South African apartheid experience confirms that such cases are not confined to the nineteenth century, and further suggests why conflict resolution may be better sought in Israel–Palestine based on the same model as found in South Africa, which was to insist on the state's territorial unity embracing one national body, rather than seeking partition based on race, and requiring that its government comply with modern human rights norms. Finally, addressing a frequent counter-argument, which is that Israel has a special privilege to maintain itself as an ethnic state because the United Nations (UN) General Assembly voted in 1947 to create a 'Jewish state' in Mandate Palestine, will demonstrate why this argument is fundamentally flawed and, in any case, does not absolve Israel of a charge of apartheid. Taken as a whole, this discussion supports the present proposal: that the only way to resolve this conflict is to alter the international understanding of Israel's status in the OPT from one of a foreign power to one of a sovereign government that is systematically imposing an apartheid regime on its territorial population.

EMPIRICAL AND JURIDICAL SOVEREIGNTY

Disputes about sovereignty are common in international affairs, but they do not usually take the curious form we see in Israel–Palestine. They normally involve rival claims between states or between states and non-state actors (such as secessionist movements) for *juridical* sovereignty: that is, international diplomatic recognition by other states that one or the other party has the right to govern a particular territory. Diplomatic recognition is the prize for which conflicts are fought, because, in the modern world system, sovereignty alone conveys the rights and privileges that accrue to statehood under international law, such as exclusive rights to administer natural resources, control borders, regulate trade, negotiate with other states to resolve regional issues, and so forth. Hence Israel's gaining of recognition by the United States within hours of its declaration of independence, ushering in recognition by a critical mass of other states, was the vital coup for which political Zionism had struggled for half a century. So vital is juridical sovereignty that states cling tenaciously to it even where *empirical* sovereignty – the capacity actually to govern in the territory – is weak or missing.[4] Where a state loses all empirical sovereignty and capacity to govern, it becomes a 'failed state', greatly worrisome to international affairs because its population cannot be held to account and the ensuing chaos spills across international borders.

International relations are not commonly worried by the opposite problem: where a state enjoys *empirical but not juridical* sovereignty, as we see in Israel's rule over the OPT. As examined here, this category does not include trust territories and dependencies, such as the Marshall Islands and Puerto Rico, as those relationships are codified. Rather, it signifies those rare cases where a state that is otherwise in complete and exclusive control of a territory may be unable to annex it formally for political or other reasons and so does not claim sovereignty there, but nevertheless holds onto and administers the territory fully as though it were sovereign. As this situation allows the state to apply its own laws selectively to the territory's population outside any constitutional framework or obligation to respect the political will of that population, it is a formula for oppression, discrimination, resistance and conflict. Such a situation emerged also in South Africa's administration of South West Africa, now Namibia, which is a case that is also relevant in considering Israel's hold on the OPT. On the purely legal question of whether Israel can be held responsible for a crime of apartheid in the OPT, the case of Namibia appears definitive, but it raises interesting questions about international responsibility in the OPT as well.

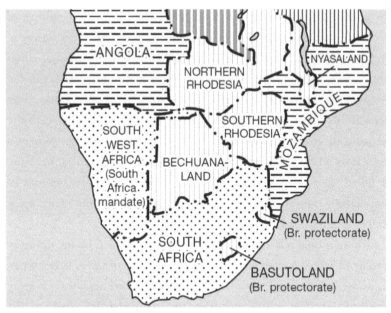

Figure 9.1. Southern Africa in 1922
Source: After Holland (1985)[5]

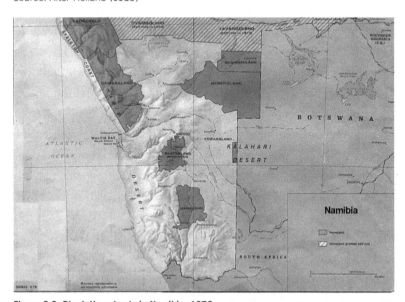

Figure 9.2. Black Homelands in Namibia, 1978
Source: United States Central Intelligence Agency[6]

APARTHEID IN NAMIBIA

The history of South Africa's governance of Namibia, long called South West Africa, must here be recalled only briefly. As in Palestine, the conflict can be traced back to a League of Nations mandate. After World War I, South Africa sought to annex what was then German South West Africa, previously a German colony, but was instead granted a 'class C' mandate over the territory (see Figure 9.1).[7] After World War II, South Africa again petitioned to have South West Africa annexed into its sovereign territory, but the UN refused and in 1950 the International Court of Justice (ICJ) advised that the mandate was still in effect and so confirmed the 'essentially international character' of South Africa's role. The South African government later attempted to annex the territory by orchestrating a petition by South West Africans for accession. The manoeuvre failed, but South Africa continued to govern Namibia effectively as a fifth province.

Thus, when South Africa's National Party developed its doctrine of apartheid into a fully blown system of racial laws in the 1950s, it extended the same system into Namibia. By the mid-1950s, the white population of South West Africa had seats in the South African parliament but the black population had no representation in any form and black African interests had been consigned to a 'Native Affairs' desk in Pretoria. In 1964, South Africa's Odendaal Commission proposed to establish black 'Homelands' in Namibia (see Figure 9.2) along lines similar to the contrived black Homelands planned for South Africa.[8] Just as in South Africa, ten black Homelands were then established in Namibia and three were eventually declared to be self-governing. All this contributed to galvanising the international anti-apartheid movement and world opprobrium regarding South Africa's racist policies in Namibia, and pressures for its withdrawal increased sharply. Between 1950 and 1970, the case came under review four times by the ICJ. In 1966, the UN General Assembly formally revoked South Africa's mandate on the grounds that the South African government was abusing the faith of the Namibian people by imposing racist policies and violating Namibia's territorial integrity. Yet South Africa did not withdraw for another twenty-three years and the 'question of Namibia' continued to absorb UN attention until the country's formal independence in 1990.

Relevant here is the fact that South Africa's lack of juridical sovereignty in Namibia did not end its empirical sovereignty there. Nor did it deflect international denunciations of its apartheid practices in Namibia. At the height of the controversy, the General Assembly passed two resolutions denouncing South Africa for practising apartheid in Namibia. In 1965, the General Assembly issued a resolution condemning 'the policies of *apartheid* and racial discrimination practiced by the Government of South Africa in South West Africa, which constitute a crime against humanity'. [9] The following year, it reiterated the charge of apartheid and demanded South Africa's immediate withdrawal.[10] In 1970, the ICJ further found that apartheid practices in Namibia contradicted South Africa's obligations to the territory's people.[11] Thus the Namibia precedent lays to rest the objection that Israel is absolved of apartheid merely by virtue of lacking juridical sovereignty in the OPT. This point was reflected in the definition of the 'crime of apartheid' in the Convention for the Suppression and Punishment of the Crime of Apartheid (Article II), which referred to 'southern Africa' rather than 'South Africa' precisely to include Namibia.

If the case of Namibia clarifies that Israel's lack of formal sovereignty in the OPT is not a legal obstacle to critiquing its policies as constituting an apartheid regime, it does not necessarily inform conflict resolution in Israel–Palestine, because Israel's legal history with the OPT is different. South Africa's empirical sovereignty in Namibia resulted from its earlier legitimate authority as a mandatory power, charged by the League of Nations with guiding the people of South West Africa to independence. Thus the UN and ICJ commanded South Africa to withdraw from Namibia on the grounds that it was abusing its role as a mandatory power by imposing policies of white racial domination and preventing the Namibian 'people' from expressing their right to self-determination. The State of Israel, by contrast, was never granted a formal mandate by any legal authority to rule the OPT – it took them by force – and overwhelming consensus (at least, outside Israel) holds that Israel remains a belligerent occupier. As in Namibia, the solution to this situation would seem to be Israel's withdrawal. The trouble is that, as noted earlier, evidence has become overwhelming that this is not to happen: Israel's annexation of the OPT is too advanced, the commitment to annexation is too embedded in the government's institutional design as well as in portions of the Jewish national fabric, and international action is far too inept to have an impact on matters of such essential internal value to Israel.[12]

Hence, legal reasoning must rationally consider other approaches. As noted earlier, abandoning the principle of withdrawal may seem highly controversial if not anathema (although, as discussed later, it was done in the 'Partition Resolution', UN General Assembly Resolution 181 of 1947). Understanding why this shift may be not only admissible but imperative therefore first requires some consideration of settler colonialism as a special category of state formation in world history.

CLASSIC AND SETTLER COLONIALISM

It is sometimes observed that Israel and South Africa are both settler colonial states, but it is not usually specified just what this means. Certainly, the significance of settler colonial state formation for international law has remained unclear. The term connotes a historical process whereby an immigrant population settled en masse in a territory outside its home country and ultimately established a state and government whose institutions and politics durably dispossess, politically demote and economically marginalise the indigenous people. Some scholars have accordingly explored cases of settler colonialism as a category of nation-state formation.[13] But its significance for international responsibility remains almost entirely unexplored and international law has not addressed it except in one isolated and carefully circumscribed instrument discussed below. The reason is unsurprising: by common definitions, many states are settler colonial states, including every state in North and South America as well as Australia and New Zealand, and not one of their governments wishes to find that sordid histories of false dealings, genocide and ethnocide and smouldering recidivist indigenous sentiments still haunt them.

This legal lacuna trips up progress in the case of Israel because the lack of understanding of settler colonialism, let alone codified ways to address it, has blocked any international understanding that Israel's policies fit the model of settler colonialism and so has stymied the identification of suitable remedies to resolve the resulting conflict. Hence, a more fine-grained definition is attempted here. Cases in the Americas and southern Pacific suggest four iconic features of settler colonialism that, taken together, reveal that settler colonialism has historically received a distinct international response and strongly suggest that Israel–Palestine requires the same one.

Before exploring this definition in detail, settler colonialism must first be conceptually situated within the broader category of colonialism, which is a very expansive term. In late twentieth-century usage – as represented by language and norms formulated by the UN Committee on Decolonisation, for example[14] – colonialism is understood as foreign rule (that is, rule over territory located outside the internationally recognised borders of the home country) that denies self-determination, or even meaningful representation of any kind, to a territory's indigenous population. As practised mostly by European powers between the sixteenth and twentieth centuries, what will be called here 'classic' colonialism was motivated primarily by the search for markets, inspiring the colonising power to seize and administer the colony and its population in all respects with the home country's interests narrowly in mind. But discursive elements were also required to provide essential moral gloss. Concepts of *terra nullius* authorised this legally, although 'empty' land usually meant 'empty of government' in the sense of European government (what the Spanish more honestly called '*sín política*' – without political order). Claims of European or Caucasian inherent superiority, regarding race and/ or civilisation, helped the coloniser make moral sense of dispossessing colonised peoples of their own governments in order to 'uplift' them, civilise or convert them, while acceding to the coloniser's appropriation of their land, resources and labour. A 'standard of civilisation' was even developed to quantify their relative standing.[15]

Settler colonialism sustains these same patterns of racism, domination and cultural denigration, but cases in the Americas, south Pacific and southern Africa, as well as Israel, suggest that it is distinguished from classic colonialism in at least four ways. First and most obvious is the evaporation of the immigrants' home country from the political equation. The hallmark of settler colonialism is a comprehensive *indigenisation* of the settler population, in which settlers detach politically, psychologically and ideologically from any extra-territorial metropole that can be held accountable for their behaviour and to whose territory they can be expected to return. In re-attaching its mythic origins and destiny to the new territory, a settler colonial society further develops a particularly tenacious understanding of its own rights to and needs for the territory, which extend to equating exclusive settler sovereignty with the settler society's physical survival. Translating into emotional narratives of natural rights and manifest destiny, this powerful identification of the settler society with the new land militates powerfully against its withdrawal.[16]

The second factor, which has distinguished settler colonialism from classic colonialism since the late nineteenth century, is the settler society's *appropriation of the right to self-determination.* In this manoeuvre, the settler society conceives of itself as the 'people' inherently holding this right and indigenous peoples as wanderers or savages who do not constitute a 'people' sufficiently coherent to claim it. Indigenous peoples' attempts to claim this mantle as peoples are thus recast as only violating and offending, rather than expressing, this important international norm by denying the right of settler society. This discursive hallmark of settler colonialism contrasts strikingly with classic colonial discourse, which routinely deprived colonised peoples of their sovereignty and subjected them to various regimes of subordination and racist exclusion, yet claimed fully to incorporate indigenous peoples under colonial authority as subjects of the crown. Since the indigenous peoples' political rights were actually acknowledged (if not met) in this formula, as decolonisation progressed, colonised peoples could ultimately challenge colonial rule on the grounds of its own contradictions and insist on their right to self-determination. By contrast, in settler colonialism, the need of settlers to make moral sense of dispossessing indigenous peoples permanently of their land in favour of settler ownership inspires locally tailored myths about why the native peoples not only lack any legitimate claim to *terra nullius* but must be excluded from the hope of ever sharing sovereignty (which might reintroduce their right to get their land back). A canon of standard devices is enlisted to this end: for example, social Darwinist logic proposing the native peoples' permanently inferior cultural status relative to the settler society (evidenced by, among other things, their very defeat). Continuing resistance by the indigenous people is thus cast as merely the irredentism of obsolete cultures: irrational, sullen, racist in motive, and beyond any moral pale in targeting the innocent, idealistic and hard-working settler people that has sought only to reclaim the land from wilderness and, by dint of its heroic pioneer efforts, has obtained the right to its own independent state. Thus indigenous claims to sovereignty are delegitimised as violating the settler society's right to self-determination. All these claims are particularly familiar to people with close knowledge of related discourse in both Israel–Palestine and southern Africa.

The third factor distinguishing settler colonialism from classic colonialism is its success in extinguishing indigenous juridical sovereignty permanently by gaining international diplomatic recognition – that is, juridical sovereignty. Diplomatic recognition is gained after the settler population has grown and embedded itself in the territory to the point of obviating any reasonable expectation by international observers of its withdrawal. The contrast with classic colonialism here is stark: international law normally rejects foreign rule and requires that an invader withdraw and restore governance to the territory's population. By contrast, at some tipping point in settler colonialism, any idea of restoring government to the indigenous people becomes unimaginable. An obvious illustration is the present United States, which no one today reasonably expects to dismantle and hand over the national territory, even if now admitted to be acquired unjustly, to Native Americans who now comprise about 1 per cent of the territorial population. This tipping point was probably reached in the eastern United States by the late seventeenth century and in the rest of the country by the early nineteenth.

Since the different proportions of settler and indigenous populations in South Africa and Israel (respectively, about 20:80 and 50:50) are often cited as obstacles to their comparison, it is worth noting here that such proportions alone do not observably determine such tipping points. Historically, the evaporation of indigenous sovereignty has been determined more by how effectively settler colonial elites manipulated evolving international standards and politics regarding purported indigenous cultural inferiority and their proposed condition as 'savages' or 'primitives', and so leveraged juridical sovereignty on the basis of *terra nullius*. In Latin America, for example, settler colonialism began in the late fifteenth century with initial sweeping claims by European powers to imperium over vast territories, swiftly consolidated through warfare and administered by a tiny colonial European bureaucracy that only over subsequent centuries indigenised as a creole elite.[17] By the time Latin American states achieved independence in the early nineteenth century, the indigenous peoples had been reduced to a labouring racial caste that, at least in creole and European views, not only lacked any right but had no inherent *capacity* for sovereignty, even where they remained a majority.[18] Thus European diplomatic recognition flowed quickly to these creole states, however small and unrepresentative their elites. In what became the United States, the process was more incremental: Native American peoples were initially recognised as sovereign powers, with whom treaties must be struck; only after they had lost all war-making and political power were they formally redefined in US federal law as never having had any standing as peoples or nations. Another variation is New Zealand, where the Maori saw their sovereignty first recognised, later eroded through deceptive treaties, and finally re-acknowledged in ways that redefined modern New Zealand as a binational state, although in practice providing only some group rights, like re-dignifying the Maori language.

Thus, the fourth hallmark of settler colonialism is its discursive success in permanently converting indigenous politics into domestic affairs. Redefining international conflicts among nations as domestic affairs (ethnic conflict) is indeed a powerful boon to any state, as it removes the international *persona juridica* of its competitors for sovereignty and prohibits direct involvement by the international community in any state actions regarding them, short of crimes against humanity such as genocide or apartheid. In this way, many nations once vying for sovereignty have found themselves redefined as ethnic groups, their legal recourse confined to human rights law involving cultural and other rights relatively innocuous for state sovereignty.

South Africa and Israel clearly fit this four-part model. That South Africa is an iconic case of settler colonialism has always been intuitively easy to spot, due to the European and white-skinned character of the settler community, but it also fits the model proposed here of settler indigenisation, appropriation of indigenous rights, international recognition and the domestication of once-international conflict. Not all of the white community in South Africa fully indigenised: the English-speaking population tended to retain its British roots. But by the early eighteenth century, the Afrikaner (Dutch-speaking) population had reinvented itself as a distinct people that, especially after persecution by the British in the Boer Wars, considered that it had no home country and, in classic blood-and-soil mode, could survive only on South African land. In Afrikaner pioneer myth, black resistance was discredited in starkly social Darwinist terms as the irrational cruel attacks by savages on peaceful heroic pioneers. By the late nineteenth century, white settlement throughout all of modern South African territory was irreversible and, save some death throes in the Zulu Wars, sovereignty by 'natives' became risible for whites (until the notion was revived by the apartheid government, in the 1960s, as the Bantustan scheme to save white statehood). International recognition flowed easily to the modern republic, converting the black African struggle for equal rights into a domestic affair.

For Israel, indigenisation has been achieved for the Jewish settler population partly by developing a distinct Israeli national character (greatly facilitated by the invention of Modern Hebrew as the national language) with a national imaginary bolstered by special claims, such as biblical sources that describe Jewish indigeneity in Palestine in antiquity and the more contemporary argument, strengthened by the catastrophic history of anti-Semitism in Europe, that the Jewish nation 'has nowhere else to go'. The Palestinian claim to sovereignty has been discredited through standard settler colonial notions: for example, Zionist discourse affirmed that the 'Arabs' in Palestine were a backward people who never used the land productively (standard of civilisation); they were not present in the land at all except as migrant labourers (*terra nullius*); they were defeated by Zionist forces due to their own cultural incapacity (social Darwinism); they therefore have no claim to be a 'people' at all; and so they are motivated primarily by irrational racist hatred for the Jewish people who nonetheless persist in resisting attack to pursue their own heroic project of nation- and state-building. The Palestinian–Arab struggle for self-determination has thus been delegitimised as antithetical to, rather than claiming, the universal human rights values of freedom, justice and self-determination that are affirmed as expressed by Jewish national self-determination in modern Israel. Famously, the whole project worked. International endorsement of the settler state came formally in 1947, when the General Assembly voted to partition Mandate Palestine into a 'Jewish state' and an 'Arab state'. In 1949, Palestinian sovereignty was permanently extinguished (within the Green Line) when the new State of Israel was granted membership of the UN, converting the problems of Palestinians inside Israel from an international crisis into a domestic issue.

Thus the international community recognised the settler colonial state in part of Mandate Palestine. As a corollary, one of Zionism's signal accomplishments as a settler colonial state has been to normalise in international discourse the idea that the Palestinian right to self-determination survives in only 22 per cent of the Mandate territory. Nor has Israel ever backed away from this stance, despite impressions given in the Oslo process. Israel's admission, initially in 2002, that Palestinian people should have a state somewhere in the West Bank and Gaza Strip has always been presented by Israeli politicians, such as Prime Minister Olmert, as a capitulation – not to justice for any 'Palestinian people' (Israel has never used 'Palestinian people' in this sense in its diplomacy) but to pragmatism, serving Israel's own security imperatives.

SEEKING JUSTICE AND HUMAN RIGHTS IN A SETTLER COLONIAL STATE

Recasting the Palestinians' dilemma as that of an indigenous people absorbed into a settler colonial state does not immediately clarify their legal rights or suggest any single correct course of legal action. Because it implicates the legitimacy of so many settler colonial states, the question of indigenous rights has proved to be a particularly sensitive matter for international law – which, of course, is written by and serves existing states. The only international legal instrument that addresses cases of settler colonialism (although without using the term and including a wider range of nation-state formations) is the Declaration on the Rights of Indigenous Peoples.[19] This instrument affirms that indigenous peoples have the right to self-determination (Article 3) but also promptly qualifies this right by limiting it to 'autonomy or self-government in matters relating to their internal and local affairs, as well as ways and means for financing their autonomous functions' (Article 4). Much of the Declaration casts indigenous rights as being similar to minority rights, carefully protecting the sovereignty of the states in which indigenous peoples have found themselves incorporated.

Recognising both the power differential and the hostile international climate regarding their situations, indigenous rights movements have therefore typically recognised the practical imperative of seeking solutions to their oppressed status other than revolution or secession. In South Africa, the African National Congress (ANC) and South African Communist Party (SACP) held lengthy internal debates about what they called 'colonialism of a special type', as discussed by Ronnie Kasrils in this volume. This extract from a 1962 thesis is pertinent:

The indigenous population is subjected to extreme national oppression, poverty and exploitation, lack of all democratic rights and political domination … The African Reserves show the complete lack of industry, communications and power resources which are characteristic of African territories under colonial rule throughout the Continent. Typical too of imperialist rule, is the reliance by the state upon brute force and terror … Non-White South Africa is the colony of White South Africa itself. It is this combination of the worst features of both imperialism and colonialism, within a single national frontier, which determines the special nature of the South African system and has brought upon its rulers the justified hatred and contempt of progressive and democratic people throughout the world.[20]

South African historian Pallo Jordan has described these debates as reflecting the last of three historical stages of black South African resistance.[21] In the first phase, which lasted from European colonisation in the mid-sixteenth century to the late nineteenth century, African peoples fought to repel European advancing assaults on their sovereignty but steadily lost ground. In the second phase, which lasted roughly until the end of the Zulu wars in the 1880s, African peoples had irredeemably lost general control of the territory to Europeans and their resistance shifted to defending their social order and local modes of production against incorporation by the European society and its economy. In the third phase, black Africans had lost even this autonomy and were fully absorbed into the settler state and its economy. They then moved to appropriating the settler society's own democratic laws and institutions and demanding equal rights and freedoms. In other words, the tipping point had passed, in the sense that the territory's indigenous African peoples could no longer anticipate the withdrawal of a white settler society that had grown to such a size and had indigenised with such nationalist passion. This last stage was formulated in 1912 as the programme of the ANC and culminated in the 1994 elections that eliminated white minority rule but affirmed the principle that 'South Africa belongs to all who live in it'. Third-stage resistance was ultimately victorious partly because it was consistent with international approaches to conflicts resulting from settler colonialism in urging that indigenous peoples' interests are a state's domestic affairs, related human rights regarding anti-discrimination are applicable, and so indigenous individuals have equal rights as citizens.

Jordan's lens suggests that Palestinians in the OPT are engaged in all three stages of resistance at once, a conflation (or confusion) possibly reflecting the relatively compressed time frame of Zionist colonisation. Some elements in Palestinian politics still cling to the notion that militant resistance can force Israel and the settler society to withdraw at least from the OPT to allow a sovereign Palestinian state (first stage). Most Palestinians in the OPT, however, follow the Palestinian Authority in using a combination of non-violent resistance and *sumud* to push back the worst intrusions of Israeli military and economic penetration and to preserve Palestinian society in a shrinking but still distinct territorial and socio-political space (second stage). Only a small (but growing) number of Palestinians is shifting to third-stage resistance: that is, accepting Israeli hegemony as irreversible and appropriating Israeli democratic norms and values to demand full citizenship and equal rights in a non-ethnic state.[22] In this final manoeuvre, they would join (although greatly complicate) a struggle for equal rights that has been pursued by Palestinian citizens of Israel for some decades, while directly challenging the (putative) first-stage posture of the Palestinian Interim Self-Government Authority. Given the stakes involved in the second-stage strategy (major funding, leadership legitimacy and the leverage of foreign powers), mixing all three stages in one volatile brew could trigger intra-Palestinian civil conflict.

The international community itself has taken a bifurcated approach to Palestinians whose status has been fragmented by war and by Israel's formation. International law has long assumed that Palestinians living inside Israel are rightly equal citizens. Since 1967, Israeli state doctrine has also affirmed this (although, in practice, Israeli law still confers a more privileged legal status on Jewish citizens).[23] Any question of resistance 'stages' or a tipping point was obviated for Palestinians living inside Israel when Israel was recognised and admitted to the UN as an independent sovereign state in 1949, a move that juridically rendered indigenous Palestinian Arab issues 'domestic' by default. Inside the OPT, however, the international community has held to the premise of military occupation, because Israel has not declared sovereignty (as it did in the Golan Heights) and because affirming Israel's sovereignty would violate the prohibition on the acquisition of territory by force.

Hence the international diplomatic paradigm for resolving the conflict generated by Israel's occupation of the Palestinian territories is not Jordan's third-stage approach (full democratisation). But if Israel has settled the West Bank past reasonable expectation of withdrawal, is there indeed no tipping point when the conflict should be reassessed as a case of advanced settler colonialism and the State of Israel held accountable for the obligations that accrue with sovereignty, including providing citizenship and equal rights to the population of the OPT?

As noted, such a paradigm shift is now eschewed partly because it would effectively reward aggression with annexation and so threaten a basic norm of the post–World War II international system. Discrediting this stance, however, is the fact that the UN effectively did just this: first in 1947, when it recommended partition of Mandate Palestine to accommodate mass Zionist settlement by granting it a formal right to Jewish statehood; and then in 1949, when the General Assembly voted to recognise facts on the ground (Israel's military victory) by admitting Israel to the UN, although within borders not yet formally set. Because the Partition Resolution is sometimes invoked to absolve Israel of both apartheid and colonialism, its terms and provisions (and politics) will receive here some special attention.

THE LANGUAGE OF GENERAL ASSEMBLY RESOLUTION 181

Although the history of UN General Assembly Resolution 181, the Partition Resolution, is a story brimming with great power and great game drama, that story is well beyond the scope of this chapter to review.[24] It must suffice here to recall merely that the Zionist movement, largely through strong lobbying by the United States, succeeded in wresting a partition resolution from the General Assembly that would serve Israel's later claims that the UN supported Israel's creation as a

'Jewish state'. The 'principle of partition' established by Resolution 181 is often invoked by Israel's defenders to suggest both Israel's legitimacy as a Jewish state and that Israel is not responsible for the rights of Palestine's residents who are supposed to be served by the 'Arab state' not yet formed. This history would appear to absolve Israel of any charge of apartheid, since the principle of Jewish ethno-national statehood received explicit international approval. Two features of Resolution 181, however, critically damage this claim. They further suggest grounds for considering that Israel's exclusive empirical sovereignty over all Mandate Palestine should be recognised as being juridical as well.

First, Resolution 181 called for partition into two states on terms that absolutely rejected ethnic statehood on the model later developed by Israel. The resolution endorsed partition into a 'Jewish state' and an 'Arab state' but these were to be ethnic with regard to only some mechanisms (such as gerrymandered borders and guidelines for citizenship choices) to encourage, not compel, titular ethnic majorities. Otherwise, the text of the resolution explicitly and repeatedly prohibited discrimination in either state on the basis of ethnicity. Thus Resolution 181 never endorsed ethnic statehood on the model that Israel would later adopt, in which Jewish ethnic rights are juridically privileged in many social sectors. A better claim today that world opinion supports a Jewish state could be UN Security Council Resolutions 1397 of 2002 and 1515 of 2003, which endorsed the 'vision' of a two-state solution and so, by implication, a Jewish state. But these resolutions refer to 'Israel' and 'Palestine' and do not use the terms 'Jewish state' or 'Arab state'. They therefore cannot be held to explicitly endorse ethnic statehood by either side.[25]

Second, subsequent General Assembly resolutions tacitly retracted the endorsement of a Jewish state expressed in Resolution 181 by calling for the return of Palestinian Arab refugees to Israel's territory: first, and famously, in Resolution 194 of 19 November 1948. Because the territory that became modern Israel had held a Palestinian Arab majority before the war (Zionist forces having seized a much larger area than

Resolution 181 had recommended, including the entire Galilee with its dense Arab population), this instruction to allow the Arab refugees to return signalled that the UN no longer endorsed a Jewish majority in that territory. In other words, the Jewish majority state proposed by Resolution 181, which gained consensus only by hedging the ethnic principle with careful qualifications to protect ethnic minorities, was rendered obsolete by the subsequent violent expulsion of most of the indigenous population and the reconfiguration of borders through war which drastically altered the impact on the region's population. This position regarding refugees, being rooted in important international legal principles, has never been retracted by any UN body and remains a hot topic in diplomatic negotiations.

Third, Resolution 181 did not constitute the General Assembly's vote to partition Mandate Palestine, as is often claimed, but only to recommend its 'partition with economic union' to the United Kingdom (the mandatory power) and to propose a plan for this. Hence the territory was never formally partitioned by any legal body: it was compartmentalised, through war, by an armistice line. Thus, after the 1967 Six-Day War, Israel held exclusive control over territory that had never been legally separated from the Mandate Palestine or recognised by any state or international actor as belonging to any other sovereign power. Indeed, Israel insists that the West Bank and Gaza Strip cannot be considered 'occupied', in the sense of international humanitarian law, precisely because they are not part of another state's territory. That Israel's status is not one of belligerent occupier has been brusquely rejected by UN bodies and most international lawyers outside Israel, but it can be considered afresh regarding the present question: not whether Israel is absolved from law pertaining to occupation, but whether Israel, having so thoroughly consolidated its settlement and integration of occupied territory, should now be held fully responsible for maintaining and insisting on exclusive sovereignty over all of it. The obvious argument against this shift is that it would deprive the Palestinian people of their right to self-determination. Given the facts on the ground, however, it now makes more sense to draw on the South African experience of advanced settler colonialism and reframe concepts of people-, nation- and state-hood as 'a state for all its citizens'.

This last point suggests a discursive question of great sensitivity but central importance: whether the real imperative regarding this conflict is not the rights of the 'two peoples in one land', including the 'Palestinian people' as this is presently defined, but how 'Palestinian people' originally came to be wrongfully defined to divide 'Palestinian' – the League of Nations' nationality category – on the basis of people's ethnic or sectarian origin. The original intent of the mandate was that 'Palestine' serve the 'Palestinian people' on a non-ethnic basis. While it famously allowed for a 'Jewish national home' within Palestine's borders, 'Palestine' was a clearly territorial national identity. Hence the more historically correct formulation – and probably the only solution to this advanced settler colonial conflict – is that this original non-discriminatory reading of 'Palestinian' be reinstated and indeed insisted upon. This idea is naturally controversial in that it suggests a profound reconstruction of key actors, but the precedent of very similar debates in late-Apartheid South Africa, regarding race, nation and state unity, could be illuminating to those involved.[26]

CONCLUSION

Israel's occupation of the West Bank and Gaza Strip has digressed so far from the terms of reference of international humanitarian law that Israel's behaviour cannot be adequately described in terms of discrete violations. Israel now controls the OPT in all ways consistent with sovereignty except the political will of the territory's population. ('Disengagement' from Gaza altered but did not end this control.) Steadily settling the West Bank, Israel's behaviour is fully consistent with settler colonialism. With half a million settlers in the West Bank, the situation could have been recognised as having passed the tipping point long ago, were not the international community still wedded doggedly to the paradigm of belligerent occupation and evolving formulations of 'Palestinian people' that have, under enormous pressure, adjusted to suit the Zionist project. The precedent of Apartheid South Africa helps to clarify that Israel's willingness to consign portions of the West Bank to a 'Palestinian state' is most accurately comparable to a Bantustan strategy: to concentrate black people within politically suffocating, disarticulated and economically crippled enclaves, where the nominal sovereignty of 'Black Self-Government Authorities' could hopefully absolve the regime of both responsibility for their welfare and international condemnation for their inevitable political exclusion, poverty and misery.

One irony emerges most clearly from the South African comparison: that the UN has actually obstructed resolution of the conflict by insisting on Israel's withdrawal from the OPT. It is incontestable that, legally, Israel holds the territories under belligerent occupation and has illegally transferred Jewish settlers into East Jerusalem and the West Bank. Yet in insisting that Israel not be allowed to annex these territories, the UN has unintentionally forestalled the normal solution to conflict in advanced cases of settler colonialism: granting full citizenship and equal rights to the indigenous people. While the Palestinian right to self-determination has ostensibly been respected and preserved by this firm position, the real-life consequences for the Palestinians have been disastrous. They are caught in increasingly hopeless limbo, in a truncated portion of the original Mandate territory ascribed to their self-determination but where no state has empirical sovereignty other than the ethnic state which took form in that territory yet is not being held responsible for an apartheid policy: excluding them from citizenship, inflicting a host of discriminatory policies on them to exclude them from life in the country, and harshly penalising them for any resistance to this system.

Diplomatic recognition of settler colonial sovereignty – here, Israel's sovereignty over all of Mandate Palestine – is not proposed here to reflect justice. In many cases it arguably represents the permanent deprivation of historical justice to peoples who have lost sovereignty, land, livelihoods, rights and collective dignity to an alien onslaught. Rather, it reflects pragmatic recognition that power differentials and facts on the ground have irrevocably altered the terms in which justice and human rights can be pursued. A settler colonial state, once it has formed, can only really be defeated if its function as a vehicle for perpetuating ethnic settler myths and racial discrimination is eliminated. This normative shift is a tough and painful one on all sides, as the bitter struggles in South Africa and elsewhere have attested. The worst outcome, however, is a situation that has passed the tipping point yet closes off this transition. Such is the situation in Israel–Palestine, where the settler colonial state has rendered obsolete one course of justice for the Palestinian people (statehood) while the international community, acting dutifully to preserve international order and norms, has helped to forestall the only logical alternative: unification. That this transition is essential is further supported if one recognises that Israel's lack of juridical sovereignty in the OPT is not only a tenet of international debate but a strategic asset to Israel in vitally veiling policies that are not legally admissible otherwise: Israel's mission to assume full and exclusive empirical sovereignty over all of '*Eretz Israel*' while neatly segregating the territory's unwanted ethnic Others and excluding them forever from citizenship.

Notes

1   The author's experience of these debates was gained while coordinating a two-year research project on the question of apartheid in Israel in 2008–09. Funded by the South African Department of Foreign Affairs, the study was initially hosted the Human Sciences Research Council; findings were later published as Virginia Tilley (ed.), *Beyond Occupation: Apartheid, Colonialism*

and International Law in the Occupied Palestinian Territories, London: Pluto Press, 2012.

2   On international consensus on Israel's status as an occupying power, contextualised in a detailed analysis of the legal status of and application of law in the OPT, see Tilley, *Beyond Occupation*, especially Chapter 2, 'The Legal Context in the Occupied Palestinian Territories'.

3   For just one notable example, see 'The Time Has Come to Say These Things', interview with Ehud Olmert, *New York Review of Books* 55(19) (4 December 2008).

4   Robert H. Jackson and Carl G. Rosberg, 'Why Africa's Weak States Persist: The Empirical and the Juridical in Statehood', *World Politics* 35(1) (1982), pp. 1–24; also see Robert H. Jackson, *Quasi-States: Sovereignty, International Relations and the Third World*, Cambridge: Cambridge University Press, 1993.

5   See www.routledge.com/textbooks/9780415438964/downloads/ihmo4c.pdf.

6   See www.lib.utexas.edu/maps/africa/namibia_homelands_78.jpg.

7   The League of Nations Charter (Article 22) established the mandate system to embrace three rough categories. Class A mandates were territories considered to have reached 'a stage of development where their existence as independent nations can be provisionally recognized subject to the rendering of administrative advice and assistance by a Mandatory until such time as they are able to stand alone'. Class B mandates were defined as territories that were less developed and so required more tutelage: 'the Mandatory must be responsible for the administration of the territory under conditions which will guarantee freedom of conscience and religion, subject only to the maintenance of public order and morals, the prohibition of abuses such as the slave trade, the arms traffic and the liquor traffic, and the prevention of the establishment of fortifications or military and naval bases and of military training of the natives for other than police purposes and the defence of territory, and will also secure equal opportunities for the trade and commerce of other Members of the League'. Class C mandates were territories considered so unprepared for independence that they 'can be best administered under the laws of the Mandatory as integral portions of its territory, subject to the safeguards above mentioned in the interests of the indigenous population'.

8   The Commission of Enquiry into South-West Africa Affairs, which conducted its work in 1962–63, was led by Franz Hendrik Odendaal, a white South African, and came to be known as the Odendaal Commission.

9   General Assembly Resolution 2074 (XX) of 17 December 1965.

10 General Assembly Resolution 2145 (XXI), The Question of South West Africa (1966).

11 ICJ, advisory opinion of 21 June 1970, 'Legal Consequences for States of the Continued Presence of South Africa in Namibia (South West Africa) Notwithstanding Security Council Resolution 276 (1970)'.

12 This argument is made in detail in Virginia Tilley, *The One-State Solution: A Breakthrough for Peace in the Israeli–Palestinian Deadlock*, Michigan and Manchester: University of Wisconsin Press and University of Manchester Press, 2005; for a summary essay, see Virginia Tilley, 'The One-State Solution', *London Review of Books* 25(21) (6 November 2013).

13 Representative titles include Caroline Elkins and Susan Pedersen (eds), *Settler Colonialism in the Twentieth Century: Projects, Practices, Legacies*, New York: Routledge, 2005; Lorenzo Veracini, *Settler-Colonialism: A Theoretical Overview*, Basingstoke: Palgrave Macmillan, 2010; Lionel Pilkington and Fiona Bateman (eds), *Studies in Settler Colonialism: Politics, Identity and Culture*, Basingstoke: Palgrave Macmillan, 2011.

14 The Committee on Decolonisation was established to monitor cases of decolonisation under the terms of the UN Declaration on the Granting of Independence to Colonial Countries and Peoples.

15 Gerrit Gong, *The Standard of Civilization in International Society*, Oxford: Oxford University Press, 1984.

16 Exceptions include the French withdrawal from Algeria, which occurred at the cusp of such a settler colonial transition. The particular viciousness with which France attempted to repress the anti-colonial movement, particularly towards the end of the independence struggle, reflected the intensity of *pieds noires* indigenisation, although withdrawal was still imaginable and so was ultimately effected.

17 Spanish conquerors in the sixteenth century considered that the great indigenous states of Latin America – for example, powers centred at Tenochtitlán in what became modern Mexico, the Mayan highland city states, Cuscatlán in modern El Salvador and the Incan empire centred at Cuzco – must be brought either to vassalage to the crown or destroyed by scorched-earth tactics and even genocide.

18 Population data on ethnicity is notoriously unreliable in Latin America, due to policies that discourage compulsory disclosure of indigenous identity and census policy not to list racial or ethnic identities. Formal censuses figures are therefore criticised for commonly under-counting or even over-counting indigenous populations. Estimates among anthropologists are that the indigenous population of Ecuador is about 50 per cent, of Guatemala about 50 to 60 per cent, of Peru about 60 per cent, and of Bolivia about 80 per cent.

19 The declaration was adopted by the General Assembly on 13 September 2007. It does not define 'indigenous peoples', but the earlier International

Labour Organisation Convention 169 Concerning Indigenous and Tribal Peoples in Independent Countries (adopted on 27 June 1989 by the ILO General Conference at its seventy-sixth session, and which entered into force on 5 September 1991) contains language that suggests the term may include colonial conditions. This convention defined indigenous peoples as 'peoples in independent countries who are regarded as indigenous on account of their descent from the populations which inhabited the country, or a geographical region to which the country belongs, at the time of conquest or colonisation' (Article 1(b)). Before the declaration was passed, Convention 169 was the only operative instrument of international law regarding indigenous peoples. Because Palestinians in the OPT have not been absorbed into the State of Israel, ILO Convention 169 has been considered inapplicable. In any case, the question does not arise normally because: 1) the appellation 'indigenous people' is avoided by some Palestinian factions as implicitly demeaning their status; and 2) Israel is not one of the twenty countries that have ratified Convention 169.

20 SACP, *The Road to South African Freedom*, 1962, London: Inkululeko Publications.

21 South African Minister of Arts and Culture Pallo Jordan, unpublished lecture hosted by the Middle East Project of the Human Sciences Research Council, Velmare Hotel, Pretoria, 12 November 2008.

22 Poll data has put support for a unitary secular-democratic state at between 22 and 30 per cent in recent years, but in 2014 support was dropping. In April 2014, a Jerusalem Media and Communication Centre public opinion poll found that '18.8% in support of it [a binational state] in this poll, while 23.4% supported it in the March 2013 poll and 25.9% supported it in the May 2012 poll': see 'Poll no. 81, April 2014 – Prolonging Negotiations, Reconciliation, Dahlan and Barghouti'.

23 For a list and analysis of these privileges, see especially the 'Discriminatory Laws Database' compiled by Adalah: Legal Center for Arab Minority Rights in Israel: www.adalah.org.

24 See, for example, the diplomatic history detailed in David Fromkin, *A Peace to End All Peace: The fall of the Ottoman Empire and the Creation of the Modern Middle East*, New York: H. Holt, 2001.

25 These resolutions are, respectively, S/2002/1397 (12 March 2002) and S/2003/1515 (19 November 2003).

26 On arguments regarding peoplehood, nation, race and statehood in South Africa, see, for example, Donald Horowitz, *A Democratic South Africa? Constitutional Engineering in a Divided Society*, Berkeley: University of California Press, 1992, Chapter 1, 'The Conflict and the Conflict about the Conflict'.

CHAPTER 10

Israel–Palestine and the Apartheid Analogy: Critics, Apologists and Strategic Lessons

RAN GREENSTEIN

INTRODUCTION

In the last decade, the notion that the Israeli system of political and military control bears strong resemblance to the apartheid system in South Africa has gained ground. It is invoked regularly by movements and activists opposed to the 1967 occupation and to various other aspects of Israeli policies vis-à-vis the Palestinian-Arab people. It is denounced regularly by official Israeli spokespersons and unofficial apologists. The more empirical and theoretical discussion of the nature of the respective regimes and their historical trajectories has become marginalised in the process. Only a few studies pursue such comparison with any analytical rigour.[1]

There are three crucial distinctions we must make in order to address the issue properly and avoid the usual conceptual and political muddle that afflict the debate:

- We need to consider which Israel is our topic of concern: Israel as it exists today, with boundaries extending from the Mediterranean to the Jordan River, or Israel as it existed before 1967, along the Green Line? Is it Israel as a state that encompasses all its citizens, within the Green Line and beyond? Israel as it defines itself, or as it is defined by others? And which definition is legitimate according to international law? Are the Palestinian territories occupied in 1967 part of the definition or an element external to it? Which boundaries (geographical, political, ideological and moral) are most relevant to our discussion? What are their implications for our understanding of the nature of the regime and its relation to various groups in the population subject to it?

Each definition of the situation carries with it different consequences for the analysis of the apartheid analogy. Perhaps the central question in this respect is the relationship between three components: 'Israel proper' (within its pre-1967 boundaries), 'Greater Israel' (within the post-1967 boundaries) and 'Greater Palestine' (a demographic rather than geographic concept, covering all Arabs who trace their origins to pre-1948 Palestine). While discussion of the relationship between the first two components is common, the third component – and its relevance to the apartheid analogy – is usually ignored.

• We need to distinguish between historical apartheid (the specific system that prevailed in South Africa between 1948 and 1994) and the generic notion of apartheid that stands for an oppressive system which allocates political and social rights in a differentiated manner based on people's origins (including but not restricted to race). To illustrate the point, highlighting different trends in the use made of indigenous labour power in the two countries (exploitation in South Africa, exclusion in Israel–Palestine) serves to distinguish between historical apartheid and the Israeli ethnic-based class society. They are indeed different in this respect. But this cannot serve to refute the claim that Israel is practising apartheid in its generic sense of exclusion and discrimination on the basis of origins. That claim has to be tackled in its own terms, independently of our understanding of the specific history of South Africa. This is especially the case as some features of apartheid in South Africa changed during the course of its own historical evolution and thus cannot serve as a benchmark in evaluating other political systems.

- We need to distinguish between the extent of the similarity of South African laws, structures and practices to their Israeli equivalents, and consequent strategies of political change. Even if we conclude that there is a great degree of structural similarity between the two states, it would not tell us much about how we can apply political strategies used successfully in the former case to the latter. Neither would it tell us much about the direction in which the Israeli system of control is heading. For that we need to undertake a concrete analysis of Israeli–Palestinian societies, their local and international allegiances, bases of support, vulnerabilities, and so on.

WHAT IS APARTHEID?

The International Convention on the Suppression and Punishment of the Crime of Apartheid, adopted by the United Nations (UN) General Assembly in November 1973, regards apartheid as 'a crime against humanity' and a violation of international law. Apartheid means 'similar policies and practices of racial segregation and discrimination as practised in southern Africa ... committed for the purpose of establishing and maintaining domination by one racial group of persons over any other racial group of persons and systematically oppressing them'.

A long list of such practices ensues, including measures:

calculated to prevent a racial group or groups from participation in the political, social, economic and cultural life of the country and the deliberate creation of conditions preventing the full development of such a group or groups, in particular by denying to members of a racial group or groups basic human rights and freedoms, including the right to work, the right to form recognized trade unions, the right to education, the right to leave and to return to their country, the right to a nationality, the right to freedom of movement and residence.

In addition, this includes measures:

designed to divide the population along racial lines by the creation of separate reserves and ghettos for the members of a racial group or groups, the prohibition of mixed marriages among members of various racial groups, the expropriation of landed property belonging to a racial group or groups or to members thereof.[2]

This is not an exhaustive list – and not all practices must be present simultaneously to qualify as apartheid – but it is based on key elements of historical South African apartheid. A point that stands out here is the notion of race: the common definition of race (indicating biological origins, usually associated with physical appearance, primarily skin colour) is not relevant to the relations between Israeli Jews and Palestinian Arabs. Both groups are racially diverse and cannot be distinguished on the basis of physical appearance.

Having said that, we must consider that race – just like apartheid – is a term that can apply beyond its conceptual and geographical origins. The International Convention on the Elimination of All Forms of Racial Discrimination, adopted by the UN General Assembly in December 1965, applies the term racial discrimination to:

any distinction, exclusion, restriction or preference based on race, colour, descent, or national or ethnic origin which has the purpose or effect of nullifying or impairing the recognition, enjoyment or exercise, on an equal footing, of human rights and fundamental freedoms in the political, economic, social, cultural or any other field of public life.[3]

Putting together the two conventions, we end up with a definition of apartheid as a set of policies and practices of legal discrimination, political exclusion and social marginalisation, based on racial, national or ethnic origins. This definition obviously draws on historical apartheid but cannot be reduced to it. The focus of attention should be on the practices of the state rather than on the degree of similarity to the situation in Apartheid South Africa.

This is especially the case since the 2002 Rome Statute of the International Criminal Court omitted all references to South Africa in its definition of 'the crime of apartheid'. In its Article 7, addressing crimes against humanity, the Rome Statute defines the crime of apartheid as:

inhumane acts of a character similar to those referred to in paragraph 1, committed in the context of an institutionalized regime of systematic oppression and domination by one racial group over any other racial group or groups and committed with the intention of maintaining that regime.

The acts referred to in paragraph 1 that are most relevant here include 'deportation or forcible transfer of population' and 'persecution against any identifiable group or collectivity on political, racial, national, ethnic, cultural, religious, gender ... or other grounds that are universally recognized as impermissible under international law'. Persecution, in turn, is defined as 'intentional and severe deprivation of fundamental rights contrary to international law by reason of the identity of the group or collectivity'.

With the passage of time and the political transition in South Africa, apartheid is becoming more of a legal than a descriptive historical term. Still, its association with the South African regime remains strong, and in the following discussion I address both its general and specific South African meanings. How the notion of apartheid, then, applies to Israel in substantive terms is the key theme to be addressed here.

WHAT IS ISRAEL? PERSPECTIVES FROM THE LEFT

But first, what (and where) is Israel? In his book *Beyond the Two-State Solution: A Jewish Political Essay*, Yehouda Shenhav of Tel Aviv University argues against the notion that there is still any meaningful distinction between 'Israel itself' (in its pre-1967 boundaries) and the Occupied Palestinian Territories.[4] He criticises what he terms the 1967 Green Line paradigm, for which Israel, a democratic nation-state of the Jewish people with a minority of Palestinian citizens, is separate from the Occupied Territories. According to that paradigm, the 1967 occupation is an anomaly that introduced a large number of Palestinian non-citizens into the system. As long as no final decision is made, the territories remain under temporary occupation. The suspension of democracy and of political rights affecting their residents is a result of the unresolved conflict, but it does not affect the democratic nature of Israel itself. The conflict can be resolved through the creation of an independent Palestinian state in the West Bank and Gaza Strip, alongside Israel. This arrangement has become known as the two-state solution: it will restore Israel as a Jewish and democratic state and give Palestinians their own nation-state.

What is the problem with this paradigm? Shenhav identifies four 'political anomalies' that make the distinction between democratic pre-1967 Israel and the Occupied Territories difficult to sustain.

These anomalies reflect the interests and concerns of specific groups in the population:

- Palestinian refugees who trace the origin of their situation to 1948. For those of them residing in the Occupied Territories, 1967 was a moment of liberation, in the sense that their ability to move within their homeland was enhanced as a result.
- Jewish religious and nationalist settlers, for whom the Green Line is not morally or politically meaningful, and Israel as a Jewish state extends beyond it, all the way to the Jordan River (and possibly beyond).
- The people of the 'third Israel', who feel marginalised by the dominant political system, and for whom the occupation has provided substantial benefits. They include settlers driven by socio-economic reasons rather than religious or nationalist motivations: primarily Mizrahim, Orthodox Jews and Russian immigrants.
- The 1948 Palestinians, who remained within the State of Israel and became its citizens; for them, 1967 represented an opportunity to reunite with their people and the Arab world from which they had been forcibly separated when Israel was established.

For all these groups, pre-1967 Israel (regarded nostalgically as a democratic haven by adherents of the Green Line paradigm) was an oppressive social and political space. A return to it would not improve their situation and might even make it worse. Although they come from different religious, political and social backgrounds, they are united in rejecting the notion that the two-state solution would lead to a sustainable resolution of the Israeli–Palestinian conflict. The refugees would not benefit from the reconstitution of a Jewish Israel from which they would remain excluded; the settlers would oppose their removal from what they see as a God-given homeland; the people of 'third Israel' would resent being relegated to a position of marginality from which the occupation extricated them; the 1948 Palestinians would be separated again from the Arab world, and be subjected to the same exclusion and oppression from which they suffered before 1967.

And who would benefit from the two-state solution? The answer, Shenhav says, is secular Ashkenazi Jewish elites, who were in political and social control before the 1967 war but who have lost their dominant position since then. The rise of new Mizrahi, religious, immigrant and Arab voices has undermined the dominance of those elites. A return to small, 'enlightened', pre-1967 Israel, in which their power was unchallenged, would allow them to reassert their position at the expense of other groups. This is why they are the main advocates for the Green Line paradigm. They have managed to make it the dominant perspective in global discourse, but underlying social and cultural currents have led to its continued decline in policy and practice. Increasing diplomatic support for the two-state solution has gone together with a growing blurring of the physical, legal and symbolic boundaries between Israel and the Occupied Territories. Most residents of the country have never experienced any reality other than that of Greater Israel.

Thus, the rhetorical victory of the paradigm, as expressed in almost unanimous international support for it, and constant invocation in UN resolutions, has disguised its demise in practice. As a result of Israeli settlement activities, which created new realities, the prospect of a viable independent Palestinian state has become more remote than ever. Through massive allocation of state resources, and a consistent policy of expansion, Israel has created a patchwork of disconnected areas in which Palestinians live, criss-crossed by settlement infrastructure. This makes the task of removing hundreds of thousands of settlers, and restoring the integrity of the pre-1967 boundaries, virtually impossible. Separation between Jewish settlers and local residents within the Occupied Territories is maintained through an elaborate system of laws and military regulations, with settlers legally and politically incorporated into Israel while Palestinians live as stateless subjects. The crucial distinction now is between citizens and non-citizens within the same territory, rather than between the pre- and post-1967 territories.

A similar argument, but without Shenhav's sociological focus on marginalised Jewish groups, is provided by Meron Benvenisti, an Israeli analyst who was the first to put forward the thesis that the occupation had become irreversible (back in the mid-1980s). Israel's hold over the territories beyond the Green Line has become permanent for most practical purposes, Benvenisti argues, even if their Palestinian residents remain excluded from citizenship and rights. This means that defining the territories as occupied is misleading, as they have become incorporated into the Israeli system of control. Disguising this reality, by keeping the pretence that the situation is temporary and there is a meaningful 'peace process' that could result in change, helps maintain the status quo. The paradigm of temporary occupation should be replaced by that of a 'de facto binational regime', which can describe the 'mutual dependence of both societies, as well as the physical, economic, symbolic and cultural ties that cannot be severed without an intolerable cost'. The binational situation does not mean parity of power, due to:

> the total dominance of the Jewish-Israeli nation, which controls a Palestinian nation that is fragmented both territorially and socially … only a strategy of permanent rule can explain the vast settlement enterprise and the enormous investment in housing and infrastructure, estimated at US $100 billion.[5]

The system is geared to undermine every agent or process that puts the Jewish community's total domination in jeopardy, and threatens its ability to accumulate political and material advantages. It has evolved as a response to the 'genetic code' of a settler society, but is no longer dependent on settlements and military occupation to entrench itself. It is sustained by Israel's success in fragmenting Palestinians and ensuring that each of the fragments is concerned only with its own affairs, with no interest in or capacity for working together with the others. As a result, a binational reality has emerged and partition is no longer a viable option, if it ever were. The two national groups are destined to live together and the only question is what kind of relations between them can and will be established.

A more complex picture is presented by Ariella Azoulay and Adi Ophir, who make a distinction between the two sides of the Green Line, in an attempt to understand how both are governed by a single internally differentiated regime.[6] This regime has a dual character: brutal oppression, denial of human and political rights and total disregard for the welfare of subjects in the Occupied Territories, combined with (qualified) democracy within pre-1967 boundaries. This duality exists within the boundaries of the same regime. Talking about Israel within its pre-1967 boundaries as a distinct social and political entity is meaningless – the regime encompasses both sides of the Green Line and they are interdependent. The Occupied Territories are included in a way that retains their exclusion from the realm of legitimate politics (rather, they fall under notions of 'security' or of 'demography'). The regime incorporates the Occupied Territories as a permanent 'outside', an 'inclusive exclusion': a space that is always subject to Israeli domination (in the Gaza Strip today just as much as in the West Bank since 1967) but is never absorbed into Israel. Neither withdrawal from the territories nor their annexation is a likely outcome. This is not a result of failure to decide on policy due to fierce internal debate, as it is usually portrayed; rather, it is a firm policy decision to retain this ambiguity forever, if possible.

While in the Occupied Territories the distinction between citizen (soldier, state official, settler) and non-citizen (Palestinian resident) is paramount, within the Green Line the ethnic distinction between Jewish and Arab citizens is crucial. In the Occupied Territories both distinctions overlap, but not so in Israel: this is why it is important not to lump them together. This tension between the principles of ethnicity and citizenship opens up opportunities for change. Israeli Palestinians are discriminated against but are not subject to the same system of domination as their counterparts who live under occupation. They can exercise their citizenship rights to campaign for meaningful political and social integration as equals. And, in doing that, they could open the way for changing the regime itself. Occupied Palestinians can resist the occupation but the road to changing the regime itself is blocked, because they have no effective leverage from the external position into which they are forced. Overall regime change thus hinges on the success of changing Israel from within through the joint efforts of Israeli Palestinians and their Jewish allies. A change there will open up possibilities for further change in the nature of the regime itself.

IS ISRAEL AN APARTHEID STATE?

Despite their different emphases and disagreements, all the views above agree that it is impossible to look at Israel in isolation from the Occupied Territories – in other words, that Greater Israel is the effective boundary of control and meaningful unit of analysis. They may also agree – but do not discuss it explicitly – that Greater Palestine is an essential part of the picture even though it is beyond the 1948 and 1967 boundaries. In fact, precisely how Palestinians from the 'beyond' came to occupy that position, and remain there against their will, is part of the system of control that is left largely unaddressed. Perhaps uniquely in modern history, the Israeli regime was founded historically – and continues to be based – on the forcible exclusion of a large part of its potential citizens. How to conceptualise this state of affairs remains a challenge.

This apparent agreement notwithstanding, many voices critical of Israeli policies retain a focus on the Occupied Territories and use the apartheid label to describe and condemn Israeli control there but not elsewhere. Famous references to the notion of apartheid in Israel–Palestine by former US President Jimmy Carter, Archbishop Desmond Tutu of South Africa and Professor John Dugard, the special rapporteur for the UN Commission on Human Rights, are restricted to Israeli practices of occupation and do not deal with 'Israel proper'. This is also true of the thorough 2009 report by the South African Human Sciences Research Council (HSRC), entitled *Occupation, Colonialism, Apartheid.*[7]

That the conceptual distinction between Israel and the Occupied Territories is still so entrenched, despite the fact that Israel has occupied the territories for forty-eight years (and had existed for only nineteen years without them), is testimony to the success of the Israeli strategy of externalising them from its body politic while retaining effective control over them. It is also testimony to the spirit of nationalist resistance to the occupation (in the territories) and the struggle for equal rights by Palestinian citizens of Israel. It is precisely this distinction that serves as the starting point for those rejecting the suitability of the apartheid analogy. I will examine in this section one such case of rejection, provided by the Israeli and South African journalist Benjamin Pogrund.

Armed with real though limited anti-apartheid credentials, and with a critical attitude towards Israeli policies in the Occupied Territories, Pogrund is perfectly positioned to present the case against the analogy between Israel and apartheid. Unlike many others who work directly in the service of the Israeli propaganda apparatus, he maintains a semblance of political independence and therefore a measure of credibility when addressing the issue in the international media (he seems to be completely absent from internal Israeli debates). Pogrund has become a key spokesperson – possibly in an unofficial capacity – against any attempt to label the Israeli regime and its practices as a form of apartheid and to borrow concepts and strategies from the experience of the anti-apartheid movement in South Africa. His approach replicates many of the taken-for-granted assumptions and blind spots of liberal-left Zionists, which need to be addressed in some detail.

What are Pogrund's arguments? In dealing with Israel inside the Green Line, he acknowledges that Palestinian citizens 'suffer extensive discrimination, ranging from denial of land use, diminished job opportunities and lesser social benefits' and so on. Yet, 'discrimination occurs despite equality in law; it is extensive, it is buttressed by custom, but it is not remotely comparable with the South African panoply of discrimination enforced by parliamentary legislation'.[8] Pogrund clearly is unfamiliar with the extensive research and advocacy work done by legal and human rights organisations such as Adalah: The Legal Center for Arab Minority Rights in Israel and Mossawa: The Advocacy Center for Arab Citizens in Israel. A look at their publications would show precisely such a 'panoply' of discriminatory practices and laws, albeit frequently formulated in more subtle language than the blunt South African legislation. It would seem that the task of a critical journalist should consist in exposing such legal practices rather than covering up for them.[9]

But, Pogrund argues: 'Arabs have the vote. Blacks did not. The vote means citizenship and power to change. Arab citizens lack full power as a minority community but they have the right and the power to unite as a group and to ally with others'. True enough, but then – as he should be fully aware of – some blacks in South Africa did have the right to vote at certain periods of history, most recently with P. W. Botha's 1983 constitution, which established the tricameral parliament. This applied to minority black communities classified as coloured and Indian, not to the majority of the black African population, and they voted on a separate roll rather than on a common one for all citizens. And yet they faced political marginalisation as minorities just as Palestinian citizens of Israel do: in both cases these groups represented about 15 per cent of the overall indigenous population and enjoyed a relatively privileged status, though in neither case have such privileges prevented them from supporting the overall struggle for national liberation. Of course, the analogy between the political status of such minority groups in South Africa and Israel is not perfect; no analogy ever is. But it does make for a potentially useful exploration that is entirely absent from Pogrund's account.[10]

Beyond these issues there is a bigger concern. Pogrund says:

> Israel now has a Jewish majority and they have the right to decide how to order the society, including defining citizenship. If the majority wish to restrict immigration and citizenship to Jews, that may be incompatible with a strict definition of the universality of humankind. But it is the right of the majority.

Missing from this statement are a few inconvenient facts. For example, Jews became a majority in the country only through the ethnic cleansing of 1948 and, long before the UN Partition Resolution of 1947, the Zionist movement created an ever-expanding zone of exclusion by removing all Palestinian-Arab residents from land acquired by official Jewish agencies, and by denying them employment in all Jewish public-owned workplaces. The crucial fact that Palestinians are not immigrants, nor are they seeking rights in someone else's country but rather in their own homeland, is ignored as well. In fact, the situation is the precise opposite: Jewish immigrant settlers are granted rights directly at the expense of indigenous Arabs, a state of affairs that Pogrund should be familiar with from his South African experience.

While recognising that 'it is clearly unfair from the victims' point of view for Israel to give automatic entry to Jews from anywhere while denying the "Right of Return" to Palestinians who fled or were expelled in the wars of 1948 and 1967, and their descendants', Pogrund claims that it is not unique to Israel: 'The same has happened in recent times, often on far greater scales, in Germany, Poland, the Czech Republic, India and Pakistan, to list but a few parallel situations'. Again, this argument deliberately ignores the fact that no European country recognises the right of 'ethnic kin' to return *at the expense of its own indigenous population.* That the Law of Return in Israel recognises the rights of all Jews to citizenship (even if they and their ancestors for millennia never set foot in the territory) and denies the same right to all Palestinians who are not citizens already (even if they and their ancestors were born there) is without parallel. No other country practises such policies, not even South Africa under apartheid.

Do India and Pakistan, then, provide any grounds for regarding the Israeli case as unexceptional? The answer is no, for two reasons: 1) there was forcible but symmetrical exchange of populations between the two countries, whereas Israel expelled the indigenous population in a one-sided manner;[11] and 2) Hindu refugees from Pakistan and Muslim refugees from India accounted for between 2 and 3 per cent of their countries' respective populations. In comparison, Palestinian refugees from the territories that became Israel in 1948 accounted for 80 per cent of the Arab population in those areas, and 60 per cent of the Arab population of the entire country. The removal of the majority of the indigenous population by settler immigrants is unprecedented. In a sense, Pogrund is right in rejecting the apartheid analogy: apartheid was about exploiting indigenous people, not expelling them from their country. This is a key difference between the two cases, but hardly one that portrays Israel in a better light.

Turning to the occupied West Bank (ignoring Gaza), Pogrund tries to create a false picture of symmetry:

> Everyone is suffering, Palestinians as victims and Israelis as perpetrators. Death and maiming haunts everyone in the occupied territories and in Israel itself. Occupation is brutalising and corrupting both Palestinians and Israelis. The damage done to the fabric of both societies, moral and material, is incalculable.

This pseudo-humanist rhetoric disguises the crucial difference between the oppressors and the oppressed: the former are perpetrators. They cause suffering, they do most of the killing and maiming, the bulk of the damage and brutalisation, and all the land expropriation and political oppression. The fact that the Palestinians are oppressed not 'on racial grounds as Arabs' but on national grounds (as Arabs) does little to offset the huge disparity in power, resources, ability to inflict damage, and impunity with which Israel pursues its settlement and occupation policies. Nor does the fact that 'The Israeli aim is the exact opposite [of historical apartheid]: it is to keep Palestinians out, having as little to do with them as possible, and letting in as few as possible to work', instead of exploiting their labour, provide much consolation. After much of their land was taken away, black South Africans under apartheid retained the prospect of finding work with white people. Palestinians in the Occupied Territories, in comparison, are deprived of land *and* job prospects. Little wonder that they do not find the notion that they are free from apartheid exploitation very comforting ...

If Israel were 'to annex the West Bank and control voteless Palestinians as a source of cheap labour', Pogrund continues, 'or for religious messianic reasons or strategic reasons – that could indeed be analogous to apartheid. But it is not the intention except in the eyes of a minority – settlers and extremists who speak of "transfer" to clear Palestinians out of the West Bank, or who desire a disenfranchised Palestinian population'. He seems ignorant of the fact that, for the first twenty years of the occupation, that indeed was the case: voteless Palestinians were a source of cheap labour for Israelis. For the last twenty years, Palestinians have remained disenfranchised, but they have been replaced by immigrant workers as a source of cheap labour. And, for the entire duration of the occupation – forty-eight years so far – Israel has controlled the territories for religious messianic or strategic reasons, regardless of the professed intentions of its population. The only difference between the scenario portrayed by Pogrund and reality itself is formal annexation.

But actual practices on the ground are much more powerful than legal formulas. Indeed, Benvenisti's argument that keeping the pretence that the occupation is temporary helps maintain the status quo comes in handy here. Empty rhetoric about the need for 'genuine peace efforts' cannot disguise the fact that the longer the peace process continues, the more entrenched Israeli control over the Occupied Territories becomes.

In summary, then, with regard to 'Israel proper', Pogrund misrepresents both the extent and the nature of the systemic formal and informal discrimination against Palestinian citizens. With regard to 'Greater Israel', he ignores the quasi-permanent nature of the occupation and the fact that Palestinian residents have been living under a system of an effective apartheid-like control for forty-eight years already, as recognised by most critical South African visitors. As for 'Greater Palestine', it plays no role in the analysis: to include it would shatter his entire construction. In other words, Pogrund provides a partial and deceptive analysis.

When we move to examine the different aspects of Israeli policies, Palestinian citizens are granted rights that were denied to the majority of black people in South Africa, occupied Palestinians are treated in much the same way as black people were treated (especially residents of the 'homelands'), and Palestinian refugees are excluded to a far greater degree than black South Africans ever were. Considering apartheid in the generic sense, then, Israeli policies and practices meet many – not all – of the criteria identified in the international legal definition of apartheid, with the qualification that they are based on ethno-national rather than racial grounds.

This does not mean that the Israeli society, state and system of control are indeed the same as those of historical apartheid, although they do bear family resemblances. No case is like any other. Even countries that shared much history with South Africa – such as Zimbabwe and Namibia under colonial rule – did not have identical systems, and apartheid itself changed substantially over time. While the technologies of rule (coercive, legal and physical) used by Israel have largely converged with their apartheid counterparts, crucial differences between the societies remain. These involve ideological motivations, economic strategies and political configurations. In all these respects, Israel–Palestine shows a greater tendency towards exclusion than was the case in South Africa. To understand why, we need to examine historical trajectories.[12]

Contemporary South Africa is the product of a long history, which saw various colonial forces (the Dutch East India Company and the British Empire, Afrikaner and English settlers, missionaries, farming and mining businesses, and so on) collaborate and compete over the control of different indigenous groups. Over a long period of expansion, stretching over centuries, this pattern brought about a multi-layered system of domination, collaboration and resistance. Numerous political entities (British colonies, Boer republics, African kingdoms, missionary territories) emerged as a result, accompanied by diverse social relations (slavery, indentured labour, land and labour tenancy, sharecropping and wage labour). White supremacy was a means to ensure white prosperity, using black labour as its foundation.

By the late nineteenth century, a more systematic approach had begun to crystallise. It was used to streamline the pre-existing multiplicity of conditions and policies into a uniform mode of control, with the aim of guaranteeing the economic incorporation of black people while keeping them politically excluded. Apartheid was a link in this historical chain, seeking to close existing loopholes and entrench white domination.

During the same period, the nature of resistance changed as well, from early attempts to retain independence to a struggle for incorporation on an equal basis, prompted by the massive presence and crucial position of indigenous people in the white-dominated economy. The exploitation of their labour gave them an important strategic lever for change, due to their indispensable role in ensuring white prosperity.

Since the 1930s at least, most black political movements aimed to transform the state rather than form independent political structures. By the late 1970s, white elites had started to realise that apartheid was becoming counterproductive in ensuring prosperity. It was too costly and cumbersome, and increasingly irrational from an economic point of view: it hampered the creation of an internal market and prevented a shift to a technology-oriented growth strategy. The resistance movement that grew after the 1976 Soweto uprising, combined with international pressure and increasing stress on the state's resources and capacity, gave the final push towards a settlement. This took the form of a unified political framework, within which numerous social struggles continue to unfold.

The South African trajectory can be contrasted with that of Israel–Palestine, which produced two distinct ethno-national groups. The formation of Israel in 1948 and the unfolding of the Israeli–Palestinian conflict have deepened the divide between the communities (but also gave rise to Palestinian citizens as an intermediary group). A major reason for this historical divergence is that settler Jews and indigenous Arabs had started to consolidate their group identities – linked to broader ethno-national collectives – *before* the initial encounter between them, whereas settlers and indigenous people in South Africa formed their collective identities locally in the course of the colonial encounter itself. As a result, the Zionist project has faced indigenous people as an obstacle to be removed from the land, in order to clear the way for Jewish immigration into the country. White settlers in South Africa, in contrast, focused on the control of resources and populations (land and labour) to enhance their wealth. Political domination was a means to an economic goal in South Africa, but a goal in its own right in Israel–Palestine.

On the basis of this trajectory, the founding act of the State of Israel in 1948 was inextricably linked with the Nakba – the ethnic cleansing of the majority of the indigenous population living in the areas allocated to the new state. This has had contradictory effects: on the one hand, the removal of most Palestinians and the relegation of the rest to the status of a marginalised minority allowed the state to adopt democratic norms premised on Jewish demographic dominance. On the other hand, the same process ensured a permanent external threat from the Palestinians who were dispossessed in 1948. Neither outcome had parallels in South Africa under apartheid. With the 1967 occupation, another component was added to the picture, moving it closer to historical apartheid: large numbers of people were incorporated into the Israeli labour market but remained disenfranchised. The state was unwilling to extend to them the political and civil rights enjoyed by Palestinian citizens, and unable to impose on them a 1948-style ethnic cleansing. They remain permanently stuck in limbo, subjects of a monstrous legal and military apparatus aimed to ensure their subordination without formal annexation and without ethnic 'purification'.

Is this apartheid in its generic sense, then? In crucial respects it is indeed – apartheid of a special type. However, it is important to understand its similarities to and differences from historical apartheid – not for purposes of labelling, but because they provide crucial clues for strategies of resistance and change. Any discussion of possible alternatives will benefit from such understanding.

APARTHEID OF A SPECIAL TYPE

By de-linking historical apartheid from its generic legal form we no longer need to retain a focus on South African racial policies and practices. And yet, I argue in this section, it would be useful to keep a focus on comparing Apartheid South Africa and Israel, in order to highlight crucial features of the Israeli system. The comparison would allow us to analyse Israeli–Palestinian relations, evaluate possible alternatives to the status quo, and devise strategies of political struggle and transformation based on South African experiences (among other things). We must keep in mind here that the point of a comparative analysis is *not* to provide a list of similarities and differences for its own sake, but to use one case in order to reflect critically on the other and thus learn more about both.

Back in the early 1960s, the South African Communist Party coined the term 'colonialism of a special type' to refer to a system that combined the colonial legacies of racial discrimination, political exclusion and socio-economic inequalities with settler political independence. It used this novel concept to devise a strategy for political change that treated local whites as potential allies rather than as colonial invaders to be removed from the territory. Making analytical sense of apartheid in South Africa in this way was relatively straightforward since there was an integrated system of legal and political control. Although different laws applied to different groups of people, the source of authority was clear.

Making sense of the notion of apartheid in the case of Israel is more complicated. The degree of legal and political differentiation is greater, as it includes an array of formal and informal military regulations in the Occupied Territories and policies delegating powers and resources to non-state institutions (the Jewish Agency, Jewish National Fund, and so on) that act on behalf of the state but in a less direct and more opaque manner, not open to public scrutiny. The fact that much of the relevant legal apparatus applies beyond Israeli boundaries (to Jews, all of whom are regarded as potential citizens, and to Palestinians, all of whom are regarded as prohibited persons) adds another dimension to the analysis. For this reason, we may talk about apartheid of a special type: a unique system that combines democratic norms, military occupation, and exclusion/inclusion of extra-territorial populations. There is no easy way of capturing this diversity with a single overarching concept.

What are some of the characteristics of this special system?

- It is based on an ethno-national distinction between Jewish insiders and Palestinian Arab outsiders. This distinction has a religious dimension – the only way to join the Jewish group is through conversion – but is not affected by degree of religious adherence.

- It uses this distinction to expand citizenship beyond its territory (potentially to all Jews) and to restrict citizenship within it (Palestinian residents of the Occupied Territories have no citizenship and cannot become citizens). Thus, it is open to all non-resident members of one ethno-national group, wherever they are and regardless of their personal history and actual links to the territory. It is closed to all non-resident members of the other ethno-national group, wherever they are and regardless of their personal history and actual links to the territory.

- It is based on the permanent blurring of physical boundaries. At no point in its sixty-seven years of existence have its boundaries been fixed by law, nor are they likely to become fixed in the foreseeable future. Its boundaries are permanently temporary, as evidenced by continued talk of the 1967 occupation as temporary, even though it has already outlived historical apartheid (which effectively lasted forty-two years). At the same time, its boundaries are asymmetrical: porous in one direction (expansion of military forces and settlers into neighbouring territories) and impermeable in another direction (severe restrictions or total prohibition on the entry of Palestinians – from the Occupied Territories and the diaspora – into its territories).

- It combines different modes of rule: civilian authority with all the institutions of a formal democracy within the Green Line, and military authority without democratic pretensions beyond the Line. In times of crisis, the military mode of rule tends to spill over into the Green Line to apply to Palestinian citizens. At all times, the civilian mode of rule spills over beyond the Green Line to apply to Jewish citizens residing there. The distinction between the two sides of the Green Line is eroding as a result, and norms and practices developed under the occupation filter back into Israel: as the phrase goes, the 'Jewish democratic state' is 'democratic' for Jews and 'Jewish' for Arabs.

• It is in fact a 'Jewish demographic state'. Demography – the fear that Jews may become a minority – is the prime concern behind the policies of all mainstream forces. All state structures, policies and proposed solutions to the Israeli–Palestinian conflict are geared, in consequence, to meet the concern for a permanent Jewish majority exercising political domination in the State of Israel (within whichever boundaries).

How do these features compare with historical South African apartheid?

• The foundation of apartheid was a racial distinction between whites and blacks (further divided into coloured people, Indians and Africans, with the latter subdivided into 'tribal' groups) rather than an ethno-national distinction. Racial groups were internally divided on the basis of language, religion and ethnic origins, and externally linked in various ways – religion, language – across the colour line. This can be contrasted with Israel–Palestine in which lines of division usually overlap. All potential bases for cross-cutting affiliations that existed early on – anti-Zionist Orthodox Jews, Arabic-speaking Jews, indigenous Palestinian Jewish communities – were undermined by the simultaneous rise of the Zionist movement and Arab nationalism to dominant positions in the course of the twentieth century. This left no space for those straddling multiple identities.

- In South Africa, then, there was a contradiction between the organisation of the state around the single axis of race, and the social reality that allowed more diversity in practice and multiple lines of division as well as cooperation. This opened up opportunities for change. The apartheid state endeavoured to eliminate this contradiction by entrenching residential, educational, religious and cultural segregation, and by seeking to shift its basis of legitimacy from race to national identity, but to no avail. Its capacity was limited and it was further eroded over time. In Israel–Palestine, there is a tighter fit between the organisation of the state and social reality, with one crucial exception: Palestinian citizens are positioned in between Jewish citizens and Palestinian non-citizens. They are the only segment of the population of Greater Israel or Greater Palestine that is fully bilingual, familiar with all political and cultural realities, and with enough freedom to organise but not enough rights to align themselves with the oppressive status quo. As a minority group (15 to 20 per cent of Israeli citizens *and* of Palestinian Arabs), they cannot drive change on their own but may act as crucial catalysts for change.

- Under historical apartheid, a key goal of the state was to ensure that black people performed their role as providers of labour, without making difficult social and political demands. The strategy used for that focused on externalising them. Although they were physically present in white homes, factories, farms and service industries, they were absent (politically and legally) as rights-bearing citizens. They were expected to exercise their rights elsewhere. Those who were no longer or not yet functional in the white-dominated economy were prevented from moving into the urban areas or forcibly removed to the 'reserves' (also known as Bantustans or homelands): children, women – especially mothers – and old people. Able-bodied black people who worked in the cities were supposed to commute – daily, monthly or even annually, depending on the distance – between the places where they had jobs but no political rights, and the places where they had political rights but no jobs.

- This system of migrant labour opened up a contradiction between political and economic imperatives. In conformity with apartheid ideology, it broke down families and the social order, hampered efforts to create a skilled labour force, reduced productivity, and gave rise to crime and social protest. To control people's movements, the regime created a bloated and expensive repressive apparatus, which put a constant burden on state resources and capacities. Domestic and industrial employers faced increasing difficulties in meeting their labour needs. From being an economic asset (for whites) it became an economic liability. It simply had to go.

- The economic imperative of the Israeli system, in contrast, has been to create employment for Jewish immigrants. Palestinian labour power was used by certain groups at certain times because it was available and convenient, but it was never central to Jewish prosperity in Israel. After the outbreak of the first intifada in the late 1980s, and under conditions of globalisation, it could easily be replaced with politically unproblematic Chinese, Turkish, Thai and Romanian workers. In addition, a massive wave of Russian Jewish immigration in the 1990s helped this process. The externalisation of Palestinians, through the denial of rights, ethnic cleansing and 'disengagement', has presented few economic problems for Israeli Jews. There is little evidence of the contradiction between economic and political imperatives that undermined Apartheid South Africa.

- Apartheid was the latest in a long list of regimes in which white settlers dominated indigenous black people in South Africa. For most of the colonial period, people of European origin were in the minority, relying on military power, technological superiority and 'divide and rule' strategies to entrench their position. Demography was never an overriding concern. As long as security of person, property and investment could be guaranteed, there was no need for numerical dominance. When repression proved increasingly counterproductive, a deal exchanging political power for ongoing prosperity became an option acceptable to the majority of whites. Can such a deal be offered to – and adopted by – Israeli Jews, for whom a demographic majority is the key to domination and the guarantee of political survival on their own terms? Most likely, no.

In summary, then, apartheid of a special type in Israel is different from historical apartheid in South Africa in three major respects:

- At its foundation are consolidated and relatively impermeable ethno-national identities, with few cross-cutting affiliations across the principal ethnic divide in society.
- It is relatively free of economic imperatives that run counter to its overall exclusionary thrust, because it is not dependent on the exploitation of indigenous labour.
- Its main quest is for demographic majority as the basis for legal, military and political domination.

In all these respects it is a system that is less prone to an integrative solution along the lines of post-apartheid South Africa. At the same time, it is subject to contradictions of its own, which are crucial to its dynamics and present potential opportunities for change:

- Its foundational act of ethnic cleansing left behind a weak and disorganised minority Arab group. With Palestinians no longer a demographic threat, the rump community could be incorporated into the political system that displayed many of the characteristics of a 'normal' democracy. Its members used this opportunity to reorganise and build a solid foundation for resistance politics, combining parliamentary and protest activities that have challenged Israel's exclusionary structures from within. This strategic location has given them a useful vantage point from which to play a vanguard role in the struggle to transform the system. The success of the joint list in the 2015 elections provides them with a good basis from which to work for change.

- The geographically expansionist drive of the Zionist project has clashed with the demographic imperative to ensure a Jewish majority. Ethnic cleansing along the lines of 1948 might provide a way to reconcile these contradictory thrusts, but it is not really feasible under the glare of international media and public opinion. Although no immediate change is likely, it is clear that the status quo is becoming increasingly unstable. Since Israel will neither incorporate the occupied population (because of the fear of 'demography') nor give them their freedom (because of the fear of 'security'), tensions are building up and it becomes difficult to contain them. This will lead to an inevitable explosion, although we cannot be sure of the precise form and timing.

- The changing international scene begins to show signs of eroding support for the regime. For two decades Israel benefited from an international context that saw the collapse of the Soviet bloc and its policies of isolating Israel in alliance with 'progressive' third world regimes. The turn of the USA and its Western allies against major Arab and Islamic forces also benefited the Israeli regime, which positioned itself as the front line in the 'global war on terror'. This period was used to entrench its hold on the Occupied Territories, divide the Palestinian people and its leadership, isolate and crush resistance to the occupation, and silence critical voices. In the last few years, though, both Israel's capacity to dominate its region and the West's support for its campaigns have declined. Although it is not yet facing real military or political challenges, expressions of weakness abound. Among them, growing international solidarity with the struggle of Palestinians against the occupation and for political rights plays an important role. The rise of civil society movements and alternative media is increasingly counteracting the unconditional support given by Western governments and traditional media to the Israeli state, although not necessarily all its policies. There is thus room for cautious optimism that the tide has begun to turn.

PROSPECTS, SOLUTIONS AND STRATEGIES

Where does all this leave us? Avoiding the temptation for easy labels and name-calling, we must examine the actual consequences of the analysis.

In Israel–Palestine there are two ethno-national groups. Israeli Jews are unified by their legal status as full citizens. Palestinian Arabs are divided by their legal status into citizens in 'Israel proper', resident non-citizens in 'Greater Israel', and non-resident non-citizens in 'Greater Palestine'. The two groups are distinct by virtue of their language, political identity, religion and ethnic origins. Only about 10 per cent of them (Palestinian citizens) are fully bilingual. Many Jews have Arab cultural origins, but that legacy was erased through three generations of political and cultural assimilation. The delusion that these 'Arab Jews' actually or potentially share any political consciousness – even if in a dormant form – with Palestinians must be laid to rest. On the face of it, this would seem an ideal argument for a separatist solution, but things are a bit more complicated than that.

The South African rainbow nation, which was based on the multiplicity of identities and the absence of a single axis of division to align them all – unity in diversity – is clearly unlikely to be replicated in Israel–Palestine. Elements such as the use of English as the dominant medium of political communication, shared by all groups, or Christianity as a religious umbrella for the majority of people from all racial groups do not exist in Israel–Palestine as a whole. At the same time, if we look at 'Israel proper' *in isolation*, the situation is not all that different from South Africa. People of all backgrounds – veteran Ashkenazi and Mizrahi Jews, new Russian and Ethiopian immigrants (many of whom are not Jews in a religious sense) and Palestinian citizens – use Hebrew in their daily interactions and largely share similar social and cultural tastes. In mixed towns, such as Haifa, Jaffa and Acre, there are neighbourhoods in which Jews and Arabs live together with little to distinguish between their lifestyles except for their religious practices. Without idealising the situation, they have much more in common with one another than white suburbanites have with rural black South Africans, during apartheid or today.

But, of course, we *cannot* look at them in isolation, just as we could not have looked at the relatively benign white-coloured interactions in apartheid Cape Town in isolation from the broader racial scene in the country. What we *can* do is use these emerging realities to build a foundation for a new political perspective, that of binationalism. Binationalism is not a 'solution' and does not compete with the endlessly discussed but vacuous one-state or two-state solutions. It is an approach based on the recognition that two ethno-national groups live together in the same country – separately within homogeneous villages and towns in some areas, but also mixed to varying degrees in other areas. Historical patterns of demographic engineering that resulted in forced population movement and dispersal (most notably the 1948 Nakba and the post-1967 settlement project) have created a patchwork quilt of mono-ethnic and bi-ethnic regions, separated by political intent rather than by natural or geographical logic.

Acknowledging this binational reality is not meant as an argument for a particular form of state. Rather, it is a call to base any future political arrangement on the need to accommodate members of both national groups as equals, at the individual and collective levels. In the words of radical Jewish activists who put together the 2004 Olga Document, 'this country belongs to all its sons and daughters – citizens and residents, both present and absentees (the uprooted Palestinian citizens of Israel in '48) – with no discrimination on personal or communal grounds, irrespective of citizenship or nationality, religion, culture, ethnicity or gender'.[13] This statement of principles must not be confused with a call to establish one state or a binational state. It is the essential condition for the success of *any* arrangement, be it one, two, or many states. The alternative would be an imposition by one side on the other, which would render a solution unviable.

It is interesting to note that the formulation above seems to draw on the 1955 Freedom Charter, which asserted that 'South Africa belongs to all who live in it, black and white'. The simple elegance of the South African original was transformed here into a comprehensive but very cumbersome language, a testimony to the difficulty of conveying unity in the face of rigid fragmentation. But it is far less difficult to convey unity – *as a first step* – among all Israeli citizens. Making Israel a state of and for all its citizens is both just and logical: just as France is a French state, the home of all French people, and South Africa is the state of all South Africans, so should Israel become an Israeli state, the home of all Israeli people. In the same way that Nicolas Sarkozy of

Hungarian (partly Jewish) origins and Zinedine Zidane of Algerian-Muslim origins can be citizens equal to the descendants of the Gauls, all Israeli citizens are entitled to an equal status regardless of their links to the ancient Hebrews.

At the same time, unlike France, in Israel people seek incorporation as individuals *and* as groups. In the Vision Documents, a series of proposals and statements written by academics, intellectuals and activists representing the Palestinian Arab minority in Israel, the quest for equality is combined with the quest for recognition as a national collective. For example, in the Haifa Declaration of 2007, they call for a 'change in the definition of the State of Israel from a Jewish state to a democratic state established on national and civil equality between the two national groups, and enshrining the principles of banning discrimination and of equality between all of its citizens and residents'.[14] There is an unresolved tension here between the call for a democratic state with no ethnic character, and the notion of equality between ethnically defined groups. A similar, though milder, tension is found in the post-apartheid South African constitution, which establishes non-racialism as an overarching principle but recognises the legitimacy of racially based affirmative action policies. It is an explicit attempt to redress historical legacies of racial discrimination, particularly regarding access to land and employment, without recognising the permanent existence of racial groups, let alone any claims to representation or resources.

The binationalist approach is compatible with either option: a non-ethnic state or a state that enshrines equality between individual citizens and provides structured representation for ethnic groups in fields such as education and culture. Both must lead to the removal of 'all forms of ethnic superiority, be that executive, structural, legal or symbolic' and the adoption of 'policies of corrective justice in all aspects of life in order to compensate for the damage inflicted on the Palestinian Arabs due to the ethnic favoritism policies of the Jews'.[15] Democratising Israel in this way is important in its own right, and also as a way to reinforce other campaigns. If Palestinian citizens are no longer ostracised as illegitimate actors, the struggle against the occupation would receive a big boost by escaping the confines of the small progressive Jewish left.

Making Israel a state of all its citizens would not change the boundaries of political sovereignty, would have no demographic implications, and would require no negotiation with external forces. It would not challenge 'the right of Israel to exist' but rather seek to modify the internal basis for its self-legitimation. In other words, it would be a process carried out entirely by its own citizens, undertaken over a period of time. Making Greater Israel a state of all its residents, and establishing common citizenship, is different in all these respects. It would mean a fundamental change in the boundaries of citizenship and the allocation of power, requiring a radical re-alignment of the political scene. It is not feasible in the short term as there are no serious political forces advocating it at present, and it cannot be seen as a substitute for the ongoing struggle against the 1967 occupation.

There is no doubt that the occupation is the biggest festering sore in Israeli–Palestinian relations. Futile negotiations over the last two decades have led to its intensification rather than mitigation. The only way forward is an ongoing campaign to put an end to it, without having anything to do with the moribund diplomatic process or with the one-state/two-state debate. The occupation manifests itself in the daily life of the population in numerous ways (both in Gaza and the West Bank, though differently), and it gives rise to localised resistance. All expressions of resistance to restrictions – on free movement, access to land, economic activity, water use, study, construction, and so on – must be supported, with the use of all means excluding armed attacks on civilians: demonstrations, sanctions, boycotts, mass defiance campaigns, legal challenges in Israeli and international courts, appeals to global public opinion. Strategically, it is important to de-link the struggle against the occupation from the relations between Israel and the Palestinian Authority (or Hamas, for that matter). A crucial lesson of the South African transition is that subordinating local struggles to the requirements of diplomacy helped the ANC gain power, but frequently led – after the 1994 transition – to the neglect of the concerns that gave rise to the struggle in the first place.

The third dimension of Greater Palestine – refugees and their rights – is the most challenging to the boundaries of Israeli citizenship and control. It can be resolved only in a staggered manner. First, the present absentees – about 25 per cent of the Palestinian population in Israel itself who were removed from their original homes in 1948 but have become citizens – must be allowed access to their property and confiscated land. This would have no demographic implications and would not involve changes in citizenship status. Second, the original 1948 refugees could be invited back: only about 50,000 of them are still alive, a small number that could be accommodated demographically easily enough. Obviously, such steps would be opposed with the use of the most potent weapons in the Israeli arsenal of internal self-justification: they would create a precedent.[16] And, indeed, the fear of the majority of the Israeli Jewish population is that any recognition – even symbolic and limited in its practical implications – of the right of return would lead to an uncontrolled influx of millions of refugees. This is highly unlikely – research indicates that only about 10 per cent of them are likely to exercise the right of return – but the issue would require ongoing educational, political and legal campaigns.[17] Again, it is strategically important that the struggle have nothing to do with the one-state/two-state debate or with grand diplomacy. The right of return is vested in individuals rather than the political leadership, and they are the only ones who can negotiate on their own behalf.

It is the refugee issue, above all, that makes the Israeli apartheid of a special type different from historical apartheid, and so difficult to overcome. As a result of it, Palestinians have been deprived of the most important weapon of struggle used by black South Africans: their strategic location in the economy and their ability to use the threat of withdrawing their labour power as a crucial political lever. Due to the historical trajectory of excluding indigenous people in Israel–Palestine, compared with their incorporation in a subordinate economic role in South Africa, they operate outside the boundaries of the Israeli-dominated economic system. This exclusion is not complete – it does not apply to Palestinian citizens or to a minority among West Bank residents – but it applies in Gaza and fully in Greater Palestine. As a result, those excluded in this way can apply pressure on the regime from the outside – using protest, diplomacy and violence – but lack any meaningful strategy of change from within. In this respect, they are dependent on the work of forces internal to Israel (Palestinian citizens together with progressive Israeli Jews) and on pressure applied by forces in the Middle East region and internationally. Solidarity and educational efforts are crucial here, as well as the evolving divestment and sanctions campaigns.

CONCLUSION

By way of broad conclusion, a political strategy that might work would anchor the concerns above in the language of democracy, justice, equality and human rights, instead of that of diplomacy and statehood. The advantage of this approach is that it can associate itself with the global justice movement and struggles of diverse independent forces, civil society organisations, media activists, and so on.

What possible form can such a strategy take? A thorough discussion deserves a study on its own, and only a brief outline – focusing on campaigns within 'Israel proper' – is possible here. First, we must recognise that progressive forces can neither ignore nationalism (risking total marginalisation) nor surrender to it (risking losing their voice). Second, in a society historically shaped by sharp ethno-national conflict, most social and political issues are affected by the conflict, but they should not be reduced to it. Third, the conflict can be seen as an overall framework, but its many dimensions may be better tackled as multiple political fronts that call for different local approaches and contingent alliances. This requires charting a course that would go *beyond nationalism* without seeking to write it off.

Concretely, a series of campaigns that position Palestinian national demands within a broader framework of rights is one way of establishing a link between particular and universal discourses and opening the way for cooperation between Palestinians and – at least some – Israeli Jews on specific issues. Examples may include questions of access to land (affecting Palestinians as well as ethnically and socially marginalised Jewish groups), questions of citizenship and immigration policies (affecting Palestinians as well as many Jews with ambiguous legal status, such as recent Russian and Ethiopian immigrants), questions of labour organisation, jobs and access to services (affecting Palestinians, socially marginalised Jews, and migrant workers from Eastern Europe and South-East Asia), questions of culture, education and social exclusion (affecting Palestinians, Mizrahi Jews and Orthodox Jews), questions of gender and sexuality (affecting everyone), and so on.

Each of these campaigns would involve alliances between different groups working for different causes, but they all share, in their specific domains, a quest for a greater equality and democracy for all, regardless of origins. They fall under the 'radical democracy' approach as advanced by Ernesto Laclau and Chantal Mouffe, though without necessarily having an overarching theme to unify them all. Unlike the traditional approach of the radical left, this strategy is not based on expectations that Jews would renounce Zionist ideology, confront state power directly, and opt for a common socialist future. Rather, it assumes that they would show some willingness to address some of the concerns of Palestinians, working jointly with them, if these were in line with their own concerns.

This approach does not tackle directly all of the core issues of the Israeli–Palestinian conflict, some of which pit Israeli Jews and Palestinian Arabs against each other as mutually exclusive groups fighting over resources and rights. In the short to medium term, there is no prospect of weakening the boundaries between these groups or constructing an identity that would transcend ethno-nationalist loyalties. No easy formulas to deal with this situation exist, and current debates over one- or two-state solutions miss the crucial point: the Palestinian population was fragmented in 1948 and further in 1967. A holistic political solution would have to address all its components (the 1948 dispersal of refugees, the 1967 occupation and the fate of Palestinians citizens) but is very unlikely ever to be implemented simultaneously. Hence, forces seeking to change the status quo need to work on each component on its own, instead of seeking in vain to solve all the issues in one big bang, with some magic formula.

Progress on one front should not be impeded by the lack of progress on another, and the final outcome cannot be predicted in advance. The key guiding principle for a solution is common to all components, however: the need for a binationalist approach, which would treat members of each ethno-national group equally, as individuals as well as collectives. The combination of a political approach operating on many different but related fronts with a new mode of activism that focuses on direct action and creative media, educational and legal strategies may be the way forward. There are no obvious answers here, but posing the right questions is a crucial step towards a solution.

Notes

1   Exceptions are Ran Greenstein, *Genealogies of Conflict: Class, Identity and State in Palestine–Israel and South Africa*, Middletown, CT: Wesleyan University Press, 1995; Mona Younis, *Liberation and Democratization: The South African and Palestinian National Movements*, Minneapolis: University of Minnesota Press, 2000; Hilla Dayan, 'Regimes of Separation: Israel–

Palestine and the Shadow of Apartheid' in Adi Ophir, Michal Givoni and Sari Hanafi (eds), *The Power of Inclusive Exclusion: Anatomy of Israeli Rule in the Occupied Palestinian Territories*, Brooklyn, Zone Books, 2009, pp. 281–322.

2   See https://treaties.un.org/doc/Publication/UNTS/Volume%201015/volume-1015-I-14861-English.pdf.

3   See www.ohchr.org/EN/ProfessionalInterest/Pages/CERD.aspx.

4   Yehouda Shenhav, *Beyond the Two-State Solution: A Jewish Political Essay*, Cambridge: Polity Press, 2012.

5   Meron Benvenisti, 'United We Stand', *Ha'aretz*, 28 January 2010: www.haaretz.com/weekend/magazine/united-we-stand-1.262282.

6   Ariela Azoulai and Adi Ophir, *The One-State Condition: Occupation and Democracy in Israel–Palestine*, Redwood City, CA: Stanford University Press, 2012.

7   HSRC, *Occupation, Colonialism, Apartheid? A re-Assessment of Israel's Practices in the Occupied Palestinian Territories under International Law*, Pretoria: HSRC Press, 2009: www.alhaq.org/attachments/article/236/Occupation_Colonialism_Apartheid-FullStudy.pdf.

8   Benjamin Pogrund, 'Israel Is a Democracy in Which Arabs Vote – not an Apartheid State', *Focus* 40 (December 2005): online version at www.zionism-israel.com/ezine/Israel_democracy.htm.

9   Among many examples, see Adalah, *The Discriminatory Laws Database*, Haifa: Adalah, 2012: www.adalah.org/en/content/view/7771; Adalah, *The Inequality Report: The Palestinian Arab Minority in Israel*, Haifa: Adalah, 2011: www.adalah.org/en/content/view/7404; Mossawa Center, *Submission to the Office of the High Commissioner for Human Rights, 17th Session of the Universal Periodic Review, Israel*, Haifa: Mossawa Center, 2013: www.mossawacenter.org/my_Documents/pic002/Final_UPR_Submission_-_2013.pdf; Mossawa Center, *The Legal Status of Palestinian Arab Citizens of Israel over the Last Decade*, Haifa: Mossawa Center, 2014: www.mossawacenter.org/my_Documents/pic002/183_The_New_Wave_of_Israel%27s_Discriminatory_Laws___Report_FINAL_2014.pdf; ACRI, *Arab Minority Rights*, Tel Aviv: Association for Civil Rights in Israel (ACRI), 2015: www.acri.org.il/en/category/arab-citizens-of-israel/arab-minority-rights/.

10 See the analogy between Palestinian citizens and coloured South Africans in Oren Yiftachel, '"Creeping Apartheid" in Israel–Palestine', *Middle East Report* 253 (Winter 2009).

11 Since Palestinian refugees did not move into countries from which Jews left for Israel in the 1950s (Iraq, Yemen, North Africa), nor did they enjoy access

to abandoned Jewish property, there was no exchange of populations there.

12   Extended discussion of these issues can be found in Greenstein, *Genealogies of Conflict*.

13   'The Olga Document', June 2004: www.nimn.org/Perspectives/israeli_voices/000233.php.

14   Mada al-Carmel, *The Haifa Declaration*, Haifa: Mada al-Carmel, Arab Center for Applied Social Research, 2007: http://mada-research.org/en/files/2007/09/haifaenglish.pdf.

15   National Committee for the Heads of the Arab Local Authorities in Israel, *The Future Vision of the Palestinian Arabs in Israel*, Nazareth, 2006: www.mossawacenter.org/my_documents/publication1/Future_Vision_ENG.pdf.

16   Another such weapon is the notion that Israelis must never lose face because it would mean erosion of their power of deterrence. So, every 'hostile' action demands an immediate counter-action, at least twice as powerful (and it is not a bad idea for the counter-action to precede the action …).

17   The work of the Badil Resource Center for Palestinian Residency and Refugee Rights stands out in this respect: www.badil.org.

INDEX

Greek Orthodox Church, Palestinian
land owned, 137
Green Line paradigm, 330-1
Greenstein, Ran, 17-19
Gross, Nahum, 62
Group Areas Act 1950, 165
Guérin, Victor, 48-50
Gush Emunim, 97
Gush Shalom, 14, 258-61, 263
Guthe, Hermann, 48

Hafrada, 9
Haifa: Declaration 2007, 355; mixed
town, 353; University, 145, 148
Halevi, Ilan, 264
Halper, Jeff, 254
Hamas, 38, 208; Gaza election of, 182-3
Hapoel Hazair, 51
haredim, 97-8
Harel, Yehudith, 261
'Hebrew labour', idea of, 146-7
Hebrew University, Jerusalem, 145
Heidegger, Martin, 73, 116
Heilige Land, 50
'Held' territories, OPT, 78
Herzilya Conference 2000, 152
Herzl, Theodor, 26, 30, 50, 290
Histadrut, 147-8
historiography, Israeli positivist and
empiricist, 43-5
Hizbullah, spying for accusations, 132
Holocaust, Nazis of the Jews, 33;
memorialisation captive of denial, 111,
113-15; memory manipulation, 18
Holy Land, 'divine right' claims, 54
homelands, Namibia, 303
'honour' murders, 192, 196, 199, 212;
Arab culture, 197; Israel profiting from,
210; Lebanese refugee camps, 214;
patriarchal excuse, 198
house demolitions, Israeli strategy of,
139
Hula Lake, drying out of, 51

human rights: Israeli sidelining, 217-18;
law, sovereignty weakness, 310
Human Rights Watch, 142
Humanitarian law, international, 296
Hunter, Roland, 251

illegal settlements, colonial strategy, 78
IMF (International Monetary Fund), 180
immigrants, Israel cheap labour, 340, 349
In'ash El-Usra Society, 204
India-Pakistan, exchange of populations,
339
indigenous people: claims delegitimized,
308; colonial essentializing, 12; labour
comparative use of, 326; rights
movement, 313
injustice, *inbuilt*, 81
Inkata, 207
Institute for a Democratic Alternative for
South Africa (IDASA), 245, 248, 251
International Convention on the
Elimination of All Forms of Racial
Discrimination, 328
International Convention on the
Suppression and Punishment of the
Crime of Apartheid 1973, 2, 173, 327
International Court of Justice, 176, 301,
303; Namibia charges, 304
International Criminal Court, Rome
Statute, 329
international solidarity, BDS, 36
ISA, mainstream academia, 43
Islamic Movement, Israel, 134
Islamophobia, 18
Israel, State of: apartheid implications, 2,
18; apartheid creation, 111; -apartheid
South Africa axis, 32; Arab education
underfunded, 142; Arab education
system, 141-2; as 'unique', 90; bi-lingual
Palestinians, 352-3; blurring of physical
boundaries, 346; boycott issue, 258;
cheap Palestinian labour period, 340;
citizenship- nationality strategic split,

South Africa, 82; black labour leverage,
342; black proletariat development,
36; British concentration camps,
278; 'colonialism of a special type',
28, 36; Dutch colonists, 29; Dutch
Reformed Church, 215; history of, 342;
Human Sciences Research Council,
336; -Israel relations, 90, 163; Israeli
OPT withdrawal demand, 37; late-
Apartheid, 319; linguistic genocide, 214;
'Making Soldiers' campaign, 200; 1910
independence, 25, 77; 1948 apartheid
birth, 22; populations ratio, 309; racial
policies, 344, 348; settler colonialism,
310, 314; specific history of, 327; Union
1911 foundation, 164; white protest
groups, 13; 'witch' 'necklacing', 11, 196
South African Communist Party, 25,
250-2, 313, 345; Central Committee, 4;
white members, 262
South African Institute of Race Relations,
246-7
South African National Party, apartheid
ideology, 303
South African 'settlement': as model,
288; Palestine not applicable, 290;
romanticised, 290
sovereignty: colonial capacity for, 310;
Israel-Palestine form, 300; non-
juridicial 'advantages', 304; Palestinian
claim discrediting, 311
Soweto uprising, 280, 343
Sparg, Marion, 220
state-social reality fit, 348
Steiner, George, 112
Suez war, 150
Sumud, 315
Supreme Court, Israel, 9, 124, 128, 135,
140-1, 143, 176

Ta'yaush, Israeli group, 258
Tal, Nachman, 148
Talmudic legalism, 97

Tambo, Oliver, 4; UN speech 1982, 32
Tamir, Yuli, 143
Tel Aviv University, 2, 142, 330
Templers movement, 53, 55, Zionism of,
63
terra nullus, settler colonial discourse,
308-11
Terrorism Prevention Law, Israel, 131
Thai immigrant labour, Israel, 349
Tilley, Virginia, 15-17
Tirosh, Ronit, 143
Toledano, Shmuel, 147
Transkei, 166-7, 178, 181; public
employment, 179
tribal chiefs Soith Africa, colonially
imposed, 166
Tuqan, Fadwa, 220
Turkish immigrant labour, Israel, 349
Tutu, Desmond, 6, 35, 219, 336
'two-state solution', 79, 239, 254, 263,
285, 331-2; ethnic rule, 284; problem
preservation, 291; unviable, 286
Tzabarm Shimon, 262

UDF (United Democratic Front), South
Africa, 244, 246, 248, 250-1, 257, 266;
white affiliates, 250
UN (United Nations): Commissioner
on Human Rights, 336; Committee
on Decolonisation, 306; Convention
Against Apartheid, 24; General
Assembly Resolution 181, 162, 170,
316-18; Jewish state creation vote 1947,
32, 300, 338; OPT withdrawal calls
real time effects, 320; Resolution 194,
1948, 38, 79, 317; Security Council
Resolutions 242 and 336, 170, 173,
255; SCRs 1397 and 1515, 317; Special
Rapporteur Human Rights Council, 38
'universality', Jewish ethics, 102
Urban Foundation, South Africa, 246
USA (United States of America), 284;
Arab and Islamic forces turn against,